76504

P9-ARV-563

The Eskimo Storyteller

FOLKTALES FROM NOATAK, ALASKA

The Eskimo Storyteller

FOLKTALES FROM NOATAK, ALASKA

Edwin S. Hall, Jr.

DRAWINGS BY CLAIRE FEJES

THE UNIVERSITY OF TENNESSEE PRESS / KNOXVILLE

Copyright © 1975 by The University of Tennessee
Press, Knoxville. All rights reserved. Manufactured
in the United States of America.
First edition.

Library of Congress Cataloging in Publication Data

Hall, Edwin S   1939–
  The Eskimo storyteller: folktales from Noatak,
Alaska.

    1. Eskimos—Alaska—Legends.   2.   Folk-lore—
Eskimo.   I.   Title.
E99.E7H22   398'.042'09701   74–17304

Drawings by Claire Fejes on pages 12, 21, 59, 67, 87,
145, 167, 185, 234, 267, 280, 310, 316. From PEOPLE
OF THE NOATAK, by Claire Fejes. Copyright © 1966
by Claire Fejes. Reprinted by permission of Alfred A.
Knopf, Inc.

For Ethel

Preface

The small plane circled the village once and then again. As we banked and turned, a jumble of confusing images was thrust at us, coming into and passing out of focus like the individual frames of a motion picture. A side channel of the river swept against a high bank sprinkled with red, green, and black roofs. The spruce-covered flats behind the village merged into the gently rolling hills beyond. Willow-covered islands barely held their own above the dirty river waters still high from the spring flood. A large complex of buildings with bright aluminum roofs stood back from the bank. The glint of the oblique afternoon sun came from everywhere there was water: from the river, the tundra lakes, and even the small spaces between the tundra plants. Many small, circular, cleared spaces lay behind each house. Our minds recorded these and other scenes, but most of them remained unfiled, not completely understood until we had spent many days in the village.

We glided to a landing on the rough gravel airstrip, stopping near the crudely painted sign that proclaimed we had reached our destination: Noatak, Alaska. My wife, Leona, and I crawled from our cramped positions in the gear-crowded plane and stepped into the bright sunlight. Smiling Eskimo faces surrounded us, mostly children but also a curious adult here and there. As we unpacked the plane the questions came. Why were we here? How long were we going to stay? Where were we going to live? We did not answer at once, for we were strangers here and it was the people themselves we had come to study. Soon the adults drifted away, leaving the children, some giggling and inquisitive, some silent and shy, to help us carry the gear to the edge of the airfield where we assembled our small tent. Then they too were gone, to see the weekly movie. We were alone—one of the few times in the year to follow that we were.

Our arrival in Noatak was Leona's introduction to Alaska, but for me it marked the end of a long journey. Two summers before I had begun an archaeological and ethnographical study of the Eskimos inhabiting the Noatak River valley in northern Alaska between A.D. 1500 and A.D. 1850. During the summer of 1962, I conducted an intensive investigation of the archaeological possibilities of the upper and middle Noatak River region. An assistant and I were flown to the headwaters of the Noatak in June. We spent the period from then until late August floating down the upper 220 miles of river searching for archaeological sites. I returned in 1963 with two assistants to survey the middle portion of the river's course and also to spend some time excavating archaeological sites discovered during this and the previous summer.

Our excavations were moderately successful and I thought it would be possible to reconstruct, with fair accuracy, the ways of life followed by the people who inhabited the region. However, my attempts to analyze the data we recovered and to commit to paper a description of the late prehistoric and early historic Noatak peoples soon convinced me that further excavation of certain sites was indicated. Additionally, I felt that it was necessary to learn more about the people themselves, information that could be gained from their descendants who still lived on the land and exploited its resources much as their forefathers had done. Besides, one cannot describe a land and a people accurately, particularly an arctic land, if he spends only the brief summer season there. It is necessary to feel the changing seasons, to know dark as well as light, freezing cold as well as warmth. For these reasons we came to Noatak village in June 1964 to spend a year completing the archaeological excavations and studying the Noatak peoples, placing special emphasis on their relationship with the land.

We spent the summer traveling up and down the river to the various archaeological sites that were being excavated. With the coming of winter we settled into a one-room frame dwelling at the northern end of the village. An oil stove kept us warm, when the fuel oil did not freeze in the outside lines. Some of our groceries came from the Arctic Research Laboratory at Point Barrow. With these exceptions our winter life was much like that of the other villagers. We participated in most of the daily activities of the village: Leona learned to sew, to cut fish, and to clean and scrape caribou skins; I built a sled, assembled a dog team, and went on a number of caribou hunting trips. We learned by doing.

We did not spend the winter alone. A young Eskimo girl, Isabelle Wesley (Ohloktune), came to live with us. Isabelle was seven, with bright black eyes, coal black hair, and a determined shyness. I think the shyness was partly because she came to us from a very large family and partly because she had little experience with strange *nalaukmis* (white men).[1] She soon grew accustomed to her new surroundings and, indeed, sometimes became a bit tyrannical with her playmates. But we grew to love her and she us. Also—and frankly this was one reason we wanted her to live with us—Isabelle afforded us an entree into the life of the village. As "parents" of an Eskimo child we were accepted more quickly than we otherwise would have been.

During the early part of the winter I concentrated on talking with the older men about their way of life, past and present. I learned how to hunt caribou with a rifle and with a bow and arrow. The postmaster taught me how to build a sled and train a dog team. I also tried to learn as much as I could about the land and how the Noatak Eskimos saw it, the names they gave to certain locations and why, the places good for hunting caribou and other game, the sites of old villages, and so on. The artifacts we recovered during the summer

[1] The spelling of Eskimo words has become a confusing issue in literature dealing with the Arctic. Here I have used the alphabet designed by Wilfried Zibell (1968), of the Summer Institute of Linguistics, for the Kobuk River–Kotzebue Sound area. However, the established spelling of place names, as on United States Geological Survey maps or in Foote (1961, 1965), has been retained, as well as the spelling of such words as *ebrulik, karigi, aŋatquq, umaypak,* and *kalovik*, already used in studies dealing with northern Alaska. To change these would only compound an already confused situation. Also, in common Eskimo fashion, plurals in English have been formed by adding an "s." This form was utilized by the translators. Syllabification rules for Eskimo words are the same as those for the English language.

were laid out on a table for the older people to look at and handle. They were able to identify the function of many tools that had been in use four hundred or more years before.

I continued to collect similar kinds of information during the entire winter, but toward spring I began to concentrate on another interest: the folktales told by the older villagers. All Eskimo groups have a rich mythology, despite the many changes that have taken place in the Eskimo way of life during the past one hundred years. Folktales are still told each evening in Noatak. As I recorded story after story I became increasingly fascinated by the way the Noatak folktales reflected the aspirations, fears, morals, and fantasies of the villagers. Each story had a meaning beyond words and plot. Soon I was lost in a world not of my own making—an alien world that sometimes frightened me with its violence, its fatalism, its acceptance of the duplicity of man and beast. And yet, the very same tales told of the special reciprocal relationship between man and the animal world, of the devotion and love of Eskimos for their kin, and of the humor Eskimos find in their harsh world. Like the Noatak villagers, I found I could smile through my fears—even laugh—and accept what would be.

The folktales collected while Leona and I were in Noatak form the basis of this study. Chapter I sets the folktales within the Noatak world as a whole by briefly describing the land and the people. Chapter II details the conditions under which the folktales were collected and compares the place of folktales in aboriginal Eskimo society to the role they play today. The next two chapters are the corpus of this study. Each deals with one Noatak informant and includes an autobiographical sketch as well as all the folktales the informant could recount. Chapter V presents a brief analysis of the importance of folktales in Noatak Eskimo life. Finally, the brief epilogue notes some of the changes that have taken place in Noatak since Leona and I were privileged to spend a winter there.

ACKNOWLEDGMENTS

The materials for this study were collected during three summers and one winter of fieldwork in the Noatak River region of northern Alaska. The fieldwork was supported principally by the Arctic Institute of North America under contractual arrangements with the Office of Naval Research. Subsidiary funds were kindly granted by the Explorers Club and the Department of Anthropology, Yale University. In-the-field support was provided by the Naval Research Laboratory, Barrow, Alaska.

Publication of this book was assisted by the American Council of Learned Societies under a grant from the Andrew W. Mellon Foundation.

Dr. Margaret Lantis, of the University of Kentucky, Dr. Harry Lindquist of the University of Tennessee, Knoxville, and Dr. Alan Dundes of the University of California, Berkeley, read the manuscript and made many helpful suggestions.

The line drawings gracing the text are the work of my artist friend, Claire Fejes, author of the delightful book *People of the Noatak*, published by Alfred A. Knopf in 1966.

My knowledge of the Noatak River region and the Eskimos of northern Alaska has been considerably enhanced by many long discussions with colleagues working there, particularly John M. Campbell, William N. Irving, and the late Don C. Foote.

The people of Noatak Village took my wife and me to their hearts. Our year in the Village gave us a sense of understanding, love, and appreciation which I will never be able to communicate fully to outsiders who have not shared our experience. All of the villagers gave of themselves to help two strangers whom they could not fully understand. Though I hesitate to single out individual Noatakers I must mention Paul Monroe and Edna Hunnicutt, who told the stories recorded here, and Martha Burns and Herbert Onalik, who translated them. Perhaps this study will partially repay our many obligations.

All royalties from this work accruing to the author will be donated to a scholarship fund established to help the children of Noatak achieve a college education.

And finally, Leona, my wife. From her first contact with a strange land until now she has been a source of strength, encouragement, and love. She deserves special thanks because she understands why this book is dedicated to Ethel Burns.

Contents

Map and Tables

The Eskimo Storyteller

FOLKTALES FROM NOATAK, ALASKA

I. The Setting

THE LAND

Northwest Alaska is a land of contrasts. The icy wind of a leaden February sky sends smokelike clouds of snow scurrying across the rough, broken ice covering Hotham Inlet. The same wind, almost silently, sweeps from a clean blue sky along the Kobuk River to break on the dark stands of spruce which shelter velvet-deep snow. Long, warm days of May start a trickle to become a flood of breakup as the Kobuk, Noatak, and Colville run once again to a sea soon to be free of ice. The July sun inspires lethargy among the Eskimos leisurely fishing at Sheshalik on the coast and among the caribou in the treeless interior seeking the cool mountain heights free of mosquitoes. The sharp nights of fall tinge the willows along the watercourses as the inhabitants of the land—caribou, grizzly bear, ground squirrel, and Eskimo—prepare for the long night of winter.

Northwest Alaska is not a natural topographically delimited region. For my purposes this area consists of all the land drained by the Kobuk, Noatak, and Colville rivers, all of their tributaries, and a number of smaller, northward flowing streams, such as the Kukpowruk and Utukok rivers. The seventy-five-thousand-square-mile area may be demarcated by drawing a line from the mouth of the Colville River south to its junction with the Itkillik River, and up the latter to its source in the Brooks Range. From here the line goes generally

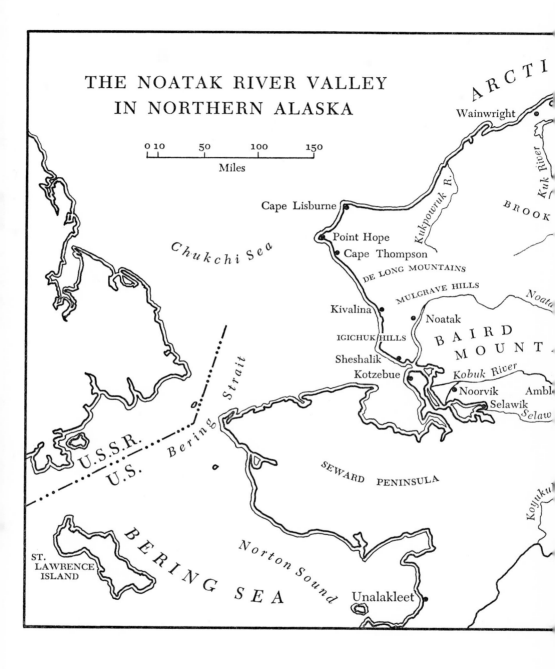

THE NOATAK RIVER VALLEY
IN NORTHERN ALASKA

0 10   50   100   150

Miles

ARCTI

Wainwright

Kukpowruk R.

Kuk River

BROOK

Cape Lisburne

Chukchi Sea

Point Hope

Cape Thompson

DE LONG MOUNTAINS

MULGRAVE HILLS

Noata

Kivalina

Noatak

BAIRD

IGICHUK HILLS

MOUNT

Sheshalik

Kotzebue

Kobuk River

Noorvik

Ambl

Selawik

Selaw

U.S.S.R.

Bering Strait

U.S.

SEWARD   PENINSULA

Koyuku

ST.
LAWRENCE
ISLAND

BERING

Norton Sound

SEA

Unalakleet

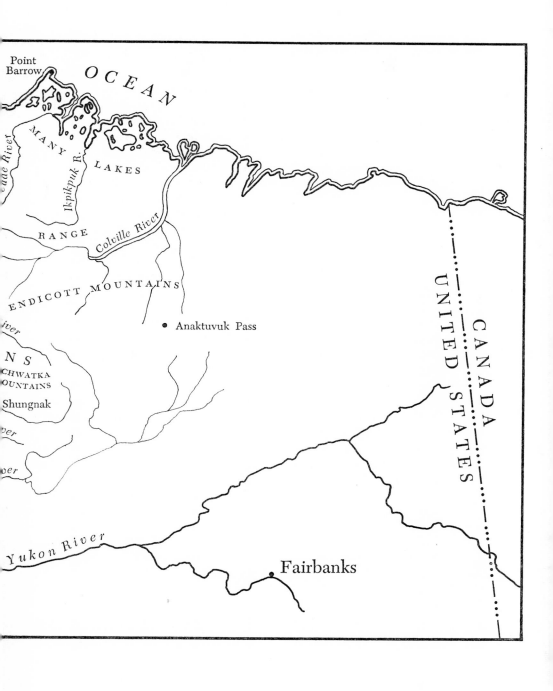

southwest along the mountainous crest of the Brooks Range to Walker Lake at the headwaters of the Kobuk River, and then west down that river to the town of Kotzebue on the coast. The line follows the undulant coast, west and north to Point Hope, north to Cape Lisburne, east and north to Point Barrow, and, finally, east and a little south to make a closure at the Colville River mouth.

This vast area, entirely north of the Arctic Circle, can be divided into four physiographic provinces. Along the area's southern fringe the Kobuk River flows west through the spruce-covered flanks of the Waring, Baird, and Schwatka mountains. East of Walker Lake, tributaries of the Koyukuk River rise in the Endicott Mountains and drain to the south (out of the Northwest Alaska area as defined here) through timbered marshy flats and gently rolling hills. Thus the main features of the southernmost province are south- or west-flowing rivers, mountains reaching four to five thousand feet in elevation and, except on high ridges and peaks, a heavy cover of spruce and other vegetation.

Immediately to the north is the Brooks Range proper, a rugged belt of mountains ranging in height between four and ten thousand feet stretching east and west across northern Alaska. The Brooks Range, considered by most geologists to be a continuation of the continental Rocky Mountains, has been divided into several subranges on the basis of regional topography. In the west the Noatak River, which flows west for the greater portion of its length before turning south to the sea, rises in the Schwatka and Endicott mountains and drains, successively, the Baird Mountains, De Long Mountains, Mulgrave Hills, and Igichuk Hills. The eastern portion of the Brooks Range is drained primarily by northward-flowing tributaries of the Colville River, including the Kuna, Etivluk, Kurupa, Killik, Chandler, Anaktuvuk, and Itkillik rivers. Large lakes, such as Etivluk, Feniak, Noluck, Tukuto, and Chandler, fill many of the mountain valleys. Spruce intrudes into this province only along the lower course of the Noatak River; elsewhere willow and other riparian species are found along the watercourses, and various sedges, grasses, and flowering species cloak the valley floors and mountain sides.

The basin of the Colville, the largest river in northern Alaska, lies north of the Brooks Range. The Colville, along with its many tributaries, drains a series of east-west trending ridges. This area has been referred to as the Arctic Foothills Province (Solecki 1951:476). In some places the relief is considerable, reaching more than three thousand feet, but the overall effect is one of long, sometimes steep, dry-topped ridges framed against the higher mountains to the south. Some of the rivers flow through deep, rock-rimmed channels; others, especially tributaries toward the lower reaches of the Colville, spread out in braided, anastomosing, gravel-filled channels. The river banks and islands in the river channels support heavy willow growth, while numerous herbaceous species cover the rolling tundra.

The northernmost of the four provinces is the Arctic Coastal Plain (*ibid.*). Low relief, sluggish meandering rivers, and myriad lakes create an almost flat, featureless landscape to the pedestrian traveler. Most of the streams, with the exception of the Meade, Kuk, and Ikpikpuk rivers, are small, and all drain northward to the Arctic Ocean. The land itself shades off almost imperceptibly into the sea along much of the coast, though bluffs and cliffs do occur. Sedges and other water-loving species form the predominant groundcover, making summer foot travel exceedingly difficult across the marshy, hummocky ground. Willows and dwarf birches are found along streams and the protected shores of lakes with high banks.

The climate of Northwest Alaska varies considerably with differing topography. In general, the climate of the interior is continental, with more extreme temperatures, lower summer and higher winter precipitation, and lighter winds than along the coast. During the summer months temperatures in the southern part of the region average between 60 and 70 degrees Fahrenheit, occasionally reaching 95 to 100 degrees. To the north, summer temperatures average considerably lower. Winter temperatures can reach 60 to 65 degrees below zero, but generally they average 20 to 30 degrees higher. Precipitation during the summer is frequent, but not very heavy, while winter snow can reach a depth of four feet in the timber and a foot or more on the windswept tundra. The total yearly precipitation rarely exceeds ten inches and averages only five to seven inches on the Coastal Plain, making this area an arctic desert despite the great amount of free-standing water. Freezeup usually occurs in early October and breakup during the middle part of May.

Along the coast summer temperatures range between 35 and 60 degrees Fahrenheit, the average at Kotzebue being about 48 degrees and at Point Barrow below 40 degrees. The maximum summer temperatures rarely exceed 75 to 80 degrees and freezing nights are not uncommon. Precipitation in the form of light rain and wet fog is a common summer phenomenon. Winter temperatures can reach minus 50 degrees in February, but usually are warmer than minus 35 degrees. Winter snowfall is light, but the constant wind moves the snow into deep drifts on lee slopes. The strong, steady wind, particularly in fall and winter, is the most dominant feature of the coastal weather.

Another notable facet of the environment is the period of continuous daylight in the summer and continuous darkness in the winter. At Point Hope the sun does not set between May 26 and July 17, and does not rise between December 9 and January 2. At Point Barrow the corresponding periods of dark and light are each seventy-two days long.

Despite the somewhat harsh climate and the rugged landscape Northwest Alaska has long supported a rich fauna. Past utilization of the area's herbaceous flora by large game animals is evidenced by the remains of mammoths and other Pleistocene species that are frequently washed from the permanently frozen sands exposed by changing river channels. Today the Cape Thompson region, south of Point Hope, contains some 30 species of terrestrial and marine mammals, 280 species of plants, 111 species of land birds, and 7 species of cliff-nesting birds (Foote 1961:11). In addition, other major mammal species, such as lynx, mink, land otter, beaver, and moose, occur in the more southerly portion of Northwest Alaska. Freshwater, anadromous, and marine fish are relatively plentiful throughout the area.

The two largest settlements in Northwest Alaska, Kotzebue and Point Barrow, serve as distribution centers for the bush villages. Both have substantial white, as well as Eskimo, populations. Other coastal villages include Kivalina, Point Hope, and Wainwright. The inland villages are Anaktuvuk Pass in the central Brooks Range; Noatak on the Noatak River; Kiana, Noorvik, Ambler, and Shungnak on the Kobuk River; and Selawik on the river of the same name. Occasionally one or more Eskimo families will be found living away from the villages, particularly during the summer season. A number of white guides and bush pilots maintain cabins in the interior. Finally, there are installations of the United States defense system in several locations.

THE PEOPLE

The Eskimos of Northwest Alaska

The antecedents of the Northwest Alaska Eskimos[1] are to be found in the distant past. Archaeologists now believe that Alaska was the end point on a land bridge that joined the Old and New worlds during glacial times. The first emigrants traveling from Siberia to North America undoubtedly passed through Northwest Alaska, across a cold land rich in flora and fauna. This was probably not a planned migration, but a slow process of population diffusion, the movement year by year of hunting peoples into new territory. During the thousands of years following both people and ideas traveled freely between the New and Old worlds in both directions, first across the land bridge and then, when the glaciers melted and the ocean waters rose, across the narrow Bering Strait.

If Northwest Alaska has served as a highway, it also has been a cultural backwater. During many periods of prehistory new ideas and cultural influences passed by or did not reach the region, which left the inhabitants to develop intensively those cultural skills they did possess. The results of these conflicting processes are slowly being scientifically reconstructed by examination of remains excavated from archaeological sites. The clues left by very early peoples are meager and sparse. However, the long continuum of culture that resulted in the modern Eskimos of the area began to coalesce during the years immediately preceding the birth of Christ. Some of the elements making up Eskimo culture can be traced back further in time, but by 100 B.C. there were already present the unique relationship of man to environ-

[1] There are a number of excellent works available dealing with the Eskimos of Northwest Alaska which the reader may wish to consult for more detailed information on the people described here. These include: for the north Alaska Eskimo, Chance (1966); for Point Barrow, Murdoch (1892), Spencer (1959); for the Nunamiut of the central Brooks Range, Ingstad (1954), Spencer (1959), Gubser (1965); for the Tigaraqmiut of Point Hope, Rainey (1947), VanStone (1962), Foote (1961, 1965), Foote and Williamson (1966); for the Kivalinamiut, Burch (1966), Saario and Kessel (1966); for the Utukokmiut, Larsen and Rainey (1948); for the Noatak peoples, Lucier (1958), Foote and Cooke (1960), Foote (1961, 1965), Foote and Williamson (1966), Hall (1966); the Kobuk River peoples, Giddings (1952, 1961). The data on the Naupaktomiut, Noatagmiut, and Tigaraqmiut summarized in this chapter come from the sources listed here and from my field notes. The section on the historic Noatak peoples draws heavily on Williamson's analysis of the village, found in Foote (1961).

ment and many of the sophisticated tools that made possible the systematic pattern of ecological exploitation characteristic of the modern Eskimo. We do not know that these people spoke the Eskimo language, but a reconstruction of their culture indicates they followed an essentially Eskimo way of life.

This does not mean there was a stagnation of culture during the succeeding centuries. New cultural elements, including the use of iron, still reached Northwest Alaska from Siberia and, to a lesser extent, from the south. There were changes, whether influenced from without or developed locally, in such things as art styles, harpoonhead types, and perhaps in nonmaterial aspects of culture. It is believed that the use of dogs to pull sleds and the idea of protracted battle, reflected in the acquisition of slat armor, did not reach Northwest Alaska until the 1500s. It was not until this late date that the people we call Eskimo achieved the total cultural expression we associate with them. Even at that, tobacco, now quite important in Eskimo culture, did not reach Alaska via the Siberian native peoples until the late 1600s, just before the white man arrived.

The first tentative exploration of Northwest Alaska took the form of various vessels skirting the coast after the 1700s. Russian trade goods, preceding the eastward exploration and expansion of the Russian Empire, reached the Eskimos of the region sometime before this. Even earlier, beginning in the mid-1600s, there were extensive prehistoric trading ties between eastern Siberia and Northwest Alaska. After James Cook first sighted the Northwest Alaska coast in 1778 there was a gap of thirty-eight years until Otto von Kotzebue visited the sound named after him in 1816. During the following years more and more exploration ships touched on the coast. In 1848 the first of a large fleet of whaling ships penetrated the Bering Strait and by 1850, though whaling and explorations were to continue for many years, the Eskimos of the region had begun to surrender their aboriginal culture.

Unfortunately, no detailed studies were made of Northwest Alaskan Eskimos until the 1880s, a long time later in terms of cultural change. However, from the few available expedition journals, travelers' accounts, and the recollections of the people themselves, we can reconstruct with reasonable accuracy the lifeways of the precontact peoples.

In 1850 the population of the region designated as Northwest

Alaska was almost entirely Eskimo, though the Ingalik and Koyukon (Athapaskan-speaking Indians) apparently penetrated the Kobuk headwaters from time to time. Eskimos were generally distributed throughout the area, living in small groups along the coast, on the shores of high mountain lakes, and along the banks of the Kobuk, Noatak, and Colville rivers and their major tributaries. The total human population is unknown; estimates range from forty-five hundred to ten thousand.

Ethnographers (Spencer 1959) have noted that Northwest Alaskan Eskimos follow one of two major ecological patterns. Thus we have the Nunamiut, the people of the land, and the Tareumiut, people of the sea. For the inland Nunamiut, caribou was the axis about which everything turned. Caribou provided food, shelter, clothing, and raw material for manufacture. The inland people formed themselves into small kinship-based bands, each exploiting the resources of a particular locality. Their only contact with the sea was a yearly trip to the coast to trade for marine products. The Tareumiut, on the other hand, were oriented basically toward the sea, though caribou and other land animals were important secondary subsistence items. The most important marine mammal was the great bowhead whale (*Balaena mysticetus*), though walrus and seals were also actively and systematically sought. Coastal villages tended to be somewhat larger and more permanent than inland villages because the rich marine resources allowed greater population stability.

There is little doubt that this was the basic economic and cultural division among the Eskimos of the northern half of the area under discussion. The Eskimos of the Noatak and Kobuk River region, however, cannot be categorized as easily. The Noatak River Eskimos participated almost equally in both the lifeways of the land and the sea. Their subsistence was drawn half from caribou and freshwater fish and half from marine mammals and ocean fish. The upriver Kobuk peoples depended on salmon and other fish to almost as great an extent as on caribou.

Though the Northwest Alaskan Eskimos themselves distinguished between Nunamiut and Tareumiut, these two terms were not conferred in a tribal sense. A man could follow either a Tareumiut or a Nunamiut way of life—or both—during his lifetime. Depending upon the ecological pattern in which a family operated they were either members of a coastal village or an inland band. A family could

choose its band of membership and residence, and indeed the population of such groupings waxed and waned depending upon the distribution and availability of resources.

In the professional literature the Eskimo population as a whole has been subdivided in three ways. The first type of division is on the basis of the name more or less distinct subgroups gave themselves, or what is termed ethnoidentification. The second is the term applied to a given band or village by other Eskimo groups. The third type of division is related to a geographic area, such as a river basin, occupied by a number of Eskimo families. The results are almost identical in each case. Most often virtually the same families were found in a named group at a given time no matter how the name was derived. Thus we have among the coastal villages the Nuwuŋmiut of Nuwuk Village at Point Barrow, the Tigaraqmiut of Tigara or

THE

Point Hope, and the Kivalingmiut of the Kivalina River area. Inland there were the Naupaktomiut and Noatagmiut of the Noatak River, the Killikmiut of the Killik River, the Tulugakmiut of Tulugak Lake, and so forth.

The cultural totality of these various groups did not differ much one from the next. Indeed, families might change geographical localities from year to year to partake of the subsistence round of a different named group. Individuals in one band or village were often related to individuals in another by bonds of real or fictive kinship. It was this kinship relationship, with its privileges, responsibilities, and obligations, that allowed peoples of one group to come into peaceful contact with those of another and to carry out trade. However, such relationships did not preclude open strife between various groups.

Minor differences between the Eskimo groups of Northwest Alaska did exist. These included slightly different dialects of the Eskimo language, different tent and house forms, and, in particular, different subsistence patterns. Thus the whale, walrus, and seal were of paramount importance to the Point Barrow people; the caribou to the Killikmiut; the beluga, salmon, and caribou to the Noatagmiut; and the seal, salmon, and caribou to the Naupaktomiut. Whatever the subsistence emphasis, however, all groups faced substantially the same environment, with its limitations and potentialities, and they all had to find a solution to the paramount problem of subsistence. The other aspects of culture were formed and constrained by the necessity of procuring daily subsistence. Thus the flavor of Northwest Alaskan Eskimo culture can be derived by taking a brief look at one local named group and noting some of the ways in which others differ.

THE NAUPAKTOMIUT AND THEIR NEIGHBORS

An Ethnographic Reconstruction

At the time of contact a group of people calling themselves Naupaktomiut lived along the Noatak River. The Naupaktomiut were the "people of the trees" or "people of the spruce," inhabiting as they did the forested flats along the lower river and, perhaps, the more sparsely timbered section of the middle Noatak between the Kugururok River and Killiktavik Creek. The locations of their winter dwellings were determined by several considerations; protection from inclement weather, proximity to dry wood, and closeness to good fishing spots. The resulting settlement pattern was one of many scattered villages containing two, three, or more houses.

Even after spending a considerable amount of time surveying the Naupaktomiut area I cannot say for certain where any of these precontact villages were situated. The encroaching forest and erosion of the river's banks have hidden or erased their traces. It seems likely that such localities as Akaekkingyorruk, Kaminik, Naupaktusugruk, and Akveexrak, which were frequently inhabited in the late 1800s because of their propinquity to important fishing grounds, were also loci of the precontact Naupaktomiut.

The population of the precontact Naupaktomiut is also difficult to ascertain because we lack archaeological data. It has been estimated (Foote 1965:251 ff.) that the Naupaktomiut population in 1850, before it was significantly altered by contact, was approximately two hundred individuals.

The nineteenth-century Naupaktomiut winter house was known as an *ebrulik*. The *ebrulik* consisted of roughed-out spruce logs covered on the outside by a layer of mossy sod with the moss in and then a layer of sod with the moss out. The single, usually rectangular, main room was as large as could be heated adequately and was connected to the outside by a short, wooden storm shed. Ventilation was afforded by the doors, both the door to the house and that to the storm shed, which were covered with caribou or bear skins, and by a skylight, approximately three feet square, which was centered in the roof over the main room and covered with the gut of a bearded seal. The floor of the room was covered with willow branches.

A bench, or platform, running across the back of the room and sometimes along the two sides, formed a place for storage, sleeping, and sitting. A fire for both heat and cooking was built in a stone-lined hearth situated in the center of the floor under the skylight. When retiring at night the inhabitants threw the remaining coals and ashes from the fire out the skylight and closed the hole. The insulated house would remain warm for hours.

Meat was most frequently boiled in large clay pots, procured by trade with people to the south, or wooden bowls which were carved locally from spruce. Stones heated in the fire were dropped into the liquid in the container to initiate the cooking process. Sometimes a stone lamp burning seal oil was used to heat a pot suspended over the flame.

The Naupaktomiut *ebrulik* generally sheltered a single extended family, that is, a man and his wife, their children, and the wife's or husband's parents, if the latter were living but unable to maintain a separate household. An aged aunt or uncle or an unmarried brother also might share the house. Sometimes two or more families lived together in one house. If so, the members were usually related in some way. A village was generally composed of the houses of related families.

In his early twenties, a man usually married a slightly younger woman. They married by taking up permanent residence together and restricting the rights of intercourse to each other. It was considered proper for a newlywed couple to live near the wife's parents for a year or so while the young man helped his father-in-law hunt. After this period the family was free to live anywhere its members wished. Sometimes a couple might exercise this option immediately after marriage and live near the man's parents or elsewhere.

Marriage was given permanence by the arrival of children; before that event separation might occur without obligation on either person's part. After children were born marriages were reasonably stable, though adultery did occur and could cause serious trouble. Wife lending was practiced, but modern informants are reluctant to discuss the subject.

Sanctions against transgressing the social mores of the group took the form of ridicule and avoidance. "To be ashamed" was something a Naupaktomiut tried to avoid; he did so by being considerate of his neighbors. It was considered good to help old people, as everyone would be old someday. To be a helpless orphan without close kin or even nonkin for protection was considered the most painful of human experiences. Thus avoiding or ignoring an individual was the most forceful sanction, though murder might be considered necessary and be carried out by the injured party if an individual persisted in his wrong-doing.

There was a definite division of labor. Men went hunting, killed the game, and carried it home. At that point ownership of the kill was transferred to the women, who butchered it and prepared the meat and hides. Fishing might be practiced by both men and women.

The operation and maintenance of the household, including collecting firewood, was the province of the women.

A Naupaktomiut's clothing, winter as well as summer, was made primarily from caribou skins and, less often, seal skin. His feet were protected by mukluks, the type employed depending upon the weather conditions. During extremely cold weather he wore *tutuliks*, boots having soles made of caribou skin with the fur facing in and uppers made of caribou-leg skins and sewn with the fur side out. Caribou-fur socks were worn along with dry-grass innersoles. During periods of thawing, when wet snow might be encountered, *ulichulyaks* were worn. These had a sole of tough bearded-seal hide and uppers of caribou skin with the fur facing in. The skin was treated with seal oil to make it waterproof. His lower body was covered with caribou-skin pants, fashioned with the fur facing in. In extremely cold weather another set of pants, with the fur facing out, was also worn. Sometimes leggings of wolf skin served to keep snow out of the mukluks. In the same fashion two caribou-skin parkas were worn when traveling in the cold, one being removed when the individual became overheated. The parkas were trimmed with a wolf or wolverine ruff. Mittens were made of wolf or caribou skin. Special clothing included a seal-gut rain parka and waterproof seal-skin boots.

Personal decoration among the Naupaktomiut included tattoos and labrets; pendants and browbands were made from ivory. Tattoos were confined to women and were usually made by drawing a soot-covered sinew thread under the skin. Girls received their tattoos, most often a series of straight parallel lines running down the chin, in early puberty. The typical man's ornaments consisted of two labrets, or lip plugs, one placed in each cheek just below the corner of the mouth. When a boy was eleven or twelve one of his male relatives held his head while another cut twice through the cheek with a flint drill or a sharp bone. The cuts were washed by taking urine in the mouth and expelling it through the holes. Wooden plugs were inserted to prevent the holes from closing as they healed. Then, as the boy grew older, a series of ivory plugs, each shaped like a hat, were worn in the holes with the "brim," or larger portion, of the plug resting against the gum. These "training" labrets were of increasing diameter, which resulted in gradual enlargement of the holes. By the time the boy reached manhood he could wear two labrets measuring three-quarters of an inch to an inch across. Some men had specially designed labrets of ivory or stone with beads or other ornaments attached to the exposed end.

Naupaktomiut subsistence activities during the winter centered mainly on fishing and trapping of small animals and birds to supplement stored surpluses acquired during the more bountiful fall months. Fish were secured by jigging a lure through a hole in the ice, by placing a net under the ice, or by sinking a cylindrical willow-frame fish trap in an eddy or backwater. The most common fish taken were "trout" (*Salvelinus alpinus* complex), whitefish (*Coregonus* sp.), grayling (*Thymallus arcticus signifer*), and ling, or burbot (*Lota lota leptura*). Ptarmigan (*Lagopus lagopus*) were taken in the fall and early spring, either by snaring or with a large net. Rabbits were snared.

Caribou (*Rangifer arcticus stonei*) were rarely taken in the Naupaktomiut area during the winter, but occasionally some men would travel to the north where a number of caribou corrals were built in traditional locations. A typical corral consisted of three rows of willows or snow blocks, one row behind another, with bearded seal-line snares set in openings between the clumps of willows or snowblocks. Two long, converging lines of decoys made of stones, willows, snowblocks, or sod clumps led to the corral. Some of the men herded the caribou into the funnel formed by these decoy lines, and the animals, afraid to cross between the decoys, moved into the corral. Men hiding in the throat of the corral then emerged to shoot into the milling animals with bow and arrow. Caribou caught in the snares were lanced rather than shot. The only other large game occasionally taken during the winter was the brown bear (*Ursus horribilis richardsoni*).

Wintertime was a period of leisure, especially when inclement weather made subsistence activities difficult or impossible. The focal point of recreational activity was the *karigi*, or ceremonial house. This was a frame building constructed of spruce logs covered with sod and was considerably larger than an *ebrulik*, though built in much the same manner. The walls were lined with benches and there was a large central fireplace. The *karigi* served as a meeting place, a spot where men might sit and talk as they repaired a bow or made a new fish spear. Sometimes in the evening men would tell stories in turn while the others worked or merely listened. Though women were not forbidden to enter the *karigi*, it served mostly as a gathering place for men. The *karigi* was also the scene of two activities of considerable import to the Naupaktomiut as well as to most Alaskan Eskimos: the Messenger Feast and the shaman's performance.

The midwinter Messenger Feast was an eagerly awaited event for the Naupaktomiut. Thus it is somewhat surprising that the accounts of modern Naupaktomiut informants concerning this ceremony vary so widely. It seems doubtful that the structure of the Messenger Feast varied much from year to year or village to village, but at this point in time it is possible only to reconstruct its bare outlines for there is considerable disagreement about the details.

The feast was initiated by sending runners, usually two men, from the Naupaktomiut village giving the feast to another village with which there were kin ties. The villagers of Kotzebue and Tigara (Point Hope) frequently were invited to Naupaktomiut villages. The Naupaktomiut runners were commissioned by Naupaktomiut men to go to the house of their partners, usually kin, in the other village. The runners carried a number of sticks, each representing one Naupaktomiut man and his partner. The runners gave a small piece of meat to each partner and promised both more of the same kind of meat when they visited the Naupaktomiut village. In turn, the partner asked for something else good to eat and also for a gift, such as a new sled or a wolverine skin. The runners then returned to their own village, where they were fed as soon as they arrived.

While the runners were gone the Naupaktomiut had been busy preparing food for the feast. They also had to obtain the food and gifts for which their partners had expressed a desire. The sticks the runners brought back helped the people remember what gifts were needed.

After a period of time the people from the invited village began to travel toward the Naupaktomiut village. They stopped to camp when they were a day's travel away. Each Naupaktomiut who had a partner coming chose a runner to go meet him. All the runners went to the visitors' camp and again gave them meat. Then the runners raced back to the village. It was an honor to arrive first. When all the runners had arrived they went into the *karigi*. As each came through the door he was given some water. Then everyone went home to sleep.

The next day the visitors arrived. There was singing as they unpacked their sleds. The visitors stayed in the house of their Naupaktomiut partners. After they had been fed, in the evening, everyone went to the *karigi*. The Naupaktomiut went in and sat down while the

visitors climbed up on the roof and crowded around the skylight. There they sang to their partners inside and lowered gifts down on a line through the hole. Then the Naupaktomiut had to give their partners the gifts they had requested.

Afterward a dance began to the sound of singing and drums. Some informants say that each group, the Naupaktomiut and the visitors, tried to "win the *karigi*" by their dancing. Late at night the feast broke up and the villagers took their guests home. The next day the Naupaktomiut men played football with the visitors. This was a rather amorphous game played by kicking a ball, usually made of skin stuffed with caribou hair, over a wide playing field. Dances, singing, and feasting went on for a number of nights until finally the visitors returned to their own village.

The *karigi* was also the place where shamans, or *aŋatquqs*, most often practiced their skills. A shaman, either male or female, had the ability to cure, to tell the future, to restore lost souls, to find game, and also to work evil. In addition a shaman made charms and prescribed individual and group taboos. Shamans served as go-betweens, protecting the common man from the supernatural. They also added an element of fear to the society because they could bring sickness and death as well as cure. It is therefore no accident that many Eskimo folktales deal with shamans.

The shaman's office was not sought; it was a calling that came to one without his bidding. Anyone could become a shaman; there was no shamanistic society or apprenticeship, though a shaman might pass on his magic songs and amulets to another. Shamans worked alone. There is little doubt that many who became shamans were in some way out of tune with reality, misanthropic, and possibly even psychotic.

A Naupaktomiut *aŋatquq* was paid when his services were required, although he often returned his fee if the patient did not live. Shamans usually worked in the darkened *karigi* accompanied by the sound of drums and mournful songs. Sleight-of-hand, ventriloquism, and other trickery were part of the performance.

According to Eskimo beliefs, illness was most often caused by the breaking of a taboo. Therefore, public confession of this transgression with the aid of a shaman often would restore health. Sicknesses of a psychological nature—and the Naupaktomiut were as subject to these as any people—might truly be "cured" by recourse to a shaman, which actually produced self-purging by acknowledgment of the violation of a taboo.

Sometime between mid-March and early April, while the snow was still on the ground and the days were growing longer, the Naupaktomiut moved from their winter quarters along the lower Noatak across the Mulgrave Hills to the coast between Cape Krusenstern and Kivalina. This sled trip usually took three or four days, as the people took their *umaypaks* (large skin boats) and kayaks with them. The pre-contact Naupaktomiut family had no more than two or three dogs, so the women had to help pull the sled along. Favorite camping places along the coast included the edges of the larger lagoons and the mouths of larger streams, such as Ukaliksuk (Rabbit Creek), Jade Creek, and Ḳiḷḷikmaḳ Creek. Population aggregations were larger during the spring than during the winter because the Naupaktomiut tended to concentrate at three or four traditional locations on the coast.

While traveling in the spring, and later on the coast, the people lived in a dome-shaped dwelling called the *kalovik*. This tent was made of bull-caribou skins sewn together and spread over willow poles which were set in the ground in a circle with their tops bent inward and tied together to form a framework. The tent was for sleeping only; cooking was done over an outside fire.

Seals were the basic subsistence item during this season. Both ugruk (bearded seals, *Erignathus barbatus nauticus*) and smaller seals (*Phoca* sp.) were stalked on the ice, speared in open leads in the ice, and caught in nets. Fishing was an important secondary source of food. Hooks and nets were utilized to secure tomcod (*Boreogadus saida*), trout, sculpins (a number of different genera), and other species from both the streams and the ocean itself. Ptarmigan and rabbits were taken. With the approach of summer, migrating waterfowl, particularly the eider and other sea ducks, offered variety in the diet. In June waterfowl, gull, and shorebird eggs were collected, as were "greens," usually young willow leaves.

The Naupaktomiut remained at their spring encampment until sometime in July when the sea ice withdrew from the coast. Then they moved by skin boat along the coast to Nuvuvruk, at the very tip of Sheshalik spit in Kotzebue Sound. Here they all camped at one spot, distinct from the tents of the Noatagmiut, the upper Noatak River people who were also at Sheshalik during the summer. The primary activity of the Naupaktomiut at Sheshalik was trading with the Noatagmiut and other Eskimo groups camped there. Sheshalik was one of the two great trading centers in Northwest Alaska, Nirlik at the mouth of the Colville River being the other. Eskimos came from as far away as Siberia and Cape Prince of Wales to trade at Sheshalik. The Naupaktomiut traded furs, blubber, seal line, and seal oil for tobacco, iron lances, and reindeer skins.

Fishing with nets, principally for whitefish, though salmon (especially *Oncorhynchus Keta*) and trout were taken, was the main subsistence activity. According to some writers (cf. Foote 1961:33) the Naupaktomiut also hunted beluga or white whale (*Delphinapterus leucas*) at this time, but my informants indicated they did not do so prior to contact. Flightless ducks were secured with a bird spear propelled by a throwing board. In the late summer, berries (*Rubus*

chamaemorus, Vaccinium vitia-idaea, and *Empetrum nigrum*) began to ripen, and the women picked them on Sheshalik and at the coast behind the spit.

Sometime in August the Naupaktomiut began to move back up the Noatak River. The period between late August and freeze-up in October was vital in terms of Naupaktomiut subsistence. The fall food quest was keyed to the acquisition of supplies of caribou and fish, although important supplementary foods were also sought. As the people moved upriver in their skin boats they seined for salmon, trout, and whitefish. If the weather were cool enough the fish were covered with willows and gravel and left on the river bank to be picked up by sled later in the winter. If not, the fish were cut and dried for later use.

The Naupaktomiut would camp at traditional caribou-hunting places along the middle Noatak River where they would kill as many caribou as possible and dry the meat for storage in seal oil. Two types of caribou drives were utilized at this time. One method involved the caribou corral described earlier. Also, converging rows of decoys which looked like men were built running toward large lakes. Forced into the water, the swimming caribou could be lanced easily from a kayak or shot with a bow and arrow. Individual hunting stratagems were probably also of some importance. Snares were set along frequently utilized caribou trails. Small groups of caribou were stalked with the bow and arrow. In addition, mountain sheep (*Ovis dalli dalli*) and ptarmigan were taken in the fall. Collecting of plant foods was an important subsidiary subsistence activity. Sometime before freeze-up the people would move back downriver to their winter quarters along the lower Noatak.

Alternative subsistence patterns did exist. For example, Naupaktomiut families might spend the spring and summer inland instead of going to the coast and then to Sheshalik. In this case they would spend the summer fishing along the lower Noatak River or, more probably, hunting caribou to the north of the middle Noatak. The latter activity was carried out on foot and was primarily for the purpose of collecting caribou skins to be used in making clothes.

The Naupaktomiut's immediate neighbors to the north and east were the Noatagmiut. The Noatagmiut, or people of the Noatak River, inhabited the Noatak River Valley, the valleys of its main tributaries, and the shores of the larger lakes between the Nimiuktuk

River and the Noatak headwaters. The locations of their winter quarters changed from year to year in response to changes in the availability of caribou and fish. Archaeological and ethnographic investigations have disclosed postcontact Noatagmiut sites at various locations—including the mouths of the Anisak, Makpik, and Aniuk rivers, at Okak Bend, in the Cutler and Aniuk river valleys, and at Desperation and Feniak lakes—and have indicated that these locations were occupied in precontact times. On the basis of explorers' reports of the number of Noatagmiut at several coastal locations during the summer months, Foote (1965:252) has suggested a population of 945 for the Noatagmiut in 1850.

The Naupaktomiut and the Noatagmiut see the basic differences between themselves in terms of distribution, subsistence patterns, and language. I am not prepared to discuss dialect differences, but a reconstruction of their culture as of 1850 discloses that distribution, subsistence patterns, and house type marked the most distinctive differences between the two peoples.

The Noatagmiut winter house, because of its domed shape, had the same name, *kalovik*, as the Naupaktomiut summer tent. A framework of willows was covered with two sod layers and a final mud layer. A skylight was cut in the top. Once the hut froze it was covered with snow to improve its insulation. A willow-burning central fireplace provided heat. The Noatagmiut summer tent, on the other hand, was pyramidal rather than dome-shaped and was made from caribou skins.

Caribou hunting was the mainstay of Noatagmiut winter subsistence. Though individual hunting techniques were sometimes employed, the caribou corral was the basic method of killing caribou. According to some informants a semicircular corral was used as well as the more common variety described for the Naupaktomiut. Mountain sheep were taken in snares.

Fishing was an alternate subsistence activity of some importance, particularly in poor caribou years. Hooking through the ice was the primary means employed in securing grayling, whitefish, and pike (*Esox lucius*). Ptarmigan were pursued in ways similar to those utilized by the Naupaktomiut. Fur-bearing animals were killed with deadfalls.

As spring approached the Noatagmiut began moving from their winter quarters to the places along the Noatak River where they had cached their *umaypak* frames in the fall. They would wait at these locations, readying the boats, until the river broke up and most of the ice had run. Then they began the trip downriver, which usually took four or five days. While traveling downstream the people seined for trout and whitefish with nets woven of caribou and beluga sinew. Waterfowl and shore birds were taken sporadically and "greens" were gathered.

Before moving out to Sheshalik the Noatagmiut would stop somewhere on an island in the Noatak mouth for a few days to prepare their summer hunting equipment and to put skins on their kayaks. When the ice left Kotzebue Sound they moved out to the end of Sheshalik spit. The time between early June and mid-August was spent here. Toward the end of this time extensive trading took place with Eskimo groups from the Kobuk River, Cape Prince of Wales, the Diomede Islands, and East Cape, Siberia.

While waiting for the beluga (*shishauk*) to enter Kotzebue Sound, the Noatagmiut fished for trout and whitefish. Although most of their seal oil came from the Naupaktomiut by trade and their ugruk skins from the Naupaktomiut and Shismaref people, the Noatagmiut occasionally took both ugruk and small seals when the sea ice came close into shore.

Cooperative hunting was necessary to insure success in taking beluga. When the white whales came into Hotham Inlet the Noatagmiut put out in *umaypaks* and kayaks. They tried to paddle out so the whales were between them and the shore and then to herd the mammals into shallow water. If they were successful the beluga, unable to submerge, made an easy target for harpoons. Often a considerable number were thus taken, and a single whale provided a great amount of meat, blubber, and *muktuk* (skin), the last a highly desired food.

In mid- or late August the Noatagmiut started upstream toward their winter dwelling locations. They would try to get as far upstream as they could before freezeup occurred. As the Noatagmiut ascended the Noatak they passed the Naupaktomiut, who were coming downstream from their annual autumn hunt. The Noatagmiut seined salmon as they went and continued to fish for whitefish and trout throughout the fall. Birds, berries, and small animals were also sought. As did the Naupaktomiut, the Noatagmiut tried in the fall to lay in supplies for the dark winter to come. The emphasis was on caribou hunting. The caribou corral and drives into large lakes were the primary methods employed.

The Noatagmiut commonly followed at least three variants to their basic subsistence pattern. Instead of descending the Noatak River to Sheshalik, some families moved north, down one of the Arctic Slope streams to Piknik, a spot near Point Barrow, where they spent the summer trading and hunting seals. Other families went by *umaypak* down the Colville to Nirlik, a small island in the Colville delta. Here they traded with coastal groups and with other inland groups while subsisting mostly on caribou and seal. A third alternative was to remain inland all summer hunting caribou.

The Naupaktomiut also had extensive trading and feasting ties with the Tigaraqmiut of the Point Hope region. The Tigaraqmiut spent the winter at Tigara, the end point of a long series of beach ridges jutting out into the Chukchi Sea. Their population in the late nineteenth century has been estimated at one thousand (Foote 1965:21).

The Tigaraqmiut winter house, or igloo, was semisubterranean, being set into a beach ridge to provide maximum insulation. The sod-covered walls incorporated driftwood and whale bones for support. A long entrance tunnel opened into the living area and, in some houses, separate storage and sleeping chambers. Seal-oil lamps provided the only heat and light source.

The Tigaraqmiut exploited an extremely favorable environment, having access to rich marine, as well as land, resources. Tigaraqmiut winter ice hunting centered around the ringed seal (*Phoca hispida beaufortiana*), which was harpooned or netted as it came to a breathing hole. Polar bears were killed with lances or bow and arrow. Caribou were taken in corrals or in a pit trap dug in hard snow. Subsidiary subsistence sources were tomcod and crabs, caught through a hole in the ice.

In the spring the subsistence quest focused on the bowhead whale. These huge animals, providing meat, blubber, baleen, bone, and *muktuk*, were taken in open leads as they migrated northward. Boat crews spent the months of April and May camped along the leads, ready with harpoons, strong seal lines, and seal-skin floats. As many as eighteen whales might be taken in one season. In early June emphasis switched to the hunting of ugruk and smaller seals. Hunters crawled along the ice to harpoon sleeping animals and speared those swimming in open leads. Migrating birds were taken with arrows, bolas, and nets.

Tigaraqmiut families had several choices when summer arrived. Some families, particularly if the members were aged, stayed at Tigara and ate stored seal and whale meat. Others camped along the coast near cliffs containing bird colonies and collected eggs, fledglings, and adult birds for immediate and later consumption. Still other families hunted caribou in the foothills behind Cape Lisburne and to the east in the Kukpuk headwaters or took white whales from various coastal locations. Some Tigaraqmiut families traveled to the mouth of the Utukok, hunting caribou along the way, where they traded oil, meat, and line to the Utukokmiut for caribou, fox, wolf, and wolverine skins. Tigaraqmiut families also traveled to Sheshalik.

In the fall the Tigaraqmiut returned to Tigara and prepared for the winter season. The Kukpuk River was heavily fished for trout and other fish species; caribou were sought if they came close to the coast.

The Historic Noatak People

The world of the Naupaktomiut began to change by 1850. This change was neither fast nor continuous. The Naupaktomiut had infrequent contact with outside influences, meeting whalers and traders on the coast in the summer and occasionally visiting white parties who wintered in the region. Besides, the Naupaktomiut, like all Eskimos, were practical, matter-of-fact people. The outsiders did offer new and wondrous things for trade, but only a few items (guns, iron, beads, tobacco, and liquor) were readily accepted. Nothing offered by the white man could change the necessity for securing subsistence, a problem which remained day after day long after the ships returned south. The Naupaktomiut were pinned both physically and spiritually to the land and its resources.

Yet, even though the change during the early historic period was slow, it was steady and cumulative. The primary agents of change were disease, liquor, and rifles. Diseases, especially venereal and pulmonary, made heavy inroads in the Naupaktomiut population. Liquor, secured both from traders and whalers and locally brewed, sometimes interfered with the food quest, particularly in the fall, causing starvation. The acquisition of the rifle caused the Naupaktomiut to change their hunting patterns and to shift the seasonal emphasis of their subsistence. Additionally, the necessity of securing furs for trade and the opportunity of seasonal wage work altered the traditional yearly cycle.

Toward the close of the nineteenth century a new problem arose to threaten the Naupaktomiut and the other Eskimos of Northwest Alaska. The constant predation by the whalers dramatically reduced the populations of whale and walrus; increased white and Eskimo hunting pressure, aided by the rifle, resulted in the virtual disappearance of caribou from the area. The Eskimo could no longer successfully pursue their traditional subsistence cycles, resulting in in economic and social changes of far-reaching consequences.

By 1897 some few Naupaktomiut still clung to the old ways of life; others had forsaken their land and subsistence cycle entirely and had moved to the coast; still others spent the winters along the Noatak River and the summers at Point Hope or Kotzebue. The Klondike gold rush had spilled over into Northwest Alaska under the impetus of gold reports from the Kobuk River. Most of the prospectors passed through the Kotzebue area and some operated along the Noatak. Also, in 1897 the California Yearly Meeting Friends Church established a mission in Kotzebue, changing what was essentially a summer camping place to a permanent village and drawing many of the Naupaktomiut during the summer. It might be supposed that the two, prospector and missionary, canceled each other out, but in actuality one group increased the incidence of disease and availability of liquor while the other offered an entirely new way of life to the exclusion of the old. The result was to further disrupt the tenuous hold the Naupaktomiut had on their traditional lifeways.

During the early 1900s the Friends decided to increase their activities in northern Alaska and they began to establish new missions. In 1908 they started a federally supported mission school at a site some seventy or eighty miles up the Noatak from its mouth. The scarcity of caribou, the disrupted economic pattern, and the desire of the Noatak peoples for schooling and Christianity drew them to the site and resulted in the founding of Noatak Village. The Naupaktomiut came first because the mission school was located in the center of their traditional hunting territory; by 1910 almost all of the Noatagmiut also had settled in the village.

From this point in time the acculturation of the Noatak Eskimos was swift, though it must be kept in mind that they had to, and still have to, operate within the subsistence possibilities of the land. By 1910 the Naupaktomiut *ebrulik* and the Noatagmiut *kalovik* were gone, replaced by one-room, split-log cabins. A store was established in the village by a Kotzebue trader in 1915. Salmon became the most important subsistence item, although caribou became of increasing importance when they again began to move into Northwest Alaska after 1913. The settled life and increasing ability to catch and store large amounts of salmon, coupled with the necessity to travel great distances in the winter to trapping and caribou-hunting grounds, led to an increase in the number of dogs kept by each family. A new type of sled introduced from the Nome area was pulled by teams of ten or more dogs. Canvas was substituted for caribou hides in making tents and kayak covers.

Another important factor in changing the Naupaktomiut culture had been introduced in 1909. A number of government agencies working together brought reindeer from Siberia to Alaska in an attempt to initiate a native-owned-and-run industry and to offset the loss of caribou. Several Noatak men owned reindeer herds during the period from 1909 to 1924, but numerous problems, including disputed ownership, arose over this individual endeavor. In 1924 the Kivalina-Noatak Reindeer Company was established and all the individual herds were merged, to be cared for by appointed managers. The herd reached its apex in 1932 when forty-two thousand animals were reported. Overgrazing, uncontrolled herd growth, and mixing between the reindeer and the wild caribou, again numerous in the region, caused a decline after this date. The Kivalina-Noatak Reindeer Company was dissolved in 1942.

New subsistence patterns arose in the 1920s and 1930s. Both the Naupaktomiut and Noatagmiut traveled to the coast during the spring and summer, following the old Naupaktomiut pattern, but now only the men engaged in the fall caribou hunt. Often many families spent all their time in the fall seining and drying fish. Trapping, aided by the extended range of large dog teams, became extremely important in the Noatak economy. Trap lines ran far north of the Brooks Range divide forcing some men to leave the village for the entire time between November and March. In the 1940s muskrat became a valuable fur source, and spring camps were made on the marshy flats along the lower river, from which the animals were hunted during their breeding season. Outboard motors were introduced in the late 1930s and within a few years became an important adjunct to hunting and fishing. The last skin boat was used in 1947, wooden river boats having replaced the traditional *umaypak*.

A cooperative native store was established in the late 1920s and continued in competition with stores run for a few years or so by various independent traders. The village council was also inaugurated in the twenties. The resident Bureau of Indian Affairs teacher (a separation between the school and mission having occurred before this time) served, then as now, as an adviser to the council. Noatak Village was incorporated in 1939, and at that time the council decreed only stores owned and operated by natives would be permitted within the village limits.

The course of Naupaktomiut and Noatagmiut acculturation between 1897 and the 1950s does not vary greatly from that of other Northwest Alaskan Eskimo groups. The initial period of disruption, disorganization, and depopulation was replaced by a time of reorganization, crystallized by the building of a mission school and the establishment of Noatak Village. Some parts of Naupaktomiut and Noatagmiut aboriginal culture—for example, *aŋatquqs*, feasts, trading partners, and dancing—disappeared early because adherence to these aspects of the old lifeway conflicted with the missionaries' concepts of Christianity. Other traditional practices and skills did not die out, primarily because they were those essential to the food quest. The tenor and manner of that quest itself shifted from time to time. The Noatak peoples' concept of the outer world was based on their contacts with missionaries, teachers, traders, and government officials. The economic health of Noatak Village ebbed and flowed around the vagaries of world commerce, particularly of the fur market.

The Modern People

The population of Noatak in 1964–65 was about two hundred people, lower than in previous years because a number of families lived in Kotzebue where regular work was available. The village is situated on two river terraces, one about forty feet and the other about fifteen feet above the water level. The majority of the houses and all of the larger structures in the village are on the higher terrace, while a few private residences dot the lower terrace. Most of the family dwellings are still log cabins; a few modern frame houses have been built. Though there are no planned streets, most houses face east toward the river and all are connected by heavily worn footpaths. The long axis of the village is north-south, with the gravel runway of the airport near the southern village limits. The river does not flood either terrace at high water, but it has actively eroded the bank, destroying over three hundred feet since the village was founded and causing the people to move many buildings back or west, away from the river. A series of log pilings was placed to form a bulkhead during 1963–64, but additional bank erosion subsequently occurred. As a result of this process the village has been forced to move west toward the marshy bed of an old lake. There is now little good ground available for expansion.

The focal point of village activities is the Native Store, located in approximately the geographic center of the village. The store is controlled by the council in conjunction with the Alaska Native Industries Cooperative Association. The bulk of the store's supplies arrives in summer, brought by barge or boat from Kotzebue. Replacements for depleted commodities and luxury items reach the store by air freight. The store paid off a loan which allowed it to expand and by 1965 had a considerable cash surplus in the bank.

Other large structures in the village include the church, the National Guard armory, and the school complex. The church is a relatively old log structure run by the Friends, still the dominant religion in the village. A native pastor holds Sunday and Wednesday services and ministers to the people's religious needs. National Guard exercises are held in a recently completed frame building. A new four-room school and quarters for four teachers were completed in 1962. This complex has its own power source, the village's only steady electricity.

Noatak communication with the outside world has greatly increased. Wien Alaska Airlines brings mail, freight, and passengers to the village on a tri-weekly schedule. There is twice-daily radio communication with the Kotzebue hospital, providing health information to the native health aids and allowing extremely sick patients to be flown to the hospital. The BIA teacher maintains a daily radio schedule with the Alaska Communication Service, which in turn has connections with Fairbanks and the southern states. The National Guard radio can be used in emergencies.

The village has another type of outside contact. Summer and winter there is a constant flow of strangers through the village. Arriving mostly by air, these include Public Health Service doctors, postal inspectors, BIA personnel, Fish and Wildlife Service personnel, and occasional tourists. Several scientific parties have spent short periods of time in the village and at least two have lived there for a year or more. Two researchers connected with the Human Geographical Studies Project, part of the U.S. Atomic Energy Commission's study of Northwest Alaska, resided in the village from May 1960 to May 1961. My wife and I spent the thirteen months between June 1964 and July 1965 there.

The subsistence cycle of the Noatak people, though very different from that of the precontact and historic peoples, is still intimately connected with the natural resources of the area. The fall months, late August to early October, are spent seining salmon, whitefish, and trout. The salmon are preserved by splitting and drying or are left in piles along the river to freeze. A good salmon catch is a prerequisite to a successful winter caribou hunt because of its use as dog food. Trout and whitefish are more commonly used for human consumption, though they may be fed to the dogs if salmon are scarce. A certain amount of caribou hunting is done on short boat trips upriver during the fall. Also moose, which have become common in the area during the past ten years, are actively sought. Moose can play a major role in the Noatak diet in poor caribou years.

After freezeup the people engage in two main subsistence activities. The women, and some men, hook for trout through the ice. Fresh fish are always welcome, and ice fishing is also of importance in years when caribou are scarce. Most of the men make sled trips of varying distances and duration looking for caribou. The animals may be found quite close to the village in some years; in the winter of 1964–65 they were not, and most hunting trips lasted from ten days to two weeks. Killing is done with a rifle. If successful, the men cache most of the meat for later retrieval and return home with fully loaded sleds. Few men now trap fur animals since low prices make trapping economically unfeasible. When not out hunting, the men repair sleds and other equipment and cut trees for wood. Propane and oil stoves are now used by a few families; however, most still depend on wood for cooking and heating.

Toward December subsistence activities slacken. Ice fishing is not particularly successful at this time, and the short days, combined with stormy weather, make hunting difficult. Besides, Christmas is probably the most popular village holiday. There is a week of celebration between Christmas and New Year, including dog races, feasts, church services, a school-sponsored Christmas program, and nightly Christmas games. The whole village is divided into two teams for the games, which consist of typical Eskimo contests of strength and agility, such as finger-pulling, high-kicking, and "Indian" wrestling.

Although the dark days of January and early February are not conducive to strenuous subsistence activities, an occasional hunting trip is made. After mid-February the days lengthen, and hunting and fishing take up much of the villagers' time. In addition to caribou hunting some men make sled trips to the coast to hunt seals in open leads. In April and early May grizzly bears emerge from hibernation and, along with mountain sheep, are killed on hunting trips. As breakup nears the trout fishing improves and migrating waterfowl appear, landing on the available open water. Geese and ducks are sometimes shot in violation of federal game laws. If the winter hunting and fishing have been poor, waterfowl can tide the villagers over until the spring hunt.

As soon as the river is free of running ice, most of the Noatak families pack up their household goods and move to Sheshalik by boat. There the men hunt ugruk and beluga from their boats during June and early July. The women tend nets set for trout and whitefish and butcher, cook, and store the game brought back by the men. Seal oil, a necessary supplement to the winter diet, must be rendered from the ugruk blubber and stored in wooden barrels. In late July and August many of the men engage in wage work while their families remain at Sheshalik or Kotzebue, continuing to fish and picking berries as they ripen. A few families stay in Noatak all summer, living on food stored from the winter and goods purchased at the store.

Most of the money brought into the village comes from summer employment. Noatak men work in southern Alaskan fish canneries, at construction jobs in Fairbanks and Kotzebue, and as helpers with various scientific parties working in the area. At least three men—the store manager, postmaster, and school janitor—are employed year around. Other sources of income include sale of mukluks and other native goods, National Guard salaries, and unemployment compensation. Federal and state agencies provide welfare assistance for blind, disabled, and elderly Noatakers, and also for dependent children. The BIA teacher is empowered to give additional welfare money to needy families.

Most of this money is spent in the Noatak Native Store. Some families purchase their staples from Kotzebue, saving money by transporting the goods to Noatak themselves. If a man has had a successful summer he might purchase an outboard motor or some other item necessitating a large cash outlay. A considerable portion of the money not spent on foodstuffs goes to mail-order firms like Sears, Roebuck for clothes and toys.

Children remain a focal point of the Noatak family world, as they always have in Eskimo society. Despite what occasionally appears to outsiders as neglect, Noatak children are wanted and loved. The villagers are extremely desirous of a better world for their children, and they often equate education with increased potential for success. The qualifications of the BIA teachers, their interest in the children, and their attitudes toward native people are carefully noted. Noatak children are actively encouraged by their parents to attend school. In 1964–65 only two teachers were in the village because of the reduced population. The school covers eight grades; for high school the child goes to Kotzebue or to native high schools to the south.

Although its people are highly acculturated, a visitor to Noatak Village would be aware of differences between the villagers and those encountered in similar small villages with different cultural backgrounds. Eskimo is still the daily language of almost all people old enough to be married, and Eskimo words are sprinkled in the conversation of youngsters. Fur-rimmed parkas and mukluks are often worn. Native foods are still eaten. But with only a brief inspection the similarities, both material and nonmaterial, between Noatak and a non-Eskimo village are more apparent than the differences.

By the 1950s, Noatak had emerged into the modern world, an almost typical Alaskan bush village. The uniqueness of its people lies partially in their continued dependence upon the land for subsistence, but mostly in the values and ideals they have managed to retain from the old way of life. The prestige due a man who secures a well-paying job is balanced by the prestige still accorded a good hunter; the desire for imported food is balanced by the continuing high value set on seal oil, salmon, and caribou; the difficulty some of Noatak's younger people have adjusting their ambitions to their potentialities in a white world is offset by the many older Noatakers who have made the transition successfully and, more important, happily. Most Noatak people describe their existence as "a hard but good life." Particularly for an outsider, it is difficult to make a measure of what the Noatak people have gained and lost over the past hundred years. Older Noatakers often sigh for the traditional way of life, though their knowledge of it is secondhand. There is a certain conservatism among the village leaders that is not met in many other Northwest Alaskan villages.

The Noatak peoples have never really consciously controlled the choices presented to them, choices which have resulted in movement toward a new lifeway. If they could have guided in any way their destiny or were free to change the results, I am not sure Noatak would be any different than it is today. One way in which the success of any change can be measured is whether or not those involved are satisfied with the results. With a few exceptions, the Noatak people seem to be so.

II. The Noatak Storyteller

INTRODUCTION

My original intention was to interview all of the older Noatak Eskimos who still told folktales. I was curious to know exactly how many folktales were current in Noatak and how many were included in each storyteller's repertory. Other points of interest were the variations of tales with a common origin or theme, and the sources from which the Noatak storytellers received the folktales they now told as their own. Finally, I wanted to know what possible roles folktales played in the culture of the aboriginal, historic, and modern Noatak Eskimos. Under what conditions were stories told? Where were they told? Who told them? Did the composition of the audience determine the story or stories to be told at a given time? Did an individual storyteller "own" certain stories or was anyone free to recount any tale he wished? How accurately were the stories passed from one individual or one generation to another?

Thus I began with my first informant, Edna Hunnicutt, and her folktales. After detailing her early life, we turned to the folktales themselves, the ones she knew well enough to relate, a total of fourteen. This was a promising beginning, so I was confident that in the few months left I could interview everyone in the village who "knew how to tell stories."

The second informant, Paul Monroe, was not much interested in talking of his early life. He maintained that his childhood was "just like Edna's." Paul, the acknowledged doyen of storytellers in Noatak Village, was afraid I would not have time to hear all the stories he knew. His concern was well founded because we spent over two months recording the 176 stories he remembered! Thus ended my plan to seek out other storytellers. However, with the folktales of Edna and Paul, the main sources of stories in Noatak, I feel the range of folktale knowledge in the village today is well represented.

THE STORYTELLERS

Edna Hunnicutt lived alone in a small, one-room, plywood cabin built by her relatives. She had no close kin in the village during the period we were there, though occasionally her grandson would come from Kotzebue for a visit. This does not mean that Edna was often alone. Called "Grandmother" by many of the villagers, whether related to her by blood or not, she almost always had company. They came to visit and brought fish or special pieces of meat they knew she would like. Her smile and "Taku, taku" (thank you) were always ample reward for any kindness.

Edna spent the inclement days of winter inside. Someone would stop at the post office for her old-age-assistance check or run to the store if she needed a can of fruit or some coffee. An older boy would come to chop some wood for the stove. On Wednesdays and Sundays people from nearby houses would walk with her to church. Many of Edna's winter hours were spent in animated conversation with Paul Monroe, who visited her almost daily.

With the coming of spring Edna moved outdoors. Wrapped in a yellow calico parka with a wolverine ruff, she sat for hours on the woodpile outside the stormshed, surveying the village in the bright spring sun. Adults and children paused for a moment to chat and laugh. As the days lengthened into summer Edna began to visit. I never could be sure then where I would find her for she was welcome in all houses. Summer was a good time for Edna, despite the heat and mosquitoes, as she was able to move about, to enjoy seeing again the village and the people she had been a part of for so many years.

Though old and wrinkled with years, Edna appeared to enjoy life. Memories of our days together flash to mind: Edna showing me how to use a seal-oil lamp; Edna laughing at my efforts to shape a moss wick; Edna coming to our house to tell stories and sticking her chewing gum on her forehead so it was out of the way; Edna's smiles when we bought black *muktuk* from Point Hope to give her; and, lastly, her infinite patience when I could not understand the translated segment of an old story.

I was never quite sure Edna fully understood why Leona and I were in Noatak or what we were doing there. We tried to explain why we were interested in her and why we wanted to record the old stories. However, there were some in the village who doubted our motives and who told Edna we would sell her stories to make a lot of money. Such notions confused Edna, who complained to Martha, the translator, that she did not know what to believe. But she continued to visit and to tell freely the stories she knew, which I felt indicated her trust. For my part, I can never remember Edna, never see her in my mind's eye, sitting outside her house in the sun, without a feeling of warmth, respect, and love.

Paul Monroe also lived alone—in an old log cabin next to the Native Store. He wore glasses and a hearing aid. These, coupled with his long white hair, led me at first to think him old and feeble. But

his stories, which came flowing forth with a vivid power that made me see the stories' actions, and his hands, which could still skillfully carve spruce wood into bowls and spoons, belied his appearance. Paul, too, received old-age-assistance money and help from his relatives. The villagers watched after him as well, inviting him to visit and bringing meat and fish to him.

Paul was not originally from the Noatak River; he was neither a Naupaktomiut nor a Noatagmiut. However, he came to Noatak Village while still young and it was there that he first began to collect stories. Always eager to retell old stories, he seemed truly to enjoy relating them to us. Often we would work all afternoon and, in the evening, I would find Paul still telling stories in someone else's cabin. He said that trying to tell me all the stories he knew made him remember even more!

I think Paul did understand why I wanted to collect folktales and he offered them willingly, demurring only to say there were others who knew more. His eagerness to talk was readily demonstrated when he sought us out soon after we arrived in Noatak. With Paul there was always the sense of wanting to impart the past, though he did not offer his stories until he knew we were interested. And that is how I remember him, his steady voice in a darkened room painting pictures of a time gone by and of things still half believed.

THE TELLING OF STORIES

In the Past

Both Paul and Edna lacked interest in the circumstances of recounting folktales in aboriginal and historic times. I was able to elicit, however, some general background information which is summarized below, indicating that the Noatak people did not differ markedly from other Eskimo groups in such matters. The only remarks Paul offered on the telling of stories without being directly questioned (which I always tried to avoid), were as follows:

> I first started telling stories when I was young. When I heard a story I always tried to tell it to other people. That's how I learned. They used to tell stories in the karigi or in somebody's house. When I heard stories they got in my head and I couldn't forget them.

When two storytellers get together they take turns telling stories. If only one man is telling stories he always tries to tell more than one. One story is simply hanging and needs a "stick" to hold it up.

Old stories are told in the past [tense]. Old true stories that happened a long time ago are called "ulipkuk." Young stories that happened not very long ago are called "itnaŋniksuit." Those are stories about something we have seen or that happened while we were alive. They also can be stories that a person gets from a person involved.

Sometimes there are two different versions of a story because one person saw it happen and made a story about it while others only heard about it and made stories from what they heard. Oftentimes two different villagers have two different versions of a story. If someone in Noatak made a story about something that happened here and at the same time someone in Kivalina made a story about what he heard had happened here, the two stories would probably be different.

A storyteller might during the story say a word in the Barrow language and his listeners would know that his story took place in Barrow. Storytellers try to talk like people from where the story took place.

Thus most stories were told in the *karigi* or someone's house, though other informants indicated that stories could be told by men in hunting camps or traveling in a boat. Apparently, anyone who so wished could tell any story; certain individuals, however, were known for the number of stories they remembered and the manner in which they related them. An individual learned a story by listening to it carefully at every opportunity.

However, there were some strictures on storytelling among the Noatak Eskimos. As Paul indicated, each storyteller tried to tell more than one story at a sitting. A story had to be told correctly, that is, exactly as it was heard. Also, relating of incomplete versions of a story was frowned upon. The emphasis was on careful, complete renderings of each story.

Despite the care with which stories were passed from individual to individual and generation to generation, discrepancies between, and different versions of, some stories are apparent in any collection of Eskimo folktales. Paul suggests in the quote above one way by which two versions of one story are created. Obviously exact recitation of folktales was a cultural ideal, not a reality. Incorrect or incomplete renderings, combination of the elements of two or more stories, recasting of stories heard from elsewhere into familiar geographical settings, and other factors have led to many ways of relating the same basic story.

The Naupaktomiut and Noatagmiut were not culturally isolated. They interacted with many other northern Alaska groups, particularly in historic times, and in the exchange stories passed between various groups as easily as seal skins and other trade items. As Paul notes, one way for a storyteller to indicate the specific setting within north Alaska where a story took place was to utilize the "dialect" of the people who inhabited that setting. Herbert Onalik, who has traveled widely in north Alaska, consulted with Paul, and together they listed the following differences in speech between various Eskimo villages as compared with Noatak.[1]

KIVALINA: same words as Noatak but slower and shorter

POINT HOPE: very slow, slower than anybody else

WAINWRIGHT: not sure, but he thinks they talk a little slower and also lower

POINT BARROW: very different words for same things, for instance, animals; a lot faster

ANAKTUVUK PASS: just like Noatak

LONG BEACH (on the Kobuk River): words are a little different than in Noatak and Kiana

NOORVIK: some words are different

KIANA: same as Noorvik

SELAWIK: words are very different and the end [terminal] sound is like that of a rock dropping in water

KOTZEBUE: some words are different and the words are generally longer

SHISMAREF: about the same as [Cape Prince of] Wales but not as fast

CAPE PRINCE OF WALES: different words and fast

KING ISLAND: different words

LITTLE DIOMEDE: different words; speech is like going up and down on waves

SIBERIA: I [Herbert] can't understand them very well. [The Siberian Eskimos speak the Yuit form of the Eskimo language while the north Alaskan peoples speak the Inuit form.]

A detailed analysis of the importance of folktales to the Noatak Eskimos and of the folktales themselves is presented in Chapter V. Briefly, a primary purpose of these stories was to provide recreation.

[1] It should be realized that these remarks on dialects are appended merely as folk judgments and are not meant to represent a serious linguistic statement on dialect differences in northern Alaska.

They were a way of whiling away the long winter, when subsistence activities were at a low ebb. However, folktales had, and still have, values beyond this. Some try to explain the universe of the Noatak Eskimos and to explicate their relationship with the environment. Some represent a verbalization of otherwise unconscious psychological stresses. Other stories detail the animosities between the Noatak Eskimos and other Eskimo groups. Finally, many of the stories told by Paul and Edna can be viewed as morality plays, reminding the listener of the importance of living within the Eskimo system of beliefs and values. For example, a man who stays too long abed with his wife in the morning will not be a successful caribou hunter. The incorporation of statements of culturally approved behavior into folktales served both as a means for enculturation of the young and as a constant reminder for all that to survive in the harsh arctic world one must abide by certain standards.

In the Present

Paul and Edna were the principal storytellers in Noatak Village while we were there, though others occasionally told a story or two. Most often stories were told in the evening after dinner. Sometimes I had the feeling that Paul, and perhaps Edna, offered stories in return for being invited to stay and eat. Their stories were always well received, no matter what the subject, even if the listeners were familiar with the ones they chose to relate. Often the audience took part in the storytelling by asking what appeared to me to be ritual questions at certain points in the stories, much as the question "What happened then?" is used in our society. Although I had little command of the Eskimo language, I found myself easily involved in the storytelling. The rise and fall of the teller's voice, the darkness of the cabin, and the interest as well as the mood of the listeners all combined to communicate the excitement and tension of the ancient Eskimo story. Occasionally I was fooled, however. One evening, after a dramatic rendition, I asked someone nearby what the story was about, thinking it might be one Paul had told me previously. The answer was disconcerting to say the least. It was a story Paul once had read in *True Confessions* magazine!

The folktales included in this study were recorded during the spring months of 1965. Early each afternoon, except Sunday, Paul or

Edna would slowly walk down the snow-covered path to the small frame house where Leona and I lived. When they arrived Leona set the table with coffee, cookies, fruit, and *muktuk* or some other local food. We then sent a child to bring Martha Burns, who usually served as translator. Edna or Paul sat on one of the metal cardtable chairs across the table from me, Martha on a big wooden chest close to the window, and various children and adults, there to hear the stories, on other chairs scattered around the room. We often had an audience, though the slowness with which the stories were told, because of the necessity of translating sentence by sentence, often discouraged the younger children. If they were too noisy Edna would ask them to go out and play.

Each session began with questions from me to clarify ambiguities in the stories collected the previous day. I also asked if Paul or Edna had anything to add to yesterday's stories. Invariably the answer was, "No, I told all I remember." Then we would begin a new story. The storyteller would ask, "Do you know the story about . . . ?" This was as much a formula to them as it is to the raconteur in our society, for Paul and Edna knew full well which stories they had told me and which they had not. When I answered "No," the story would begin.

Paul knew a little English, so we could carry on a reasonable conversation if no translator were present. Edna, however, spoke almost no English. In either case a translator was necessary for me to follow the folktales and to transcribe them accurately. Martha Burns, a lovely, soft-spoken Eskimo woman in her thirties, translated most of the folktales. Herbert Onalik, an older Eskimo man, translated at several sessions when Martha was not available. Both Martha and Herbert had only a limited amount of formal schooling, but their ability in English was sufficient for my purposes and, indeed, I was often surprised at their range of vocabulary. Herbert, because he had traveled widely, was the better translator in terms of technical matters and geographic locations; Martha's almost unfailing good humor, her patience with me, and her rapport with Paul and Edna, however, made her an ideal translator. Most importantly, she greatly enjoyed hearing the old stories and often said to me that if she could only remember those she had heard from Paul and Edna she would one day be the best storyteller in the village.

Paul and Edna began by relating a few lines of the story in Eskimo.

Then they waited while Martha translated and I transcribed. If Martha were not sure of some point she referred again to the storyteller for further clarification. When I finished writing, the story continued. Undoubtedly this method of recording lacked spontaneity, though both Paul and Edna still became enough involved in the stories they were telling to visually act out the storyline.

When a story was finished I quickly read my notes to make sure all was clear. Usually I reread the stories each evening so that inconsistencies could be checked at the beginning of the next day's session. Approximately once a week Leona typed my notes, and at this time we again checked for clarity and consistency.

Storytelling sessions lasted between two and three hours. For reasons explained above, both Paul and Edna preferred to tell at least two stories at each sitting, and they often told more. Occasionally Paul would tell only part of a story, saying that he could not remember the rest. He knew I was interested in the total number of stories he knew, including the fragments, but he was always careful to distinguish between full stories and partial ones.

I did not directly pay Paul and Edna for storytelling. However, we kept them supplied with canned fruit and vegetables. I also brought them caribou, fish, rabbits, ducks, or seal oil whenever I was successful in hunting, and I occasionally chopped wood for Edna when her supply ran low. Such payment in kind was consonant with the pattern of reciprocity in the village. The translators, however, were paid by the hour. Translating interrupted the daily routine of subsistence activities for both Herbert and Martha, and hence I felt compensation was necessary.

ORGANIZATION OF DATA

The data I received from Edna Hunnicutt and Paul Monroe are presented in the next two chapters, the first dealing with Edna and the second with Paul. Each chapter begins with an autobiography and then continues with the folktales. Each folktale is numbered and given a title. In most cases the titles are mine; I chose a name mentioned in the story or a phrase reflecting some aspect of the story. Occasionally the title reflects the earlier-mentioned question from Paul or Edna, "Did I tell you about . . . ?" Each story ends with the name of the individual from whom Paul or Edna first heard the version he or she was recounting. Sometimes Paul or Edna had a comment on the story or an additional fact to bolster its veracity; if so, such comments are also included at the end.

The final paragraph following each story contains a number or numbers referring motifs found in the folktale to Thompson's (1955–58) comprehensive motif index. References following the numbers are to other folktales, in studies cited by Thompson (*ibid.*) from the Eskimo area only, that contain similar motifs. Additionally, I have compared, in terms of similarities of *major* motifs, of whole episodes, or of entire stories, the Noatak folktales to those found in the following sources: Ostermann 1942 (Mackenzie River); Ingstad 1954, Gubser 1965 (Anaktuvuk Pass); Spencer 1959 (Point Barrow); Ostermann 1952[2] (Colville River, Utukok River, Noatak, Point Hope, Kotzebue, King Island); Rasmussen 1932 (Colville River, Utukok River, Noatak, Point Hope, King Island); Curtis 1930 (Noatak, Kobuk River, Kotzebue, Selawik, Cape Prince of Wales); Lucier 1958 (Noatak); Lucier 1953 (Buckland); Giddings 1961 (Kobuk River); Nelson 1899 (Norton Sound, Sledge Island); Keithahn 1958 (Seward Peninsula); Ray 1968 (St. Michael); Gillham 1955 (Hooper Bay) and Lantis 1946 (Nunivak Island). Thus the distribution of particular motifs and folktales within the Eskimo area can be seen. Finally, any comments on the folktale content follow the references.

The autobiographies and stories are printed almost exactly as I recorded them. Too many possibilities for distortion are already present, including the use of a translator, the telling of the stories in a somewhat artificial setting, and the recording of them by an individual not of Eskimo culture, for me to take the further liberty of recasting them in a form that might be more elegant or grammatical. I have substituted a few words here and there to avoid confusion. If I felt further clarification of a point was necessary I inserted an explanation in brackets (an elaboration or explanation by the informant or translator is enclosed in parentheses within the text proper). Beyond this the stories retain the flavor of the way they were told to me in the carefully chosen words of the translator. If the reader bears in mind that these folktales were told by two individuals at a certain

---

[2] Ostermann (1952) contains fuller, original versions of folktales also found in Rasmussen (1932).

place and a certain time, translated by two other individuals, and recorded by still another, then the folktales may stand as my rendering of the repertories of two Noatak storytellers.

I should stress that perhaps not all the stories told by the Noatak Eskimos strictly fall within the categories of myth or folktale. Though I refer to the selections that follow both as stories and as folktales, my sole criterion for their collection was that Paul and Edna chose to relate them. If the reader wishes to categorize the stories or to distinguish between story and myth, or folktale and myth, or *ulipkuk* and *itnaɲniksuit*, he is free to do so.

III. Edna Hunnicutt

AUTOBIOGRAPHY

I was born on the coast at Uḳaliḳsuk in May when the ice was break-ing up [around 1880]. The white men call me Edna Hunnicutt, but my Eskimo name is Iraahuruk. My father's father was a Noatagmiut [properly, the singular is Noatagmi], married to a Naupaktomiut. My father, name Itigvruk, was a Noatagmiut. He married a Nau-paktomiut named Simiuk. His brother also married a Naupaktomiut.

I had two older brothers, but my parents threw the second one away [infanticide]. I was the third child. There were quite a few children born after me, but they all died.

When I was born my father was hunting seals with a kayak. He used a spear with an antler or ivory point. He also used to net for seal through a hole in the ice and get lots that way. We had seal oil plenty. Father might get enough ugruk to cover the boat and he would try to get all the seals he could for the winter.

He also had a gun when I was born and made shells out of powder. People got guns and steel traps from white people when they first came on a ship. Before that they got bears and caribou with snares and bow and arrow.

We stayed on the coast through May, June, and July. Plenty of families stayed at Uḳaliḳsuk, both Noatagmiut and Naupaktomiut. They lived in dome-shaped skin tents made over a bent-willow frame, a kalovik. It took six bull-caribou skins to make one. The door was made of a caribou or a bear skin. The tent floor was made of cut willow branches covered with skins on top. People slept anywhere on the skins. There was no stove in the tent and no heat.

The fire was outside, away from the tent. Cooking took place there. To cook, people made stones red hot and put them in a spruce bucket. They also broke caribou bones for marrow.

My father and other people netted the rivers when the fish went out. They got trout, flounders, and tomcods. Kids collected eggs. At one time people did not eat eggs because a long time ago old people died from eating them. I sure could eat eggs when I was young, especially ptarmigan eggs. Eggs were cooked underground—put in the sand with a fire built on top.

Around the end of July we moved by umaypak to Nuvuvruk, at the very end of Sheshalik spit. We did not hunt beluga there. My father did not hunt beluga because we moved around so much. Naupak-tomiut did not go to the beluga hunting place. They got no seals at Sheshalik either.

We stayed at Sheshalik until early September and just fished for trout, salmon, and whitefish. We had lots of food then which we would dry up and store for the winter.

One day we moved across to Kotzebue. I was a little girl, about three, and my brother, Aargun, was five. My grandmother was with us. The Noatagmiut and people from up Kobuk way always go to Kotzebue sometime during the summer.

At Kotzebue we always stay up at night, out playing someplace. Three girls (two sisters and another girl) were not quite ready to get married so they still played. They had me for a play daughter and my brother for a play son. Those girls were walking on the beach after they played for awhile. They found a dead baby beluga that had a cut in his flipper. They didn't work on that beluga but started play-ing with me again as a play daughter and my brother as a play son. My brother got sleepy (he never used to be sleepy before when we were playing) so I got sleepy too and we went to sleep.

Those girls went to the beach and found a naulayuk [least weasel, *Mustela rixosa eskimo*]. They killed it and tried to skin it. Then they started to play tan it just for fun, even though it still has meat.

My father woke us up and told us that the girls got sick. When I went out from the tent I saw my father working on those two girls, trying to make them well. He was trying to let them have breath by putting their tongues out. This happens, people dying, when they work on things they shouldn't (that's the time when the devil walks around before the Bible covers this world). And that other girl that played with them died too.

Suvalik, the father of those two girls that died, wanted to kill my father. He was mad because my brother and I went home. He thought that if we stayed with the girls they would still be alive. People sent a message to my father's cousin, Ḳavun, living where the army camp is now [a couple of miles south of Kotzebue]. Ḳavun heard that that man wanted to kill his cousin so he came with a boat and took me and my whole family to his camp. My family was poor then. We had no white man's food and not many clothes.

Ḳavun brought along some young men. He had a rifle [probably a single-shot .44] to protect us. The young men loaded up that boat. Ḳavun hid my father, brother, and me in the boat, covering us with some of the gear. He had his rifle ready.

We knew we had to pass Suvalik, who was getting ready to bury his daughters. The bodies were by the water. I saw Suvalik putting clothes on them. He had one of his daughter's legs and he stroked it. He put long mukluks, up to her hip, on her. The mukluks were made of white-and-black reindeer skin. He cut his other daughter's hair and stretched it out to show how long it was. That dead girl had real long hair, almost six feet.

The dead girls' mother went to see them. She had hung some things in her hair. Some dried fish, some flowers, some other things. They did this in the old days when a relative died.

After Ḳavun took us to his place we watched closely to see if Suvalik would come over. We watched day and night. Finally people decided someone should go across to Sheshalik to tell another of my father's cousins, a Naupaktomiut name Tikiliauruk. Ḳavun unloaded his boat and took off for Sheshalik. He put a sail on his boat when going across.

Ḳavun told Tikiliauruk about the man who wanted to kill my father. Tikiliauruk came across from Sheshalik with his two wives. The first was named Nanauk and the second Innuwuk. Tikiliauruk was a real aŋatquq. We kept watching for Suvalik. After staying for awhile, Tikiliauruk wanted to go back to Nuvuvruk, so he took my whole family with him.

After we got to Nuvuvruk we put up our tents. Then a young woman named Siichak, my female cousin named Iiḳaluḳ, the same age as me, and I walked over to the point. We found a straight cut bank along the lagoon side of the point. My cousin and I started playing in the water, after we took off our clothes. Siichak sat on the bank watching us. I stepped on what I thought was a rock. I sank to my neck and slowly kept sinking farther. I got weak and couldn't breathe. My cousin started sinking too. The girl sitting on the beach didn't try to help us. We hollered for help, but that girl couldn't move. When I couldn't make it I thought it was going to be the end. Just my hand waved above me out of the water. I noticed my stomach was full of water; I drank a lot. I kept putting my hand up again and again, but that girl wouldn't help.

After awhile I decided I had one last chance. My cousin stepped on gravel under the sand and managed to tiptoe to shallow water. When she got out she was looking for me. She saw me close to her, saw my hand and tried to reach it, but the hand went down again. I tried once more. I felt someone grab my hand and felt myself being dragged through the water. That girl still sat on the beach.

When my cousin got me out I tried to know what I was doing. I started crawling along the sand. Iiḳaluḳ grabbed me and put me with my stomach over a hump of grass and pushed on my back. Soon I started throwing out water, lots of water, every time my cousin pushed. When we both finally got good that girl was still sitting there. We went home and slept. I think that if we both drowned that girl still wouldn't have talked. My ears haven't been good since I stayed in the water so long.

About this time my father's youngest brother died; I remember him. He put my chin tattoo on. I was about Bertha Burns's age [four]. I remember when the needle got in my chin and I started crying.

One spring we were at Uḳaliḳsuk. There was Nellie Woods and Nellie's sister, Agnes, and their mother and me there at one time. So we (Nellie's mother, Agnes, and me) went down to the ice and played seal. Nellie's mother has a baby on her back (Agnes) so she and I played seal. One boy came along and play hunt seals with us. He told us to play sleep and he plays trying to get the seals. Then we put our heads up, hear something coming, and that boy would get low and hide himself. He would play scratch the ice to put us to sleep so we put our heads down, pretend we're sleeping. There was a little crack in the ice near us so I said to that baby, "Pee your mama, pee your mama." So pretty soon Nellie's mother says, "Alapah, alapah!" [Cold, cold!]. Then we both fall on that crack. That boy got up and he really laughed and we all laugh.

When we were at Uḳaliḳsuk I had my first period. I was about fifteen when my period started. When women have their period they have their parka drawn down over their faces [the hood of their parka pulled a little beyond the edge of their head] and they look down, not anywhere else. They don't move around or pick up food or anything. A woman stays in the house. If they are at the coast she can't get close to the fireplace outside. Also, animals are scared of weapons that have women's menstrual blood on them. A man and woman don't do it because the man gets funny and dies.

When a woman has her first period she doesn't go to people, has her own pots and dishes, can't go out and play with the kids. After I had my first period I didn't feel like playing with the kids. I felt like a woman. We used moss to catch the blood; spread the moss all over down there.

When I had my first period, my brother was hunting with other men. When he came home, my mother came out to meet him. She told him that I had my period. He went in. He took two seals home. When he heard that I had my period he told me that he would hunt ducks with me because I always went with him when he went seal hunting.

There was a family whose father had just died on the other side of Uḳaliḳsuk. Nobody goes over to comfort them after their father dies or talks to them, all except me and Agnes' mother.

My family used to stay on the ice in a tent near the open water and when we get a seal they bring it to Uḳaliḳsuk (a short way). After we were down on the ice the whole family moves up to Uḳaliḳsuk. On the way when they're moving I lose lots of blood and I had to use a stick to walk with behind my parents. I was very weak and almost fainted on the way.

When we went to Uḳaliḳsuk we put up our tent on the rocks. We build a fire and start cooking and eat outdoors. We used to take small, smooth, flat rocks with us for a fireplace when we went seal hunting, on the ice. We put an old skin on top of the rocks, then sand on top of the skin and niggerheads [sedge tussocks] around the edge.

When we stayed at Uḳaliḳsuk, after we put all our stuff up from the ice, then the ice starts breaking. There is a lake at Uḳaliḳsuk and a river going out to the ocean, and that's the place we get lots of fish. When there's no more ice and we can't go dogteaming, we go hunting ugruk and seal with kayak and bring back a full load. We hunt with guns. When we're ready to, we "skin" the boat; put a new ugruk skin on. We put new skins on every spring when they're ready to go to Sheshalik and up the Noatak River.

After we put a new skin on a boat we went to other people with our boat to get more seal oil. We went to Uukruruk (near Uḳaliḳsuk). Me, my brother, and Paul Monroe's brother went to Carl Luther's uncle. He was living at Uukruruk where we went to get the seal oil. After we get a load from that man and come back to our camp we get ready to take off.

My family (father, mother, and brother) and Paul Monroe's family (Paul, brother, mother, and sister) all take off in the same boat. Just when we took off from Uḳaliḳsuk all the other boats take off too. It got windy and big waves came. The waves hit the boat and put them on the beach; all their stuffs, seal oil and other things, were spilled in the water. Some people's boats were broken. All the people get to a high place except my and Paul's families, who get to a low place.

Everybody fixes up their boats and waits for it to get calm. When it calm down again they take off again with all the Sealing Point [Cape Krusenstern] people. It got windy so we went into Aaniigak [between Cape Krusenstern and Sheshalik]. Everybody stayed in Aaniigak for a few days. We're expecting two boats from Uukruruk, Carl Luther's two uncles (each had a boat). One of Carl Luther's uncle's wives was pregnant, so we were expecting the two boats while we were waiting in Aaniigak. When the boats were coming the wind catches them and they went into Ḳiḷḷikmaḳ. When they were there, the pregnant woman got sick, not with labor pains. She had a little boy already. While they were in Ḳiḷḷikmaḳ that woman got sick and she told her husband she always works seals and ugruks on top of big rocks where there is no sand. They call these rocks taupuk. She died while they were in Ḳiḷḷikmaḳ and they bury her on top of the taupuk instead of in the ground.

When those two uncles got to Aaniigak, they told us that one's wife died at Ḳiḷḷikmaḳ. They let my brother hear that his atuk (namesake) died and he feels funny about it and he was going to cry, but he didn't know what he was doing [he had fainted] and when he "wake up" people were working to make him get good. He got weak and never worked for a long time.

My brother used to pull the skin boat by its string [rope] but now Paul's brother takes over because they don't want my brother to work. When we went as far as Itiiptiḵviiruk [a part of Sheshalik] we put our boats through the lagoon and went to Nuvuvruk. When we went to Nuvuvruk we put a sail and went across to Kotzebue.

We stayed in Kotzebue for a few days; then we start coming up the Noatak River. When we reach that place, Kaḵlik [on the lower Noatak], where spotted seals always stay, Paul's brother wanted to stay there. He asked for my brother's kayak and he said if you go as far as the place you're going to stay for camp I'll reach up there.

When we went as far as Amaktuk (three big rocks that look like they're packing each other) we start seeing a man on the beach walking with his hands holding his sides. When he gets close to us he calls out that he has a pain in his side. That man is from Wales [Cape Prince of Wales]. That man keeps walking back and forth. We went farther up, saw a boat on the beach, and went to the boat. There were two Eskimos, one from Kobuk way, one I don't know from where, in that boat and a third man [a white man whom the Eskimos called Auyiiruk] who found gold in fall time and was taking those three Eskimos that summer to find more.

When we put our boat close to that other boat one man said to my father, "I don't think that man (from Wales) had pain." After we stayed there awhile, we take off for that place where Paul's brother told us to stay. All night we sleep and Paul's brother didn't show up. When he didn't show up to us, Paul's brother stayed with those four men. That other boat take off the next morning and pass us who were waiting for Paul's brother. When we saw that boat the white man was in the back with the oar and that man with pain (Wales man) was in the front and had a gun with him; the other two men were walking, holding the string. The man with the gun was aiming all over at anything and soon he shot that white man who was in the back with the oar (the white men that brought Auyiiruk to Alaska told the Eskimos not to kill him; if they killed him something would happen).

Paul's brother was coming along with these four men; his kayak was behind their boat and he was on shore pulling it. The men who were on the shore pulling (including Paul's brother) all run and hide in the willows. They don't have guns with them. All their guns were in the boat and kayak. That man that killed the white man went down to the beach and tried to pull the boat. Those other men were hiding and that Wales man kept calling them to help him put the dead white man up to the beach. That Wales man say, "I thought I saw a spotted seal; that's why I shot."

He keeps calling those men for help and Paul's brother says, "You killed him. There's no spotted seals this far." Then that Wales man forgets about the other men while he was trying to pull the boat up; the three men ran to the boat and kayak and got their guns. The Wales man kept pulling the white man and put him in the trees. Paul's brother got his kayak back. Paul's brother ask one guy from that other party (the Kobuk man) to go with him to his (Paul's brother's) family. That Kobuk man said he doesn't care what happens to him. He said he's not afraid to tell the other white men who killed Auyiiruk. So he didn't go with Paul's brother.

One of the four men takes off through the hills (walking along the river) and he says there are lots of blueberries; Paul's brother went with kayak through the river toward us. It is that third Eskimo in the gold-hunting party—the one that I don't know where he comes from —that goes with Paul's brother. We are still waiting for Paul's brother. When Paul's brother and this other man get tired they take turns, one goes through the hills and one takes the kayak. When they get close to us, but on the other side of river, Paul's brother doesn't want to leave that man, so we put the skin boat down and go to the other side of the river and get those two men. When we reach those two men Paul's brother calls out, "They killed one of our men."

About those two men down there with the boat. Those two men (man from Wales and man from Kobuk way) are getting ready to go to Kotzebue. The Wales man says to the Kobuk man, "If we go to Kotzebue, are you planning to say I killed Auyiiruk?" So that Kobuk man said, "No, I won't tell them that you killed him." That Kobuk man is scared. When they're going down to Kotzebue that Kobuk man tries to oar, turning his back to the Wales man. He tried to keep his back turned, but he was afraid of that Wales man so he turned towards him. That Kobuk man notices that he doesn't have much shells in his gun but that Wales man has lots of shells under his seat, so Kobuk man runs along edge of boat, grabs some shells, and runs back to other end of the boat. After he went back to his place that Wales man says, "Well, friend, I'm not going to do anything to you."

They reach Kotzebue, and when they landed in Kotzebue a lot of people come to meet them because they knew they were going to hunt gold. When the people see them Carl Luther's aunt misses two people in the boat. "Where those two men?" she asks. "Maybe you killed them and then came down to Kotzebue," she says. That Wales man says, "No, we didn't kill them. Paul's brother took them up the river."

When they reached Kotzebue that Wales man's villagers take him to their tents. So those Kobuk people take that Kobuk man to their tents. That Kobuk man starts eating when they put the food down, that Wales man starts eating when they put the food down (they are in different tents, not together). Before that Kobuk man starts eating, the white men living in Kotzebue come to him and ask him if he killed Auyiiruk. He said, "No, I didn't kill him. That Wales man killed him." In first place that Kobuk man said he wouldn't tell them [the white men] about Wales man, but he tells the white men he told the Wales man that to protect himself. He said, "That white man and that Wales man were in the boat and those two other men were pulling the boat; they hear a shot and find out that Wales man killed the white man."

After that Kobuk man tell the white men the truth, the white men take that Wales man to the ship and they tie him up. They get a knife and white men cut pieces of his skin off. When the ship goes they take him.

A year after that white man was killed [the following summer] they take Paul's brother in a big ship as a witness and they take that Kobuk man. While they talk that captain of the ship always lets Paul's brother drink (whiskey). The people on the ship (some people from Diomede going to jail) start making trouble for Paul's brother. The natives tell him they'll kill him. They want to protect the Wales man. They [the natives] like the Wales man; they tell the white men that Paul's brother is lying. Paul's brother knows he's telling the truth, but the others don't believe him so he cuts his throat.

There is a man from Shismaref who had been around the Noatak and knows Paul's brother. That Shismaref man was going to eat. He is "in the states," in some tent [house] with other Shismaref people. They tell him that the men that went to jail had one person from the

Noatagmiut. After he eat his meat the man from Shismaref says he'll go see that Noatagmiut man; he knows him. While he was eating he heard that a man had already cut his throat. It was Paul's brother. After the Shismaref man eat he went to jail to visit. He went into the jail; he saw Paul's brother with his throat cut suffering from pain. His stomach was cut too. That man that watch Paul's brother [a guard] didn't know Paul's brother had a pocket knife. This man from Shismaref was going to bail him out. It was too late.

Auyiiruk wanted to take only two men from Kotzebue and go hunt for the gold. That Wales man really wanted to go; they didn't want him to go, but he got back in the boat. One time Wales men went down to a big ship from their village and the white men killed all the Wales men, including that man's father. So he hated white men.

That same fall I saw Auyiiruk killed we came upriver and stopped at Naupaktusugruk for the winter. When we started coming upriver we used both paddles and poles (iuktun); we also pulled the boat with ugruk rope. In September we went up to Kuguruk or Nimiuktuk. We pulled the skin boats upriver—never used sails—used two or three dogs to pull boat. Men pulled the boat while women poled. We got salmon and ducks that could not fly along the way. My father had a skin boat. Everybody that went down to the coast had a skin boat. If we went up the Kuguruk we would walk the next day to Siyaḷiññik (north, to the land beyond). In my family all went there, leaving the boat at the Kuguruk mouth. When we went home from hunting we would get the boat and go back downriver. If we didn't see any caribou we went as far as the ocean (we could see the ocean when we climbed the mountain—it looked like smoke). This trip took a long time, maybe a month.

We dried up the meat, fat and all, over a fire and tried to carry it all back with us. The hunters were using rifles and hunted like people do now. If my father was lucky he might get four or five caribou; if we got more we would just have to throw them [away] because this was all we could bring back. We would kill any much [any number], but we usually didn't get lots and sometimes didn't get any.

My family didn't hunt sheep, but others did. We took only ugruk-gut shelters with us. After hunting we went downstream to Naupaktusugruk.

After we got to Naupaktusugruk the Noatagmiut came, traveling the same way. Even if there were only two persons (no kids) they travel the same way (by umaypak). On the way some people always throw those who starve or who are too weak to go farther. They leave them on the trail.

We always stopped at Naupaktusugruk for the winter. There were a few houses at Naupaktusugruk and a few at other places. At Naupaktusugruk we made ebruliks. Everybody helped. We always put a window and then put the fire in the middle of the house so that the smoke went out of the window. We made a window of ugruk gut and then put rocks on it to hold it. We didn't use spruce for fuel, only willows. Just before the fire went out we threw the remains of the fire out through the window and then covered the window with the ugruk gut. We had this house for two years and then it got funny. We would make a new one every couple years.

The ebrulik was heated and lit with a seal-oil lamp. One will burn all night with one load of oil. I used one when I was young until I married my first husband. Mine is an old one used by my grandmother and I carried it with me saying that was just like having my grandmother along. When my family went I have to take it along. When they stop I have to use it. It was used for both light and heat. I melted snow in a pot on a string above a lamp. Point Hope people also did it this way. I never cooked above it and used only seal oil (like gas). For a wick I used moss rolled and shredded like tobacco. The height of flame was adjusted like in a kerosene lamp.

Many lamps could be used in a house. The lamp was called aulanguluk. We let the lamp burn out at night. The coal oil lamp came with first white man. You could use any number of lamps in a house. I had only one. It would keep my present house [approximately seven by ten feet] warm. One would keep an ebrulik warm.

We stayed at Naupaktusugruk all winter until we moved across to the coast in April. At Naupaktusugruk we used to fish in the fall, hunting fish with spears and traps and later hooking. My father did not hunt at Naupaktusugruk; he only fished. He used a gaff to get salmon and trout. He also used a spear with a point which came out of the shaft so that the fish could be played with a line. We did not use a seine for salmon; used spears and still got enough, all we want. After it froze up we fished with hook and line and traps. When food was scarce we'd dig for dead salmon. That's how we lived. We always put snares, but frequently rabbits would chew the sinew up.

We got a few rabbits and ptarmigan. Other people would hunt them more than my family.

When I was young I used to walk upriver with the men. We never saw a moose or moose tracks. Moose only came around recently. My father does not know about moose. We didn't get enough food when I was young, no moose. When I was up Kobuk way (as far as Kiana) I saw a moose hide, but no moose. I don't know where they came from.

There are lots of people at Naupaktusugruk that winter. We stayed down there and one man's wife died in the house next to ours. There was an old woman; she was sick. That old woman lives in an ebrulik. Her stepdaughter stayed with her for awhile and that woman's step-daughter's husband was with them, too. Then that man went to Point Hope alone. When that old woman got real sick her step-daughter stayed with her. While that old woman was real sick the stepdaughter's husband's family had the girl move in with them. After that old woman's stepdaughter moved, she and I and another girl went over to the old woman's window and listened and that old woman called for Ikuluk (the stepdaughter's name). That old woman would call from inside that she wants water and I would say to those two girls that they should go in and give her water, but the other two girls didn't like to go in, and that old woman's house was locked from outside by other old people because they don't want her to go out. Because we go to the window that old woman still calls for water —that old woman hears us [Edna and other two girls] coming. I think this old woman was probably an aŋatquq. I told those two girls they should go in to give her a cup of water, but those other two girls don't want to go in. I am not scared to go in with other girls, but scared alone. Everybody at Naupaktusugruk was scared of her.

When we go over to that old woman's window another time we listened and there was no sound. When we could not hear that old woman anymore she had died. She's got a big stone lamp. They don't take the old woman out after she dies. After that old woman was dead, her stepdaughter's husband came back from Point Hope. After that woman died everybody moved a little farther upriver from Naupaktusugruk.

Carl Luther's uncle, whose wife died at Ḳiḷḷikmaḳ, and his little boy moved in with my family when we left Naupaktusugruk after that old woman died. When we move they build new ebruliks. Other people cook indoors at round stone fireplaces, but my family cooks outdoors. We had no coffee or tea or whiskey because these people don't trade with the white men at this time. When we boil fish we drink the "juice" from this fish. When we're going to bed the little boy always prays, "Dear God, can I go to my mother too? Can I go to my mother right now?"

My father works on his kayak and skin boat during the winter— he gets the pieces of the frame ready and puts it together when we go to the coast. He doesn't build a new frame every year, just when it goes old. My father would put his boat frames together before we went to the coast. He took the old skins off the skin boat during the winter, put the old skins inside the frame, and put whole thing on the sled to carry it to the coast. He never used the old skins again on the boat. We used these old skins for other things. My father left the old skins on the kayak and used them until new skins were ready.

In the springtime we went to Ukaliksuk. It took three days to dogteam from Naupaktusugruk to Ukaliksuk. The first day we went to Iḷḷiŋnuk. The next day to Tiŋmakpuk, then to Ikarriak, the edge of the overflow ice on Rabbit Creek. We sometimes stayed for a few days at each place and always stayed at Ikarriak for a few days. When the ice was good for hunting we went to the coast.

My father did not have any dogs and he pulled our sled to the coast. We had big sleds. When we went to the coast I remember walking. Sometimes kids would ride.

Sometimes old people had two or three dogs. They didn't have dogs like people around here now; had one, two, or three. People always had to pull the sled themselves, and when there was little food had to kill the dogs. During the summer people fed the dogs water and a little food. In winter they fed them one-half salmon, dried or green, each day.

The time people were most likely to starve was falltime before they started upriver. The ones that didn't go from here (Naupaktusugruk) to hunt in the spring at the coast were the most likely to starve. I had all I want from seal oil and other things.

There is a story about when the people starved. My father was still alive and I was a teen-ager. There were several families living together. From Naupaktusugruk they moved to Kotzebue and from there to Siŋigraachuk on Kobuk Lake, where the reindeer herders

used to stay. My mother adopted four kids while they were at Siŋigraachuk̇. My mother's uncle wanted to come up the Noatak River. His name was Autuyuk and his wife's name was Iiuŋnuvluk̇. Iiuŋnuvluk̇'s father, Kaapaaluk̇, wanted to come too. Kaapaaluk̇ wanted to bring his daughter upriver and leave his own wife at Siŋigraachuk̇. Kaapaaluk̇'s family wanted to take Iiuŋnuvluk̇ along with them even though she was married. The couple cried because they wanted to stay together, but Kaapaaluk̇ didn't want Autuyuk to come along.

They came upriver and the Noatagmiut started to starve. They had no food. The people at Kotzebue heard that the Noatagmiut had no more food. Kaapaaluk̇'s daughter (Iiuŋnuvluk̇) was up the Noatak too. Some Noatagmiut starved to death.

It got towards spring. Autuyuk started walking upriver to look for his wife, to see if she had lived. The weather was nice and he stopped anywhere when he got tired. He walked along the west side of the river. When he got somewhere around the Kelly [River] he saw somebody sitting under a tree leaning against it. It was his wife.

He got close and saw the upper half of a body hanging from a branch in the tree. He sat down and told his wife, "You still live. Let's go home from here." She said, "No, I am not fit for that anymore now." He wanted to take her, but she didn't want to go. He asked, "Where

are your parents, your sisters, and brother?" She answered: "They all starved except for my brother. He is still alive. He took a knife and tried to kill me for food. That half body up there is one of my parents. I took it along for food when I ran from my brother."

The girl had a younger brother too. Her husband asked, "Where's your younger brother?" She said: "He was alive, but my older brother killed him. Maybe he has eaten him already. I am going toward Point Hope. You go home. If I get real hungry I have that half body yet. I'll take it along and if I'm hungry I'll eat from it."

They left, she going towards Point Hope and he downriver. She got married to a white man when she got to Point Hope. Autuyuk got another wife too, named Uŋguk. After he got married they had a big family. They had a daughter, my cousin who married Tuḳtuk from Kivalina. She had a big family too.

I had to drag my own father through the water to the graveyard in Kotzebue. The people wouldn't help me. Dogs ate him. When Robert Sams (the first missionary) came he told me not to cry for my father because he was already in heaven. That's why I tried to be Christian too.

My father was sick while at Kotzebue so I had to make hot water. After a few days he died there. When he died my brother and my mother and I alone took him from the place where he was through the water (I put on long mukluks), covered him with cloth, and dragged him to the other side of the lagoon. His back was torn from dragging him. My father's dog started hollering, so we set him loose and he went to his master.

We didn't use the tent. Afterward, we used cloth for a shelter. Just left the tent there in that place. When we woke up in the morning Robert Sams came for the first time with a translator. He came and asked why we didn't wake him up when my father died. He went into the tent and told us to come in and he drank water from the bucket (a long time ago people used to die from this). He let us move back into the tent. Before this people told us to move away.

Robert Sams asked my mother, "Is that your two kids?" She answered that her eldest son was upriver hunting caribou in a boat. Robert Sams told us he would have made a box for us to put my father in, but it was too late, so he taught us how to pray—"Our Father who art"—so that we would be forgiven. He said that even though we shed our tears in this world God will wash them away. This was the first time we had heard about the gospel.

After that there were big meetings in Kotzebue, like quarterly meetings. About two months after that a man died and they buried him in a box. Now they always do that.

After my father died, and that other man, we heard that there was a big ship down the coast and that the white men were going to take a boy and girl down there. A man named Pausina also went. They tied Pausina with his hands behind him on the big ship. A woman named Kiinak was sorry for Pausina and told the white men to untie him. They told her to stand on the ship's side and look ashore with a looking-glass, and she began to see people going back and forth. She recognized them and saw another man, Saŋnak, that the white men were looking for hiding in a little lake. They couldn't find him and she saw him through the looking-glass hiding behind Kotzebue. She must have been some kind of aŋatquq.

Pausina was tied up for making homebrew. Later they turned him loose. They were looking for Saŋnak for the same reason. The boat was anchored way down from Kotzebue. They couldn't even see land. This is a real true story.[1]

I never saw the boat. Three of my relatives planned to take me, my mother, and my younger brother away from the white people be-

[1] Hadley (1969:22) notes that on August 27, 1899, an Eskimo man named "Pashona" was taken out from Kotzebue to the Revenue Cutter Service ship *Bear* for punishment for making whiskey.

cause my younger brother said they might try to get us to the boat also (the Eskimos never let the white men take the boy and girl).

My relatives took us up the Noatak River. My mother took over the steering on the river, but she got the boat stuck on sand bars all the time. The men took over. Their names were Sikuḵsiraluḵ, Iḷḷya-ġuniḵ, and Iyaayuk.

The boat was a wooden boat with a keel; it was my mother's boat. My father sold his skin boat to some Kobuk people for one wolverine skin, one pair of pants, one box we never opened, and "some other stuff." We stopped at Aaliktuññuk [on the lower Noatak] and left seal oil and berries at Agashashok [a tributary of the lower Noatak]. At Aaliktuññuk my elder brother and Aŋnuyaḵ (Grace Bailey's uncle) got us in kayaks and brought us to Akveexrak for the winter. There I got married for the first time.

I was about fifteen when my period started and three years later I got married. Ever since I was ready to get married my father looked for a son-in-law. He looked for a long time. I don't know why I didn't want to get married. Maybe because it cost too much for men.

I got married when my father died. Before that I hunted for my parents. I didn't sew. I just went fishing to feed my father and grandfather. I hunted, that's why I don't know how to sew.

I was eighteen when I first married. My husband's name was Taluk. His English name was Clarence Allen and he was a Naupaktomiut. He worked for my grandmother. When women get married their husband works for the women's family as long as the women's parents are living. The husband can help his family, but he has to go back and help his wife's family. When I got married the first time my grandmother and Taluk's mother lived with us.

I was pregnant with my first child when we got married. I had only two children. I had my first baby, a boy, alone, and when he was born the head was cracked because nobody would help me. At this time people believed that if they helped deliver a baby they would die, so none of the women around would help me. I had no water when I was having the baby.

Maggie, my second child, was born about two years after the boy died. She was also born outdoors. At this time the people had fish and masu [root of *Hedysarum alpinum*] stored in one place, but they died from eating it. It was like poison. This was when I had Maggie, Clarence Allen's mother [another Clarence Allen]. After I had the child they didn't think I was alive; they pulled my hair and broke both little fingers, but I would not wake up. Finally they gave me an enema and I came alive.

When a woman had a baby she would have it outdoors, away from the house. Sometimes they made little snow houses for birthing. A woman had to stay away from the house for five days if the baby was a girl or four days if it was a boy. Sometimes women may have four or five children at once. I know of two women that had five babies and one woman who had four. The kids didn't live. When somebody had a baby they'd use moss for diapers in seal-skin pants.

Taluk, my husband, had kidney trouble and died while Maggie was young. I stayed in my own house here in Noatak until I remarried. I married my second husband, Kusik Hunnicutt, two years later. He was from Kotzebue. I hardly slept, that man went after me so much. After marrying we stayed around here.

Paul Monroe has been my help ever since I was small. When Maggie was about four I got sick with a big stomach (not pregnant). At this time Paul Monroe did not know how to speak much English. He and my brother took me to a white man. The white man was called Kiŋaaliluk. We went by dog team from a place below Naupaktusugruk to Itgitchak (a little above Kikmik, on the lower Noatak). The white man gave me a little piece of medicine and I went home. Later I threw out pus from down there. I had no children after that.

I started hearing that teachers and preachers will come ever since I was small. Some real old good people knew about this way before the white man came. They knew about God and knew that the missionaries were coming, and it was true because Robert and Carrie Sams came. When Robert Sams came I had my first period; he came the second year after [when Edna was about sixteen and a half]. Robert and them came in a big ship. In 1897 they built the Friends Church in Kotzebue. Later they came to Noatak and had a little ebrulik; then they built the old mission.

Uuyaksak is what the missionaries were called before they came. They weren't the first white men I knew. I don't know how old I was when I saw the first white man up Kobuk way. Lots came in big boats. The first white man was called Muuwaa.[2] His youngest brother

---

[2] Murdock (1892:52) notes that the Point Barrow Eskimos refer to Commander Maguire of the British ship *Plover* as "Magwa." Maguire wintered at Point Barrow in 1852–53 and 1853–54 while waiting for Sir John Franklin, who was lost in the eastern arctic. Edna's account may refer to Maguire.

came to Alaska first and when he didn't return home to the U.S., Muu-waa came to find him. I met him [her first white man, not Muuwaa] on the Kobuk. I was scared, had to run to my father. I don't know how old I was, but I was about as big as Bertha Burns [who is four]. I wouldn't be scared if I was as big as Aku [who is twelve].

Before the missionaries came there was an Eskimo man from Kobuk who had a pole outside his place at Sheshalik. Every seventh day he put up a flag. That man's name was Maanilyuk.[3] He rested on the seventh day. Other people and I used to visit him. He told us, "Some-day we'll have strangers, maybe white ones. We'll have a free coun-try, too, by that time, not like today." He took the flag off when sunset came.

That man that had the flag always told us when we were small that the world was wicked long ago. When people ate anything dif-ferent they always died. If the world would turn over like a hotcake everything would get good. He was just like the weather bureau, telling what is going to happen tomorrow and even next year.

Maanilyuk was an aŋatquq. He used to tell us that if the world didn't end something white was going to be flying in the air. He meant airplanes. He used to tell us that the Sheshalik peoples wouldn't stay there anymore, so the Naupaktomiut would move in then. This happened. The Naupaktomiut only started hunting beluga a few years ago. Before that the Noatagmiut always let them eat be-luga. I never cut beluga when I was small. When Maggie was small I started cutting beluga.

There were a lot of rules before the missionaries came. Especially at the coast. As soon as people put their tent up women would have a play mitten ready and they put a small pot and the mitten to hang (because they wanted their husbands to get ugruk and seal).

My father or some men would go down to a crack of open water and put their stomachs to the water (low enough just to touch the water), and they would turn over on their side out of this crack and get up on one side of the crack on their back, and that means they wanted to have open water for the spring. So it would always be open water for hunting season.

When a person first gets ugruk, as soon as they put it on the beach,

[3] Maanilyuk is further described by a Kobuk River Eskimo in Giddings (1961:31–34).

the women cut it and start cooking it in big pots. First thing they cook is lungs. They all eat a piece of the lung and drink the juice from cooking it. After they eat the lung they eat any part they want. When they bring the first ugruk to the beach they put a piece of grass in its mouth and let it drink water (fresh water) because they want more ugruk, and so when the soul leaves it it will be more comfortable. The head is left facing the water for a few days and then is turned around to face the other way. Some seals and ugruks have a mind, too, and when they hear a woman quarreling or complaining to herself the seal or ugruk say if that woman's husband hunt them they'll be scared because his wife won't cut them up right away. Those seals or ugruks that hear that woman complaining make it harder for her husband to hunt them, and sometimes he won't get any. Some women are good and don't fuss about when their husband hunt; they get seals and ugruks.

At the coast you couldn't go into anybody else's tent. A family always puts all the ugruk and seal bones together in one pile so when there was no more ice, when they don't hunt, they burn those bones, and some bones burn real bright and fast and some people's pile of ugruk and seal bones doesn't burn bright, and that family's pile of bones that don't burn good the family will "be missing" again ["be missing" means one of the family will die or something will happen to the family], and the family's bones that are burning brightly always have good luck. After they burned the bones they could visit other tents.

Animals have souls. If people don't cut it in the throat the animal won't go away. Anything they catch they have to cut the throat. It's wrong to work on animal skins with meat still on them because they have a "soul." I know two people who died from trying to dry a reindeer skin before preacher came.

In the old days they made clothes in winter, around Naupaktusugruk, because they could not do any sewing on caribou skins at the coast. They could only work on sea animals there; for instance, they could sew on the umaypak. If this rule were broken the person died. They even had to cut caribou skins that they were going to use on the coast before they got there. If a woman cut caribou skins at the coast she would die right there. They had certain pots for certain things. A woman had a pot just for taking food to the karigi and her own pot for herself and family. After eating seal or ugruk meat in the karigi you had to clean your teeth with a piece of wood before you went home. You could sew seal-skin pants on the coast.

You can't even pull grasses at Sheshalik, before preachers come, without dying. From the start it was like that, but when Carrie and Robert Sams came and tell about Bible it get good.

I have seen lots of kariyit [plural of *karigi*]; there are big ones and small ones. At Ukaliksuk there was a place outdoors where people all ate, not covered with a tent or anything. The same at Sheshalik. All the families ate there. When they quit using the kariyit, when the preachers and teachers came, they started eating outdoors.

The Akveexrak and Kotzebue people had a big meeting at Akveexrak and decided to make a karigi. This was after I had my period. Some old people thought of it first. They built it in the wintertime. The women helped.

The wall logs were spruce trees cut in half. To make the karigi they put logs on the side and then piled turf up. They made a sloped roof. This karigi was about sixteen feet square. There was a pole in the middle of the karigi to hold the roof up. The fireplace was nearby. There were whale bones around the fireplace so that the smoke would go out the window. In the evening when there was no more fire in the karigi they threw ashes out the window and then covered it with a hide.

This karigi had a big, long entrance passage. The only door was at the far end of the entrance passage. Some kariyit had no entrance passage so the door was at the karigi itself. The door was made of caribou hide. Kariyit were quite high because they had benches in them. The people who sat on the benches were called top people. I was in the Akveexrak karigi when the bench by the door fell and killed one man. He was made alive by an aŋatquq.

People didn't go to the karigi every day unless they were getting ready for a big meeting. Then men and women went to get presents ready. When they finished the presents they brought them up to the karigi. First they asked the other people what they wanted; then a few months later they brought them that and gave it to them. Pretend: Martha's [the translator] father has died and she hollers for him. I ask her what she wants. She says she wants parka, mukluks, socks, and mittens. I finish them and then at a big gathering give them to Martha. Martha puts them on. Then I give Martha food. Later Martha

gives me skins to make things for myself. After the gift exchange we would all dance. This was the last thing that was done. Both men and women danced.

When Maggie was a baby I didn't go to the karigi anymore. They didn't have them anymore after the teachers came.

If a person got sick with a pain or bad cold the aŋatquq would use a drum around him to try to make him well. Anybody could treat headaches and cuts. For headaches they used to poke in the back of the head to let some blood out. If somebody broke his arm they bound it up with wood until it healed up, until he could move it. If someone cut himself badly they would sew it up with human hair. If you used sinew the wound would have pus.

I can show you how aŋatquqs work. I will take a small willow and stick it under Martha's mukluk strings. Aŋatquqs do this and lift the foot. If somebody wants something they ask for it. If the leg is easy to lift the answer is "no"; if the leg is hard to lift the answer is "yes."

This is how a man I know was born. The aŋatquq let his mother have her baby through aŋatquq. I used to see aŋatquqs work this way occasionally.

People would ask all kinds of questions. They would pay the aŋatquq for this. They would always ask if some person wanted to-bacco. The aŋatquq lifted the leg of the person, then asked the question. If the person wanted that tobacco the leg would be real hard to come up. The aŋatquq used a stick like a cane.

A woman is lying down on the floor trying to have a baby, but she is having a hard time. The aŋatquq takes his stick and makes a digging motion at the floor. If she is going to have the baby the stick will be hard to pull up, just as if it had a big fish on it. If she is not going to have the baby the stick is easy to pull up.

In another case, when they don't know if a woman is going to have her baby, they tie a string around her head as she is lying there. They put the stick through the string. If her head is heavy to lift she is going to have the baby. If it is light she won't. If it is light even though the aŋatquq keeps working his aŋatquq the woman is going to die because she can't have her baby.

They'd put a string around a mitten and insert the stick under it. If the mitten was heavy to lift the answer was "yes"; if it was light to lift the answer was "no." They'd ask the mitten if it wanted seal oil or something, and if the mitten wanted some seal oil some was taken from a container with a finger and spilled on the ground. If the mitten didn't want the seal oil, the woman didn't have her baby.

A woman I know was going to have her first baby and the aŋatquq had to work on her. Her husband crawled all over the floor because he was suffering when she couldn't have the baby. She was about ready to die. The aŋatquq worked on her, but they never let her have the baby. The woman's mother-in-law took off her parka when the aŋatquq gave up. She had no clothes on. She started holding her daughter-in-law, trying to let her live. There were graves farther up. These people had a place by the [present location of the] Federal Aviation Agency in Kotzebue.

Her mother-in-law kept working on the woman and finally she had her baby. It was a big boy. The woman's husband didn't see her for four days. That's how a man is when a woman has a baby. When a woman has a baby in a house by herself she can't come back to the family for five days. Something will happen if this rule is broken.

After that woman had her baby she went home the fifth day. Her mother-in-law went to her tent, but she didn't even live through the night. She died because she let her daughter-in-law have her baby and the aŋatquq's devil got her. There were bad and not real bad aŋatquqs.

Martha's grandfather's first wife was an aŋatquq. I saw this. When she talked to her aŋatquq she asked the people for a knife. When they gave her a knife she stuck it in her belly button. I saw this with my own eyes. When it went in the point came out through her mouth and started moving just like a tongue. When the point came out farther she'd swallow it again and just let a little bit show. Finally the handle came back out her belly button and she pulled the knife out. There was a man with her who worked on his aŋatquq too. I saw the man walking around. Finally he stopped and took his jaws off. He put them down and tied things to them as if they were a sled. He left and then came back in awhile saying he had gone way out someplace. This happened in the karigi at Akveexrak. It was in the evening during wintertime. There were a few seal-oil lamps. I was younger than fourteen. This was before I planned to get married.

In Uŋgalaklik (Unalakleet), way down south, was Kusik Hunnicutt's birthplace. Kusik Hunnicutt and two more men left Kotzebue to take Kusik's mother some meat in Uŋgalaklik. They went through the hills; Uŋgalaklik was across the hills. They dogteamed down. They saw Uŋgalaklik from a hill. Kusik asked one of the men with him, "Which way would you go to there?" That man had never been there before and Kusik was trying to check if he was some kind of aŋatquq. The man said, "I would go that way." It was the way Kusik always went. When they got to Uŋgalaklik, Kusik went to see his mother. He had three brothers. He'd been adopted to a woman in Kotzebue, but he was from Uŋgalakik. The teacher in Uŋgalaklik found out they came and had them bring some food over because they were going to have a meeting. I think that maybe they went home after that because Kusik always stopped here when he told this story. About a year later Kusik's mother burned in her house.

Carl Luther's aunt was an aŋatquq. She had an aŋatquq with an eagle. Wilson Ashby's uncle was hung and killed by some people. Carl Luther's aunt let him become alive through her aŋatquq. She used a drum. I saw this.

Carl Luther's uncle was also an aŋatquq. When I was upriver

someplace we heard Carl Luther's uncle's dogs calling from clear down here (Noatak Village) even though he was dead.

A woman was dying. Her relatives gave Carl Luther's uncle gifts to have him work on her. They said that if the woman got good he could use her. This was before I started having my period, when I was about nine or ten. It was in the wintertime. The aŋatquq worked in the house where the woman lived with her parents. Sometime they took the sick person to the karigi. It was evening. They had a few seal-oil lamps burning, but it was not too bright. There were a lot of people. Anybody could come. This took place way up the Noatak somewhere.

The aŋatquq stood her soul on his drum and it kept falling. The soul was a small thing, something like a crust of bread and kind of darkish in color, maybe shaped like a little doll. He started using a drum, and after he played it the cover would always come off. He put it back on and played it again. He kept playing it and when the cover didn't come off anymore he tried to inhale something. He had it in his mouth for awhile, and then he took it out and set it on the drum. It was inuksuk, her soul. A lot of people were around watching. It fell and he put it back up. It was falling because the woman was dying. Finally the soul stood up by itself. It started going around, jumping by itself, all over the drum. The aŋatquq got ahold of it and put it on the dying woman's head. Then it went into her and they didn't see her anymore. The woman became alive.

People sang when the aŋatquq beat the drum. The woman had bad pains. She would have died if the aŋatquq hadn't worked on her. Carl Luther's uncle had an aŋatquq with dogs and with the devil himself. When she got well he used the woman.

Aŋatquqs never tried to continue after Christ came. A person became an aŋatquq when the devil got into him. That's how strong the devil was long ago. There was no really good aŋatquqs. People went to see aŋatquqs because they wanted to listen to the devil talk. Aŋatquqs always helped when they let a person live, but they couldn't help when a person died. Some aŋatquqs got rich when they helped people. If a person got well the aŋatquqs kept his payment; if not, he had to give it back. They all quit aŋatquqing and threw their aŋatquqs when they heard about the Bible.

This is all I can remember.

All the Noatagmiut I knew have died, all except me. My grandmother always tell me I should help old people so my life will be longer. Don't make fun of them; if you make fun of them your life will be shorter. I always tried to help old people, bring water to them and meat, so that's why my life is long. My grandmother says that people who try to boss people and not help them, their life will be shorter. My grandmother always tell me if a person come from other place, let him come to your house, give him coffee, tea, or hot water; your life will be longer.

FOLKTALES

EH1. Kiññuk

Way up the Noatak River there was a man with his kayak. His name was Kiññuk (crazy). As he came down the river with his kayak the water was swift, so he traveled fast. As he traveled he heard something in the trees making noise. It was a voice saying, "My friend, there is a hair on your shoulder that I can see. Kivilik." He went to the shore and went up into the trees. There were some old houses there and he went inside thinking that he would see somebody. When he didn't he went back to his kayak. Just when he was going to go he heard the same voice say the same thing. He went up the bank again and went into the houses. He started hitting the broken bones, old posts, and everything else that was lying there to see if they would make noise. They didn't, so he went back to his kayak. As he got there he heard the same voice again. As he went back up he saw a mousehole on the trail. While he watched a mouse came out, closed its eyes, and started saying what he had heard. Just when the mouse got to "kivilik," Kiññuk got ahold of him. He built a fire and started burning the mouse's nose and lips. When they were brown he let go of him, and the mouse went back in its hole. He didn't hear the mouse again.

He went farther down the river. He caught some fish and put one fish on the point of the kayak and one in the middle. He got as far as Agashashok when he saw smoke coming from the ground. Just then an eagle came, took one of his fishes away. He got to the beach and went up to the smoke. When he got close he saw a hole. While he was standing there he saw a white fox's nose come out. The white fox said, "Come in. They want you to come in." Kiññuk said, "How can I come in? The hole is too small." The white fox went back in. Fox after fox came out and told him to go in, but Kiññuk kept saying, "Too small. I can't go in." Finally another fox came out and told him to go in. When Kiññuk said "Too small," the fox said, "Put your legs in first, then close your eyes and you'll come in."

Kiññuk tried, even though the hole was too small, and he slid into the stormshed. He opened his eyes and saw all kinds of animal skins hanging on the stormshed wall. He went into the house and saw an old man sitting on the other side. Someone with a sheep-skin parka on was sitting by the door. The man in the sheep-skin parka told him to sit down, so Kiññuk sat close by him. The old man got up and asked, "How come we never try to feed the stranger? Get food for him." The man in the sheep-skin parka nudged Kiññuk in the side when they put food down for him, to tell him not to eat. Kiññuk played that he eat them, putting the food inside his parka, and when the plate was finished the old man said, "Put some more food in front of Kiññuk."

Kiññuk saw a lot of people inside the house where he was eating. The old man knew that Kiññuk was not really eating the food but pretending, and so the old man sang a song about something dropping from a wall and Kiññuk would want to look up, but the man in the sheep-skin parka nudged him in the side to tell him not to look up. The old man kept singing and Kiññuk wanted to look up, but the man in the sheep-skin parka was still nudging him, so the old man said, "I remember when you burned my lips. After you burned my lips you don't want to look anywhere." The old man's lips and nose were real wrinkled.

The people in the house kept going out until Kiññuk and the man in the sheep-skin parka were left alone. The man in the sheep-skin parka said, "We're not going to stay in here alone. Let's try to go out too." When they went out the man in the sheep-skin parka said to Kiññuk, "When you came down the river I'm the one who took your fish off your kayak." Then the man in the sheep-skin parka said, "You can go down the river and I'll fly." So the man in the sheep-skin parka became a nauyak̦ (seagull) and flew. The man in the sheep-skin parka told Kiññuk before he went, "I'm the one who saved you. That old man gave you food with worms and I didn't want you to eat them so I saved you."

Kiññuk went down to the mouth of the Noatak River and began seeing people. He thought the trees became people. We always think nauyaḳ go home [meaning south] for the winter, but they go into holes. After Kiññuk went close to those people he found out they were trees. THE END.

I heard this from Aŋasuk (my first husband's brother).

B211.3 Speaking bird; B450 Helpful birds; B521.1 Animal warns against poison; C221 Tabu against eating meat (Mackenzie River—Jenness 1924:76; West Hudson Bay—Boas 1901:327; Greenland—Holm 1912: 93; Rasmussen 1921:I, 233); D150 Transformation: man to bird (Greenland—Rasmussen 1921:II, 14; Rink 1875:148, 287, 327); D310 Transformation: animal (fox) to person (Greenland—Rasmussen 1921:III, 205; Rink 1875:450); D315.2 Transformation: mouse to man (Mackenzie—Jenness 1924:74); D352.2 Transformation: eagle to man; F513 person unusual as to mouth; J585 Caution in eating; J1050 Attention to warnings.

"Mouse" refers either to a lemming or a vole (family Cricetidae). The explanation for the absence of seagulls in the winter is somewhat unusual as the Noatak Eskimos (now, at least) know that most avian species spend the winter to the south.

EH2. THE MAN-WHO-BECAME-A-CARIBOU

In Wales (Sagmalaruk) Village there was a man and his wife and their two sons. The woman's mother also lived with them. The man had snares on a hill. Every time the man went out to check them his mother-in-law always said behind his back, "That man has a big bladder." He heard her call him nakasuḳtuḳ (big bladder). He began to get tired of her calling him that. When he went out again he heard that name again behind him and he got mad. He went to see his snares and never came home. Before that they had never been out of food because the man had always hunted.

When he left his snares he walked to the mountain. He heard people laughing. He was climbing up a hill so he got up on top and then went down to see who was laughing. It was ptarmigan making noise just like laughing and talking. He thought that the ptarmigan were people. When he went down the ptarmigan got in one bunch and started eating rocks. He went farther on. As he went around a bend by a little lake he heard people laughing again. He went closer and saw geese fly from the lake.

He went farther on and when he saw some wolves he followed them. When they stopped, he stopped. When they moved on, he moved on. That's how he traveled. One time when the wolves stopped again he stopped a little ways away. The wolves got in a circle and had a meeting. One of the wolves came from the circle toward the man. When it got to him, the wolf put his nose to the ground and pulled his face skin back like pulling a hood back and asked him, "Why do you keep following us?" The man answered, "I want to become a wolf and join you." The wolf went back to the rest of the wolves and after staying with them awhile came back over to the man. When he got back to the man he put his nose to the ground again, pulled his face back, and said: "You want to join us, but my friends say that when it is stormy and we have no food we always eat another wolf. When we see a man hunting and we are short of food we always eat him. Why don't you try to become some other kind of animal and not stay with us?"

When the man decided not to join the wolves he started to follow the caribou. He saw the way the caribou pawed the ground to take the snow off and eat moss. He saw the smaller of the two bones in the front legs (called the needle). He followed the caribou for a year, winter and summer. One time when he was following them a caribou came, put his nose to the ground, pulled his hood back, and asked, "Why have you been following us?" The man answered, "I want to join you." The caribou went back to the herd where he stayed a little while and then started back towards the man carrying a caribou skin. When the caribou got to the man he took his hood off and told the man, "You can put this caribou skin on." The man put the skin on and he and the caribou sewed it up down the middle of the underside. Then the man tried to walk, but he always fell. He didn't know how to walk in the skin. The caribou told him, "If you put your head up and look toward the sky you will probably start walking." He looked toward the sky and started walking, but still not very well. He still fell every time he looked down. The caribou told the man-that-became-a-caribou: "You started walking, so now you stay close behind me. We always have trouble with people because they always hunt us, so I'll tell you if people come. If I say there is a man coming, stay close behind me if I start running. Watch closely. If anything happens run ahead. If men get caribou and don't cut their throat after they kill them, the soul never comes back."

After awhile the caribou said, "There is a man coming hunting caribou." The man-who-became-a-caribou looked back at the man coming. The caribou said, "He's not going to get one of us." The man was carrying a whole bunch of willows from a house floor. The caribou said, "When he was little his mother fed him from her breast instead of letting him go out early in the morning. He's not going to get any of us." The man didn't get any because the caribou ran away. They saw him because of the dark willows he carried.

When they got together in a big herd again the caribou said, "There is a man coming again." The caribou saw him coming. The caribou said, "That man coming has something dark again. Every morning before that man goes out hunting he puts his hands between his wife's legs and lays down with her instead of going out early." They ran away again and the man didn't get any [caribou].

The caribou rebunched and started eating from the snow. When they dig down they always get fat from the ground [eat enough to get fat]. You can see it along their stomach. When the caribou saw another hunter he told the man-who-became-a-caribou, "A man is coming. If he gets close to us he's going to kill lots of us." The man-who-became-a-caribou turned around and saw the man as a thin stick, not as a large, dark spot. Before they knew it he was close and he killed lots of the caribou. After the rest had run and got together again the caribou said: "When that man was small his mother let him go out early in the morning. But when a hunter never cuts the caribou's throat that caribou never comes home. When a man does cut the throat the soul is like a feather and when it comes back we can see that feather even though the caribou is missing. Some of them are not home because that man didn't cut some of their throats."

In the summertime the man-who-became-a-caribou was always alone. The other caribou went off somewhere. In the fall they got together again. When they did they saw a man coming. They told the man-who-became-a-caribou, but he couldn't see him, and before he knew it a lot of caribou were dead. Then another man came and the caribou said, "There is a man coming." The man-who-became-a-caribou tried to see him, but he couldn't. The caribou said, "He is going to kill a lot of us. If he starts shooting just stay behind me."

The hunter got closer and the caribou went towards him just as if the world was tipping to him. When the caribou started going towards him he killed a lot. The man-who-became-a-caribou and his

friend ran away and didn't get caught. This hunter got more caribou than the first one. The caribou said: "That man's mother got him up early in the morning. She told him to take a few pieces of wood to the old men and the old women in the village and put it by their door while they slept. She told him, 'Early in the morning you should always go down to the river and make a hole so people can get water.' That's how this man learned, and after he got older he always gets lots of caribou." All of the caribou the man got came home. They saw their feathers because he cut all their throats.

After the bunch regrouped they stayed together all winter and in the spring they left the man-who-became-a-caribou. He started thinking about where he had put his snares when he was a man. He thought that he should look there, so he went and he recognized the place. While he was looking he stopped all at once. He tried to get out, but was caught in his own snare. When he couldn't get out he thought to himself, "Somebody must be watching my snare." He put his head down and stayed there waiting for someone to take him out.

While he waited he heard men's voices away off. He put his head up and, listening, heard the talking coming towards him. He saw two young boys coming with bows in their hands and arrows on their backs. They got close and he heard them say, "We got a caribou again." They were surprised because they were really too young to hunt.

They got close. One boy took an arrow from his back, put it in the bow, and was going to shoot the caribou because he was alive. Just as he was going to shoot, the man put his head to the ground and took his hood off. The boy stopped and the man-who-became-a-caribou said, "Don't be scared of me. Please take the snare off." The boys didn't move, so the man said again, "Don't be scared. Take the snare off." They went to him and took the snare off. After they did the man-who-became-a-caribou said, "I've just got a sewn-on skin on. Take it off." The boys took the stitches out. Before they got it off the man asked, "Whose snares are these?" One boy said, "Our mother always told us they are our father's snares. When he went to see them he never came home." The man told them, "You are my boys. When your grandmother always talked behind me I didn't like it, so I went to see my snares and ran away. Did your mother get married again?" The boys told him she had gotten married. They took his skin off and he had no clothes, so they gave him some of theirs. They had to get ahold of him, one boy grabbing him under each armpit, because he couldn't walk like a man anymore. He walked like a caribou. He told them, "I want to go to the village and tell the people how I ran away." When they took his clothes off one of his shoulders had become that of a caribou.

When they took him home and he went inside the house it smelled of people so much that he couldn't stand it. The man who had married his wife told him, "You came home so you can go back to your wife." He said, "I am not going back to her because I have already become a caribou. Make a house outdoors for me. I'll have a meeting with all the villagers and tell them how I traveled when I went away." They made a house for him. He told the people what he saw when he was with the caribou. He told them how he tried to become a wolf but they didn't want him, and about his mother-in-law and why he had run away. He told the young boys and young girls not to follow his trail, not to do what he had done. After he told them the story he starved because he couldn't eat people's food. THE END.

This is a real true story. Just a few years ago that man down that way became a caribou. I have forgotten where I heard this story.

B211.2.2 Speaking caribou; B211.2.4 Speaking wolf; B435.3 Helpful wolf; B443 Helpful wild beasts—ungulate (caribou); D114.1.6 Transformation: man to caribou (MacKenzie River—Jenness 1924:56); D531 Transformation by putting on skin (Kodiak—Golder 1903:95; Bering Strait—Nelson 1899:468; Central—Boas 1888:617; Cumberland Sound—Boas 1901:181; Greenland—Rasmussen 1921:I, 364; 1921:II, 13; 1921:III, 75, 143, 262; Rink 1875:146); D682 Partial transformation (shoulder to that of caribou); E715.4.1 Separable soul in deer (Greenland—Rasmussen 1921:II, 55); E745.1 Soul as feather; J130 Wisdom (knowledge) acquired from animals; S51 Cruel mother-in-law. Similar to story in Keithahn 1958:90–96 (Seward Peninsula), Gubser 1965:327–30 (Anaktuvuk Pass), and to PM109 in this volume.

This story addresses a number of moral precepts still current among the Noatak Eskimos, including the dangers of insulting comments (by mother-in-law) and the various rules a man must follow if he is to be a successful hunter. Note the literary convention of equating the appearance of a hunter as a dark spot with the knowledge that the hunter will not be successful; this of course is true in fact. The Noatak Eskimos' keen observation of the natural world is suggested by the depiction of how caribou run. Finally, note that the man-who-became-a-caribou specifically tells his story to the younger people, thus telling them not only "not to follow his trail," but also giving positive advice.

EH3. The Point Hope Boy and the Man-Who-Always-Kills-People

There were people in Point Hope. A rich man there had a son who got all kinds of animals when he hunted. When men hunted in the hills they didn't come home. When they didn't come home the rich man's son tried hunting up that way and he never came home. A grandmother and her grandson lived in Point Hope too. The rich man's son had been liked by that grandson. When the rich man's son didn't come home the grandson went to the rich man and asked him if he had any old snowshoes and a bow and arrow and a spear. The rich man gave the grandson snowshoes, spears, and a bow and arrows. The rich man told the grandson, "Behind the hill there is a flat. Long ago my parents gave me that flat. There is always a lot of caribou up there."

The grandson went up the hill. He saw the flat, but he didn't see caribou even though the rich man said he saw some every time he went up. The grandson walked farther up and he saw a fog bank in front of him. He went to the foggy place and got up on top of a hill. He saw men playing football below him and farther over a house. He went to the house. Inside there was an old man and his wife. The old woman said, "If the man-who-always-kills-people finds out about you he'll call for you. He always takes strangers up to the top of the hill and challenges them to a race. The man-who-always-kills-people stays on the right side because he has a knife in his right arm, and when he reaches the flat he kills the strangers there or takes them to his house and then kills them. When he takes them to his house there is a rock there where he kills men. It has blood and hair on it."

While she was talking a voice came through the window saying, "The stranger has to go over to the man-who-always-kills-people." The old woman told the grandson to watch out. The man-who-always-kills-people took him up to the hill to race. He stayed on the right and kept the grandson on the left. The grandson watched him closely. They started racing down the hill. When they got to the flat the man-who-always-kills-people was going to knife him, but the grandson kept away.

When they finished the race the grandson went back to the old couple's house. He went in. After the football game the old couple's three boys came in. Pretty soon two other men came in and said, "The man-who-always-kills-people wants the stranger." The three boys said, "Yes, we'll all go up." The old people said, "We'll go too, so he'll have to kill all of us."

They went up to the man-who-always-kills-people's house. They went to see if the man-who-always-kills-people would kill the grandson. They all wanted to be killed if he killed the grandson. The-man-who-always-kills-people told two of the boys to bring that rock, and they did. It was a real sharp rock with dried blood and men's hair on it. The man-who-always-kills-people went to the grandson, got ahold of him, and whirled him around. He was going to throw him on the rock, but the grandson just missed the sharp edge and landed on his hands and knees on the floor. The grandson said, "You beat me." This happened again.

After the man-who-always-kills-people did this a third time the grandson said, "You are not the only one who's going to go around.

Let me try you." He got up and went to the man-who-always-kills-people. He got ahold of him, whirled him around, threw him on the rock, and killed him. After he killed the man-who-always-kills-people he said, "Anybody that's thinking about my killing this man-who-always-kills-people come on down." Nobody came down. The grandson and his friends went home. He stayed for a year and then went back to Point Hope. The Point Hopers said, "If there was still a man-who-always-kills-people up there, Point Hopers wouldn't come home even now if that grandson hadn't killed him." THE END.

I heard this story from Paul Monroe today. Paul forgets where he heard it. [Paul said, "Edna told this story right even though she only heard it once. Everything was right."]

H1562 Test of strength; K800 Killing or maiming by deception; K1626 Would-be killers killed; L111.4.1 Orphan hero lives with grandmother; N825.3 Old woman as helper (Greenland—Rasmussen 1921:II, 162); Q211 Murder punished (Cumberland Sound—Boas 1901:168; Greenland—Rasmussen 1921:III, 76, 111, 294); Q411.6 Death as punishment for murder; S118 Murder by cutting. Similarities to Curtis 1930:230–35 (Selawik), Nelson 1899:499–505 (Sledge Island), and EH7 and PM53 of this volume.

The man-who-always-kills-people appears in a number of Noatak stories and will be discussed in chapter V. Relations between the rich and the poor seem, as here, to have been friendly in north Alaskan Eskimo culture. The grandson (granddaughter) is also a stock character in these stories.

EH4. THE DEAD SEAL

There was an old seal on the beach, a dead one, named Kaasiigak. It's been on the beach for a long time, drying up. A man was walking on the beach so he saw that dead, dried seal; it's been there for a long summer. And that man went to it; he wants to know what it is. When that man touches that old seal, that old seal puts his head up. So that seal told that man, "I'm tired; I'm suffering. If you need help sometimes I'll help you. Cut my throat off." So that man cut his throat. THE END.

I don't know the rest of this story, but when a man gets some ugruk and seals he takes the meat and hangs it up and cuts the throat off and puts a grass in its mouth because he wants more ugruk. If they don't do this they won't get more.

B210 Speaking animals; B390 Animal grateful for other kind acts.
The slitting of the throat of an animal to release the soul is a rule that still has some force in Noatak. Martha says they still cut the throat today.

EH5. The Woman Who Became a Caterpillar

In Point Hope there was a village. This man has a wife and he always gets seals. He always take his wife through [along] the Kukpuk River. When they get to that place for hunting they stop and that man always gets caribou. When he gets caribou they both work on them and dry them up. His wife had a mother and brothers. When they go down to the village in falltime with their boat, that woman's brothers always welcome their brother-in-law. When they go down to the village they always stay with that woman's mother.

After they stay down there for the winter hunting seals, they go up the same river (Kukpuk) and hunt caribou. They dried meat and fat and skins. When they get ready to go down to the river and to the village, that woman's brothers always welcome them. They would stay down there and hunt seals; in the springtime they go upriver again and dry some meat. The wife always pack [carry] some meat. After she get some meat she's going to get another load of meat and she stopped for rest. While she was resting some woman go to her. That other woman that go to her want to trade her parka. She didn't want to trade. That woman really wanted that parka and tries to take it off from her.

When that other woman take that parka off from her, she left. That woman whose parka was taken become a caterpillar so she couldn't move. She didn't know what to do, so she start to try walking a little bit. She knows her trail down to her house. Well, she's been trying to reach their house and she saw that other woman going down to her husband. That other woman takes that woman's place and she start working. When they go to bed that man ask her why she smell so much. She said she worked too much today, sweating.

Every evening when they're going to bed he still asks her why she smells. She tells him the same story; she works too much. And that woman-that-becomes-a-caterpillar was finally getting close to her house. He still ask that other woman why she keep smelling like that. She keeps telling him she works and sweats. And that woman-that-become-a-caterpillar is getting closer. That woman finally reach her house.

When she go in the house she was still a caterpillar so she went close to her husband to see if he will step her and crush her, but he didn't care because he doesn't know. They're getting ready to go to the village, so he gets six caribou skins and ties them together [translator explains he tied them with two laid north-south direction, two east-west direction, and finally two north-south again]. When that woman-that-become-a-caterpillar doesn't know what to do, she went into the ear of the dried caribou skin.

When they are going down to the village they put their boat down to the river and bring their stuff, and they bring those dried skins and that woman-that-become caterpillar was still in that ear. When they get down to the village they put the skins on racks [translator says like fish racks now used]. They put those skins on top and that woman-that-become-caterpillar doesn't know how to get down. She saw her mother's house; she saw that other woman working. When she doesn't know what to do she starts thinking to herself. She wants to try to make it down, so she starts going down along that pole when the people go to sleep. When she goes down through that pole she went to where they cook outdoors, not inside to her husband.

When she goes to that place where they cook, she want them to step on her, but they can't and she sees her mother and that other woman working. When they're working she wants them to step on her, but they can't. She sees her husband, her mother, that other woman working, and she gets close, but they can't step on her. She had tried to go to her mother's place where her mother steps more. When she cooks that's the place she steps more, so she starts going over. She went to the place where her mother steps all the time. That other woman went to get some snow and they always call to each other through the window. Her mother was cooking; finally her mother steps on her. When her mother steps on her, she bursts; she becomes a woman and her mother recognizes her. That other woman that go get snow called and said, "Mother, here's the snow what I get." When that woman find out about her daughter, she gets hold of that caterpillar skin. She gets the caterpillar skin and throws it through the window at that other woman that gets snow. That mother said, "Here, caterpillar, you have a mother." So when she throws that skin that other woman becomes a caterpillar.

When her husband find out about that woman he tells his wife that time when she comes home from packing some meat that man find out that woman was smelly. That woman tell her husband another woman come while she was resting and get hold of her and start fighting, so that woman take her parka and she become a caterpillar. When she become a caterpillar she went down to the house. She said to her husband, "You didn't know I was caterpillar." She went down through the pole and went to that place where her mother cooks and her mother finally steps her. They forgive each other and that man get her back and that mother get her daughter back. THE END.

I heard this from Ralph Gallahorn.

B653 Marriage to insect in human form; D192.1 Transformation: man to caterpillar; D380 Transformation: insect to man; K1310 Seduction by disguise or substitution. Similar to PM34 in this volume.
    Note that "false" people smell.

EH6. THE RAVEN MAKES DAYLIGHT

In a village there is a rich man. He has a pole outdoors. That rich man has a daughter. Those village people always hunt for wood. It was dark, so they put their finger to their tongue and to the wood to see if it is green wood or dry wood. That rich man has two balls (uuglugruk), one big and one little. Some other villagers always hear that rich man got two balls, one small and one big.

That rich man's daughter, when everybody quit bringing some water home, always goes down to get water by herself. After the other women get some water a squirrel and a raven came to the well, and that squirrel make a hole by the well and start staying in that hole. That raven becomes dirt and gets inside the well. When the women start getting some water that rich man's daughter was the last to get water again. She starts filling her bucket. That raven starts thinking, "I wish that woman gets thirsty and takes a drink from her bucket." First time that woman puts her hands in her bucket and takes a drink with her hands, she didn't know she had a dirt [translator always says "a dirt," but I suspect she means feces] in her hands. So she swallowed that dirt. She tried to take it off from her throat. [Edna makes coughing sound and translator says she tried to take it off by coughing].

When she went home she tells her father that she swallowed a dirt. That woman becomes pregnant. That woman was pregnant and she has a baby boy with a tail. That squirrel that had a hole by the well went to that woman's house, and under the door he made a hole. That woman had brothers. That boy's uncles always say, "Our nephew, he's got a little tail, he's got a little tail." That boy when he starts walking around starts hollering to his mother that he wants her father's balls. He wants that big ball, but his mother tells him that he might bust it, and they give him the smaller ball. He kicks it and plays with it. When he was going to bed he gives that ball to his grandfather.

In the morning when he wakes up he hollers for that ball again. When he plays with it on the floor his uncles always say, "Look at his tail; look at his tail." When he wakes up the day after he plays with that ball he wants the bigger ball this time. His mother said, "You might bust that ball." Anyway his uncles give it to him, so he starts playing with it and kicking it again. When he wants to play ball they (his uncles) always give him the smaller one, but he wants the bigger ball. So every time he plays with that bigger ball he starts kicking it towards the door. He starts playing with that ball again after he sleeps. They give him the smaller ball, but he wants to play with that bigger ball. He kicks it, the bigger ball, towards the door and it went out.

And when he kicks it out that squirrel catches it with his teeth and he (squirrel) starts running with that ball, and the boy runs out after that ball, and that old rich man starts running after them. And when the old man gets close to the squirrel, the squirrel throws it to that boy, and when that old man gets close to the boy that boy throws the ball to the squirrel. So that old man gets tired of running after them. He starts resting. That old man starts shouting, "Raven, let your friends have half of it. Dirty Raven, dirty Raven."

That old man said if the raven gets the smaller ball we'd have short days, so the raven takes the bigger ball and we have long days. THE END.

We have the daylight now because the raven took that ball and he ran away with it. I heard this story from many different old people, from anybody, old people.

A1170 Origin of night and day; A1411 Theft of light (Smith Sound–Kroeber 1899:205); A1411.2 Theft of light by being swallowed and reborn; B631 Human offspring from marriage to animal; D437.4 Transformation: feces to man (Greenland–Rasmussen 1921:III, 85); D830 Magic object acquired by trickery; F518 Person with tail; K311 Thief in disguise; K640 Escape by help of confederate; T512 Conception by drinking (Bering Strait–Nelson 1899:461). Also known from Ostermann 1942:70–73 (Mackenzie River); Spencer 1959:385 (Point Barrow); Gubser 1965:35–39 (Anaktuvuk Pass); Lucier 1958:92 (Noatak); Giddings 1961:69–71 (Kobuk); Curtis 1930:216–17 (Kobuk); Nelson 1899:452–62 (Bering Strait); and Ray 1968:52–53 (St. Michael). Shows some similarities to PM47 in this volume.

A classic, widespread tale.

EH7. Kutmvumavik

Kutmvumavik is the name of a place at Uḳaliḳsuk. There were quite a few people in Kutmvumavik. A boy and his grandmother lived in one house. In another house there lived a man-who-always-kills-people. When some men in the village who went out caribou hunting came home, that man always went and asked them, "Did you kill any caribou today?" A man would usually answer him kind of sarcastically, "Yes, I got caribou today." Then the man-who-always-kills-people said, "When you talk to me like that you're talking funny."

When the man who came home from the hunting was having supper, the man-who-always-kills-people had a woman call through the window and say that he wanted to see him. The other man would go up to the house of the man-who-always-kills-people, go in, and sit down. The man-who-always-kills-people would say, "I'm stiff today because I never went out." He would stretch. Pretty soon he would get up, grab the other man, throw him against a big rock in the house, and kill him. He did this several times.

The old woman decided to take her grandson away from that place. When they went they followed the river up between two mountains. It was winter. While they were walking they found running water and they stopped. The grandmother started hooking flounders. There were lots there. She built a little ebrulik. After she made it they started hunting for wood and found green wood. The boy always tried to pack heavy wood. He dragged them and tried to reach the house. Every time they went to get wood his grandmother would give him heavy wood to pack. She was trying to get him strong.

After awhile the boy started growing bigger, and soon he could pack heavy wood and bring it home. Once after he got to be a big boy he went into the ebrulik and asked his grandmother, "What are those things in the willows that have big horns that stick out?" His grandmother went out, looked around, and said, "Those are caribou." He asked his grandmother to make a bow and arrow for him, and she did so. When she finished he went outside to try it, and he got one caribou. When he got it he grabbed it by the legs, put it on his back, and went home. So they started eating it.

In the evening one time the boy asked his grandmother, "Grandmother, you don't know about other people too?" Every evening when he came home from hunting they would eat and he would ask, "You don't know about some other people around somewhere?" She would answer, "I don't know about any other people." One evening he asked her again and she got tired and answered, "I took you away from the village because one man was going to kill you."

She told him about that man-who-always-kills-people and said that he had also killed the boy's father. The boy decided to take his grandmother back to Kutmvumavik. When they left they stopped overnight and he got a caribou. They ate a little bit and went on in the morning, leaving the rest of the caribou. They reached their village.

The boy and his grandmother went into the house to stay with three women whose husbands were killed by that man. They were probably sisters. There were only a few men left in the village now. The boy planned to go hunting and left early in the morning. He saw quite a few caribou and got them all. When he went home the man-who-always-kills-people went to him and asked, "How many caribou did you get?" The boy answered, "I got all the caribou that I saw." The man-who-always-kills-people replied, "When you talk like that to me you're making fun of me."

When the boy started to eat a woman called through the window, "That man wants you up there." He left his food and walked out. One of the three sisters ran after him, took him back in the house, and said, "That man will kill all of us." She started sharpening her ulu and told him to wait. He didn't want to and went out. The three sisters all started sharpening their ulus in case the man-who-always-kills-people came to their house. As the boy left he said, "If I really need help, I'll call for you."

They put their ulus in their sleeves and went up to the house of the man-who-always-kills-people with the boy's grandmother after the boy went in. They went in and saw the boy sitting there. The man was stretching and saying how tired he was. By the wall was the rock all covered with men's blood. The man got up, grabbed the boy, and tried to swing him around and throw him on the rock. He threw him, but the boy landed on his feet. The man got mad and tried again, and the same thing happened.

The boy said, "Let me try you." The boy was mad and he grabbed the man by the shoulders and pushed his one side on the rock until the man's bones started breaking up. Then he pushed his other side on the rock until those bones broke. The man was really suffering from pain and the boy left him there. When he went out he said, "If you heal up I will come back." Every time the boy comes home from hunting he always checks up, and soon he finds that the man is getting better. He asks, "How is he?" And the answer is, "He starts walking around a little bit."

When the boy heard that the man was getting well he went up

again one evening. Before he went the three women told the boy again that the man had killed all the men of the village and also the boy's father and mother. So the boy got really mad, went up, and grabbed the man and really smashed him up. He killed him this time. THE END.

I heard this story from Ralph Gallahorn.

H1562 Test of strength; K1626 Would-be killers killed; L111.4.1 Orphan hero lives with grandmother; P233.6 Son avenges father; Q211 Murder punished (Cumberland Sound—Boas 1901:168; Greenland—Rasmussen 1921:III, 76, 111, 294); Q411.6 Death as punishment for murder; Q450.1.1 Torture as punishment for murder. Similar to EH3 and PM53 in this volume.

Note common themes of flight from aggression, self-sufficiency, and revenge. The idea that hard work in childhood will make one strong also occurs in a number of folktales. The phrase "things in the willows that have big horns" appears to be a literary convention to denote a person's first sighting of caribou.

EH8. THE WOMAN WHO KILLED HERSELF

Two Noatagmiut had a baby boy with them. They always traveled last when the people were coming upriver. I know who they are, but I won't say all the names. After everyone else had unloaded for the night those two Noatagmiut would come along. They got up by the canyons [of the Noatak].

After the people went again in the morning those two would follow. When they all stopped for the night the couple used their boat for shelter. The woman got some food from the poke [a sealskin container for oil or food] because they were going to have a big supper. She filled a tray with dried ugruk panuktuk (meat) and took it over to her husband. After she brought that tray over she went back to the boat. The other people called her over to eat with them. She said she didn't feel hungry.

When the other people began eating that woman was in her place. The people got quiet, busy with food. The woman put her baby on her back and started walking through the canyons. She walked up to a hill, got on top, and started dancing and crying at the same time. The people didn't know she was gone. The woman was walking backwards. She knew there was a cliff and she was walking backwards towards it.

When she almost got to the edge the other people saw her. She sang a song: "My poor son / Your dad hit you with that pole / sonny / sonny." The song was about her baby. Her husband always hit the baby with the stick he used for poling the boat. He was mean to her and hit her too. The woman knew the cliff was close. Her leg went down and then she fell in the water. What does her husband have left after that? Maybe that man still travels alone. THE END.

I don't know where I heard this story.

S62 Cruel husband; S410 Persecuted wife (Cumberland Sound—Boas 1901:198; Greenland—Rasmussen 1921:I, 365; 1921:III, 104; Rink 1875:441).

Apparently a historical tale.

EH9. THE LAKE OF WORMS

This is a story about Point Hope Village and a place inland from there called Kukpuk. A man got married to a Point Hope girl and started going upriver to Kukpuk. When they reached the hunting place he began to go out, and on the first day he got a bull caribou. When he got it he cut off one whole hindquarter and hung it on a pole to dry. All fall it hung there getting real dry.

The man still hunted caribou, and when they got some he and his wife would dry it up. When they had dried up lots of meat they began to plan to go down to the village. They got their boat ready and filled it up with dried meat and skins, all that they had. When they got ready to go the man told his wife, "There is a lake up over there, and every time I go home from hunting I go up there to see it and give thanks." The man took the dry hindquarter of the caribou and went with his wife to the lake. When they got there he threw the hindquarter into the lake. After a minute they could see only the bone, no meat.

Then the man grabbed his wife and threw her into the lake and soon just her bones showed. There were some kind of worms in there. The man took off downriver. When he got close to Point Hope they could hear him crying. He said, "My wife died because the sickness was too strong. I really liked my wife, but death was too strong." After he got down to Point Hope he told the people that his wife had died and he had had to leave her.

In the spring that man was married again and went upriver to the same place. When they first got there he got a bull caribou again and hung a quarter to dry. All fall he hunted caribou, drying it up. As he and his wife were getting ready to go back to Point Hope he told her about the lake. Again his wife went with him and after he had thrown the meat in, they saw just the bone. He grabbed his wife and threw her and just bones were left. He went down the river alone and said the same things that he had said before, that the sickness was too strong for his wife. He stayed in the village for the winter, married in the spring, and went upriver again where the whole thing happened all over.

The next spring he married again, but this girl had two elder brothers and a younger brother. The two elder brothers said to the younger brother, "Why does that man have wives? How do they die?" They want the younger brother to find out, so he goes upriver with the man and his wife. If anything happens they tell the younger brother to call them because they won't be far away. The three went upriver to the hunting place; the man got a bull caribou and dried one quarter. The man hunted all summer and in the fall, after they had loaded the boat, he took his wife up to the lake. The woman was kind of scared and wouldn't stand close to the water. The man noticed it. He threw the meat and in a minute only bone was left. He called to his wife, "Come closer and see the meat."

He grabbed her and at the same time the woman tightly grabbed some willows. He pulled her and the willow roots started to come out of the ground. She still kept holding onto the willows. He said, "Go ahead and hold on. See if I don't throw you down." The woman started sweating. He kept pulling at her. She started calling, "Where's my youngest brother and my older brothers, after they told me to call them?" The man said, "They won't hear you. They are too far away. Go ahead and call them."

He didn't know the brothers were standing there. They grabbed him. He told them he was just making fun with his wife. They didn't believe him and threw him into the lake. Then just his bones came up. After that all the women's bones got up and waved. The brothers and the woman went downriver with the man's boat. THE END.

I don't remember where I heard this story.

D1827.2 Person heard call for aid from great distance; K640 Escape by help of confederate; K950 Treacherous murder; K1626 Would-be killers killed; N820 Human helpers; P251.6.1 Three brothers; Q211 Murder punished (Cumberland Sound—Boas 1901:168; Greenland—Rasmussen 1921:III, 76, 111, 294); Q411.6 Death as punishment for murder; R156 Brother rescues sister; S62 Cruel husband. Similar to Ostermann 1942: 69–70 (MacKenzie River); Lucier 1958:100–1 (Noatak); and PM69 in this volume.

A third version, which I did not fully record, is current in Noatak Village.

EH10. BELUGA HUNTING FAILS

When the Noatagmiut came down the river from its end they went to Nuvuvruk at the end of Sheshalik and got lots of belugas. There were two old people—Amii, a woman, and her husband, Aaluk—at

Sheshalik near the base of the spit. Amii and Aaluk were from Wales or somewhere down that way [the translator says Edna is talking in the Wales tongue]. Aaluk wanted to go to Nuvuvruk and have some muktuk (beluga skin).

The Noatagmiut have seats made of logs; they always ate outside and had heavy sandstone pots. The Noatagmiut women were cooking muktuk and the inuksuks (meat racks) were full of white muktuk. Aaluk went there and saw the people eating muktuk outdoors, but they wouldn't offer him any. He walked by the women cooking, but they didn't say for him to eat. All day this went on. Finally Aaluk went home and he didn't feel happy. He said to Amii, "I'm hungry." She said, "They didn't let you eat all day?" He answered, "They didn't. I walked by them while they were eating and they didn't offer me anything. Next year the Noatagmiut won't get any beluga."

The Noatagmiut left some caribou (dried) down in the Amaktuks so that when they came back upriver they could load them in the boats. They started up the river with enough muktuk in the boat for the whole winter, picked up the dried caribou, and went up the river.

They stayed up there all winter and in the spring started down to Nuvuvruk.

When they got there they unloaded their things. Looking across to Kikkikkichak they saw the waters full of beluga. They unloaded quickly and started that way with kayaks and skin boats. They tried all day to get beluga and could not get even one. They came home empty. They slept and in the morning saw belugas in the same place. Again they went to hunt; again they came home empty. Every day this happened. Finally they started getting short of food. Still they saw belugas.

They started putting fishnets. Each family wanted to have their net first so they kept putting theirs in front until the nets went as far as Aakuluk. They got no fish so they went to Kulagak [on the coast] and started seining there. They got nothing there so they went upriver. Upriver they hunted all winter, but they got no caribou, so they spread out in various places. Some went to Point Barrow, Kakaktaruk, Kaktuvik, and other places. THE END.

I know about some of these people that spread out. I know one man named after one of them. I think that Aaluk must have been an aŋatquq. I don't know where I heard this story.

D1711 Magician; D2090 Destructive magic powers; Q210 Crimes punished.
 For the Noatak Eskimos, refusing to share is a crime in social terms.

EH11. THE RAVEN AND THE WHITE FOX

There were a lot of people living somewhere at the coast. They had a karigi. A raven and a white fox always stayed in this karigi. In this village there were five children, three older brothers, one sister, and a younger brother, all in one family. Men would come from all over the villages to try to marry the girl. She didn't want to get married.

The younger brother hunted and every time he came home with a load. The older brothers didn't hunt; instead every night they had aanuktuk (games). The younger brother didn't play; he hunted.

One night when there were no more people in the karigi the raven said to the white fox (they were iilyuk, or special friends) that they should try to get the girl. The white fox said to the raven, "As if you could get her when all those men couldn't." After they all went to sleep the raven melted ahnuk (feces) and when it was melted he put it in the girl's pants. He woke her up and she saw he is going to tell all the men that go after her that she has dirt in her pants. He is going to tell all this if she doesn't get married to him. So finally she marries him. Then she becomes pregnant and they had a baby boy.

The younger brother always goes hunting early in the morning. The raven figured to hunt so his wife started to make mukluks. She sewed the bottoms and then sewed them up. After he hunted the raven came home with holes in the bottoms of his mukluks. Every time he went he came home this way. She kept sewing new bottoms.

One man in the village looked every day at a pile of rocks (ipnuk). When the raven left to go hunting again he went towards the rocks and the man watched him. He shuffled his feet when he went through the rocks and let his mukluks have holes again.

The raven wanted to go hunting earlier than the younger brother, but he never could catch him. One time he really tried to go first. When he got to the open water the boy already had one seal. When he got there the raven said, "Let me have your seal." The younger brother answered, "It's mine; I got it." The raven said, "Let me have it." They started fighting.

The younger brother got weak and the raven threw him in the water. After the raven threw him in he heard somebody behind him yell, "What are you doing with that boy? Why did you throw him in the water?" The raven turned around and saw the white fox. The raven told him, "Don't tell the other brothers about it. That baby of mine is yours if you don't tell about it."

The raven went home with the seal and the fox didn't tell. The boy didn't come home. The brothers and the other men started hunting for him on the land and on the ice, but they couldn't find him. In the summertime they looked along the beach. The white fox wanted to tell them, but he was scared of the raven. They gave up looking in the fall.

The brothers had nobody to hunt for them. They gave up looking for the boy's body, started the karigi again, and started games. The raven and the white fox were there. The karigi had benches all around the walls. People sat on the benches and on the floor below them. They were having games and the raven's partners lost.

When this happened the raven's partners began singing songs. Each man sang alone in turn, the leader singing last. The white fox's partners sang after the raven's partners got through. The man behind the white fox began singing. The raven and the white fox were on different sides. Raven told the white fox, "If you start singing, sing everything you think about. Sing all you think." The fox started singing: "My iilyuk and the boy were hunting / so the boy got a seal / when the raven gets to that boy he got the seal / he killed that boy / when I got there the boy was in the water already / I was scared of my iilyuk / I was scared to tell / my iilyuk gave his son to me." After the white fox sang the three brothers jumped up from where they were sitting and tore the raven up. Then they gave the little boy to the white fox so that the white fox could help him. THE END.

I heard this from Ralph Gallahorn.

A2493 Friendship between animals; B210 Speaking animals; B211.3.6 Speaking raven; B430 Helpful wild beasts; B602 Marriage to bird (Mackenzie River—Jenness 1924:52, 75; Cape York—Rasmussen 1921:III, 57, 83); B631 Human offspring from marriage to animal; F1015.1 Shoes miraculously worn out; K926 Victim pushed into water; K958 Murder by drowning; P250 Brothers and sisters; Q211 Murder punished (Cumberland Sound—Boas 1901:168; Rasmussen 1921:III, 76, 111, 294); Q411.6 Death as punishment for murder; S131 Murder by drowning (Central—Boas 1888:637; Labrador—Hawkes 1916:152; Greenland—Holm 1912:56; Rasmussen 1921:I, 363; 1921:III, 200); T40 Wooing; T110 Unusual marriage; T311 Woman averse to marriage.

This story is somewhat unusual because there is no indication that the animals, who partake of human activities, are human in form. The haughty girl (or boy) who refuses to marry is common in Eskimo folklore. Note that he who goes early to hunt is successful. *Iilyuk* apparently is the same as *iilyaaruq* which is a north Alaskan term for joking partner. Spencer (1959:173–76) discusses the institution of the joking partnership at some length. One aspect of the joking relationship was to exchange songs which often contained sarcasm and irony hidden in humor. Such insult songs were not nearly as formalized or as important an outlet for aggression as among the more easterly Eskimos, but were part of interpersonal relationships in northern Alaska.

EH12. THE TWO RICH GIRLS

Once in a village there lived two rich couples. Each couple had a daughter. Another old woman lived there with her grandson. When the girls started to play ball the young boy would always go to play with them. One of the girls didn't like the boy and always picked on him. The other girl always brought a little food to the old woman and the boy because they were short of food and the rich people always had lots. Morning, noon, and night she brought something for them to eat and called them through the window. Both rich couples always gave food away until finally everyone was short of food and some people were starving. The girl still brought some food to the old woman and the boy. The other girl who didn't like the boy brought nothing. The first girl told the second girl to be nice to the boy.

Finally all the people starved except for the two couples and their daughters and the old woman and the boy. One evening the old woman started making a play black whale. She finished it and put it by the door. When they woke up it was a real whale, a whole one. They started cutting it and stored it away. Still the girl brought food to them since she didn't know they had a whale. Their house looked like a little lump in the ground; it was covered with earth.

One time when the boy was going to play ball with the girls again the old woman put blubber in his mouth to chew. The girl who didn't like him started looking at him when he began to chew. She asked him, "What are you chewing?" He answered, "A piece of my grandmother's belt." The girl started fighting with him about what he was chewing, took it out of his mouth, and put it in hers.

The old woman started sewing pretty clothes for the boy. Everyone stayed in that village for a few months. One day the boy said to his grandmother, "You should ask those people if I can have that girl." He meant the girl that liked him. His grandmother said, "I don't think they will take you." The boy said, "Just go ask anyway." The old woman went over to the house of the girl that didn't like the boy, went in, and sat by the door. The rich man said, "When you start starving you come here." The boy's grandmother replied, "I go ask about your daughter. That boy over there want me to go ask." The rich man said to his daughter, "Put a stick in that old woman's nose and throw her out." The old woman said, "I'll go out myself."

When she returned home the boy asked, "What did they say to you?" She told him. A few days later he told her to go over again and ask. She went to the house of the girl that brought them food, went in, and sat by the door. The rich man asked if she had come for food. She said, "That boy want me to come over and ask about this girl." The rich man put his head down for awhile and then called his daughter and said, "You can go with that old woman." The girl started following the old woman to her home. She wasn't happy and went out crying because she knew that the boy didn't have any good clothes.

When they went in the house that girl started seeing a lot of food. The boy said, "Grandmother, you get something to eat for us." After they ate the boy asked, "Grandmother, where are the clothes you are making? Let the girl put on the spotted white parka and mukluks, real long ones with white strips." The boy put on new clothes too, as did the old woman. Then the boy said, "Where are the clothes you made for that girl's parents? Bring a piece of muktuk with us so we can take it over." When the boy and the girl took the stuff over, the rich man told them to get the boy's grandmother so that they could all live together.

The other rich man heard about this and wanted to sell his daughter to the boy so that the boy would work for him and give him food. The boy didn't want the girl because he remembered what the old man said about the stick in his grandmother's nose. The rich man tried to sell himself to the boy, and still the boy didn't want him. He couldn't forget. A few days later that other rich couple didn't show up. They must have starved. THE END.

I heard this from Ralph Gallahorn.

D1470.2 Provisions received from magic object; L111.4.1 Orphan hero lives with grandmother; N825.3.3 Help from grandmother; Q2 Kind and unkind; Q40 Kindness rewarded; Q272 Avarice punished (rich man starved). Similar to Spencer 1959:402–13 (Point Barrow).

Generosity and sharing are expected and are rewarded; meanness and stinginess are punished.

EH13. THE WAR BETWEEN POINT HOPE AND NOATAK

There is a placed called Oksuruk located between Point Hope and Sealing Point. An old man and an old woman lived somewhere between Sealing Point and Oksuruk and another old couple lived between Oksuruk and Point Hope. These two couples always talked to each other. They said that if there are strangers from Point Hope way the couple located between Oksuruk and Point Hope should tell them to stop with them. If strangers come from Kotzebue way the couple located between Oksuruk and Sealing Point should let them stop with them. [The translator henceforth referred to the latter couple as the "Noatak couple" and the former as the "Point Hope couple".]

The Point Hope couple and the Noatak couple talked more with each other. They said that if there is a stranger let him leave his "killing things" with you before he comes farther on. Later on strangers come from both directions. The Point Hope man told the strangers from Point Hope way to leave their weapons and to then go to the top of Oksuruk. The Noatak man told the strangers from Noatak way to take their weapons to the top of Oksuruk.

The strangers started climbing the Oksuruks; they sat on top and started having a war. The Noatakers [identified as Noatagmiut by Edna] killed all the Point Hope men but two. One Point Hope man was shot in the leg with an arrow. This wounded man started singing a song when the Noatakers came up to him. They killed him.

Another Point Hope man that the Noatakers did not know about escaped. After this a Noatak man saw him, ran after him, and caught him at Umagachak [up the coast]. The Point Hope man laid on the ground on his back with his hands and feet in the air and gave up. The Noatak man saw that the Point Hoper's mukluks were all torn from running. The Noatak man stood over him with his arrow drawn and was going to shoot him, then he recognized that the Point Hoper was his katunun—they had shared the same wife. The Noatak man told the Point Hoper to take off his mukluks and to put on the Noataker's old ones and then to go home and stay there. If the Point Hoper came back and the Noatak man saw him he was going to kill him.

The Noatakers turned back up the Noatak River after this fight. They went over to Tuturuks [across the river from the modern village of Noatak]. In the fall they started seeing people because one person had escaped from that war. The people could not sleep because they innukoned (were afraid of strangers) too much. They knew the Point Hopers were around. One old man lived by himself farther away from the rest of the tents.

The lake (slough) just behind the tents started freezing up just beautifully. [The translator said that since Edna used the word "beautifully" something must disturb this beauty.] When the men could not sleep anymore they planned to make ditches at the base of the bank on the other side of the slough from the tents in which to hide themselves. They dug hiding places, took their wives to the other side of the river, went back, and hid in the ditches.

The old man stayed by the tents. That night they put him in a tent with a seal-oil lamp. They told the old man that if the dogs started to holler he should scold them like a woman or cry like a baby. He was to go to each tent and do this. They told him that if the Point Hopers started coming they were going to start fighting at dawn, and if they start that old man can hide any place.

They started hearing a lot of people stepping on leaves and making noises. The Point Hopers started jumping over the bank not knowing that there were people underneath. They started going toward the tents with the light in them. When they got close to the tents the men from the bank came out. There was water with beautiful ice between the bank and the tents. When the Point Hopers saw the Noatakers they started running, got onto the slough covered with thin ice, fell in, and started crawling to get out. One man got up from the water. A Noataker started following this man that got away.

The Point Hope man who ran off started ferrying himself across the big river on a small floe. The man following said that he could do it too, and he went across. The Point Hope man started to run towards Alutunituk [a place between the Noatak River and the coast] where the Noatak man caught him. The Point Hope man surrendered the same way as before, with feet and hands in the air. He was the same man as before and so was the Noatak man who caught him. The Noatak man stood above him with his arrow strung and told him he was going to kill him because he had told him not to come back. He killed him. All the other Point Hopers drowned and the Noatakers dragged two out and froze them with open mouth and eyes. They stood them up on either side of the trail leading to the water. THE END.

When I was small I used to hear those dead people in the fall, but they can't hear them anymore. I have heard this story lots of time. I do not know where I first heard it.

H79 Recognition by physical attributes; J1050 Attention to warnings; K1626 Would-be killers killed; P310 Friendship; Q325 Disobedience punished; R260 Pursuits; T141.2 Wife exchanged (Cumberland Sound —Boas 1901:223; Greenland—Holm 1912:75); W11.5 Generosity toward enemy.

The sparing of the Point Hope man because he stood in a *katunun* relationship to the Noatak man is an example of the extension of kinship so important in northern Alaska. The recognition by the translator of the literary device of equating beautifully flat frozen ice with impending turmoil is unusual because similar conventions were not noticed, or at least not commented on.

EH14. THE WOMAN AND THE EAGLE

On Point Hope there lived two older people with a son. On the north side of the village lived a woman with no husband. Behind Point Hope there was a big karigi, or meeting place. The Point Hope man always went up to the karigi when they were going to have a meeting. Every time he came home he told his wife that whenever he put his mittens on, in order to go, the kids always talked to him and let him stay a few hours. Whenever he came home he told his wife that again, but every evening he stayed longer.

Finally, when he was going again, she was suspicious and followed him. She found out that he went to the widow's house on the north side of the village. When he came home late again it was daylight. He told her the same story. He went out the next night and she followed again and saw him go to the widow again. Her heart broke right there. This happened another night and she started to think that she will get a seal skin and make a boat cover. [Edna used the word for dried seal skin; the translator remarked that it must be winter or spring.] When her husband came home she always put her sewing away so he couldn't see. She sewed with small, waterproof stitches. Finally she started making the boat. She finished and put a string to tie the boat above her head (some kind of round boat).

She started thinking that the wind should be from the east [to drive the ice away from shore]. She went out from the house one morning before her husband came home and saw open water. She went back inside. The second time she came out she saw more open water, so she went and got her boat. She put the boy on her back and went down toward the ocean. When she got to the beach someone yelled "Akham" (wait for me). It was her husband, but she wouldn't wait, saying he should have said "Akham" long ago, before he visited that woman.

When she got to open water she put the boat down, got inside with the boy, and tied it up. She knew the waves would take them away from the shore. She didn't know where they were heading. They had no food. All summer she spent on the water, her child crying for food, but they had none and he got skinny. Finally they stopped, as if the water couldn't move them anymore, and she tried to rock the boat, but she couldn't. So she opened the boat and saw ground.

After she opened the boat they both got out. She couldn't stand, so she put the boy on her back and started to crawl. She saw a little lake. She crawled there and started cleaning her boy and herself. There was ahnuk all over her back. Then they rested until she began to feel stronger.

She got up and started walking along the beach. Farther on she saw a house with two high inusuks (meat caches, also called ikigut). One was filled with beluga and one with black whale. When she got to the house she stood outside for awhile and then went in. She saw only one parka hanging in the stormshed. It was a long parka. She stayed in the stormshed for awhile, then went into the house. It was obvious that there was only one person living there. Food was ready. She went to the corner and sat down, putting her baby on her stomach under the parka. There was lots of food around, but she was scared to eat.

She heard someone outdoors. A man came in and said, "You poor thing." Then he said, "Why didn't you try to eat when you came in? The food is all for you. Put your baby down and feed us." She cooked and they started eating. The man started liking the boy when he saw him. They stayed together and the man didn't want to let her go. He started hunting. When he came home he'd have one-half beluga. He'd also bring home black whale.

The boy kept getting bigger. Finally he got big and wanted to hunt also. The man started taking him along, putting the parka in the shed on him. Every time they got beluga and black whale. The man started telling the boy not to try to kill the black whale that spit out red flames.

When the boy got older, he started thinking, "Why doesn't father want me to get the black whale that spits out red flame?" He saw the black whale that spit out red flame and got ahold of him by turning into an eagle (the man was an eagle when out hunting). The boy got his claws into the whale and got stuck there. He couldn't get loose. While he was trying to get free the water came up to his waist, so he began to call for his father. When the water got up to his neck his father came and pulled him off the whale. After that the boy didn't hunt the black whale that spit out red flame. The woman and the boy stayed for a long time and the old man couldn't talk much anymore. Sometimes he didn't say a word in the evening. Finally he didn't speak for a long time. Finally he said that he started hearing the boy's true father's voice.

The boy flew away again looking for his real home. He started seeing kayaks with seals or ugruks lashed to them. He recognized Point Hope so he started flying close to the kayaks until he recognized his father's kayak. The kayaks started home full speed when they saw the eagle. The boy started flying close to his father. He flew above him, got very close, and then would turn and his father's kayak would try to tip. His father started yelling for help.

When they got close to the houses the eagle started his diving again and the man in the kayak yelled louder. Finally the boy clawed his father in the shoulder and picked him up, kayak and all. He flew low over the houses. He dropped his father somewhere in the mountains. Then he went home to his mother and stepfather. His stepfather said something when he went in the house. He said to the boy's mother that when he found out that the boy's true father went to the widow, the eagle knew and pitied that woman and boy, so he took her mind and made her ready to make the boat and get in it. He made her go away. The man and the woman forgave each other. THE END.

I heard this story from Ralph Gallahorn.

C841 Tabu against killing certain animals; D152.2 Transformation: man to eagle (Kodiak—Golder 1903:94); D531 Transformation by putting on skin (Kodiak—Golder 1901:95; Bering Strait—Nelson 1899:468; Central—Boas 1888:617; Cumberland Sound—Boas 1901:181; Greenland—Rasmussen 1921:I, 364; 1921:II, 13; 1921:III, 75, 143, 262; Rink 1875: 146); D1532.1 Magic flying skin; N731.2 Father-son combat; Q241 Adultery punished (MacKenzie River—Jenness 1924:87; West Hudson Bay—Boas 1901:223).

May be the same story told by Paul Monroe (PM73), but told from a woman's viewpoint; also similar to PM5 in this volume.

IV. Paul Monroe

AUTOBIOGRAPHY

My name is Paul Monroe or Pulungun. I was born on Ḳuvañik River close to the Utukok River.[1] My birth date is April 1 and I am now seventy-three or seventy-four [in 1965]. My father died while I was small.

Before I knew anything, my parents stayed up the Noatak River. When caribou were hard to get the people started starving. My eldest brother, the one that killed himself outside, took us to Kobuk way to hunt rabbits. When they went there I can remember little things. I remember some people, a man named Kutalaruk and his family. When we went over Kobuk way my eldest brother and my elder sister and Kutalaruk's son and daughter always hunted rabbits. When they saw the rabbits, the rabbits were snowblind because of the spring sun. They made a thin, circular board of wood and put charcoal all over it. It was about eight inches across and called "kavhwuk."[2] They threw it over a rabbit. The rabbit thought it was a goshawk and would go into its hole. Then they would run over, dig it out, kill it, and put it on their backs. Those four always came home with full packs. That's how we were saved.

[1] I believe the Ḳuvañik is part of the Colville headwaters.
[2] The ḳavhwuk has been further discussed in Hall (1968).

In the springtime, after the ice broke up, we went down the Kobuk River. Farther down we saw a house and we stopped. We went inside. It was a big house and it had two trees on the floor inside. These logs marked off two big rooms, one on each side of the house, with another room or a hall in between. I saw a man sitting with his legs tucked under him. He had three strings tied around his neck. One went to a man in front and one to a man on each side. They were pulling him.

Every time they pulled the string the man said, "Aahaha." He never choked; he just made that noise. I passed out and don't know the rest. I heard the man's head come off because they were pulling him. They threw his head outside down the step. They threw the body down to the head and the body and the head stayed there for awhile, and then the body came up with the head on. The man was trying to become aŋatquq. I know that man. His name was Kipmayluk.

Just after it was like I slept, I woke again. I started hearing singing ("Come to Jesus, Come to Jesus just now . . ."). Then the song went to my head. I saw people standing in a row. I saw ice with water on it (spring). It was some Eskimo missionaries going by singing that song. They were going past people hooking sheefish [*Stenodus lencichthys nelma*]. My mother was hooking. Then I passed out again.

I woke up again in Kotzebue. There were only a few people there. The rest were at Sealing Point and around hunting. Kuyuḳ and some old people didn't go. We stayed the summer. In the falltime, before freezeup, my brother took us up the Noatak. We stopped at Uyyuḳ [across from Noatak Village]. Farther down we had met Auyiiruḳ [the white man whose death Edna described].

We built a real big house. My family lived by the door. On one side lived another couple with their kids, in the back lived a man and his kids, on the other side lived a couple and their kids, and someone else lived by the other side of the door. In the spring we went to Sealing Point through the mountains. Then to Sheshalik and up the river again.

I have heard about my brother's death from other people. I was small then. While I was upriver (in the falltime) at the south side of Kugruruk with my family (sister and mother) a boat came downriver. When the boat comes to my family they take my sister away (the Nunaluk family was in the boat). Me and my mother are alone now.

We stayed up at Kugruruk all winter and in spring my brother-in-law (the Nunaluk boy who married my sister that winter) came to get us. When my brother-in-law takes mother and me downriver to Pisiksuaktuglimpaŋaanii [on the lower Noatak] the old man Nunaluk was dead already.

When it's getting longer days [probably March, says translator] we went from Pisiksuaktuglimpaŋaanii toward Kivalina direction. When we get to Igisugruk I hear that my brother is dead. We stayed in that place for awhile and then my brother-in-law brought us down to Siñnugak, a place very close to Kivalina. We hear more about my brother while we're in Ivruktusugruk. After we hear about my brother we went to Kivalina.

When we're ready to go, we went through the beach with the boat. We took off from Kivalina and went to Kotzebue. When we go to Kotzebue a ship comes with white people. That same captain that take my brother away on that ship was again captain. My mother went down to the ship and the captain finds out my brother's mother was on the ship. The captain tells her she can have anything as long as they're on the ship. The captain gave them one ton of flour. My mother probably asked for that. She asked for guns and traps, and anything she asked for he gave them to her. She sold some of the flour for five cross-foxes [fox pelts with dark crosslike marks].

I came to Noatak way before the mission was built. The first teacher was both preacher and teacher. His name was Elmer Harnden. I came after Elmer Harnden settled here. After the second teacher came I got married. They put twenty-five years old on my marriage certificate. Elmer Harnden stayed about three years. I have lived around here since.

When the teachers got here the Noatagmiut and the Naupaktomiut started coming to the village in the wintertime. When Elmer came they made a log-cabin school soon after. I still went over to Ukaliksuk and then down to Sheshalik during the spring. I did this until about fifteen years ago. My first rifle was a .44 black powder which I got when I was about twelve. I got it after my brother killed himself. The captain told the people to give my mother anything she wanted. She wanted a gun for me.

I have traveled as far as Point Hope to the north and Deering to the south, and then up the Kobuk when I was small. My wife's maiden name was Mary Jones. Mary and I had ten kids, but some of them died. The most dogs I ever had was seven, but dogs used to be real big. I got enough food for them.

I went to school for a year and a half in Noatak. Kids used to go to summer school in Kotzebue and I went there for about two summers. We used to go over to Kotzebue as soon as we had finished hunting at Nuvuvruk and the women had put the things away. Some people would go upriver while the caribou still had thin skins. I never got a moose. I shot sheep by Ikalugrok. I always went to Point Hope by dog team and never stayed long.

One time my father-in-law went out hunting shishauks in a kayak. I followed behind with a short spear for seal. A big shishauk went under my kayak. I wounded it and followed it way down. A Selawik kayak speared it, but didn't kill it. There were two shishauks together and John Adams got one. I hollered for another spear and John Adams let me use his. I kept spearing the beluga and finally killed it. This is the first one I got in a kayak.

This is the way my early life went. Edna tell us from that time.

FOLKTALES

PM1. NAAKUN AND ḴUVAAYRUK

Around here there were two old people. They went up the Noatak River close to the headwaters and there they stopped for overnight. The next day the man went hunting. He hunted all day until it finally got dark, but there was moonlight. This was in wintertime. They were traveling by dog team. The man was out all night; he walked and walked in the moonlight.

Finally he saw another man walking, and though he looked at him the other man didn't see him. The other man was pulling something. It was a seal. It was soft and it wiggled as he pulled it over the soft ground. The first man went behind that man with the seal. He walked behind him for awhile and then stepped on the seal's flipper. The other man didn't look back because he thought it was a willow catching the seal. The quick pull almost made him stumble.

The first man stepped on the flipper again, but harder this time, and the other man really almost fell. The third time he stepped on the flipper the other man really pulled, and finally he fell down. He got up, but he didn't look back or turn back. He took his belt off and whipped backwards with it. The first man moved back a little so he just felt the end of the belt on his forehead. If he hadn't moved back he would have been killed. Then the man with the seal started walking again. The other man got scared and went home.

The man who made fun was called Naakun. The people near the Noatak headwaters were just like invisible people, they moved so fast. People could not even see them hunting, they went so fast. That's why they got so many seals. That's why the seal in the story wasn't frozen. [It is 150 miles from the Noatak headwaters to the sea.]

Naakun and his younger brother were aŋatquq. The younger brother planned to go up Kobuk way. He told Naakun, "If I reach the Kobuk some place up there you watch and see how the weather is. And if the sky turns kind of red it means that I have died." They made more plans and Naakun said, "If we live for awhile you watch the sky also, and if it turns kind of red that means I have died." So the younger brother took off for Kobuk way. After the younger brother went, for years Naakun lived and watched the sky. Finally one day when he woke up and went out the sky was kind of reddish. So he thought to himself, "My younger brother is dead." He lived for a few more years and people noticed that when he died the sky turned red. That's what Ḳuvaayruk noticed when Naakun died.

A boy knows about Naakun. This boy was a Naupaktomiut. His name was Ḳuvaayruk. He was small when Naakun died, but he grew up to become a man. He started hunting alone and walked as far as Kangiguksuk [small tributary of middle Noatak]. He always felt like hunting. He started along the little creek inside Kangiguksuk. He was walking along the high ground along the creek. When he came to one point he saw two men on the next. He stopped and they turned back so he couldn't see them. Ḳuvaayruk started running through the flat along the creek, and when he got near the third point he saw two little men. As he got closer to the point he couldn't see them again, so he started walking slowly, looking around.

Soon he heard someone whispering close by him, but he couldn't see anyone. There were lots of rocks around making a shelter under the cliff. He saw two little men there. He pretended he couldn't see them, but watched them out of the corner of his eye. He heard them say, "Gee, that man is so tall." Suddenly he pretended to discover them and started to walk towards the rock. The two dwarfs stood up and started talking to him.

While they were talking Ḳuvaayruk saw that one was a young boy with no whiskers and one was older with whiskers. The two little men asked Ḳuvaayruk what his name was. He answered, "Ḳuvaay- ruk." He asked their names. "Ḳaḳuchuk and Tuklivak," was the answer. Then the dwarfs asked him, "Where's Naakun?" Ḳuvaayruk answered, "When I was a boy I remember that Naakun died." The dwarfs said that they had met Naakun up there when he was a young boy.

Ḳuvaayruk started thinking that he had heard that some little men were tough and liked to fight. Just then, as if he knew what Ḳuvaayruk were thinking, one of the little men said, "Us, we can't fight. We don't try to scare people away." Then he said, "Let me see your bow and arrow." So Ḳuvaayruk gave it to him. The bowstring was tight, but the little man could pull it easily. Then the little man said, "Now give me your arrow." It was a long arrow, as long as Ḳuvaayruk's arm. The little man said, "This arrow is too long. It won't even kill an animal, but will break if I hit something."

The little man wants to try the arrow with his own bow. When he does the arrow breaks in two in the air. Then the little man gave Ḳuvaayruk his bow and arrow. And Ḳuvaayruk tried, but he couldn't even pull the string; it was too tight. The dwarf tried it and Ḳuvaayruk didn't even know he had fired the arrow, the little man did it so swiftly. The dwarf said, "We'd take you to our home, but one of our chief's sons just died and he wouldn't like to have strangers around." Their home is the highest point of Maymumirits [mountains northeast of Noatak Village]. They talked for awhile further and decided to all go home. They parted and went home. The little men said that they met Naakun when they were young. When Ḳuvaayruk got home he told people that those little men must never get old because Naakun was real old when he died and that was when Ḳuvaayruk was young.

Little men are called "Inugaakaliḳurit."

This is also about Ḳuvaayruk. He got married. After awhile his wife died. The people he was with started staying in the trees some- where across from the present village of Noatak. One fall they started seeing innuḳons. Ḳuvaayruk planned with the other men that they should go up a little ways from the village and cut some trees. They did so. Ḳuvaayruk told the men, "Don't watch for anything, just cut trees. I'll watch."

There was a tree close by with branches clear to the ground and he crawled inside there to watch. It was daytime. They were cutting trees and he was watchng. He said, "I see some men way over there. Don't watch, just keep cutting trees." Pretty soon he said, "They are getting closer." Then: "They are getting close. They are getting ready to shoot with their bows and arrows. They are standing all in a row. Don't worry; keep working; I'll take care of it."

Just when they were getting ready to shoot Ḳuvaayruk ran out towards them. Surprised, they ran away. He had nothing except a short knife (saavitluk). He kept running after them through the willows. Pretty soon they jumped over a bank. He stopped on the top because he was afraid that they might be waiting for him underneath with their bows and arrows. Ḳuvaayruk's crew went home. After they slept they went to that bank to search and found nobody, just a lot of broken arrows around. Going a little farther along the bank they saw the men. Ḳuvaayruk went up to them and told them to go home and not to bother the Naupaktomiut. He recognized some men. They were from the Kobuk. So the Naupaktomiut didn't see any more innuḳons. THE END.

I heard these stories from Frank Burns.

F451 Dwarfs; F451.3.8 Dwarfs are strong; F451.4.1.11 Dwarfs live in hills and mountains; F451.8 Names for dwarfs; F681 Marvelous runner; F960.2 Extranatural phenomena at death of hero; P251 Brothers.

A string of incidents held together by common actors. Dwarfs, or little people, still populate the Noatak Eskimo territory and occasionally their footprints are seen along the riverbank.

PM2. AKSIḲUKUK AND ḲUKRUKUK

Down at the coast there were people. There were two brothers there. These people always hunted for black whales. Each of those two brothers had a boat, and one time when they were hunting whale the youngest brother's boat caught one. After they caught the whale the eldest brother's boat came along to help. The whale took the boats far out into the ocean. When they got far out they killed the whale.

They tied it to the boats and tried to bring it ashore, but the wind changed and blew strong from the east. The younger brother always had a whale shoulderblade with a stick in it for his paddle. He always took it when he went out. The other men in the two boats of the brothers were paddling. They were trying to bring the whale ashore, but it got to be too stormy so they took the rope off and left the whale to drift. The younger brother started using his whale paddle; he used it a few times, but the waves were so rough that the stick broke and the shoulder[blade] dropped off into the water. The men in his boat tried to paddle with the small paddles, but they couldn't make it because it was too rough, so they returned to the whale.

When they got there they took a large piece of black muktuk off and they started drifting out to sea. They drifted so far they couldn't even see the hills. All summer long they drifted. One day they were drifting in the fog, and after the fog cleared up they thought they saw a black cloud just ahead. They got closer and found out it was land. When they could see the place well, they discovered it was hills and water. Rounding the point, they landed near a village.

When they got the boat on the beach they got out. People came, put their hands all over the boat, shook it, and pretty soon it was completely broken up. Then the people took them to the karigi. They went in and saw a man with only his pants on, leaning on the bench. He looked pretty tough to them. He had them sit down and said, "When you get to the beach after being on the ocean you are always thirsty and hungry. So bring them some food."

The women brought some food to the men. After they had eaten, that man said, "When there are strangers in our village some people like to wrestle to see who is stronger." That man was a man-who-killed-strangers. He was leaning on his side and he straightened up. He talked to them saying that he never did anything, that he always stayed home, and he was getting old and stiff. He finally got up, moving as if he were very stiff. He went to those men, grabbed one, twirled him around, and threw him against a sharp-edged whale shoulder bone that was on the floor on one side of the karigi. He grabbed another and did the same.

He killed all of them except the captain, the younger brother. The

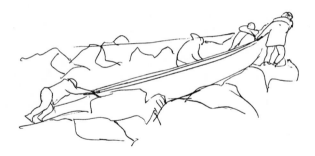

younger brother was kind of heavy and the man couldn't throw him. When the man couldn't kill him he said, "I can't kill you. You are too tough." So he gave up and put the man by the side of the karigi door saying, "When people come in they will bow to you. If the women come and bring some food they will bow down to you."

The elder brother was an aŋatquq and he started looking with his magic through the villages for his younger brother. He couldn't find him. Finally he went to the village where his younger brother was. He had never noticed that village before. He landed on top of the karigi by the window. He saw a man standing by the door with his head down. That man couldn't look up. The elder brother decided he should spit in front of that man to make him look. He spit and the spittle landed just in front of the man by the door. The man wondered where the spit came from and looked towards the window.

The elder brother recognized his younger brother standing by the door and so he left for home. When he got home he started building a new boat. He finished it all by himself and put the skin on all by himself. When he finished the boat he put it in the water when it was real calm. He wanted to try it out by himself. He drifted out and had the boat stay still, waiting for some ducks to pass. When some ducks came by, the boat started to move all by itself, following those ducks. They were iḷḷiktiuruk. The ducks started leaving the boat behind. Then the elder brother went back to the shore and said to himself, "This boat is too slow."

So he took the skin off, put another skin on, and went to the ocean again to test it. He put the boat in the water and waited for the ducks to come. The boat moved off by itself, again following those ducks.

They were iiŋaagiiruk (stay in the ocean all winter). He followed for awhile and then turned back to the beach. He said, "This boat is fast enough now."

He started getting ready to go to his younger brother. He got some young boys who had no whiskers to go with him. He also got one man with whiskers who was going to pretend to be his father. When they were all ready to go the elder brother became a little boy, smaller than the other young boys, through his aŋatquq magic. He wore a raincoat made of ugruk skin that was dyed red and long ikakliks (seal-skin boots).

When they left the old man went to the back of the boat and the elder brother got on his lap. The boat moved by itself out into the ocean. The young boys sitting in the boat pretend to paddle, but the boat went by itself. The old man sat still with the boy in his lap. They went way out into the ocean until they came to a place where two opposing currents went by each other. There was a lot of uksruks [sea birds] there. The boat stopped because there were so many birds. The young boys got their paddles and started moving the birds to the side of the boat so that they could make their way through them.

Finally they got through and moved farther on. Soon they saw a dark cloud, just like the first boat had. Coming closer they saw it was a mountain in the water. They went around the bend and saw the village. When the villagers saw the boat they yelled, "There's a boat, aahee." When they were going to beach the villagers wanted to get ahold of the boat, but it backed out from the shore by itself. The little boy said, "When we get to the shore, all you boys get out and pretend to lift the boat into the air. It will lift up by itself." When they got to the beach the boys got out and pretended to lift the boat up. The boat went up into the air so high that the people couldn't reach it.

The villagers took them to the karigi. The older man in the crew carried the little boy all the way. When they went in the younger brother was still standing by the door with his head down. He saw the little boy and said, "Aanaŋah, little boy, so cute." He didn't know it was his brother. He said, "These young boys have a small boy with them, aanaŋah."

When they went in the older man and the boy sat down. The older man picked up the small boy and put him in his lap. The man with only his pants on was still leaning on the bench in the karigi. He said, "If you've been out on the ocean for a long time and you get to the beach, you are always thirsty and hungry. Bring them some food and water." The women brought it. After they ate it the man that was sort of leaning on the bench said, "Me, I'm always tired. I never do anything." He straightened up and they could hear his bones crack. He stretched and finally tried to get up saying, "Some people from other villages like to wrestle or try to fight."

He started to walk towards the boys and at the same time the little boy got up and started to walk towards him. When they got close together the little boy pushed the man in the thigh and said, "You and I, let's fight. All year you have been killing people, so let's try, you and I." The man said, "No, I don't want to fight you. I'd rather raise you." He wanted to get to the other boys, but the little boy was always in his way and said, "No, you and I, let's fight," and kept pushing him back. Finally the third time the boy became a big man.

They started bearhugging each other. The boy got a good grip and started pressing very hard. The man's bones started breaking and he began spitting blood. Finally he got weak and the elder brother put him down because he couldn't stand up anymore. After the elder brother put the man on the floor, he went to the young brother saying, "Now it's your turn if you want to do anything to these people." The younger brother grabbed a stick and began hitting the people in the karigi. He killed them all. Then he went outside and killed all the people in the houses. He went back to the karigi with his brother.

They all stayed in the karigi for awhile. Then they started hearing someone in the kanichuk (stormshed) of the karigi. They waited and waited and finally two old men came in. One had a man's lower arm bone in his hand; the other had a small bag or pouch over his shoulder. When the little old men got inside they both stood by the door. The one with the bag opened it and pulled out a man's toe bone and put it in the middle of the floor. He brought out more and set them up in a row until there were as many as there were boys and the older man there. The other little old man took the arm bone and said he was going to swing it and hit one of the bones, and then the boy opposite that bone was going to die. He hit the bone and a boy died. He kept hitting those bones until all the boys died and only the elder and younger brother were left. Then those two old men left. When they ran out the aŋatquq started working on the dead boys and they came alive again. They became themselves again.

Soon they started hearing someone in the shed again. They waited and waited and two old women came in and stood by the door. They looked really fat. Their parkas were all puffed up and they had ropes tied around their middle. They let the ropes loose and a whole lot of feathers flew out. There were so many feathers that the whole karigi was smoky. The younger boys started dying because they couldn't breathe. The feathers got in their noses and their mouths. Only the two brothers lived. The two old women ran out. When the feathers had settled down the aŋatquq worked on the young boys again and soon they were alive.

They waited for awhile and nothing further happened. They left the karigi and went to the boat. It was still up in the air. They pretended to put it down and it came down by itself. They put it in the water and headed for home. They had to go through the uksruks again and they used their paddles to put them aside. Thus they made their way, got through, and reached home. The eldest brother was named Aksikuḳuk and the younger brother Ḳukrukuḳ. The End.

I heard this story from Kakan (Grace Bailey's grandfather).

D55.2.5 Transformation: adult to child (MacKenzie River—Jenness 1924:40; Greenland—Rasmussen 1921:I, 103); D1121 Magic boat (Kodiak—Golder 1909:17; Bering Strait—Nelson 1899:500; MacKenzie River—Jenness 1924:41; Central—Boas 1888:628; Cumberland Sound—Boas 1901:181; Smith Sound—Kroeber 1899:171; Greenland—Holm 1912:43; Rasmussen 1921:III, 102, 294; Rink 1875:154, 300, 417); D1606 Magic object automatically keeps out of reach (Central—Boas 1888:622; Cumberland Sound—Boas 1901:183; Greenland—Rink 1875: 264); D1711 Magician; D1889.7 Rejuvenation by conjuring (Greenland—Rasmussen 1921:I, 272, 322; 1921:III, 248; Rink 1875:238); D2060 Death or bodily injury by magic; D2135 Magic air journey (MacKenzie River—Jenness 1924:40; Greenland—Rasmussen 1921:I, 87); H1385 Quest for lost persons; K950 Treacherous murder; K1626 Would-be killer killed; K2010 Hypocrite pretends friendship but attacks; P251 Brothers; Q211 Murder punished (Cumberland Sound—Boas 1901:168; Greenland—Rasmussen 1921:III, 76, 111, 294); Q411.6 Death as punishment for murder; R155 Brothers rescue brothers; S116 Murder by crushing. Similar to Keithahn 1958:47–51 (Seward Peninsula).

PM3. Iŋaagiruk

Down at the coast there was a village A rich man lived there with his daughter. There was a karigi in the village. An old man had a place in the karigi; he was an aŋatquq. People went to the karigi and paid the aŋatquq when they needed help. There was also an old couple in the village who had a son. Every time the son went hunting he brought something home. There was another boy in the village and that boy married the rich girl. When the boy who was always successful at hunting brought something home, the rich girl always went to help him cut it up. The rich man's wife always helped her son-in-law. Every time that girl would go up to the first boy's home to work on the game he got, even if her husband also got lots.

One day when she went over her husband started to get jealous. He went to his father-in-law, and when he went in his father-in-law asked, "What do you want?" he answered, "I want one wolverine." He went right straight to that aŋatquq and said, "I'll give you this." The aŋatquq took it and put it by his side. Then he asked the man, "What do you wish for?" The man answered, "If that boy who is always successful when he hunts goes to the coast, let it get foggy." The aŋatquq put his head down; he felt funny because he didn't want that boy to get in trouble, but he had already taken the wolverine. So finally he said, "All right."

The boy who was always lucky at hunting went out on the ocean in his kayak. He got one ugruk and tied it on his kayak to go home. When he went a little ways it got foggy, so he couldn't see his way. He tried, but he couldn't reach land. He paddled for a long time, lost, not knowing where he was going. Then he saw something under the kayak in the water. He couldn't make out what it was so he kept kayaktuking (paddling along in the kayak). He'd see something black in the water, first on one side of the kayak and then on the other, but he couldn't make out what it was. Suddenly the kayak stopped. He was on the sand and it had been the ocean bottom that he had seen.

There was a small boy on the sand whom he hadn't seen before. The boy pulled the kayak part way up on the sand. Then the boy who was always lucky at hunting could get out, and the little boy helped him pull the kayak up the rest of the way. The little boy said, "Let's go to my house up there and see my grandmother." They went inside the house and there was an old woman there. She got up and welcomed the stranger. She put out some food so he could eat. After he ate she said, "You can stay with us." He did so.

Every day the little boy went out and brought a lot of fish home on a string. He didn't stay out long, but he always brought home fish.

The man stayed there all winter. In the spring the ice started going away. One evening the old woman said: "It's about time you go home. You can go now. Your parents are worried about you. They need your help. You didn't know when you were back home that that man got jealous because his wife always worked for you and not him. He went to his father-in-law and got a wolverine to pay the aŋatquq. Then the aŋatquq made it foggy so that you drifted away. If you are going home you have to follow the beach to beyond that mountain that you can barely see the top of from here. There is your home. While you were lost I saw you and pitied you, so I let you land here." She was aŋatquq too.

After she told him how to get home she said: "If you get home don't say anything about what has happened. This grandson of mine will go with you. I'll stay here. Don't say anything if you go home. Don't go to your parents. Go to that rich man and stay with him. If you go in and people ask where you have been, don't tell them. Tell the rich man the story first. Have him gather all the people in the karigi so that you can tell them how you got lost. If they go to the karigi and sit down, tell them about that rich man's son-in-law. Let the villagers take that aŋatquq from the karigi. He is no good." The last thing she said was, "The one that sent you to the fog, if he goes hunting some-time he'll travel in the fog himself." Then she let him go.

He went to the beach, got in the kayak, and waved for the boy. The boy didn't come. The man was going to paddle off when suddenly the kayak went by itself. It went along the beach and by the middle of the day he reached home. When he got his kayak half way up on the sand he noticed that the little boy was there again. The little boy helped him pull the kayak up and they went to that rich man. The rich man asked what they wanted, and the man answered, "Let all the people go to the karigi." The people did. When they went in, the man looked around and saw the aŋatquq, but he didn't see his parents. He told the story of how he got lost. The rich man said, "Take that aŋat-quq and throw him out of this karigi." He had his men take ahold of the aŋatquq and throw him out.

When everybody went out from the karigi the man started looking for his parents. When he went towards the house he saw them on the top facing towards the sea looking for their son to come home. Their tears couldn't dry. Their noses had dirt dripping down. They would look down to work at something, then look up again with tears coming down. He went to them, stood by their side, and said, "Here I am. I'm home." They looked up and wouldn't believe him. He told them the story of how he got lost. Finally they believed and went inside with him and the small boy.

After awhile the rich man's son-in-law went hunting with kayak. He caught an ugruk and tied it to his kayak. When he started off the fog came and he never returned home. When he didn't return the rich girl married the boy who was always successful at hunting. The little boy stayed with him and his wife and every time the little boy went out he brought home fish. That little boy was Iŋaagiruk, a bird that became a boy. THE END.

This story was told by Charlie Goodwin's wife.

D350 Transformation: bird to man; D1121 Magic boat (Kodiak—Golder 1909:17; Bering Strait—Nelson 1899:500; MacKenzie River—Jenness 1924:41; Central—Boas 1888:628; Cumberland Sound—Boas 1901:181; Smith Sound—Kroeber 1899:171; Greenland—Holm 1912:43; Rasmussen 1921:III, 102, 294; Rink 1875:154, 300, 417); D1711 Magician; D1814.1 Advice from magician; D2143.3 Fog produced by magic (Greenland—Rasmussen 1921:I, 109; Rink 1875:451); F1041. 21.1 Illness from excessive grief; H10 Recognition by common knowledge; N825.3 Old woman as helper (Greenland—Rasmussen 1921:II, 162); Q211.8 Punishment for desire to murder (Cumberland Sound—Boas 1901:62; Smith Sound—Kroeber 1899:177; Greenland—Holm 1912:47; Rink 1875:157, 222); Q411 Death as punishment.

The ambivalence of the aŋatquq reflects the general ambivalence concerning this type of individual in Eskimo society. The extreme sadness of the couple at the loss of their son reflects, beyond normal emotional bonds, the particular dependence of an elderly couple on a provider and the general dependence of any Eskimo individual on kin. The difficulty the son had in perceiving the shoreline in the fog is a common phenomenon in parts of the arctic, where the shallow ocean floor grades into low sand or mud banks.

PM4. KUPKUK

I don't know the beginning or the end of this story.

There was a man named Kupkuk who had two brown bears for dogs. He traveled to the beach where there was a house. He saw it and stopped close by. This was the house of a man and his wife and

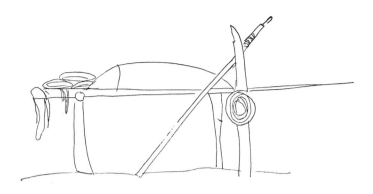

their daughter. As soon as Kupḳuk went to the house, that same day he got married to that girl. There was no ice at this time so it must have been summer (brown bears come out in the summer too). He tied his bears to poles.

In the falltime Kupḳuk started getting ready to go. The ice had started to form along the ocean beach and some of the lakes had started freezing along the edges. One morning Kupḳuk told his wife that he was going to take a trip, that he would be back. He went with his sled and his two bears through the beach for awhile, and then he went up to a lake behind the beach. The lakes were all frozen now. When he got to the end of the lake he went back to the beach again and drove along it. When it got to be night he camped, using just a caribou hide to cover himself.

After he woke he drove down to the beach and drove along there again; then he went up and went along another lake. When he got to the end of that lake he was going down to the beach when all of a sudden it got real stormy. He couldn't see anything. He tried to go, but he couldn't. Then just as suddenly it got clear again and he saw a house down at the beach with two inusuks. One had a whole lot of food on it while the other had only a little.

He went down to the house but stopped before he got there and tied his bears in the willows, hiding them. He told them to stay there. Before he went inside he noticed two dog poles by the side of the house. They were real thin ones, like the ones he tied his bears to. He also saw a dog-team trail going down to the ocean. He went to see the

inusuk with only a little bit of stuff on it. It was farther from the
house than the other one. He went under it and saw it was covered
with people's bones, some of them with meat still on them. He went
back to see the bigger inusuk. He went under and saw that it was
covered with a lot of seals.

He walked around outdoors for awhile, thinking of how to go in
the house. Houses on the coast have a door on the top because when
storms come it is easier to keep the snow away from the door. He
went through the door and down the ladder. When he got to the floor
he looked around the kanichuk and saw lots of seals all around the
walls. Looking around more he saw a door with a big pole on either
side of it. Above this door was a big rock. The rock was moving back
and forth ready to fall any time. When he looked closer he saw a man's
head on top of the rock. It was looking at him, the eyes moving. He
saw strings by the poles. The head winked at him and he decided
that the man didn't want him to go in because if he did so the rock
would fall and hit him.

He went out and waited on his sled to see what would happen.
After awhile he saw someone coming behind the house. It was a man
with a big white ruff. Behind the man followed a polar bear, and
behind that Kupkuk saw another polar bear. The bears were pulling
a sled full of seals. The man stopped at the inusuk and started throwing the seals up. He threw those heavy seals just as if they were small
pieces of wood. The man was tall and really strong.

After the man unloaded the sled he noticed that his polar bears
weren't lying down but were standing up listening instead. The man
walked back and forth. Kupkuk began singing real softly and the
polar bears stopped listening, lay down, and went to sleep. Then the
other man went in the house. Kupkuk got his bow and arrow ready.
Then he took his long spear, went to one of the polar bears, and
speared it while it slept. Then he went to the other polar bear and
speared it.

He went inside the kanichuk of the house. The teetering rock was
still there above the door. Kupkuk pretended he was going through
the door, then suddenly jumped back. The rocks fell and blocked the
door. Kupkuk tied the rock to the two poles with the ropes there.
Then he went out and went to the window to open it. As he did so
he felt the touch of a hand on his forehead. The other man had almost
got him. Then the man inside went to the door and tried to get out,

but the rock was too heavy. The man went back to the window and Kupḳuk shot him with his bow and arrow. It didn't hurt him; the arrow just broke on his chest.

He disappeared inside somewhere and then went back and tried the door again, and Kupḳuk shot him in the back with another arrow, but this arrow broke too. This happened several times. Then the man inside went to the door and started making a noise, started pounding on it. Kupḳuk then saw blood all over the floor. He had hurt the man even though his arrows had broken. Finally, when the man came back to the window again, Kupḳuk shot him in the chest, and this time the arrow stuck. The man slipped on his own blood and fell to the floor. He didn't get up; he was dead. Kupḳuk waited for awhile to make sure the man was dead.

Suddenly he heard a noise from inside the house. He waited and saw a little old man with just his pants on. The little old man started looking up at him, staring at him. The man said, "Yes, you killed my boy. The one that hunts for me. Yes, go ahead and kill me." The man in the window (Kupḳuk) had only one arrow left because the rest were broken. He broke the point off the arrow and shot just the shaft. It hit the little old man in the forehead and he fell down. Kupḳuk went to his sled and thought to himself that the old timers always peed after they killed a man and washed themselves in the pee. He did this, and then he took off again, still going away from home along the trail.

This time he went through the beach all the way. After going not too far he saw a village where a lot of men were playing football. These people saw a dog team and started running towards him. He told his bears not to bother the people if they got close. The people got closer, and finally three young boys reached him. The bears stopped at a big house with a large inusuk and a large single pole in front. This pole meant that it was the house of a rich man (umaylik).

They all went into the house. The three boys that had reached him first were brothers and this was their house. Their parents also had a girl, the boys' younger sister. Kupḳuk went in, stayed, and got married to that girl. The father gave him the girl the same day. When Kupḳuk started eating someone called through the window that his bears had already killed a little boy. He was going out, feeling sorry, when the three brothers said, "Don't feel sorry, that's not the first time it's happened." After they ate, someone called through the window saying, "That strange man has to go up to the karigi." So Kupkuk, the three brothers, the girl, and her parents all went up to the karigi.

When they went in there were a lot of people there sitting all around the sides. They sat down and Kupkuk started looking around. He saw a middle-aged man by the door who was looking sad and holding his head down. When they got settled the middle-aged man put his head up and asked, "Did you see anybody over that way where you came from?" Kupkuk answered, "I saw a house with a strong man and a little man living there." And he went on to tell what had happened to him.

He said that when he went into the house he saw the head on the rock and that head winked at him. The head had a tutuk (labret). Then the middle-aged man said, "It was my son. He hadn't come home for quite awhile and I was lonesome for him. Now I found out what happened to him." Continuing, he said: "Every time one of our young men went out hunting they didn't come home. That man grabbed them and their seals, took them home, and killed them. Then he put the men on one inusuk and the seals on another. That's why he got lots of seals." After that when the men of that village went out hunting they always came home with heavy loads.

Kupkuk stayed with them all that winter and the following summer. Then fall came and one morning Kupkuk asked his wife, "Do you know about people close by?" She answered, "No." A few days later he asked again and received the same answer. The third time he asked his wife did not answer for quite awhile. Then she said, "I like you so much I don't want you to go. I want you to stay with me. There is a village one day's travel away from here and every time someone goes there he doesn't return home. I am afraid you won't come home." Then she told him: "They have a pet there, a tirichik. (This is a dragonlike animal with lots of legs and small sharp horns on its back. It has large tentacles, one on each side of its big mouth to grab people so that it can eat them.) When that tirichik got big it began to kill people and eat them. It has a place in a little lake in the middle of the village. When it begins to get dark the people of the village bring some food, meat, and water up to him. There's a karigi behind the village. I didn't want you to go but to stay with me, that's why I didn't answer you at first."

Kupkuk decided to go to that village. He got ready and told his wife, "I'm going to leave a pair of gloves (tanned caribou) in my sled under the cover. If I am still alive a fox will come outdoors around here, so tell your brothers not to try to kill him. It will go away and then it will come back again if I am still alive. If it doesn't come back you can search for my gloves in the sled." Kupkuk went, taking only his spear with him. He used it for a walking stick when he was tired.

He left early in the morning and by alternately walking and running was close to the other village in the middle of the day. Towards evening he saw it clearly. He didn't go to the village, but stayed close by to see what the villagers were doing. As he rested he saw women take plates to a little lake and then they brought little buckets of water to the lake. He saw one big house with a light. It was the karigi.

When it got dark there was one more light down by the lake. He looked in the lake, but he didn't see the tirichik. He peeked into the big house through the window and saw the tirichik's head right by the door. He looked around. The house was full with the tirichik's body and the tail was by the door on the other side of the house from the head. He looked in the window and pretty soon the tirichik's tentacles started moving. That tirichik smelled something.

Kupkuk closed the window and started singing the same song that he used to quiet the polar bears. After he sang he opened the window and saw that the tirichik was sleeping. Quickly he ran to the door and went in. The sleeping tirichik's head was close to the door. Kupkuk noticed a soft place by the tirichik's neck. He poked his spear hard in this place and ran out. There was a lot of noise inside and then silence. He knew that the tirichik was dead. To make sure he went on top and looked in the window. The tirichik was dead. He noticed that one of the door poles was chewed up, bitten clear through by the tirichik's head when the tirichik first felt the spear.

Kupkuk went up to the karigi. Going inside he found the men sleeping. He carefully got in the middle of the sleeping men and pretended that he was sleeping too. Pretty soon someone called through the window, "Somebody killed our pet." The men woke up and said, "The guards slept. They were supposed to watch." They all ran out, including Kupkuk, who had killed the tirichik. They didn't know him. They checked, saw that the tirichik was dead, and went back to the karigi. They all started talking and blaming each other. Kupkuk said to another man, "You were supposed to watch the tirichik."

Finally one man said to two boys there, "You should go get the

mother of our pet. She will know who killed him." The boys got ready and went. It didn't take them long. Soon they heard a noise coming from way up. Then the tirichik's head came inside the karigi, breaking the poles of the karigi door. Then the tirichik's body came in. It started moving towards Kupkuk, even though there were a lot of other people around. Its tentacles went towards him. Kupkuk grabbed another man and threw him at the tirichik's mouth. It swallowed the man. He did this again and again. Soon there was only a few men left, and finally Kupkuk was left alone.

There was a lot of room now so he ran around trying to hide, but the tentacles kept following him. He didn't know what to do. He could see no way to get out. He started running around the karigi benches, but the tirichik kept following him. Finally Kupkuk jumped out the window. He was sweating. Still the tirichik came after him. Every time Kupkuk met some people he threw them to the tirichik. Finally he was getting kind of tired, and when the tirichik opened its mouth Kupkuk jumped over its back. He did this several times, and then when the tirichik opened its mouth again he jumped inside before the teeth could get him.

The inside of the tirichik was real bright. Her stomach was full of dead people. Some were chewed real good, some were not. Kupkuk stayed for awhile, trying to think of how he would get out. He took out his knife and started cutting the stomach bone of the tirichik. He cut all over. Soon it got real dark inside, but he kept cutting. Finally it was like the tirichik couldn't move anymore. Kupkuk stopped cutting. He still didn't know which way to get out. He took his magic bone hanging around his neck and changed himself into a little black bug (miñnuk) and started to crawl out the tirichik's nose. He saw light and went out.

When he got to the ground he felt weak and couldn't go any farther. So he changed himself into a wolverine. After he cleaned himself on the ground he started to go home. When he got home he was still a wolverine. When the brothers saw him they set out traps for him, even though Kupkuk's wife had told them, "If any kind of animal comes around here don't bother it." He almost got caught in the traps. The boys also started to hunt him. After three days they didn't see him again. So his wife went to his sled, got the gloves, and started looking for something in them. In the little finger she saw a miñnuk.

It was weak. She put the glove back in the sled and covered it up real well.

After they slept the woman checked again. She saw the miññuk again and it was getting livelier, so she covered it up and went inside once more. Every time she checked the miññuk was getting better. On the third morning she went out and her husband was sitting on the sled. She took him in to her parents. He had become a man and gone home to his wife and her parents. THE END.

This story was told by Makan.

B10 Mythical beasts and hybrids; B575.1 Wild animals kept as dogs (Central—Boas 1888:599; Greenland—Rasmussen 1921:I, 318, 363; Rink 1875:248); B877 Giant mythical animals; C841 Tabu: killing certain animals; D124.3 Transformation: man to wolverine; D184.1 Transformation: man to beetle; D1364.24 Music causes magic sleep; F501 Person consisting only of head; F610 Remarkably strong man; F911 Person swallowed without killing; F912.2 Victim kills swallower from within by cutting; H1220 Quest voluntarily undertaken; K952 Animal (monster) killed from within; K1626 Would-be killers killed; K1860 Deception by feigned death (sleep); L161.1 Marriage of poor boy and rich girl; P253.0.3 Three brothers and one sister; Q211 Murder punished (Cumberland Sound—Boas 1901:168; Greenland—Rasmussen 1921:III, 76, 111, 294); Q411.6 Death as punishment for murder. Similar to Curtis 1930:201–3 (Noatak).

The method Kupḳuk used to travel along the beach, sledding across frozen lagoons when available instead of the beach itself, is still utilized today. Note that the middle-aged man's sadness was mitigated somewhat when he found out his son's fate. I could not ascertain the import of a single large pole in front of a rich man's house, though this association is noted in several other stories.

PM5. THE NEPHEW'S REVENGE

There were some people down at the coast. There were two brothers who had no parents. The younger brother had a wife and kids. Every time one of the youngest brother's eldest boys grew up his uncle took him hunting. The uncle would come home alone. The youngest brother's boy would not come back. The youngest brother and his wife were scared of the elder brother. Every time he took their eldest son out hunting the elder brother would come home alone.

The couple started planning. She was pregnant. If it was a boy they were going to treat it like a girl and see what happened. Even when the child got older they were going to clothe it like a girl. They were scared to ask the elder brother what happened to their sons. The woman had labor and had a baby boy, but they said, "It's a girl." So they made clothes just like for a girl. The baby grew and they always said, "This girl is so cute," and so forth, even though it was a boy.

The boy got big still wearing girl's clothes. Soon he was bigger than the other boys were when they were lost. The elder brother said he wanted to walk with that girl. They let him go. The boy/girl and the elder brother walked through the beach. The elder brother was carrying an ax. Not far along they found a log and the elder brother cut it the same length as the boy and split it in half. Then he started cutting the inside, hollowing it out. When he finished he made a top for it. Then he got ahold of the boy. The boy didn't want to get in the box. The elder brother grabbed him, took his pants down, and found it was a boy. He put him inside the box and covered him. Then he put the box in the ocean and pushed it out.

The wind was offshore and that box went farther and farther out. The boy didn't know how many days, how many months, he drifted. He started getting weak. He didn't eat or drink. He peed in his pants and got wet all over. He cried, but nobody could hear him. Finally it seemed like he stopped. It was just like little waves were rocking him on a beach. He couldn't open the box. Soon it seemed like he heard two people talking. He couldn't move. He was weak and real skinny. The people came closer saying, "I wonder what's that over there on the beach." They got the box and moved it up to where it was dry. They tried to open the box, finally did so, and saw the little boy. It was two girls who found that box. They felt sorry for the boy because he was so skinny. They said, "Let's take him home to our parents." They helped him out of the box and one of the girls put him on her back.

They took him home and their father said, "You girls have no brother, so clean him up and try to raise him as your younger brother." So they started cleaning him up. The father said, "Don't give him too much food at first since he hasn't eaten in so long. Just give him a little bit and a little water and tomorrow give him the same, just a little meat and water." In a few weeks the boy got his strength back.

He was fat and strong, just like before his uncle put him in the water. When he started going out to play the two girls always went out with him. In the stormshed he always looked around and saw four eagle skins hanging there.

When he got to be a big boy the father said, "Take him out and teach him how to fly. Let him put my skin parka on." They went to the shed, got the eagle skins, and went out. They had the boy put on his stepfather's skin. They put their own on, grabbed his wings, and flew way up in the sky. They showed him how to fly, then dropped him. His head hung down because it was too heavy. He kept falling, and when he got close to the ground the girls caught him and took him up again. They dropped him again, telling him to keep his head up and use his wings. He got better and kind of flew side-slipping, like a duck. They told him more and he got better. They flew and he followed their trail. It didn't take them long once he learned to use his wings. The third time they took him up and dropped him he really flew well, so they landed near the house. They had taught him in one day. They took him out every day for practice. When he was able to fly well alone they told him he could go fly any time.

So one day he went out alone and in just a little while he brought home one caribou. The sisters cut it up and dried it. They were proud of him. The girls stayed home now and sewed instead of going out hunting. They had someone to hunt for them. He started bringing home all kinds of animals. One time he brought home a whole black whale. His stepfather told him when he hunted far from home he should not try to get the black whale with red flame in its mouth. He said, "Those kind are real strong. If you ever get that kind and you can't bring it home, cry like an eagle."

Then the boy went hunting again. He thought, "I wonder why my stepfather doesn't want me to get a whale with red fire in its mouth." Just then he saw one. He grabbed it from behind and tried to fly off with it. He didn't move. He kept trying to fly, but he kept sinking deeper in the water. His legs went in the water, his wings started touching the water, and then it was up to his waist. Suddenly he remembered that his stepfather had said to call if he needed help. He called real loud and kept calling. All of a sudden two eagles came, put their claws in the water, pulled the whale up, and flew home with him. The stepfather came out to meet them. When he went to the boy he said, "I didn't want you to get that kind of whale. You didn't listen to me. They are strong. If you didn't holler you wouldn't have come home." The boy didn't try to get that kind of whale anymore.

He went hunting again. One evening when he came home his step-father said: "It's about time you got married. There are people one day's walk away, not very far. There are three brothers and one younger sister. If you want to get married to that girl you can go up there. You are old enough now. If you get married to that girl you can stay up there as long as you want." So one morning the boy started out; he walked all day and in the evening reached a house and went in. The three brothers, their youngest sister, and their parents were all there. He stayed with them and married that girl. He stayed there for a long time and finally his wife had a baby boy.

When that baby got a little bigger he decided to visit his stepfather. When they went they took the youngest brother with them, leaving two older ones. They left in the morning and arrived in the evening. They went inside the house and the boy's stepsisters saw their step-brother's baby boy. They really liked him. They stayed for a long time and the boy really hunted every day because his stepfather was making an umaypak. The stepfather worked on it and his stepson started making a chair for himself. He broke caribou longbones [leg bones] and put them with the sharp edges up on the seat of the chair. He also kept hunting and they dried up lots of caribou. He worked on the chair in the evenings when he came home. His step-father got the boat ready and they started loading dried meat in it. They made a house in the middle of the boat. The stepfather said, "When you get in the house don't look out or get out. Don't go out until you land someplace." The man and his wife, the baby boy and the wife's younger brother got in the boat.

The stepfather pushed the boat out into the ocean and it moved by itself. They went for one day and in the evening they stopped. Then they got out and saw a village close by. They walked over and went into the first house they saw. The family living there had girls and one boy. The man of the house said, "There is a man around here who kills people. He lost his son when the son was small and he became an iñnukaknaaluk" (man-who-kills-people). They stayed in the house for awhile. Someone called through the window, "The strangers have to go to the karigi."

They all went up, the people from the house walking up with them. They went inside the karigi and sat down. The boy looked around. He saw people and then he saw his uncle, the one who had put him in the box. One man who looked real mad got up and went to the strangers. He went towards the boy sitting there with his son in his lap. When the man who was mad got closer the boy said, "Kill your namesake first, and then you can do whatever you please with us after that." The man who was mad got closer. When the boy said "kill your namesake" that man didn't believe it. So the son said, "When I was a little boy my uncle took me for a walk. He put me in a box and I drifted." The mad man still didn't believe it, but finally began to believe and he got weak and fell on the floor.

They all went out from the karigi and the boy, his wife, his wife's younger brother, and the small baby went to the first house they had come to, unloaded the boat, and took all the meat to that house. The boy told his wife to cut up any kind of meat she could find in the house and put it in a big wooden tray (aaluyuk). So she cut all the different kinds she could find and put it on a tray. When she got ready the boy got the chair he had made and they went up to the karigi. He carried the chair himself. Everyone was there.

The wife put the tray in the middle of the floor. The boy put the chair by the tray so that a person could reach from it to the tray. Then he stood behind the chair, looked around, and called his uncle. He said: "When I was a boy you took a walk with me. You had an ax on your back so I took a walk with you. When we reached the tree we stopped and you cut it in half, the size for me, carved it out and made a lid. I didn't want to go in. You made me and pushed me into the ocean. You didn't think you'd ever eat meat that I got."

The uncle came over and the boy stood behind the chair. The uncle was going to sit down. When he started to do so the boy pushed him down by his shoulders so hard that the caribou bones on the chair were broken. The uncle started eating. His blood started spreading all over. He got weak and fell. They went out from the karigi and started planning to go back to the boy's stepfather. He took one boy and one girl from the house where they were staying. When they got in the boat they went up. The boy he brought married one of his stepsisters. Later they went to the village of the parents of the girl he had married. They stayed there for awhile and he took home a boy to marry his eldest stepsister. From then on all the families in this story visited each other. THE END.

I heard this from Daniel Walton.

C841 Tabu: Killing certain animals; D152.2 Transformation: man to eagle (Kodiak—Golder 1903:94); D531 Transformation by putting on skin (Kodiak—Golder 1903:95; Bering Strait—Nelson 1899:468; Central—Boas 1888:617; Cumberland Sound—Boas 1901:181; Greenland—Rasmussen 1921:I, 364; 1921:II, 13; 1921:III, 75; Rink 1875:146); D1121 Magic boat (Kodiak—Golder 1909:17; Bering Strait—Nelson 1899:500; MacKenzie River—Jenness 1924:41; Central—Boas 1888:628; Cumberland Sound—Boas 1901:181; Smith Sound—Kroeber 1899:171; Greenland—Holm 1912:43; Rasmussen 1921:III, 102, 294; Rink 1875:154, 300, 417); F786 Extraordinary chair; F1041.21.1 Illness (psychological) from excessive grief; H10 Recognition through common knowledge; K1626 Would-be killers killed; K1836 Disguise of man in woman's clothes; K2211.0.1 Treacherous elder brother; P251 Brothers; P252 Sisters; P253.0.3 Three brothers and one sister; P293 Uncle; Q211 Murder punished (Cumberland Sound—Boas 1901:168; Greenland—Rasmussen 1921:III, 76, 111, 294); Q261 Treachery punished (MacKenzie River—Jenness 1924:87; West Hudson Bay—Boas 1907:551f.); Q411.6 Death as punishment for murder; S71 Cruel uncle; S118 Murder by cutting; S143.1 Child abandoned in hollow tree. Similar to Lantis 1945:281 (Nunivak) and to EH14 and PM73 in this volume.

This story offers advice on how to feed an individual suffering from starvation. Also noted are observations on the erratic flight of young eagles. Here, too, a man's grief at the loss of his son is so great that the man becomes a man-who-always-kills-people and thus deprives others of kin.

PM6. THE WAR BETWEEN THE ḴUVAÑIK AND BARROW PEOPLE

At a place called Ḵuvañik on the Utukok River [probably actually on the Colville River] is my birthplace. There were people living in Ḵuvañik. In the falltime they made houses, ebruliks, and igloos there. Innukons started coming in the evening. When the innukons came an old couple took their grandson to their boat and went downstream. Before they went they listened to and understood the strangers. They sounded like Barrow people. When the couple and the boy got farther down the river they went inside some thick willows and hid there.

Later they made a house there and started raising the boy. When the boy got a little bigger he started following his grandfather, staying out. They would walk up from the house to get wood, and when returning the grandfather gave the boy heavy wood to carry. Even though he was tired the boy tried to reach the house. Every time they went home from a walk the grandfather would pile heavier wood on the boy. They raised him that way.

Finally he got bigger and tougher. He started walking alone farther away from the house. He always saw something in the willows like horns. One time when walking he saw something in the willows again. He went home and asked his grandfather, "What are those things that always walk in the willows; they look like trees?" His grandfather answered, "Those are caribou." He asked his grandfather how they hunted caribou and his grandfather answered, "They always shoot them with a bow and arrow." His grandfather started making a bow and arrow for him. He made only one arrow. One time the boy went out with the bow and arrow, saw a caribou, and shot it. This was the first caribou he ever got. He started getting a lot of caribou and helping his grandparents. One time when he was out he came home with a whole caribou on his back. He started packing home a whole caribou. Every time he went hunting he brought a caribou home. His grandfather made more arrows. The boy became a man and didn't grow anymore.

One time he started walking up the river, and after awhile he started seeing some cut willows. He kept walking, seeing those cut willows, and farther up he came to an old village with broken houses. When he got there he started going in the houses when he could. He started finding people's bones. He kept looking and going inside, finding bones. Finally he went over to a bank. On the top there was a big fireplace. Around the fireplace he saw big sticks. They had been used for cooking people because he saw foot bones by the ends in the ground. His throat got tight; he was sorry, so sorry for those people who got burned. He felt lonesome and sad after he saw those burned bones. He felt weak and turned back.

He walked home really slowly. When he reached the house he went in and they noticed that he felt real sad. He didn't talk all evening. His grandmother brought him some food, but he didn't want to eat. They asked him what was the matter. He didn't answer for awhile, then he told his grandparents what he found when he walked upriver. That was why he felt unhappy. When he had told about what he had seen and finished talking his grandparents said, "We were up at that place when those people came in the evening. When we heard them

we took you away in our little boat. When we reached here we settled down. Your parents are up there." After he heard that, it was like
he didn't care because they had already died. He started hunting
again. He killed a brown bear with his bow and arrow. After that he
began killing brown bears with his knife.

One time he was hunting and while walking along he thought he
saw somebody hiding in the willows. He turned back and ran away
to hide. When he got a little farther he thought to himself, "What am
I afraid of anyway? If that man wants it that way, anyway, why run
away?" He went and found the man who looked tough too and killed
him. Then he tied the man up on his back and packed him home. His
grandfather recognized the man he killed because it was the son of a
man from Barrow who-always-killed-people. That boy was tough in
Barrow, tougher than all the Barrow boys. The boy cut the Barrow
boy's head off and cooked the body. Then he stored them away where
they wouldn't spoil. The grandparents of the boy stayed in that place
for some years.

One summer two strange men came. He welcomed them and they
talked. He brought some meat in and they ate some. They said it was
the first time they had had this kind of meat. It tasted real good. After
they ate, the boy got the head and put it in front of those men. One of
the men was kind of young and the other was a man. The older one
recognized his son. He looked at the head and said, "I raised my boy
to be tough and you killed him." The boy answered: "He tried to kill
me first. I didn't want to kill him. He was hiding, waiting for me and
I started to run away, but then I thought if he wants it that way, that's
the way it should be, so I went back and killed him. That's the meat
I gave you fellows. That was the boy's meat you ate."

After the man-who-always-killed-people found out about his boy
he said that he had been looking all over for him when he didn't come
home. He was glad that he had finally found him. The boy said, "If
you guys want to fight we can. I can do anything you want." The
man-who-always-killed-people didn't want to fight or anything. He
was just glad to find his son. The two strangers went back home.

After they left the boy started thinking of those Barrow people. He
started hunting caribou for his grandparents. He was getting ready.
He got a lot of meat. In the fall he let his grandmother make him
mukluks. He was planning to take off for Barrow. When the ground

was hard he left for Barrow. Before he left his grandfather said, "There is a trail you should follow which will take you to Barrow. If you can go there your anna (grandmother) lives there." The boy always stopped at night and got a caribou for his supper.

Once when he started again in the morning he saw a village. While he waited for it to get dark he noticed a house alone. He went down, put his pack on top of the stormshed, and went in. There was only an old lady in the house. The old woman welcomed him because he was a stranger. She asked, "Why did you come here?" He told her about the time he discovered the ruined village and the burned people and said, "Whenever I think of it my throat gets tight. I am sorry for those people, so I am looking around for people." The old woman said, "Who are your parents?" He told her their names. She knew them because his grandmother was her half-sister.

She felt sorry for him coming to Barrow because there is a man-who-always-kills-people there. He replied, "I don't care what happens to me. That man can kill me. My throat is always tight." He stayed there overnight. He went out in the morning to pee. Then he went back in the house. It wasn't long before somebody called for him to go over to the karigi.

They went in and he looked around and saw the man-who-always-killed-people. That man asked him why he came, and he told him about the burned people and how his throat always got tight all the time. When he told this the man-who-always-killed-people got mad. He had his other son start fighting with the boy and the boy quickly killed him. His grandmother said, "That's enough," and kind of scolded him. She told him to quit. The man-who-always-killed-people gave himself up to the boy, saying that if he wanted to kill him he could. When the man-who-always-killed-people gave up he said, "There's a lot of women in this village. I have a daughter, too." The boy went to his daughter and stayed with her. When she got pregnant he left her and went to another woman. When the second woman got pregnant he left her and went to a third. When the third got pregnant he moved again. Finally when he had five women pregnant he went back to the first girl and started staying with her. All the girls had their babies.

He planned to get his grandparents. When he went he brought them back and they became Barrow people. When the five women had their kids they grew up and became tough boys. Barrow people and Ḳuvañik people used to have war. Now they quit and became friends. The End.

Daniel Walton used to tell this story.

G61 Relative's flesh eaten unwittingly; H79 Recognition by physical attributes; H1220 Quest voluntarily undertaken; K1626 Would-be killers killed; L111.4 Orphan hero; P233.6 Son avenges father; Q211 Murder punished (Cumberland Sound—Boas 1901:168; Greenland—Rasmussen 1921:III, 76, 111, 294); Q411.6 Death as punishment for murder; T617.1 Future hero as child isolated from world kills increasingly larger game.

In PM19 the meat of a dog is saved to feed the murderers, while in PM41 a man's head is cooked and eaten—again, the importance of knowing what has happened to kin.

PM7. Kaḳun

There was a village down at the coast. A man and his wife lived there. Their son and his wife lived there too. They stayed there winter and summer hunting for a couple of years or more. Their boy couldn't talk in the evenings when he came home from hunting. He would start getting ready to go hunting early in the morning. Before he said anything he took off in his kayak along the beach.

Once he paddled along the beach for a ways and then turned straight out into the ocean. He paddled all day, then he saw a big white iceberg floating in the ocean. When he got to it he got on top of it. He saw one ugruk and he speared it. He stayed on the ice, cut the ugruk up, took the stomach out, and ate the ingaluk (the gut).

He stayed overnight and in the morning took off. He paddled along the ice. After awhile he started seeing seals with no heads on them. Then he saw walrus, black whale, and beluga with no heads. After he saw these animals he paddled on, going close along the ice. Soon he came to a real tall section of the iceberg (naguyuk). As he was paddling under it he started hearing someone singing up on top. He noticed it was a man's voice.

He passed and went farther on. He climbed up on the iceberg. He found another ugruk and killed it and then stayed there overnight. That iceberg was a seagull. He had landed on the seagull's wings. It was a seagull that he had heard singing. The naguyuk was really its neck. The ugruk, seals, and other animals without heads that he saw were the seagull's food. After the boy stayed there overnight (he still thought it was ice) he took off again in his kayak. He stayed on the water all day. In the evening he saw something that looked like a black cloud. He got closer and knew that it was land. It was a rocky mountain in the water. He got there and wanted to land, but the cliff was too steep and there was no place to put his kayak. He got his spear ready and threw it up to the top of the cliff, with a rope attached. The spear landed and he tried to pull it back, but it was stuck, so he started pulling himself and his kayak up.

He got on top and got out of his kayak. He looked around and saw some large plants (ikusiks). He cut one off and went inside the stem. He covered the hole in the stem with his parka and went to sleep. After he slept for awhile he woke up. Two people were talking outside. He listened and when they got close he heard them say, "We've come to get you. Our dad wants you." After awhile he went out and saw two boys, two brothers. He went with them and they went down off the mountain to low land. It wasn't far. If he had gone around the corner he would have been able to land with his kayak.

They followed a trail down from the mountain. He saw some houses. They took him up to the karigi. The two boys' father was there and he said, "It's me that let you come. I took your mind away." He was a rich man, an umaylik. They gave the boy food. He didn't recognize it; it was black on top and white underneath. They told him that it was whale muktuk. They had got a whale just yesterday. The rich man said, "You can go home to my wife. I am always in the karigi."

The boy went to the house and the woman was home. He told her, "That rich man up there told me to come down here, so I came." They went to bed but not in the same bed. He couldn't go to sleep and he tossed and turned. That woman was sleeping in the bed over him. He was underneath on the floor. He took out his knife and showed it to her. He said that he wanted to pay with his knife so that he could sleep with her. She grabbed the knife and said that she was going to let her husband see it first. She didn't come back for a long time. He got worried, got up, and went to the karigi. He went in and saw the rich man and his wife fighting over the knife. He said that he had two knives so they shouldn't fight. The rich man got the knife. The boy and the woman went home and she got the other knife.

The boy stayed three or four days with the young woman. Then he said, "I can start home now." The rich man said, "Take your kayak to the karigi. From there I will send you home." The boy took his kayak to the karigi and the rich man said, "Put it down and turn it towards the door." The boy got inside and got his paddle ready. The rich man said: "Close your eyes. When I say to, paddle two times on the left and then take the paddle and paddle two times on the right before you open your eyes. If you reach your home and go to your wife, don't say any bad words to her. Don't be mean to her." The rich man went to the boy's back and pushed him. He paddled as he was supposed to and when he opened his eyes he was already on the beach at home.

When he got out of the kayak there was a woman there cutting ugruk. He went up to her. She didn't know there was anybody around so she kept cutting. He recognized his wife and said, "I'm glad somebody gave you an ugruk." Even though he spoke she never looked up, but just kept on working on the ugruk. Again he said he was glad that somebody brought her an ugruk. He said it louder this time. She still didn't look up. The third time he said it real loud. Suddenly it was just like he was knocked down. He didn't know what was happening. Finally he woke up in a little house. The house was very bright. He stayed for awhile and finally the house started getting smaller and smaller.

He went out and started hearing people talk. A woman said, "That little baby that just got born has no water for bathing in." He heard a mean voice say, "Give him a bath in pee." Then he said, "I'll bathe myself." Suddenly he was knocked out again. He was on a woman's back. He recognized his wife, the one that was packing him. When he had said the third time real loud, "I'm glad someone brought you an ugruk," he had gone into the woman's womb and she'd become pregnant with her own husband.

That woman had gotten married to another man when the boy had gone off in his kayak. When he woke up again he was on his mother's back. He saw some men in a circle outdoors talking. He looked around farther and saw a man and a little boy coming. The little boy was dragging a baby seal. The baby starting jumping around on his mother's back. He wanted to get that baby seal, he really likes them. He tried to jump down. Suddenly he jumped into that circle of men. He had become a man. He found out that his wife was married to another man. He didn't go back to her; he went back to his parents. The boy's name was Kaḳun. THE END.

I heard this from Grace Bailey's grandfather.

B872.2 Giant gull (Cumberland Sound—Boas 1901:195; Greenland—Rink 1875:455); D55.2.5 Transformation: adult to child (MacKenzie River—Jenness 1924:40; Greenland—Rasmussen 1921:I, 103); D1121 Magic boat (Kodiak—Golder 1909:17; Bering Strait—Nelson 1899:500; MacKenzie River—Jenness 1924:41; Central—Boas 1888:628; Cumberland Sound—Boas 1901:181; Smith Sound—Kroeber 1899:171; Greenland—Holm 1912:43; Rasmussen 1921:III, 102, 294; Rink 1875:154, 300, 417); D2121.2 Magic journey with closed eyes (Bering Strait—Nelson 1899:511; MacKenzie River—Jenness 1924:52; Central—Boas 1888:629; Smith Sound—Kroeber 1899:171; Greenland—Rasmussen 1921:II, 14; 1921:III, 103, 124, 257; Rink 1875:147, 196, 219); E607.2.2 Rebirth by crawling into woman's womb (Greenland—Rasmussen 1921: III, 57); F815 Extraordinary plants; J1761 Animal thought to be object; P150 Rich man; P251 Brothers; T281 Sex hospitality.

PM8. The Baby with the Sideways Head

There were some people living down at the ocean. A rich man there had some kids, including a daughter. In another house lived a grandmother and her grandson. When the grandson played out other kids would try to play with him, but he always went inside to his grandmother. Nobody ever saw him close; he always ran inside. He never visited anybody. This happened even when he got bigger. No one knew how he looked. One winter his grandmother got sick and died. The boy put her in the stormshed.

The rich people always brought food to the poor boy. Every time they were going to eat they handed it through the window. They never saw him. One day after he got big someone called through the window, real loud, "There are two tirichiks coming, eating up people." He couldn't stay still after he heard that. He walked back and forth in the house and finally went out. He went to the rich man's house and called through the window, "Come to my place, even though the tirichik might eat you in my house too." Then he went home. They didn't see him. He stood his frozen grandmother up in the kanichuk by the door. Then he got ready. He got out his bow and two arrows. The rich man, his kids, his wife, and his daughter came over to the poor boy's house.

When they came in it was the first time anybody had seen him. His head was placed on sideways on his neck [90 degrees from proper position]. They fainted when they saw him. He started working on them and made them conscious again. Then he went out to check to see if a tirichik was coming. Finally the tirichik went to the rich man's house. It didn't stay there long because there was no one there. The tirichik came towards the poor boy's house and started coming in the shed. The poor boy could hear it chewing the wood of the stormshed. He said, "Go ahead, come in. Open your mouth wide. You've got no food here. I'll give you my dead grandmother." He got his stiff grandmother and waited.

The tirichik started coming in. Its mouth showed in the door. The poor boy said, "Go ahead, come in; open your mouth wider. You've got no food here except my dead grandmother." The tirichik opened his mouth wider and the poor boy threw his grandmother in real hard. The tirichik choked. The poor boy shot one arrow up in the air through the window and his other straight down into the floor. The tirichik couldn't move forward because the frozen grandmother was stuck in its throat, keeping its mouth open, so it backed out of the house. When they couldn't hear it anymore the poor boy went out. He saw the tirichik down by the beach, dead. The smaller tirichik, her baby, went along the trail towards the ocean.

The rich man took the boy home and he stayed there and married his daughter. In the wintertime the people that ran from the tirichik started coming back. They heard that the poor boy had killed the tirichik. In the springtime the boy built a house for himself. He and his wife moved in there and he started hunting. He got lots of wolverine and wolf and became a rich boy. THE END.

Charlie Allen told me this story.

B877 Giant mythical animals; F511 Person unusual as to his head; L111.4.1 Orphan hero lives with grandmother; L161.1 Marriage of poor boy and rich girl; N825.3.3 Help from grandmother; Q40 Kindness rewarded.

This story suggests that Eskimo individuals with physical aberrations tend to shy away from social contact, but by performing good deeds can be integrated into normal society.

PM9. Sayuk

There was an Indian man called Sayuk that was a brave fighter. He had two wives. One of them had a boy. Sayuk killed people. He was tough and killed Kobuk people. He always took young boys with him, went up Kobuk way, and killed people. From there he took an Eskimo boy home with him for his son. He had killed the boy's parents.

He started raising him and let him follow when he went hunting. The Eskimo boy got to be big and started putting snares for rabbits. Every time the boy went up he'd bring rabbits home. Every day he'd spend a little longer at his snares, coming home before dark. One time he went and they waited, but he never came home. He had gone back to the Kobuk, running away from Sayuk.

He stayed up at Kobuk and became a man. He couldn't forget that Sayuk had killed his parents. He took a couple of men with him and went to the Indian village. They went to have war. They reached the village and waited for morning. The man said, "When the Indians are going to have war they go to the houses early in the morning." One house had a light. It was Sayuk's. The men went in another house and killed some people. The others thought that the house having a light was someone having a baby, but the Eskimo man recognized it as Sayuk's and went in. He saw Sayuk sleeping between two young boys.

He took his bow and arrow and killed one boy. Then he wounded Sayuk in the kidney. The wounded man grabbed a bucket that was close and put it in front of himself. The Eskimo man shot again and the arrow flew around the bucket hitting Sayuk on the upper lip. The flint stayed in, but Sayuk broke the shaft off. Then Sayuk ran out. The Eskimo discovered that Sayuk had gone, followed him, and shot him in the leg. He lost him then.

The Indian went to his two wives. He took them to a bank and hid underneath. The Eskimos settled down because they thought they had killed everybody. They got on top of the meat caches where there was caribou meat and skins. The Eskimo man said, "I didn't kill Sayuk. Watch for him; he might come back." The others didn't pay any attention. They just kept letting the meat and skins drop to the ground. Then the Eskimo man saw two arrows coming through the air close together. They hit one man on top of the cache and he fell.

Sayuk went down from the bank to the clear sand along the stream and started moving slowly along, dragging one knee. He was trying to make the Eskimo man that had lived with him mad, but all the men were scared of Sayuk and nobody went down, so Sayuk went back to his two wives under the bank. The Eskimos went back to the Kobuk. Sayuk got sick. His wounds festered. The flint in his mouth poked out like a tooth and he could hardly eat. The women pushed it back so he could eat.

Sayuk's wife's son started getting big and Sayuk said to him, "Don't make fun of people. Look, I made fun of people and killed them and see how I got paid. If you get big don't kill people." He started talking about the Eskimo boy he had taken and how he should have killed the boy when the boy was small. He should have hung him in a tree. Sayuk died from his wounds. The reason Sayuk had looked tough was because he wore armor [probably slat armor, made from caribou antler] on his chest and back and even though men shot him he couldn't be hurt. Sayuk called the Eskimo boy Uulararuk. Sayuk said that when he was young he looked for trouble; that's what he gets for being tough.

Uulararuk stayed in a place by Noorvik when he came back to the Kobuk. He started hearing from people. They said, "When Uulararuk was small I should have hung him in a tree." When he heard what Sayuk had said he put a caribou-skin cover, like a coat, over himself. Then he took it off and said, "If he had tried to kill me, I would have run like this." He ran and jumped across a wide river. Then he jumped back again. THE END.

I heard it this way; other people tell it another way. I heard it a few years ago. I have heard it from Aalunik (Jennie Mitchell) and also from Jack Porter.

F680 Marvelous powers; L111.4 Orphan hero; P233.6 Son avenges father; Q211 Murder punished (Cumberland Sound—Boas 1901:168; Greenland—Rasmussen 1921:III, 76, 111, 294); Q411.6 Death as punishment for murder; R10 Abduction; R210 Escapes; T145.0.1 Polygyny. This story also appears in Giddings 1961:99–103 (Kobuk).

According to a number of stories, a light left on in a house at night meant someone was having a baby. Though Sayuk was an Indian, his advice about "not making fun of people," or not interfering in their lifeways, is consonant with Eskimo philosophy. During the historic period (post A.D. 1850) the Kobuk River Eskimos frequently came into contact with various groups of Athapaskan Indians (Hall 1969), so this story may be based on fact.

PM10. THE BOY WITH THE MITTIKLUK

A grandmother and a grandson lived in Oksuruk. They stayed there for a few years. One spring the grandmother got sick. She told the boy, "Don't stay here if I die. Don't stay alone. Go straight towards those hills to the north." She got something from next to her pillow and told her grandson, "Here, you take this if you go." He took it and it was a mittikluk (a springy piece of hardwood used to flip small stones). She got something else and gave it to him. It was two little rocks.

She didn't live long, and after she died the boy started walking towards the hills. She told him to go to File Creek [south of Kivalina]. He saw a bump on a little rock. When he got closer he saw that it was an eagle. This eagle was looking all over. When it looked away he walked fast. Finally he got under the eagle and said, "Who are you looking for? Why are you watching? You can't watch good. You didn't even see me when I came up. Why are you sitting there?" The eagle answered, "I am the watch bird. I am looking for people that pass and this is the first time that I didn't see someone who came by. I have a big boss up there and he wants only women. I take only women." The boy said, "You should go home; you can't watch good." The eagle said, "I wanted to go home long ago, but my boss made me stay." So he took off from his place towards Kivalina, towards Elaygutisuk [near Kivalina]. He flew there.

The boy started walking again. After not too far he heard a siksikpuk (marmot) make a real loud noise. He hid. A man came out of a house, looked around, and said to the siksikpuk, "Did I tell you to make a noise when there was no one around? You always try to fool me." He went in, and the boy shot and killed the siksikpuk with his mittikluk. Then he went into the man's house. When he opened the door he saw a lot of women, all over the house, all busy. On one side of the house he saw two curtains. The man said, "How did you pass my watch bird and my siksikpuk?" The boy said, "Your watch bird and siksikpuk are blind. They can't see me." The man got mad and said, "My watch bird and siksikpuk were good all of the time."

One of the curtains started opening and a brown bear came out. The boy got his mittikluk and shot it, and before the women knew what hit the bear it fell dead. From the next curtain came a bigger brown bear, really big. The boy really pulled the mittikluk, shot real hard, and killed that bear. When the rock came back it hit one of the women and killed her. The boy saw a hole in the floor. When he looked there was no bottom. The boy got ahold of the man who wouldn't let the women go home and threw him in the hole. Then he said to the women, "If you have a home you can go home now."

So all the women went out and started walking home. The boy went out and started walking the way that his grandmother told him. Finally he reached a little house. Inside were a young man and an older man. The older man wanted to kill the boy. The younger man said, "This boy let me go home when I was an eagle. That man let me lose my mind, made me an eagle, and let me watch. This boy told me to go home." So they let him stay. THE END.

Kenneth Flood used to tell this story.

B211.3 Speaking bird; B390 Animal grateful for kind act; B575.1 Wild animals kept as (watch) dogs; D152.2 Transformation: man to eagle (Kodiak—Golder 1903:94); D810 Ownership of a magic object: a gift; D956 Magic stick of wood; D1445 Magic object kills animals; D1653.1.6 Unerring stone missile; K1626 Would-be killers killed; L111.4.1 Orphan hero lives with grandmother; Q411 Death as punishment; R10 Abduction; R169.10 Unpromising hero a rescuer. A story that may be similar is found in Ingstad 1954:79–80 (Anaktuvuk Pass).

The *mittikluk* is known from Point Barrow (Murdock 1887:379). I do not understand why one of the women was killed in this story unless as an expression of the ambivalence surrounding women who are abducted by a man, perhaps not entirely against their will.

PM11. The Boy Who Didn't Like Girls

There was a village somewhere on a river. An old man and an old woman had a son there. The boy always brought home meat. The old woman worked what he got. Finally she took a girl home for her daughter-in-law. When the boy was home he never paid attention to girls. The girl tried to get close to him, but he wouldn't pay any attention to her, so she went home. This happened several times. Finally he told his mother that he'd rather hunt than get married, but his mother never gave up. She always brought him girls home and he always didn't want them.

Summer came and he wanted mukluks because he was going to travel. In the fall he started walking. He kept walking for a few days, sleeping when he was tired. One day he saw some people, but they couldn't move. He watched them, but they couldn't move so he passed by. He went down to a river and walked along the shore. As he walked he began to see tracks in the snow, but they were covered by a little fresh snow and he couldn't figure out what they were. He went farther down the river and saw a water well. There was a woman coming with a bucket to get water. He waited until she came and asked her for a drink. She gave him one in a cup made of sheep horn.

She went back along the trail and he followed her. She went into a house. He stayed outside for awhile and then went in. It was a big house with two rooms. On one side of the door sat a woman with a baby, sewing. Farther over an old woman was working on something. On the other side of the door another woman was working. The woman who got water was sitting between the old woman and the woman with the baby. The boy sat beside the woman who got water, close to her. The woman with the baby went out with the baby on her back. Soon she came back with a man who was her husband. Another man came and went to the other woman by the door. Then an old man came in and went to the old woman.

Finally a young boy came in and went to the stranger. The young boy said, "Bring some food here. He should be hungry." The girl who got water went out and got some fish. The boy didn't like them because he had never had fish before. The woman brought dried caribou meat and he ate it. While he was eating he heard someone making a funny noise behind the curtain. He stopped to listen and the young boy said, "Don't listen, that's our old grandfather. He's ready to die." The young boy was watching over his grandfather.

A woman came out from behind the curtain with a potty. She kept looking at the strange man, but she didn't say anything. She went outside with the potty and then came in and went behind the curtain again. All the people went to bed. The young boy stayed with the man all evening. The boy slept with him and they talked all night. While talking the man asked the boy, "Is that woman who got water your sister or relative?" The young boy said that she was an orphan and that is why the old couple took her home. She worked for them. And then the man asked about the other girl, the one that had carried out the potty. The young boy said she was his youngest sister. She was watching the old grandfather too. The woman who had gotten water got up during the night and came over to them. She was trying to get close to that man. The young boy told her to go to her room, saying, "This man has to sleep." She went away.

Then the man asked the young boy if he could go in to his sister. The young boy said that he could go in. He went in and when he opened the curtain he saw a real old man lying down. The man was so old that his forehead had moss on it. The stranger said to the women, "I can watch this old man if you want to work or something." The old man couldn't move or help himself because he was too old. The stranger started watching the old man and after a few days he and the woman got together.

One time the stranger was staying outside and a little boy came to him and said, "My grandmother wants to see you." He went over, went in, and found an old woman. He stayed there all day and went home in the evening. His wife asked him where he was all day and he answered, "With that old woman and her grandson."

That girl who went to get water always served food. One time she said, "We are out of food, even the neighbors are out of food." This was in the spring. The man asked his wife, "Where do you get caribou from?" She answered, "We always got them from just behind those trees, but in the springtime the caribou go far and we don't hunt." He took off towards the trees. He walked up beyond them and just to under the mountains, where he saw a few caribou (these people must be Naupaktomiut). He said, "There are not very many caribou here."

He went farther up into the mountains and saw a lot of caribou. He got behind them and started driving them towards the village. He met the first caribou he had seen and drove them along with the rest. When he got to the trees he started killing the caribou. He killed them all with his bow and arrows. When he came home that evening he told his wife to go tomorrow and get some of the caribou. The old woman's grandson went up to get some caribou with them. They got enough so that they had meat all spring.

The old grandfather finally died. The man put him in his arms and took him and buried him. He was so skinny that he was real light.

Every time the man went out, the orphan girl went out too. When people weren't around she would always grab him and say, "I was

the first to see you when you came." She wanted to get close to him.
It kept happening. He always tried to get away from her, and when
he did he went inside. She kept after him. He decided that he wanted
a sled and let his father-in-law make one for him. His father-in-law
finished the sled (unaypak). He and his wife got ready and put their
stuff on the sled.

The orphan girl really wanted to go with them. She even got ready,
but the young boy didn't want her to go and he held her while the
man and his wife left. The wife pulled in front of the sled while the
man pulled from alongside. They were going to see his parents. After
they had gone away they found that the orphan girl was running after
them. When the orphan girl got close she went straight to the man's
wife and took the tow rope away from her. She wanted to pull herself.
They started fighting over the rope. The man took his rope off, went
over, and stopped them. He got ahold of the orphan girl and kind of
hurt her. She said, "Go ahead and push me around. Pretty soon you'll
become birds and fly away." They became birds and flew away. The
orphan girl became a cross-fox. THE END.

Makan told me this story.

D113.1.1 Transformation: man to fox; D150 Transformation: man to
bird (Greenland—Rasmussen 1921:II, 14; Rink 1875:148, 287, 327);
D2072.0.5 Person paralysis; F571 Extremely old person; T311.1 Man
averse to marrying; T320 Escape from undesired lover; W181 Jealousy.

The relative paucity of dogs in aboriginal Noatak Eskimo culture is
suggested by the pulling arrangement for the sleds. I do not fully understand this story. The large number of characters and lack of detailed
action lead me to believe that the story is incomplete or was not well
known to the storyteller.

PM12. NAPAARAK

In Point Hope lived a young boy named Napaarak (sled stanchion). He lived in one of three houses that were a short ways from
the main village. His mother was real tall and pretty. Napaarak always
walked from his house to Point Hope proper and stayed there for
awhile visiting people. Then he went home again, then back to Point
Hope. He was getting big. He kept going back and forth. Sometimes
he didn't come home for a couple of days. He couldn't stay home anymore. His mother found out he had a girlfriend and he was staying
with her.

One time Napaarak was in Point Hope and went home in the
evening. When he got close to the three houses, one had a light while
the others did not. His had a light, and when he went in he saw his
mother sitting very stiffly and his father lying on the floor. His mother
said, "I couldn't understand those men when they came in. I couldn't
understand how they talked. After they made fun of me [rape] they
left me. They killed your father." After she had spoken she died. He
looked and saw that she was covered with blood. He looked closer
and saw a walrus tusk under her. They had put it under her and
shoved it up all the way inside of her. That's why she sat stiff.

Napaarak went out from the house and went down to Point Hope.
He married his girlfriend and stayed there. They had killed the people
in all three houses and left the light on in Napaarak's house to rape
his mother. Napaarak started building a boat in the summertime. In
the fall he and his wife went up through the Kukpuk. They stopped
at a place where another river joined the Kukpuk (Keyak [a few miles
up the Kukpuk from coast]) and built a big house in the willows on
the point. They stayed for awhile and hunted caribou. Napaarak made
a long stormshed and he built a deep hiding place along one side. Just

before the ice came down they got ready and left for Point Hope with the boat loaded with dried meat. They stayed at Point Hope until the ice got solid; then Napaarak alone went back to the house, leaving his wife at Point Hope. He stayed there watching for people to come.

Finally one moonlit night he listened and heard people walking in the willows. He hid in the stormshed. He had made his bed so that it looked like two people were sleeping there. He watched and men with spears came. They came in and one man with a spear got close to the bed, stood above it and said, "Ahohohoho," trying to wake the people ("ahohohoho" means they were Indians). When they found nobody in the bed they started out of the house. Napaarak had a spear and when the first man came out he speared him and the Indian fell on the stormshed floor. He speared and killed them all. They lay there in a pile.

He started out and by the door of the stormshed saw two spears. He grabbed them, one in each hand, and broke them. When he went out he saw two Indians. They ran off in different directions, but he speared them both. Then he went back into the stormshed. He saw two spears again by the door and broke them again. Two Indians outside ran into the willows and Napaarak ran after them and speared them. He had killed them all. He piled all the Indians away together (like salmon for dogfood). There were seventeen Indians.

Napaarak went towards the east looking for people. He was not satisfied. He kept thinking of his mother and how they had killed her. He walked, stopping for overnight. He kept walking until one day he saw a village. He looked around and saw one house apart from the others. He went down and went in. There was an old woman and an old man there. The old man asked him, "Where did you come from? What place?" Napaarak didn't look like he had come from that village.

Napaarak told the old man that he had killed seventeen men, but that he wasn't satisfied. He still wanted to kill men. "I can't forget my mother. I can't forget how they put a walrus tusk (tuwak) in her." The old man said, "I'm sorry to see that you came because there is a man here who doesn't like strangers." The old man talked as if he had come from the Kobuk. While they were talking someone came in and said that the man who didn't like strangers wanted him to come up to the karigi.

He and the old man went up. They went in, and before Napaarak sat down he looked around. His eyes met those of a young boy. The young boy didn't seem to be scared of the aŋatquq or anyone, so Napaarak sat down and the old man sat real close to him. The aŋatquq asked him, "What village did you come from and why?" Napaarak told him about his mother. He said that he had killed seventeen men but that he was not satisfied after they had played with his mother. He wants to find those people who talked in the way his mother couldn't understand. He wants to find those people and that is why he came. The aŋatquq said, "Yes, we heard about it this fall. We heard that those seventeen Indians didn't come home. They were all tough."

Then he said, "Bring some food for him." They brought some in an aaluyuk. When they put it in front of Napaarak the old man nudged him with his elbow and Napaarak knew that the old man didn't want him to eat. Napaarak looked at the food for awhile and then said, "I don't eat this kind of meat." So the aŋatquq said, "Take it away and bring him another tray." They did so and the old man nudged him again. Napaarak looked at the tray and said he didn't eat that kind of meat either. The aŋatquq said, "Take it away and bring another kind." This time they brought him dried caribou meat on a tray. The old man didn't nudge him so Napaarak ate it. After he ate the aŋatquq said, "You are welcome as long as you want to stay here. People, treat him nice."

While they were in the karigi the young boy was real friendly and mentioned that he wished to see Point Hope sometime. Napaarak went home with the old man. The people of the village told him not to go to the Indian village because of extremely deep snow, so he decided not to go and turned back to Point Hope. After he went to his house on the Kukpuk he went back to Point Hope. That summer he and his wife stayed in Point Hope. In the fall the young boy came and stayed with them. The old man of the other village had relatives in Point Hope. Those two trays were poisoned; that's why the old man didn't want Napaarak to eat from them. Napaarak was a tough guy and the other Point Hope men always asked if he wanted to go to other villages and kill people. He always answered, "No, I don't like to bother people in other villages." THE END.

I heard this from Daniel Walton. Napaarak died just a few years ago in Point Hope. Some archaeologists found that woman with the walrus tusk in her [I have not been able to confirm this]. When they found it they couldn't pull it out because it was caught between her ribs.

D1711 Magician; H1220 Quest voluntarily undertaken; J585 Caution in eating; K800 Killing or maiming by deception; K950 Treacherous murder; K1626 Would-be killers killed; L111.4 Orphan hero; P233.6 Son avenges father (and mother); Q211 Murder punished (Cumberland Sound—Boas 1901:168; Greenland—Rasmussen 1921:III, 76, 111, 294); Q244 Punishment for ravisher; Q411.6 Death as punishment for murder; Q411.7 Death as punishment for ravisher; T471 Rape.

PM13. KIPPUKLUKUN

There was a grandmother and her grandson living along a river. They were living on ptarmigan. The grandson had a puppy that he always took outdoors walking with him, letting the puppy follow. He always called the dog different names, but the puppy didn't listen to him. He took the puppy out every day. He started getting big and so did the puppy. One time when they were out playing he called the puppy Kippuklukun and it turned around and started running to him, wagging its tail. It liked that name.

Another time when the boy was out playing with the puppy, he saw some willows moving. He went in and asked his grandmother, "Why are those willows moving?" She answered, "Those are caribou." He asked, "How do they always get them?" She started making a bow and arrow for him. When she finished he went out and got caribou. He started helping his grandmother. He always got caribou and brought them home.

When he got big he fixed his bow and arrow up real well. When he went out again he didn't take his dog. He got one caribou and, leaning over, started cutting it. He saw a man's feet close by, just standing there. He dropped his work and brought his eyes up, and he saw a man standing there with his bow and arrow ready. The boy said, "I'm not looking for trouble." The man put his bow down and they met. The man said, "When I meet people I always put my bow and arrow up first because I am afraid of people." They talked and found out they were cousins through their grandmothers. The stranger gave the boy a piece of muktuk that he had taken for his meat. The boy took it home and gave it to his grandmother. He didn't know what it was. She said, "It's muktuk." The boy told his grandmother that he had met a man up there. His grandmother and that man's grandmother were relatives. That man's grandmother lived under that big mountain down there by the mountains.

One day the boy started walking up through the river. While he was walking along the beach near the mountains he began to hear two people talk. It sounded like two men talking at first, two men with one wife because they called each other "apuk." One of the people said, "There is a boy down there that we can kill. His dog's name is Kippuklukun." The other person said, "Uh huh." They got closer and the boy hid, listening to what they said. After he hid he saw a little boat coming from upriver with two old women in it. They were calling each other apuk.

They started passing. They were both paddling, one in front and one in back. The one in front seemed like she was watching carefully. She kept saying, "Apuk, there is a boy up there we can kill. His dog is dumb." The boy always carried two rocks. When they got in front of him he threw one rock and the boat tipped over. His dog jumped in the water. Pretty soon he saw one old woman come up. She was dead. The other one came up dead too, and the bodies drifted down the river.

He went home. He didn't think about those old women. He didn't even tell his grandmother. He hunted and made a big ikigut to put the meat on. He always got lots of meat. His grandmother never went hungry. He started planning to visit his relatives. His grandmother sewed him a parka out of mixed seagull and raven skins. When she finished she took out a bag and gave it to the boy. He didn't know what was inside. She had put in a parka made of spotted skin and also some wolf and also some wolverine skins. It was full. She let him put the spotted parka on, then the seagull- and raven-skin parka.

When he was going to go his grandmother said, "You can stay with that man and his grandmother. You will know the house because it is set apart from the others. There is a rich man in that village and he has a daughter." When the boy left he ran and walked until he got close to the big mountain. When he got to the village he went to the man's house. The man and an old woman were there and they recognized each other. After awhile someone came and said they should go up to the karigi. They went up, in, and sat down. The rich man saw the boy's parka and the other boys in the karigi (there were a lot, too) saw it too. The rich man noticed there was another kind of parka under the seagull-and-raven parka, but he couldn't figure out what kind it was.

They brought some food to the boy. While he was eating he noticed that the other young boys were laughing at him. They were laughing at his parka. They said, "When a poor boy is poor he is really poor. He wears funny clothes." Then the rich man said, "When ilaypuruks (orphans or children without parents) are poor they never get anything. They can't use good clothes." The boys quieted down when he said that. The rich man took the boy home. He kept seeing the raven-and-seagull parka and the under-parka. He found out the boy had a spotted-reindeer-skin parka. [Reindeer skins were brought from Siberia and were valuable.] The rich man wanted the boy to marry his daughter and he did.

They went and got his grandmother and moved into the rich man's house. These villagers were Kinitmiut, Wales people. In the spring they started hunting seals at the coast. The boy followed them. One time he went out on the ice and he was drifted. He didn't come out all spring and the people began to get worried about him. The ice started breaking up and the beach had no ice. They were really worried. The boy's dog, Kippuklukun, inside the house always turned his back to the wife, but she couldn't understand yet what was wrong. He went out and came in again. He got close to the woman, turned his back, and looked over his shoulder at her, but she couldn't understand. There was no ice in sight on the ocean. He went out again and came back. His harness was hanging in the house. The woman grabbed it and put it on him. As soon as she did so the dog went out.

Meanwhile the boy was on a piece of ice. It wasn't too big and there was no other ice. It was a calm day and he was watching out over the water. He started seeing whitecaps as if a boat were coming. They got closer and he thought it was a boat. When they got real close he recognized his dog. That dog swam so fast he was just like a boat. When the dog got to the ice he turned around, the boy got on his back, and the dog took off again. The dog took him home. THE END.

Ralph Gallahorn tells this story.

B300 Helpful animals; B541.4.1 Boat towed (boy carried) by dog (Bering Strait—Nelson 1899:505; Greenland—Rink 1875:196); F536.3

Remarkable stone-thrower; F982 Animals carry extra burden; J1072 Man to be judged by his own qualities, not his clothes; K958 Murder by drowning; K1626 Would-be killers killed; K1815 Humble disguise; L111.4.1 Orphan hero lives with grandmother; Q211.8 Punishment for desire to murder (Cumberland Sound—Boas 1901:62; Smith Sound—Kroeber 1899:177; Greenland—Holm 1912:47; Rink 1875:157, 222); Q411 Death as punishment; T145.0.1 Polygyny.

Making fun of people is considered bad behavior.

PM14. THE MAN WITH THE SNARES

Only one man lived along a river. (I don't know how he grew up to be a man alone.) He always put snares for ptarmigan. His ik̦igut was always full with ptarmigan and fishes because there was no one to eat them. In the fall he set his ptarmigan snares again. He went to see them and when he got close he heard someone choking as if there were a rope around their neck. He was kind of scared because it sounded like a person. He was scared because he had never seen people before, so he turned back home. He went the next day to see the snares. He got close and didn't hear anything, so he went closer to the snare. He saw a black thing caught in it. It was a person who had gotten caught in the snare and died. He looked and it was a man. He took the snare off from the man's neck, laid him out, and hoisted him to his shoulders, took him home, and put him on the ik̦igut because he got him just as if he'd caught a ptarmigan.

In a few days he went to see his snares again. He heard the same noise he had heard before. He went closer and from the top of a little hill he saw two black shapes in his snares. One of them saw him and said, "He's coming." One wasn't in the snare, just trying to help. He took off. The man called for him to come back. The boy (they were both young boys) came back and the man took the snare off from the other one. The boys said, "Our brother-in-law hasn't come home for quite awhile. He was out hunting." The man said, "Well, I got one man from my snares and put him on my ik̦igut. Maybe that's him." He took them to his place to see the man he had caught. After they took him down the boys looked and said, "That's the one that was lost." They got him ready with rope to pack him, and the man put him on his back. The two boys took the man to their home to show that he hadn't really meant to kill their brother-in-law; the snare had gotten big without the man's knowledge.

When the man started walking the boys had to run to keep up. He was fast. They reached the boys' house and went inside. The boys related what had happened. Their father said, "Bury my son-in-law behind us." They put him up in a scaffold burial. The man started staying with them. He stayed with them for a year and got married to one of their girls.

In the spring the sun started melting the snow. The man in the grave sort of woke up. The water was dripping in his face. When he can open his eyes he doesn't know where he is. He sits up. He was under the wood of the grave. When he can move he goes out from his box. He looks around and sees his house a little way. He went down and went in. They were all there, including a man strange to him. The strange man said, "If you want to go back to your wife you can." (The man who had snared him in his net had then married his wife.) The once-dead man said, "I don't want to if I can stay here with you. You already got married. I don't mind." So he stayed with them and they started living together. The man who had the snares was tough. He hunted a lot and was very fast. He can even keep up with rabbits. That's why those boys couldn't keep up with him. THE END.

I heard this story from Daniel Walton.

E1 Person comes to life; F560 Unusual manner of life; F681 Marvelous runner; K730 Victim trapped; N320 Person unwittingly killed; P251 Brothers.

As Paul remarks, living alone is exceeding unusual (if not impossible on a long-term basis) in Eskimo society. The equating of being frozen and death is found in a number of stories; thawing brings life again. In this particular story revival comes with spring, the time of rebirth in the natural world.

PM15. TAYYAKNIGLUK

At Naupaktusugruk there was one big house, no other. One couple lived on each side of the house. They all lived together. One man was named Tayyaknigluk. He always had a fish trap in the river towards the left of the house. He always covered his trap with willows to keep it dark. He went to see it in the evening and found no fish. It seemed like there was blood in the trap, but no fish. The next time he went there was still no fish. The willows over the fish trap were arranged differently than before. He thought he should hide and watch.

After he hid he heard two people talking upriver. They came and went inside his willows. When they went in they said, "Gee, lots of fishes." One finally said, "Maybe we have enough now." Tayyaknigluk got his snowshoes and tied them together and then said, "Let me eat them, let me eat them," real loud. He came out and went to the fish trap. When he looked in he saw just sacks full of fish. The two had gotten so scared that they had jumped into the water through the fish-trap hole (they thought the devil was coming). Tayyaknigluk got two bags of fish, put them on his back, and went home.

His wife was outdoors waiting for him. When she saw that he had fish she went inside and told the other couple, "Tayyaknigluk got fish. When he gets the first fish of the year other people cannot eat them until the next day." Tayyaknigluk and his wife had some ḳuk (fresh frozen fish) that evening. The couple on the other side of the house didn't eat. After they went to bed and woke up, the other couple ate ḳuk with them. Tayyaknigluk started getting lots of fish after that.

In the springtime a man and a woman with a small boy just old enough to walk came from upriver. They stayed overnight. Tayyaknigluk was the last person to go out in the evening to toilet. He looked around for awhile and then he got an Eskimo fishhook from beside the door and hung it in the doorway. This was to keep people from coming in during the night. He was worried because strangers had come. In the morning the boy wanted to go out badly and finally his parents let him go out. The boy didn't come back for a long time. Tayyaknigluk got worried and went out. He saw that the boy had the hook in his mouth and was already dead. He went in and said, "That boy got a hook in his mouth and he died." They all went out and worked on the boy, but he was really dead. After they buried him his parents stayed for a few days and then went away.

Tayyaknigluk went out again in the spring. When he came home he brought two frozen ptarmigan. He took them inside. He put one in his hand and threw it out the window saying, "In springtime you should always come back." The frozen bird flew away. Then he threw the second one saying, "You should always stay around here in wintertime." Again the frozen bird flew away. That's why we always have a lot of ptarmigan now. THE END.

I don't remember who told me this story.

C221.1.3 Tabu: eating fish; D1711 Magician; N330 Accidental killing or death.

This story was told in Noatak in the 1920s (Curtis 1930:200–1). The devil is, of course, a post-contact concept.

PM16. THE MAGIC SLED

There were people living in Point Hope. There was a rich man there who had a son who always got a lot when he went out hunting and brought it home. An old woman and her granddaughter lived in the village too. The kids had a sliding place on the hill. They slid on small sleds made of walrus tusks. A lot of kids were playing there. The rich man's son got lost and they couldn't find him. The boy used to give the grandmother and the granddaughter a lot of food. The rich man and people looked for his boy, but they couldn't find him.

The girl was playing inside the house. The grandmother was working there. The girl said, "The rich man's son's sled went through the ground." The grandmother understood what she said, but she asked, "What?" The girl said it again, and the grandmother then knew what she was talking about. The grandmother couldn't stay still after she heard her say that. She went to the rich man's house and went in. The rich man asked, "What do you want?" The grandmother answered, "I think your boy slid and went through the ground. When my girl is playing she always talks about that boy." The rich man said, "I wonder what that girl wants."

After she heard that the grandmother went home and said to her

granddaughter, "The rich man wanted me to ask what you wanted." The girl didn't answer for awhile, and then she said, "I want a walrus-tusk sled just like the other kids, but it should have a circular enclosed place in it with a top (kavsuk, like a toy top) that goes around inside."

The grandmother went to the rich man and told him the kind of sled the girl wanted, with a top in the middle. The rich man said he would have it made that way, the way the girl wanted it. It was finished in a few days and he took it over to the girl. She went out and over to the place where they slid. A lot of people watched. When she was on top of the bank she got on top of the sled. She started the top going around; it got going really fast and then started singing. The girl started sliding and suddenly went through the ground. The people watched, but she didn't come up.

The girl started following the rich boy's trail. The top let her follow it. The trail was rough and went any old way through the ground. She kept following it and finally saw light ahead. She got close to the light and saw water and land. It was the ocean. When she got to the sand she put her sled up. She saw a house close by and went over, leaving the sled. There was no sound. She stayed outside for awhile and then went in. She saw the rich man's boy and recognized him. He was real skinny. He asked her why she came. She answered, "I came to get you. Your father is worried about you." He said, "You may have come to get me, but the one that took me is too tough for you." The girl said, "Try to get on my back." She put him on her back. She went over to her sled and they got in. The girl was in the back, the boy in front, close to the top. The girl started the top. It went around faster and faster and started singing again. All of a sudden the sled went towards the sea and into it. They went by sea worms (ḳupuluk), seals, walrus, and all kinds of animals. They traveled through the water until they saw light ahead. When they came up they were close to Point Hope. They came up through the open water and took the boy home.

They started feeding the boy. He was so weak that he couldn't stand up. Soon he started gaining weight. They watched him real closely. When he got strong and started hunting again he always took food to the grandmother and granddaughter. The granddaughter and he got married. They made a house and stayed all winter. In the spring everybody was short of food. There was no caribou or anything. One time the girl said, "I hid my sled under my grandmother's floor. With that sled maybe I can get some food someplace. Somebody might give me some." She told everyone to go up to the karigi. She said that she would go from there. So everyone went and she took her sled up. She told the people, "Until you hear me coming back don't go out too much."

She set two snares for caribou between the back stanchions of her sled. She turned the sled towards the door and got inside. The top started going faster and faster and started singing. The sled started going around the karigi floor. Pretty soon it started going around the karigi in the air and then went out the window. The girl flew through the air, kept flying, and pretty soon she saw a river where she landed. She saw a house with nobody around it. She put the sled up, took the top off, and put it inside her parka. She started walking toward the house and a girl as big as her came out. The girl from the house was real excited, crying, "Hi, sister, my sister, let's go inside and see our grandmother. She's home." That girl didn't know this was her sister.

When she went inside she saw her own grandmother. The girl from the house said, "Let's play tops." She said she had no top, even though she had hers in her parka. The girl from the house really wanted to play and finally got her own top, which was made of brass (patupuk). She started it around as the other girl watched her. It whirled around real fast and started going towards the girl from Point Hope. She got kind of scared. So she got her own top out from under her parka and started it. The tops started spinning close together, not moving. Then they started moving sideways by each other. Then they tried to bump each other and the brass one broke. The other top started towards the girl from the house, got close, and killed her. Then it went to the grandmother and killed her.

The Point Hope girl got her top and started out. She got to the stormshed and walked and walked, but she couldn't find her way out. It was so dark and she couldn't see any light. Finally she gave up and stopped because she didn't know which way to go because she couldn't find the door. She started the top, and after it got going real fast it made a noise. It moved off and she followed the noise. Finally she saw light. The top led her out to just in front of her sled.

She went again with her sled, up the river. She saw a village and stopped. She left the sled and went into the first house where there were people. She said, "I have come to get food. We are all out." The man of the house said that all the men of the village could get food for her. They all went out and drove caribou alive to the village, where they killed them. They put one caribou in each of the snares behind her sled. Then they tied the hair of the rest of the caribou together, one to another, and tied them to the caribou in the snares. They got her ready to go. She spun the top while the people watched. It went real fast, made noise, and she flew off with the caribou behind. She went to Point Hope and landed where there were no tracks of people. She took the caribou off and went to the karigi where people were waiting. So those people got a lot of food to eat. She had saved their lives.

Winter came. The girl didn't talk to her husband. She was feeling lonesome. She had again hid the sled under the floor of her now-dead grandmother's house. Her husband asked her why she wasn't happy anymore. She answered, "I want to go see my parents." He asked, "You have parents?" She said, "Yes." Her husband said that he wanted to go with her. She said, "How can you go? You've no way to go. The trail is real rough." Her husband said he didn't care if the trail was rough; he really wanted to go. She got ready and walked out from the house. They went towards the ocean, walking until they saw open water. They stopped and she said, "Do you really want to go with me?" He answered, "Yes, I want to go no matter how rough the trail is." She said, "All right, I'll try to take you with me. You can get on my back. When I say ready you close your eyes and don't open them until I say stop."

They were going to cross that open water, so he got on her back and they went. He closed his eyes and she started making a lot of noise. Then they stopped and she said, "You can open your eyes." They were on the beach. There was no ice, just water and sand. They started through the beach. Soon they started seeing a lot of people on the beach working on kayaks. They got close, but the people paid no attention to them. They passed and the man said, "Why didn't they pay attention to us?" She said, "Those were the ones who drowned in their kayaks in the ocean." They walked farther on and saw some men working on umaypaks. When these men didn't pay any attention to them he again asked about them, and she answered, "When they were out on the ocean their boat tipped and they never came home." They went farther and he heard one man say, "Why does that man ask so many questions?" They went still farther and saw a lot of friendly people.

They met them and started talking. It was sunshiny and real bright. They saw a house beyond the people. A man came out from the house and the husband saw that the man's forehead was real shiny. The girl said, "That's my parents' house over there." He said he wanted to go, but she said, "I don't think my father will let you live. You stay here for awhile and I'll go over. After awhile I'll come back to you." The girl went back from her parents and told her husband, "My father won't let you live; he almost killed me, too, so you can stay with these people and I'll go back to my parents, and if these people go you go with them." (She doesn't want to go back to his parents.) Then the girl said "If you ever go home to your parents, if you get married, don't treat your wife rough. If you don't treat your wife good I'll go there to you." After the girl talked she went back to her parents and the husband started staying with these people. Finally these people start getting ready to leave, put the boats in the water, and he went with these people in one of the boats, and when they went he hears people singing in the other boats. They were happy.

He starts seeing a white wall way over where they are going, and they go towards it, and when they get close to that ice, under that ice, these people tell him, "Jump up, use all your strength." And if he doesn't make it, they tell him he's going to become one of these people. When they get under that ice they tell him to get ready, and he gets ready. When they said, "You can jump," he uses all his strength, and jumps to the top holding on the edge with his hands. He tries to move his body to go up. He makes it, climbs up that ice. And when he climbs up the iceberg he noticed it was close to Point Hope.

When he goes up he goes home to his parents and starts staying with them. He stayed a year with his parents. He starts planning to go and he gets his wife's sled where she told him it was, in her grandmother's house. When he gets it he lets the top spin when he gets inside the sled and he takes off through the air. While he was going he saw a village close by, so he stopped near, kind of hid his sled, and went over to the village and sees a lot of men playing football. He went closer and when he got closer they saw him. When they saw him they said, "Let's run to him and see who's going to be the first." They start running toward him, and when they got close he saw three men in the lead and behind those three men was a girl running close by. They got closer and closer as he walked towards them, and one man came up to him, touches him, and then turns around and runs back to the village. All three of the men run up to him and touch him, and one man said, "If this girl comes to you and touches you and then turns around, you start running behind her and try to keep up with her." When the three men and the woman and the man behind her start running and got close to the village he wants to find out where she lives. When he found out where her house was he runs in front of her and into her house. When the man went in the girl went in and looked sad and was crying. There was nobody in the house. This man found out this girl was the fastest runner and the three men running with her were her brothers. These three men came into the house and told this man that this woman never liked to marry the men that ran behind her. She was looking for a faster runner than herself. They got married because he ran faster than she.

He stayed with the three brothers and their sister. These people were from Barrow. They stayed in this village and finally this boy said to his wife that he wanted to see his parents, so this woman wants to go with him and they take off walking. While they were walking he picks up the sled he left. After he picks the sled up they keep walking and after awhile they stop to rest, and while they are resting both of them start getting bossy. This man starts saying nasty things to his wife.

Then they see a girl walking on the ice close by the shore. The girl had one hand inside her parka, the other had a mitten on. When she got close the wife starts running to her, and when she got close to her she starts kissing this girl. The girl is stiff and doesn't feel happy. After the wife was kissing the girl that came from the ocean, the girl told this man and his wife: "I told you not to do that if you found a girl for your wife. I've come to kill you both, but this woman likes me, really likes me, so I'm not going to kill you. Why do you let her walk even though you have a way to take her home quick with your sled? Next time you treat her rough or funny I'll come to kill you both." The girl walks towards the ocean.

And this man and his wife got ready and got inside the sled, and they flew. They went home to Point Hope with this sled and they go back and forth to both sets of parents. The people that he went with in the boat were bugs that swarm together (niivakruuk) and the first girl he married was a bumble bee and so were her parents. THE END.

I don't remember who told me this story.

B653 Marriage to insect in human form; C35 Tabu: offending animal wife (Central—Boas 1888:616; Greenland—Rink 1875:145); C901.1 Tabu imposed by certain person; D380 Transformation: insect to man; D382 Transformation: hymenoptera to person; F511.1 Person unusual as to his face; D382.1 Transformation: bee to man (Greenland—Thalbitzer 1904:2); D801 Ownership of magic object; D1110 Magic conveyances; D1520 Magic object affords miraculous transportation; D1533.2 Vehicle travels above or below ground; D2060 Death or bodily injury by magic; D2089.9 Trail magically closed; D2121.2 Magic journey with closed eyes (Bering Strait—Nelson 1899:511; MacKenzie River—Jenness 1924:52; Central—Boas 1888:629; Smith Sound—Kroeber 1899:171; Greenland—Rasmussen 1921:II, 14; 1921:III, 103, 124, 257; Rink 1875:147, 196, 219); D2131 Magic journey underwater; E400 Ghosts and revenants; H1220 Quest voluntarily undertaken; H1385 Quest for lost persons; K2212 Treacherous sister; L111.4.1 Orphan hero(ine) lives with grandmother; L161.1 Marriage of poor boy and rich girl; P253.0.3 Three brothers and one sister; Q325 Disobedience punished; T311 Woman averse to marriage.

The brass top indicates white contact as brass was unknown in aboriginal Eskimo culture.

PM17. THE GOOD AND BAD AŊATQUQ

In Point Hope there were two houses, somewhat apart from each other. In the first lived an aŋatquq. Early in the morning this good aŋatquq always heard a tuutlik (loon) fly over his door. It was a bad aŋatquq trying to work on him. The good aŋatquq thought to himself, "That aŋatquq is bothering me too much."

When he went out in the evening to toilet he set a net on top of his window through his aŋatquq. He went to bed. In the morning he woke up and started listening. He heard the loon come again, close, close to that net. Suddenly the loon made a noise like it had hit something hard. The aŋatquq listened and heard the loon trying to get out. He heard it try real hard.

Finally he heard the loon say, "Come take me out of this net." The good aŋatquq didn't care; he let the loon holler. The loon kept hollering, "Take me out, take me out." Finally the loon said, "I'll give you my ulimun (adze) if you take me off." The good aŋatquq went out and took the loon off. He got the ulimun. After that time the loon didn't come again. The bad aŋatquq got scared because his aŋatquq didn't work good. THE END.

Carl Stalker told this story.

B211.3 Speaking bird; D150 Transformation: man to bird; D1711 Magician; D1719.1 Contest in magic (Greenland—Rasmussen 1921:II, 222; 1921:III, 111; Thalbitzer 1904:7); K730 Victim trapped.

PM18. THE PEOPLE WITH NO HEADS

A man and his wife were staying down at the coast alone. The man always hunted and always came home early. One time he didn't come home when he should and the woman got restless. She went out and watched the way that he always came, looking for him. Finally she saw someone coming. It was a man and she heard him say, "Little woman, you think you're going to live?" She got scared and grabbed her husband's ṭuk (ice chisel). She climbed up on the iḳigut and started waiting. When the man came closer she saw that he had no head. He just had eyes on his chest. He said again that she wasn't going to live. The man came up to her and climbed up the iḳigut. She jumped down to the snow. He came down and she went down and started running back along his trail. He followed. She ran and ran and finally got to a place where there were lots of tracks. There she found her husband dead. The man with no head had killed him.

She saw a single track going away from there and followed it, the man running behind. When she looked back he was far behind, but still chasing her. Finally she started going uphill and sliding down the other side. When she looked back she saw that the man always slid down on his stomach. She kept running. Finally after she slid down the hill she put the ṭuk with its point facing uphill where she had slid. She ran on. She turned around and saw the man sliding down on his stomach. She ran farther and then looked again. The man had slid down and stuck himself on the ṭuk. She watched and he didn't move.

The woman kept going. She walked through the man's tracks and finally up a hill. Ahead she saw a house by a river. She went down and, hearing no noise, went in. She saw a woman with no head and also some kids. They all had eyes in their chests. The woman with no head asked, "Did you see a man back there?" She answered, "I didn't see anyone." The woman-with-no-head's big pot was boiling.

There was fat on the surface. The other woman looked at the pot and said, "What's that boiling down there?" The woman-with-no-head came close and looked into the pot. The other woman went behind her, grabbed her legs, and dumped her in the boiling liquid. The woman-with-no-head moved for awhile and then stopped. The other woman grabbed the kids, hit them, and killed them. THE END.

I heard this story from Kusik Hunnicutt.

F511.0.1 Headless person; K832.1.2 Dupe induced to look about, seized and killed; K955.2 Murder by burning in hot oil; K1626 Would-be killer killed; Q211 Murder punished (Cumberland Sound—Boas 1901:168; Greenland—Rasmussen 1921:III, 76, 111, 294); Q411.6 Death as punishment for murder; S111.2 Boiling to death; S118 Murder by cutting. Similar to Gubser 1965:243–46 and PM124 in this volume.

The pot in this story must have been considerably larger than known Eskimo containers.

PM19. THE POOR BOY AND THE BIG DOG

At a place where a river empties into the ocean there was a village. A rich man and his son lived there as well as a grandmother and her grandson. The people of the village always told boys not to go up the river with kayaks. One time the rich man's boy didn't come home. This rich boy had liked the grandson, a poor boy, and so the poor boy started planning to go look for him. He asked the rich man if he had an old kayak. The rich man answered, "Yes, I have one, but don't take it up the river. Just hunt some ducks for me. Take the place of my boy who never came home."

This was the first time the poor boy had ever used a kayak. He practiced all day and then went across the river and got some ducks. He went home and gave them to the rich man. The rich man said, "I'm so glad that you can take my son's place." The poor boy liked the rich man's son, too, and he couldn't sleep much at night. He always woke up before other people. So early one morning he started up the river. He paddled up a long ways and then went close to the bank where he started seeing broken kayaks all over, in the water and on the beach. He landed and got out.

He fixed the kayak so that he could jump in it and go if something happened. He looked around and saw a cut trail through the willows. He followed it, looking around and watching closely. Farther up he saw a village. He went down towards it and all of a sudden in front of him he saw a big dog. The dog noticed him, turned, and started running after him. The poor boy ran real fast towards the river. When he got to the beach he noticed a big rock, barely showing above the water, out in the river. He grabbed two big boulders and turned around to find the dog just behind him. He jumped to the rock in the water and landed on top of it. The big dog jumped after him. He threw one boulder and hit the dog on the head and it fell in the water close to the rock. It came up and the boy hit him in the head with the other rock and killed him. The dog drifted down the river. The dog was what kept other men from coming back upriver. It had killed them.

I may have forgotten some of this story.

The boy doesn't know how to get back to the beach. His kayak was ready so he motioned to it with his finger. The kayak came to him. He followed the dog's body, got it, tied it to his kayak, and took it home. He let the women skin it out. They took the head off and he let them boil it and the body and let them store them away where they wouldn't rot. A few days later two strangers came from upriver in two kayaks. The poor boy welcomed them. They said that their boss dog was lost and they couldn't find him. The poor boy said, "I don't know about that dog." He took them to the karigi and got food for them. He let them eat the dog's meat. They didn't know that's what it was. He went out and locked the door and shot the men through the window. He let the women put the men in their kayaks and set them adrift down the river.

A few days later four men came with kayaks from upriver. The poor boy went down and met them. They told him that two of their men hadn't come home to the village. He said, "I don't know about those men unless they are staying down there somewhere hunting caribou." He took them to the karigi and fed them dog meat. He went out, locked the door, and shot them through the window. He had the women clean up the karigi and set the men adrift in their kayaks.

In a few days an umaypak came downriver full of men. The poor boy met them. They asked about the men who had come before and the poor boy said he didn't know where they were, unless they were down caribou hunting. He took them to the karigi and brought them food. Then he shot them through the window and killed them all. The women cleaned the karigi, put the men back in the umaypak, and let it drift down the river.

A few days later one kayak came. The poor boy went down. He looked at the man and thought that it must be the umaylik of the village upriver. The man said, "That skin boat didn't show up. Which way did it go?" The poor boy answered, "I don't know, maybe caribou hunting." He took the umaylik to the karigi and gave him the dog's head. While the man ate the poor boy went out and locked the door. Then he went to the window and shot the umaylik. In this way the two villages on that river killed each other's men. THE END.

Tiŋuk (Agnes Towkajhea's brother) told me this story.

D810 Ownership of magic object: a gift; D1121 Magic boat (Kodiak—Golder 1909:17; Bering Strait—Nelson 1899:500; MacKenzie River—Jenness 1924:41; Central—Boas 1888:628; Cumberland Sound—Boas 1901:181; Smith Sound—Kroeber 1899:171; Greenland—Holm 1912:43; Rasmussen 1921:III, 102, 294; Rink 1875:154, 300, 417); F536.3 Remarkable stone-thrower; H1220 Quest voluntarily undertaken; H1385 Quest for lost persons; K1626 Would-be killers killed; L111.4.1 Orphan hero lives with grandmother; Q211 Murder punished (Cumberland Sound—Boas 1901:168; Greenland—Rasmussen 1921:III, 76, 111, 294); Q411.6 Death as punishment for murder. Similar to Curtis 1930:220–21 (Kobuk).

In PM6 a human body is preserved and fed to evil persons; in PM41 a man's head is cooked; and in PM80 a boy goes upriver to save the rich man's son.

PM20. KIYAK

This is a story about an aŋatquq who had a son. The aŋatquq was a Unŋaluklikmiut (from Wales or Shismaref way). His name was Kiyak. His son got big and then died. Kiyak lived for a few more years and then he died. Kiyak's family and the other people in the village

worked and lived for a few years. Another aŋatquq planned to aŋatquq (work his magic).

The people met in a house (not a karigi) and the aŋatquq started
to work. He put a cover made of sewed ugruk gut over himself and
said that he was going to talk to his aŋatquq. He turned towards the
door and started to work. He called and called, but his aŋatquq never
answered. He kept calling and the people began wondering if he was
really an aŋatquq. Then they started hearing a voice from far away.
The aŋatquq could not hear his voice from under his iñgaluk (gut
cover). The people understood the voice. It said, "Aaraa, aanii, alapah, I am suffering. Nagliksauknaknikpuk."

The voice got closer, close to the long stormshed. It said, "Aanii, I
am thirsty." The voice started coming into the stormshed. When it
got to the door it stopped making noise. The people wondered what
had happened. Then they heard the voice inside the iñgaluk. They
started seeing a shadow under the cover. Finally the voice said, "Did
you people know Kiyak when he died, that old man, that aŋatquq
who died long ago?" The people said that they all knew him.

The voice continued: "I am Kiyak. When my boy died I died too
after a few years. When I died I looked for my boy all over, through
my aŋatquq. All these years I have looked and I have never found
him." Then Kiyak asked the people, "Can I join you; can I sit with
you?" The people replied, "No, because you will scare our kids. You
look different now; you are not a person anymore." This is because
Kiyak's soul did not go home to heaven.

Kiyak asked for a drink of water and the people gave him one in a
sheep-horn cup. They put it under the iñgaluk. After Kiyak drank,
the cup came out from under the iñgaluk and the place from which
he had drunk was frozen. No voice came forth for awhile. Then from
the door came the voice fading away out the house saying, "Alapah,
I am cold. I am thirsty, I am suffering." THE END.

This is as far as I heard this story from Wanda Stalker (Amisimak).

D1711 Magician; E380 Ghost summoned; E541.4 Revenants drink;
E578.1 Revenants want to warm themselves; E721 Soul journeys from
body (West Hudson Bay—Boas 1901:326; Greenland—Rasmussen 1921:
III, 171, 178); H10 Recognition through common knowledge; H1220
Quest voluntarily undertaken.

Note again the correlation between death and being cold or frozen.

PM21. The Boy Who Was Raised by Wolves

Up Kobuk way there was a village. It was on the river across from a big bank. Two brothers lived there, of which the youngest brother was married and had kids. When the youngest brother's wife had their youngest baby they went out berry picking on the high bank. The woman always left her baby on the ground. She would dig a little hole and put some berries in it, then leave the baby alongside so that he could eat if he wished.

One time when they were picking berries they went back to check the baby and he wasn't there. They looked all over and couldn't find him so they went home. The boy's father had bought a bead band (with one bead) from an old man and it was tied to the boy's wrist. The man looked all over for him.

The baby boy was crawling. He didn't know which way to go. He could not find his mother. He was crying, but nobody could hear him. He didn't eat. Finally he got to running water, a little drip running down a bank. He stopped to rest and saw some trees a little ways farther and crawled up there. He sat on top of a big hump and rested; then he went into the trees. When he got inside he saw a little ebrulik. He thought there was someone inside so he went through the door. He found nobody there so he went in and went to sleep. When he woke there was food and water on the floor. He went over and ate and drank. There was no sign of people and he did not know how the food had gotten there. He stayed in the ebrulik and every time he slept he woke up to find new food and water. This happened for many days.

The boy got bigger and his clothes were tight on him now. Early one morning when he woke up he found new clothes as well as food and water. He put them on and ate breakfast. He grew bigger and now was walking around, but it was hard being away from people. Still he stayed there. When he got to be a big boy he woke up and found a bow and arrow. He went out and saw some birds (kerlaluk, Canadian jay) in the top of trees which had been cut off. He tried to shoot them with the bow and arrow. He tried all day. He wondered why the birds stayed on those cut trees. He went over and looked and saw pieces of caribou fat tied there. The birds were trying to eat them. The boy didn't know who had put them there. He practiced with his bow and arrow and finally he began to kill jays. He stayed out every day trying to kill birds.

He was a big boy now and his clothes got small again. One morning he got new clothes and put them on. He started walking farther from the ebrulik than he had before. He came to the dripping water where he had stopped when he was a baby. He followed it downstream. He saw something moving in the willows, with long legs, a little tail, and horns. He aimed at it and shot it. He took it home and dried it up. After that he got caribou every time he went out walking.

One morning before he had left the ebrulik he heard two people talking. They came up to and in the ebrulik. It was two boys. One said, "We have come to get you. The one that raised you wants you." The lone boy said, "I'm not going even though you come and get me. The one that raised me let me suffer, not taking me home in the first place when I was a baby. I am not going." The two boys went out saying, "If you don't come the one that raised you will come and kill you." The lone boy answered, "If he comes, maybe I'll kill him."

The boy stayed there. He got caribou and brought them home. He is expecting the man that raised him to come and is watching closely. One morning he heard people talking. He got his bow and arrow, ran out of doors, and hid in the shadow of a tree. He saw three men coming. They got close and one went around the house. When he got to the door the boy shot and killed him. The other two were going to run, but he shot one more. The third ran off. After a while the boy went to check on which way the man had run off. The man was already way up there. Those three men were wolves that had become men. When the boy saw that man running he had changed back to a wolf.

The boy stayed there in his little place for awhile. Springtime came and it seemed real warm, so he started walking in the morning looking for something to hunt. He went towards the river. He started climbing a hill and when he got on top he saw the river. He looked around and saw a man walking. He sat down and watched the man. The man clapped his mittens together. The man walked back and forth clapping his mittens together and the boy saw ptarmigan in front of the man. The man had willow traps (puaak) nearby and was chasing the ptarmigan towards them.

The boy came down to the man chasing the ptarmigan and when they met they started talking. The man told the boy that he had a wife down there and took him home. When they went in the man's wife fed him, and the boy started telling the man that when he was a baby he crawled and didn't know which way he was going. He told them that when he got to a little house he went in and stayed there until he grew up. The man said that there was a whole group of people in the place where he was now living. Once when a baby boy had gotten lost the people had moved farther up the river. But this man and his wife had stayed behind. They were expecting the boy to return home sometime.

They talked further and the boy let the man see his wrist. The man recognized the bead that his youngest brother had bought from another man and had given to his baby boy that was lost. The boy had met his uncle. The man found out that the boy was his nephew. Then the man told his nephew that his parents were in a place called Siksikpuk, not far from that present place. The boy said, "I am going to see my parents." His uncle told him, "If you go up to your parents, I don't think you'll come out alive because your father has become a man-who-always-kills-people. When you got lost he suffered so much he became a man-who-always-kills-other-men." The uncle wanted him to stay, but the boy wanted to go and he told his uncle, "Maybe I'll kill him." He said, "He never looked for me; he let me suffer. If he had looked he would have found me."

When the boy wanted to go over to his parents his uncle took him to Siksikpuk and they went straight to the karigi. When the boy went in he looked around and saw a young boy who looked just like him. That was his brother. The man-who-always-killed-people asked the boy all kinds of questions, and finally the boy let him see the bead on his wrist. After the man-who-always-killed-people saw the bead he still didn't believe that the boy was his son and said, "You killed my boy and then put the bead on your wrist." He got mad and said, "You're not my son. I'm going to kill you." And the boy said, "I will kill you. I killed the one that raised me and his son. They were wolves. I can kill you; you are only one."

The man-who-always-killed-people still didn't believe the boy and told him again, "You killed my boy and then put this bead on." While they were arguing the uncle said not to kill the boy but to see where he got the bead from. So the man-who-always-killed-people took the bead off from the boy's wrist and showed it to the older people in the karigi. They looked at it and one old man said that he had sold this bead to the man-who-always-killed-people.

After they found out that about the bead the man-who-always-killed-people still did not believe the young boy's story. When he still didn't believe the story, the other young boy in the crowd who looked like the first young boy got up and came over to his side. The boy from the crowd said to the man-who-always-killed people, "Don't we look alike?" And the man-who-always-killed-people said, "You boys look alike." And he went to the boys and begged them to forgive him. He had found his son. When they found each other the two young brothers started wrestling to see which one was toughest. They both were the same; they both had the same strength. Their father took them home from the karigi. THE END.

Frank Glover told this story.

D113.1 Transformation: man to wolf; D313.2 Transformation: wolf to man (MacKenzie River—Jenness 1924:76); F1041.21.1 Illness (psychological) from excessive grief; H79 Recognition by physical attributes; H80 Identification by tokens; H1385 Quest for lost persons; R13 Abduction by animal; T617.1 Future hero as child isolated from world kills increasingly larger game. A variant of PM154 in this volume.

PM22. Naaluḳtuak

There were people on the coast. There was a little river with a village on one side and a grandmother and granddaughter living on the other. In the village lived a man and his wife who always had kids, but when their boys grew up and went hunting they never came home. The boys always got lost. This couple started watching their youngest boy, named Naaluḳtuak, real closely. They didn't want him to get lost like the other boys. He grew up and was old enough to hunt.

His father went across to the old woman. She asked, "Why did you come?" He answered, "I want something for my son so that he won't get lost." The old woman gave him two small dried flounders, one dried northern pike, one small pot, and a wood spoon (kaivtuk). Then she told him to put them on the boy's parka. The northern pike was to go on the front, on the boy's chest, the flounders on the backs of his shoulders, and the pot and the spoon on his back by his neck.

The father took them home. Before he left the old woman said, "Every time his clothes get small put them on his new clothes." The boy grew and every time that he got new clothes they put those things on them. He got big and everybody watched him. His father or the other people were always watching him.

When Naaluḳtuak got big he wanted to go on the ocean in a kayak. He wanted to go out. Finally his father couldn't hold him anymore. He let him go, but he followed him. They walked through the ice and finally got to open water, where the boy started swimming. He never stopped. He swam all winter and all summer and he couldn't find land. Winter came again, then summer, and finally in the falltime he saw land. He went to the beach. There was a lake nearby drained by a small stream to the ocean. The mouth of this stream was frozen with snow on top of the ice. He went there and saw people's trails. He followed the tracks. The person was running with his toes in, so it was a woman's trail. He saw a ṭuk in the river. When he got to the ṭuk he saw several trails coming from the willows on the side of the river to the hole made by the ṭuk. It was a waterhole.

Naaluḳtuak quit following the trail of the running woman and followed the water trails up to a house. He went in and saw a fairly old man and his wife. The old man said, "It's me that let you come up." The old man started telling him about the running woman's trail. Before he came in he had seen another house behind the old man's.

The old man's son had gotten married and had built a house behind his father's. The old man said, "If you kept following that running woman's trail you would have gone to that house over there (a third house) and that woman would have killed you."

While they talked three boys came in. They were the old people's sons. Between the old couple and the running woman lived an old woman and her granddaughter. The old man said, "When people go in that old woman and her granddaughter's they can't come out, maybe because that old woman had a granddaughter with her." Naaluk-tuak started planning to go to the running woman's house. The youngest son of the old man started following him. When they walked over the man saw that the old woman and granddaughter's house with the door on top (like a little ebrulik). The man wanted the boy to wait outside while he went in. He said, "You wait for me out here. I'll be back." He knows that people who go in don't come out.

When Naaluktuak got into the stormshed he found it was dug out into the ground. When he went farther down the ladder he saw a big worm coiled around in the stormshed. He saw its head. He thought of his little pot and took it off and covered the worm's head with it. The pot got big and the worm couldn't move. Then he went inside and saw the old woman and her granddaughter. The granddaughter was kind of small. She went out to the stormshed and came in feeling sad. The old woman said, "I don't think my granddaughter wants her pet to be treated like that. Please take that pot off her pet's head. Sometime if you need help we might help you if you take it off." So he took it off and the old woman said to the worm, "This is your master; don't bother him." The man went out and found the boy still there.

They went to the house of the running woman and went in. The running woman was big and tall. She said, "Come and sit down by my side; your place is here." Naaluktuak said, "I didn't come to stay, just to see you." She kept saying, "Come to my side; this place is yours." She started getting rough when he didn't sit down. He kept saying he just came to see her. When she got real rough he got the wooden spoon hanging on his parka and waved it in front of her. She couldn't see; she was blinded. She started begging to see. Naaluktuak waved his spoon again and she could see. She didn't want to kill people anymore. Naaluktuak and the boy went out.

The boy told Naaluktuak that there was a house farther over. They went in and saw an old man and his wife and a man that was blind.

When Naaluktuak started talking the blind man started listening. Naaluktuak kept talking and the blind man kept listening. He listened for awhile and then said, "I recognize my parents' voices from way over. It's just like my parents' voices."

They started talking and found out they were brothers. The blind man was one of Naaluktuak's brothers that had gotten lost. The blind man told his brother that the running woman had taken him home and had married him. When she had gotten tired of him she had tried to kill him, but he was tough. She cut his eyes out and sent him away. The old people had found him and helped him. They let him stay with them. The old man always took the blind man hunting. The old man had made a bow and arrow for the blind man, and when they saw animals the old man would aim the arrow and the blind man would shoot and get the animals. Naaluktuak brought the blind man, his brother, to the place where he was staying. He took the old woman's granddaughter with him for a wife. They all went to the first house he had come to and stayed there.

After awhile somebody came in. It was the running woman. She said to Naaluktuak, "I want you over there." She kept after him. Naaluktuak said, "I'm not going over. I already have this girl for my wife." While they were talking the girl went out and saw a polar-bear skin on the ikigut. She went up and talked to the skin, saying, "If we need help you will help us. If that woman in there does anything you will eat her." The running woman came out and the skin didn't eat her, but she got real sleepy. She always used the polar-bear skin for a cloak. When she got to the polar-bear skin she tore it to pieces. After that she went home to her house. The girl went out again and saw the skin all torn up. She sewed it together and then it belonged to her.

The next day the running woman came to Naaluktuak again and said, "Let's go home. I want you." He answered, "I'm not going over. I have a wife." The running woman got mad at him. The girl went out and saw an eagle skin on the ikigut. She went up and said, "All these years your master has killed lots of people. (The running woman became an eagle.) I'll have you. I will keep you." She went back inside the house. The same thing happened as before. The running woman came out, got sleepy, tore up the skin, and went home. The girl sewed it up and kept it.

Naaluktuak sent his brother to his grandmother-in-law to see if he could get his sight back. She worked on him and soon he could see.

The running woman didn't come back. The two brothers started wrestling to see if they were really brothers. In any kind of game their strength was the same, so they were really brothers. They stayed there through the winter and when it was spring they always went away and hunted caribou. They dried it up. Naaluktuak's wife would use her skin and become an eagle and take the meat home. When everything was dried up they went back home and stayed all winter. They stayed there for a few years.

Then they planned to make an umaypak. The brothers cut wood for the boat and other people helped them build it. When it was time to put on the skins the girl became a polar bear and went out to hunt ugruk for skins. Naaluktuak took his flounders and put them under the boat. He put his northern pike in front of the boat. They got ready to go. They put dried meat and stuff in the boat. The running woman came and sat real quietly by the boat. She had been quiet since she had torn up her skins. She sat there feeling real lonesome while they got ready to go.

Naaluktuak had a big pole set up in the boat. He put the worm by the pole and let it encircle the pole around the base. Naaluktuak asked his brother, "What are you going to do with your wife (the running woman)?" His brother ran up to his wife, got ahold of her real roughly, and started dragging her to the boat. He got inside and tied her behind the boat in the water by her hair. They started dragging her when the boat went. They dragged her that way all summer. In the fall when the ice started coming the worm made a trail for them. They went all winter with the worm cutting the ice. Then it was summer again and the running woman was still being dragged behind the boat. The second winter the worm again cut their way through the ice. Then the next fall they reached Naaluktuak's home.

When they went up to his house his parents took the rope off the running woman's hair and brought her up too. Her husband treated her real roughly and hurt her, but she didn't say a word. He said, "That's how you treated people when you were going to kill them. It's a lucky thing I don't kill you." They put their gear up and stayed there. The running woman stayed with them. They all treated her roughly, but she still stayed. Finally Naaluktuak's father started treating her roughly too. He hit her and hardly fed her.

The girl saw that and didn't like it, so she started sneaking the running woman food. One time when they didn't know, she told the running woman to go. She felt sorry for her. She said, "I will give you my old clothes and you walk out from here. Later on I will come to you." The running woman left. Later the girl went to her, gave her better clothes, and flew her to her home. She came back before the others knew she had gone. They didn't miss the running woman. They didn't even ask where she was. Naaluktuak let his brother marry the granddaughter that lived across the river. Those two brothers lived and hunted together. They made a house for the worm and a trail for him to the ocean. The worm always got meat from the ocean for them. THE END.

I heard this from Frieda Goodwin.

B877 Giant mythical animals; D113.2 Transformation: man to bear (Kodiak—Golder 1907:297; 1909:10; Bering Strait—Nelson 1899:493; West Hudson Bay—Boas 1901:326; Cumberland Sound—Boas 1901: 251f.; Cape York—Rasmussen 1921:III, 124, 211, 297; Greenland—Rasmussen 1921:I, 184; 1921:III, 96, 184; Rink 1875:193); D152.2 Transformation: man to eagle (Kodiak—Golder 1903:94); D531 Transformation by putting on skin (Kodiak—Golder 1903:95; Bering Strait—Nelson 1899:468; Central—Boas 1888:617; Cumberland Sound—Boas 1901:181; Greenland—Rasmussen 1921:I, 364; 1921:II, 13; 1921: III, 75, 143, 262; Rink 1875:146); D801 Ownership of magic object; D1170 Magic utensils and implements; D1171.1 Magic pot; F696 Marvelous swimmer; H79 Recognition by physical attributes (voice); H151.10 Combat of unknown brothers brings about recognition; J151 Wisdom from old person; J652.4 Warning against certain people; L111.4.1 Orphan hero(ine) lives with grandmother; N825.3 Old woman helper (Greenland—Rasmussen 1921:II, 162); Q210 Crimes punished; Q261 Treachery punished (MacKenzie River—Jenness 1924:87; West Hudson Bay—Boas 1907:551f.); Q450.1.1 Torture as punishment for murder; R155 Brother rescues brother; W11.5 Generosity toward enemy; W181 Jealousy.

The physical separation between the house of the grandmother and granddaughter and the rest of the village noted at the beginning of the story may also represent social distance, a village of individuals bound together by kin ties versus two individuals who have no other kin. Physical separation of this type is part of several stories in this collection.

PM23. THE GRANDDAUGHTER AND THE RICH BOY

There was a place to the south in which lived a rich man and his son and a little old woman and her granddaughter. The granddaughter had only one eye, which spread clear across her face [there was no bridge of nose between]. This girl had a necklace with a little ulu hanging from it. She started playing out with other kids. When she came home she was crying because her parka was torn [this seems to have been a bird-skin parka, perhaps duck skin].

Her grandmother said, "Why are you crying?" The girl did not answer. Then the grandmother asked her who tore the parka, and the granddaughter finally answered, "That rich man's boy tore it." She took off her parka and her grandmother sewed up the holes. She went out to play and again came home with her parka torn. She told her grandmother that the rich man's boy had torn it again, and her grandmother sewed it up. This happened a third time and the grandmother got mad and said to her grandaughter, "This time you watch him and see if he pees somewhere. After you find out where he pees, if there is nobody looking, put some of the pee in something and bring it home."

The girl went out to play and watched to see where the boy peed. She found out and after everybody went home she went over and got a piece of snow with the boy's pee on it and took it home to her grandmother. Her grandmother wrapped it up in something and hung it up to dry. After a few days the grandmother started hearing that the rich man's son couldn't pee good anymore. A few days later she heard the boy died. The girl had fooled her grandmother when she told her that the boy had held her and torn her parka up. Actually she had done it herself. She had gone to the willows and torn her own parka.

All the people moved away from that place except the grandmother and granddaughter, because people move when someone dies. The girl started going to the rich man's house every day. One time when she got inside it was so dark that she had to feel everything with her hands. She felt some ropes hanging from the ceiling. When she grabbed one she took the little ulu from her necklace and tried to cut it. Finally she did so and it made a lot of noise. She got so scared she felt weak. She went out crying, "Aatakahi."

She got better outdoors and went inside again. She felt another rope hanging from the ceiling, grabbed it, and cut it with her little ulu. Again there was a lot of noise and she felt weak. She went outside until she felt better and then went in again. Those ropes had held boards up in front of the bed to make a grave for the rich man's boy.

She found the dead boy lying in the bed and she started warming him up. She took the bedding off and started making him warm all over.

Finally he started to get soft and unfrozen. She pressed on his stomach and fire shot out of his mouth. She was so scared she fell down on the floor and started crawling out, crying, "Aatakahi." After she got better she went back in again and worked on the boy some more. He started coming alive. When he started moving the girl said, "I want you for my husband." She took him home to her grandmother. They got married and stayed with her grandmother through the fall. In wintertime the rich man heard that his son was still alive and all the people moved back to their homes.

The boy started hunting, getting ugruks and seals as he did before he died. One time his wife told him not to get any female ugruk or female seals. He went out hunting, but he couldn't find any ugruk or seals. He went farther down the beach with his kayak. A female ugruk came and started bothering him. He didn't want to kill it, but it kept bothering him, so he finally killed it. He knew that it was a female. He went home with the female ugruk tied to his kayak.

When he got close to the beach he saw his wife coming down. She said, "I always told you not to get female ugruk or female seals. You're not going to live. I'm going to kill you." She kept saying this as he paddled closer and closer. When he was nearly to the beach he untied the ugruk, pushed it ashore, and took off. He paddled way down the beach, running away from his wife. He traveled in his kayak for many days.

Finally he saw land and went close. He put his kayak up on the beach. He saw a house, left his kayak all ready to go, and went to it. There was nobody outside so he went in and saw two old women. As soon as he entered one of the old women started braiding sinew, and while he stood there she made it real long. When she finished she put a hook on it and went to the door and started hooking. After awhile she hooked a mitten. It was his wife's. A little while later she got his wife's other mitten. Then she hooked his wife's mukluks, then the rest of her clothes.

The other old woman said: "You should go away before she finishes piling up your wife's clothes. I don't think she'll let you live. If you go right now you'll be saved. There is a house over there not too far away. If you go to that house you have to go down through a door on top, down a ladder. When you get to the bottom of the ladder you'll see a polar-bear head. Step firmly on the top of the head; if you don't it will eat you. Then go through the long entrance passage. By the inner door is a brown bear's head. Step on it hard, too, or it will eat you. Then you can go inside that house."

He got his kayak and paddled towards the other house, got close, stopped, and walked over. There was nobody around, so he went in. He saw the polar bear's head as he climbed down the ladder. He stepped on it hard as the old woman had told him. There was no hair on the top of the head because people had stepped on it too much. After he had passed the polar bear made a noise. He went through the entrance passage and saw the brown bear's head. It didn't have any hair on top either. He stepped on it, passed, and went inside the house.

When he got inside he started hearing his wife's voice from outside the house saying, "You think you are going to live? If I catch you I'm going to kill you." After that old woman had hooked all her clothes she had hooked her body. His wife got closer saying all the while that she was going to kill him. She got close to the house door and then suddenly her voice started getting farther and farther away. The man heard chewing in the stormshed. The polar bear got her and killed her. She hadn't stepped on the head the right way so the polar bear ate her. THE END.

I heard this story this far and then people started talking and I did not hear the rest. I hear it from Wanda Stalker.

B15 Animals with unusual limbs or members; C841 Tabu: killing certain persons; C901.1 Tabu imposed by certain person; D810 Ownership of magic object; D2060 Death or bodily injury by magic; D2061.2.1.1 Murder by sympathetic magic; E1 Person comes to life; F512.1.1 Person with one eye in center of forehead; K800 Killing or maiming by deception; L111.4.1 Orphan hero(ine) lives with grandmother; L161.2 Marriage of rich boy and poor girl; N825.3 Help from old woman (Greenland—Rasmussen 1921:II, 162); N825.3.3 Help from grandmother; Q211.8 Punishment for desire to murder (Cumberland Sound—Boas 1901:62; Smith Sound—Kroeber 1899:177; Greenland—Holm 1912:47; Rink 1875:157, 222); Q261.2 Treacherous wife punished; Q411 Death as punishment; R210 Escapes; S60 Cruel spouse. Shares elements with or is similar to Curtis 1930:221–23 (Kobuk); Rasmussen 1932:150–56 (Noatak); Ostermann 1952:191–93 (Noatak); and PM32 in this volume.

Though the conflict in this story might be interpreted as being between the rich and the poor, I think that depiction of sexual antagonism is intended. Rich-poor relations are generally good in the Noatak stories. Note again that a dead person is revived by thawing.

PM24. Katak

A young boy named Katak (waterbucket) had a small polar bear for a pet. He lived somewhere between Point Hope and Point Barrow. Along with the polar bear he also had a sled, like a bobsled. One day Katak and this polar bear were going out to look for wood. They went along the ice such a way that a strip of open water separated them from the beach. The polar bear was pulling the sled and all of a sudden he headed for the beach, but it was too late. A strong offshore current had taken the ice out.

They went along the ice for a long ways, even going over thin ice. They came to an ice-covered bump and the polar bear dug inside and found fishes. Katak brought them up to the surface of the ice and put them on the sled. Then they traveled again, traveling over thin ice all day. After awhile they found another ice bump. The bear put his paw inside and pulled out a seal. They went farther, the polar bear leading Katak over the thin ice. After awhile the polar bear got an ugruk from an ice bump. It wouldn't have been easy for Katak to get food, but it was for his polar bear. The polar bear never let Katak be out of food, but always got all all kinds. They started traveling again.

Katak always slept on the polar bear's stomach so that he wouldn't be cold. All winter they traveled. They couldn't find land. It started getting warm and the sun started melting the snow on the ice. The ice started breaking up. While they were traveling Katak saw a piece of log and they went and got it. Katak made a boat out of it. The polar bear got some ugruk and Katak put ugruk skins on the boat. Every time the ice they were on got small, Katak would get in the boat and move to a better place.

Finally when he got to a good thick section of ice he and the polar bear went to sleep. When he woke up he didn't see the polar bear close. He looked around and saw the polar bear on a piece of ice farther over. When the polar bear saw his master he waved at him. He waved again and then left. This meant good-bye. When they had gotten close to people the polar bear had gone.

Katak kept going and pretty soon he saw a village. He went there. People came to him and told him to go to one house. He went there and ate and then stayed there all winter. In the spring when the ice left the ships [white men] came. He got on a big ship and went home.

Katak made a story about himself when the white men came. The white men read his story and were pleased with him because he had written his own stories and told them how he lived. THE END .

Carl Stalker told me this.

B435.4 Helpful bear; B575.1 Wild animals kept as dogs (Central—Boas 1888:599; Greenland—Rasmussen 1921:I, 318, 363; Rink 1875:248).

The ending of this story suggests a historical incident, but given the premise of the storyline I think the conclusion may have been tacked onto a precontact tale.

PM25. THE BOY WHO HOOKED A WHALE

Down at the coast lived a grandmother, her grandson, and some rich people. A lot of people lived there and they always hooked [fished]. When a lot of people were hooking the poor boy always watched, and one time he told his grandmother he wanted to go hooking but he had no hook. His grandmother made hooks for him. He went down to hook and found the rich man's son there hooking too. The poor boy went to him and the rich man's son said, "Alapah. You're going to get cold. It's cold out. Why did you come hooking?"

The rich man's son had a few fishes so he said to the poor boy, whom he'd always liked, "Here, take my fishes and go home. You don't have to hook." The poor boy put the fishes in his bag and went home to his grandmother. The same thing happened the next day. The day after that the poor boy went down real early and found nobody there. He went to the rich boy's hole and found a few things there, but no hook. He found out that the rich boy hadn't come home. He told his grandmother and they went to the rich man. They looked all over for his son, but they couldn't find him.

The poor boy got worried and said, "That rich boy always used to help me." He got lonely and one moonlit night went out after his grandmother had gone to sleep. He went down to the beach and started walking. He found some little pieces of wood and gathered lots of them. He took them home. He cut them, making them round and real thin. He made a hole in the middle of them, strung them on a string, and put them around his body over one shoulder. He made a string for his other shoulder too. When he finished he hung them on the wall.

In the evening when his grandmother went to sleep he walked out on the ocean ice in the moonlight. He kept walking and went way out. He saw a real big shiny thing ahead of him on the ice. When he got close something black came out from the middle of the shiny thing. He knew it was somebody, but he didn't know who it was because it was too dark to recognize the face. The person and the shiny thing sunk down into the water until it was just like salt ocean ice again. It was the rich boy.

All of a sudden the poor boy grabbed the rich boy, got ahold of him, and tried to put him on his back. He got him and started running towards home. The rich boy was heavy, but still the poor boy ran with him. He ran a ways and then looked back and saw broken ice coming towards them, piling up and breaking. He really ran, but the broken ice started catching up. He took off one of the rich boy's mittens and threw it back. Then the broken ice stopped for awhile.

He ran on and the ice started following their trail again. When it got close he threw another mitten and the ice stopped. He ran on and the ice followed again. He threw off the rich boy's mukluks to make it stop. He kept throwing the rich boy's clothes and finally he had nothing left to throw, but he could see their home so he kept running and got close. He went inside, taking the rich boy with him. He put him on the floor and grabbed his two strings from the wall. He ran out.

The broken ice was on the beach trying to come up towards the house. He ran down and got close to it. He couldn't recognize the water because it was so black. Suddenly it looked like a person. He got close and saw a lot of hair all over the person's face. He went down there and the long-haired person said, "Do you want to see my face?" While she was trying to take her hair away he threw one of his little pieces of wood, which had real sharp edges, at her and she went limp. Every time he threw one the woman would drop her head. Finally he started running out of pieces of wood. Every time he stopped throwing, the woman would say, "Do you want to see one side of my face?" Finally he finished his two strings of wood and ran inside saying to his grandmother, "Go outside with your ulu." They both went out and looked around and saw a dead black whale.

They started cutting it up, and every time the grandmother cut a big piece the boy would take it to the cache. He filled the cache and the stormshed. They worked all night while people slept. In the morning people saw the whale and came to help. Everyone took home lots of muktuk. That's how that poor boy got a whale. While the rich boy was hooking the whale came, got his hook, and took him away. That's why he never came home. The whale that got him wanted him for a husband if he died and became a whale. After they worked on the whale they worked on the rich boy, who was dead, and brought him to life. He got healthy and walked around. In Point Hope people always find these little pieces of wood in the ground. These people were Point Hope people. The End.

Austin Thomas, Bernice Wilson's half-brother, told me this story.

B600 Marriage of man to animal (suggested); D110 Transformation: man to mammals; D672 Obstacle flight (MacKenzie River—Jenness 1924:79; Greenland—Rasmussen 1921:I, 106); D801 Ownership of magic object; D956 Magic stick of wood; D1445 Magic object kills animals; D2165.3 Magic used to prevent pursuit (MacKenzie River—Jenness 1924:82); H1385 Quest for lost persons; L111.4.1 Orphan hero lives with grandmother; P310 Friendship; Q40 Kindness rewarded; Q411 Death as punishment; R10 Abduction; R169.10 Unpromising hero as rescuer; W11 Generosity.

The obstacle-flight motif, also found in PM125 in this volume, is a classic folktale motif.

PM26. A Naupaktomiut Aŋatquq

A Naupaktomiut aŋatquq went through his aŋatquq towards the ocean. While he was flying he met another aŋatquq in the air. He was going to pass, but the other aŋatquq wanted to meet him. They jostled back and forth for awhile. The Naupaktomiut aŋatquq couldn't get by, so he flew straight up and got above the other aŋatquq. The aŋatquq from the other side got scared and turned back. The Naupaktomiut aŋatquq followed above him. Finally they came to the ocean and saw a little open water, and the other aŋatquq flew into it. The Naupaktomiut aŋatquq circled above the open water. Every time the other aŋatquq put his head up the Naupaktomiut aŋatquq tried to grab him. Pretty soon the other aŋatquq drowned.

The Naupaktomiut aŋatquq was Kirgavik (goshawk, the bird that chases ptarmigan). The other was Ingagiruk (a small sea bird). The Naupaktomiut aŋatquq went on his way. He saw a house and started hearing people inside talking. They said, "Here comes that aŋatquq back that went from us." Then they said, "It's not our aŋatquq that's coming back; it's another kind of bird." He landed on a pole and started looking around. He looked up and saw two little dwarfs trying to shoot him, so he slid down the pole and went inside the storm-shed. He hid there. The people inside started talking again. One man said, "Burn him." The Naupaktomiut aŋatquq had a little amulet on his neck, and he covered himself with it when the aŋatquq(s) inside the house made a fire on him. The cover burned instead of the bird. When the fire stopped he looked around and then started home. When he reached the open water he looked and saw the same bird that he had killed there. It was still dead. He went home to Naupaktusugruk. The bird that got killed lived in Samalarruk (Shismaref). THE END.

I heard this from Frank Burns.

D150 Transformation: man to bird (Greenland—Rasmussen 1921:II, 14; Rink 1875:148, 287, 327); D152.1 Transformation: man to hawk (Ungava—Turner 1894:263); D615.4 Men transformed to animals fight; D801 Ownership of magic object; D1385.24 Amulet protects against sorcery (Bering Strait—Nelson 1899:511; Greenland—Holm 1912:54; Rink 1875:151); D1711 Magician; K958 Murder by drowning.

PM27. YUKYUŋNAK

Somewhere by Shismaref lived a man, his wife, and his mother. They stayed there and the couple had a baby boy. They got their drinking water from a lake. The lake had ice, but it was thin, and they chopped through it to get the water. The ground was covered with snow. The wife went to get some water. When she didn't come home for awhile her husband got worried. He went to the lake to check, but he saw only the water bucket and a few tracks in the snow. He also saw where an eagle's wings had brushed the snow. He had no way to find his wife, so he, his mother, and his son stayed there.

Finally his mother said: "I can't go without my daughter-in-law. I want you to start looking for her. Try, and if you don't find her we'll do something else. Get a light pole, clean it up, and stand it up outside. In the morning when you go out see which way it falls. Go straight the direction it falls."

His mother started packing his things. She put some dried caribou meat in the pack, the meat from along the backbone which lies above the sinew. Before she packed it she wet the meat with her mouth saying, "Even if you eat this meat it won't finish; it'll stay the same." Then she made a pair of mukluks and wet the bottom in her mouth saying, "Now they won't tear or get funny." She also put a polar bear's nose inside the pack. Thus she got him ready.

When he went out in the morning he saw that the pole had fallen towards the mountains, away from the ocean. He started that way. He traveled all day until it got dark. He stopped and ate some dried meat, saving a little. Before he slept he set the pole up and then slept all night. When he woke he saw that the pole had fallen towards the mountains again. He looked in his pack and saw that the meat had grown as large as it was before he ate from it. He kept traveling on that way, following the pole. He walked for many days, but his mukluks stayed new and the food in his pack renewed itself each night.

One day he walked up a hill, and when he got to the top he saw in the distance a village on a river. It was fall and the river was covered with ice. When he got close he started watching. Toward evening, before it got dark, a man came out from one of the houses in the main part of the village. There were lots of houses on both sides of the river and farther downriver one house alone. The man had a ball (auksauk) and he kept throwing it up in the air and crying, "Hiii." It was a football and he wanted people to come out. Men started coming out of the houses and going down to the river to play football. When a lot of men were down at the river, three men came out of the house by itself, followed by a girl.

The man started watching how they played football. He noticed that one man, when he was happy, would grab a man by the collar in each hand and start running with them. He thought, "That man is strong if he can hold two men." After it got dark they quit playing football and the man went to the house that was alone. He put his pack in the stormshed and went in. The whole family was there, a man and his wife, their three sons, and a younger daughter. The old man said, "I'm sorry to see you come because there is a man-who-

always-kills-people here who has an eagle and a tirichik. That eagle
has already taken two boys home from other places. If that man hears
you are here you won't live." Two boys wearing nice clothes came in
for awhile and then went out. The old man said, "If those two boys
get fat, that man-who-always-kills-people will kill them. When he
kills strangers he always kills boys from this village too." Later one
man came in and said, "The man-who-always-kills-people wants to
see the stranger." The old man replied, "Tomorrow we'll go up," and
the man went up and didn't come back.

They slept and the old man gave the stranger his daughter for a
wife. In the morning they got ready to go up. The old man and his
sons looked for weapons they could carry, like ulimuns and other
tools. A little short man stayed with that family too. He got a pick
(siikluk) and tried to hide it somewhere on his body, but it was too
long so he put it across his shoulder under his parka. They went up to
the karigi, went in, and sat down. The stranger carried his ulimun.
He looked around and saw a curtain behind which the man-who-
always-killed-people had his bedroom.

As he sat there he suddenly remembered the polar-bear nose and
said, "I forgot that polar-bear nose which is in my pack in the stormshed." Everybody in the karigi wanted to help him, so two boys ran

out, got the polar-bear nose, and brought it to him. He started wetting it from his mouth. He told the people in the karigi, "If I become a polar bear be sure to tie my ulimun on my arm. If I win the battle take the ulimun off right away or I might kill somebody else." After he wet the nose he pretended to put it on over his head, and suddenly became a polar bear. The men in the karigi got scared. He told them not to be scared. Quickly they tied the ulimun on his arm.

From behind the curtain something started making a noise. When the polar bear heard it he made a noise too. From under the curtain he saw the tirichik's tentacles coming along the floor towards him. He hit one with the ulimun and cut it off, and the other one went back inside the curtain. While he was looking around it came out again. He saw it and hit it, drawing the ulimun back towards him and taking some of the floor off in the process. Then he saw the tirichik's head already above him with its mouth open. When he saw the tirichik's teeth he started hitting the tirichik's head by swinging his ulimun above him. Finally the tirichik went back behind the curtain. The stranger had killed it.

The man-who-always-killed-people called for his eagle, but the eagle didn't show up. It was scared. The man-who-always-killed-people gave up and the polar bear told the people to take the ulimun off right away, but they were scared of him and some tried to get out of the door. Finally one man came and untied it. The little man with the pick on his shoulders tried to get out of the door, but he got stuck. The stranger won, so the man-who-always-killed-people said, "You can do anything to me." The stranger asked, "Where is my wife?" The man-who-always-killed-people answered, "She's around here." He had always told his eagle to look for food for the tirichik and that was why the eagle brought people home. When they got fat the man-who-always-killed-people fed them to the tirichik.

The stranger started living in the village. He got his wife back and now had two wives. The man-who-always-killed-people was good to strangers now when they came. He was real friendly and fed them. After the stranger had stayed for a few years the old man started building a big sled. He put a house on it. He told his son-in-law to go and to take both wives with him. He told them not to go out from the house, that his daughter would take them. They left and didn't go out of the house unless the sled was stopped. They never went out while the sled was moving. The stranger's second wife was out all the time making the sled go.

They traveled for several days and then stopped and the stranger got out. He looked around and saw a house and they walked over towards it. They got close and saw someone going in and out. It was a boy, and when he saw them he went in again and then came out and went towards them. He got close and got his bow and arrow ready to shoot. The stranger kept walking towards him until they met and the stranger said, "Son, what are you going to do with your bow and arrow?" The boy answered, "I don't know about people. I have never seen them before. I can kill you all right now." The stranger said, "You don't have to kill us. You're my son. Don't kill."

The boy wanted to kill them, but the stranger said, "When you were young your mother got lost and I went to look for her. Finally I found her and she is here." The boy said, "You named me when I was small. You can say my name. If you don't I will kill you." The stranger answered, "Your name is Yukyuŋnak." The boy said, "You are my parents." He got weak and dropped his bow and arrow. Then he took them home. His grandmother had died and he was living alone. He was strong and they saw a lot of animal bones piled in one place by his house. They started living there, visiting back and forth with the stranger's second wife's parents. THE END.

Nellie Woods' half-sister's husband told this story.

B552 Man carried by bird; B877 Giant mythical animals; D113.2 Transformation: man to bear (Kodiak—Golder 1907:297; 1909:10; Bering Strait—Nelson 1899:493; West Hudson Bay—Boas 1901:326; Cumberland Sound—Boas 1901:251f.; Cape York—Rasmussen 1921:III, 124, 211, 294; Greenland—Rasmussen 1921:I, 184; 1921:II, 96, 184; Rink 1875: 193); D531 Transformation by putting on skin (Kodiak—Golder 1903: 95; Bering Strait—Nelson 1899:468; Central—Boas 1888:617; Cumberland Sound—Boas 1901:181; Greenland—Rasmussen 1921:I, 364; 1921: II, 13; 1921: III, 75, 143, 262; Rink 1875:146); D801 Ownership of magic object; D956 Magic stick of wood; D1065.2 Magic shoes; D1110 Magic conveyances; D1313.5 Magic stick indicates road; D1652.1.9 Inexhaustible meat; F610 Remarkably strong man; H10 Recognition through common knowledge; H1210 Quest assigned; H1385.3 Quest for vanished wife (West Hudson Bay—Boas 1901:180; Greenland—Rasmussen 1921:I, 222; 1921:III, 75; Rink 1875:180); R13.3 Abduction by eagle; R151 Husband rescues wife; T145.0.1 Polygyny. Similar to Spencer 1959:397 (Point Barrow); has elements in common with Curtis 1930:198–99 (Noatak).

The obvious humor (in Western terms) of the little man who got stuck in the doorway is somewhat unusual, at least in this collection.

PM28. Upumipaŋgunkiisiitah

On a river lived some people. There was a rich man and his son. The rich man and his son lived in the village and a little farther up-river lived a grandmother and her grandson. They lived by a stream that emptied into the river. The grandson is a poor boy, without mother and father. The poor boy always went up the stream by his house. He carried a play kayak with a play person inside it with him. In the middle of the stream was a small island, and the poor boy would put the play kayak in the water and tell the play person, "Cousin, you go up that way around the island and I'll go along the bank and meet you up there." All summer he played with the kayak and the doll. Finally winter came; he put the kayak and doll away. He had nobody to play with now.

When the poor boy quit playing with the kayak and doll in winter the rich man's son always came to spend the night with him. He liked the poor boy. This rich man's son sometimes stayed over days and, when he'd spend the day with the poor boy, he and the poor boy would walk along the stream. They did this all winter. Finally springtime came and when the ice went the poor boy started playing with his kayak again. One time when the river had no more ice he brought his play kayak down and pushed it into the river. He pushed it real far and said to the doll, "When you get in front of the village become a man-who-kills-other-people."

After the poor boy let his kayak go the people in the village stayed where they were a few days and the poor boy started getting lonely. Then he started hearing that a boy from the village went downriver with his kayak and never came home. Again after a few more days he heard that another boy who went downriver with a kayak never came home. After these boys never came home the poor boy heard that the rich man's son was one of the two boys who never came home. The poor boy got restless then and one day he finally started thinking,

"Why did I let my cousin go downriver and become a man-who-always-kills-other-people?"

So he went over to the rich man, his friend's father, and when he went in the rich man asked him, "What do you want?" The poor boy asked him, "Do you have a kayak?" The rich man told him he had an old kayak that the poor boy can use. The poor boy gets inside the kayak and goes downriver. While he was kayaktuking he went farther from the village, where the water was getting swift. It got swifter and stronger and ahead of him he saw the water going around in a circle [a whirlpool]. This poor boy tried to go backwards with his kayak, but he couldn't because the water is too strong. He started getting closer to the whirlpool and his kayak started going down, and when he went down halfway he said, "Cousin, it's me you're going to kill."

When he said that his kayak stopped all of a sudden and a man came halfway out of that whirlpool and the poor boy said, "Cousin, you almost killed me." The man-halfway-out-of-the-whirlpool said, "I don't know I have a cousin; ever since I was small I don't know. I'm going to take you down. There are lots of boys down there." This man-half-way-out-of-the-water kept telling the poor boy that he doesn't know about having a cousin. The poor boy kept on begging the man-halfway-out-of-the-water that he wants to turn back, and the poor boy said, "I know your name." The poor boy kept saying, "I know your name."

The man-halfway-out-of-the-water keeps saying, "Go ahead and say my name; see if you say it right." The poor boy said his name, "Upumipaŋgunkiisiitah." And after the poor boy said his name, Upumipaŋgunkiisiitah said, "That's right, that's my name. You're my cousin." After the poor boy said Upumipaŋgunkiisiitah's name right, the poor boy asks, "Where is the rich man's son?" Upumipaŋgunkiisiitah said, "He's down there." The poor boy said, "Bring him up." So Upumipaŋgunkiisiitah went down, and after he stayed for awhile he brought the rich man's son up in his kayak. After the rich man's son came up the poor boy said to his cousin, "Cousin, you make me feel funny when the boys never come home. You go someplace way far." So Upumipaŋgunkiisiitah went down after they were talking and the rich man's son and the poor boy go home. The village gets back to the same way after Upumipaŋgunkiisiitah goes. People go out and come back. When the rich man's son and the poor boy go home, the rich man lets the poor boy and his grandmother move in to his home. He was happy his son came back. So they start living together. THE END.

I was told this story by Frank Burns (Akuġuruk).

D283.6 Transformation: man to whirlpool; D1412 Magic object pulls persons into it; D2060 Death or bodily injury by magic; F420.1.1 Water spirit as man; H10 Recognition through common knowledge; H1220 Quest voluntarily undertaken; H1385 Quest for lost persons; L111.4.1 Orphan hero lives with grandmother; P310 Friendship; Q261 Treachery punished (West Hudson Bay—Boas 1907:551f.).

I am not sure if "cousin" is merely a casual form of address or if some deeper meaning is intended. One possible moral of this particular story is that one should not treat society or thoughts of deviation from societal norms lightly. A man-who-always-kills-people was a real and present danger and the poor boy's evocation had serious consequences.

PM29. THE GIRL WHO MARRIED A POLAR BEAR

In Point Barrow lived a fairly rich man and his three sons. His niece also lived there. She lived in the house with her husband. They had no kids. They all decided to move a one day's trip away from the village. When they moved they made houses and caches and got everything ready. They stayed there for a few years and the girl's husband died. She was alone, and when the rich man decided to move back to Point Barrow he left the girl behind all by herself. There was nobody around. She wanted to go but her uncle didn't want her to, so he left her.

One morning in the falltime she went out to go walking on the beach and found a fresh ugruk lying there. So she cut it up and put it in her cache. She went to bed and the next morning went out on the beach again. She saw a black whale lying there right next to the trail from her house to the beach. It was fresh and she worked on it all day. She piled the muktuk on the beach, after she cut it off. Towards evening she looked towards Point Barrow and saw two men walking towards her. They got close and she saw that it was two of the rich man's sons. They reached their cousin and started helping her take muktuk to the cache. When they were half done it began to get dark and they started home. They had filled her cache and put some

muktuk in her uncle's. She gave them a piece of muktuk to take with them.

The next day she saw one person coming while she was working. It was the rich man's youngest son. He got to her and told her, "My father sent me to you to get married." She said, "I'm not planning to get married. When I wanted to go your father left me, so I can stay alone. Go home and tell your father I don't want to get married." He went home and the girl stayed for a few days. She saw someone coming again. It was the young boy and he said, "My father told me to stay with you and help you." She let him stay because they were cousins. One night she was sleeping and she woke up with someone on her back. It was the boy. She sat up and was going to move. He didn't move; he was dead. She fixed him up and buried him.

Towards evening a stranger came. It was a man and he came from the direction away from Barrow. She told him her cousin died and the man said, "I killed him. I was jealous of him. I put that ugruk, walrus, and whale here because I wanted to marry you. I was jealous." The stranger was a polar bear. They got married and the girl's cousins visited her and found out about their youngest brother. The polar

bear and the girl moved to Point Barrow. The rich man and his sons started picking on the polar bear. But the polar bear was too tough for them. The rich man said, "Why didn't he let my boy live?"

One time the polar bear and his wife were home when they heard people outdoors. The people wanted to kill the polar bear. The polar bear told his wife, "I'm not going to try to fight." He went out without weapons and they shot and killed him. She felt sad because her second husband had died. She started thinking that her husband could have fought back, but he didn't. That girl was somewhat of an aŋatquq because after that the Point Barrow men got no meat even though they hunted hard. They were all starving except her. She still had a cache full of muktuk. She didn't feed them either because she kept thinking of her husband. THE END.

Daniel Walton told me this story.

B435.4 Helpful bear; B600 Marriage of man to animal; B651.7 Marriage to bear in human form (MacKenzie River—Jenness 1924:76; Central—Boas 1888:638f.; Smith Sound—Kroeber 1899:176; Greenland—Holm 1912:82); D313.3 Transformation: bear to man (MacKenzie River—Jenness 1924:58; Greenland—Rasmussen 1921:I, 134; 1921:II, 11; 1921: III, 52, 86; Rink 1875:196); D1711 Magician; D2060 Death or bodily injury by magic; L111.4.2 Orphan heroine; P251.6.1 Three brothers; Q211 Murder punished (Cumberland Sound—Boas 1901:168; Greenland—Rasmussen 1921:III, 76, 111, 294); Q261 Treachery punished (MacKenzie River—Jenness 1924:87; West Hudson Bay—Boas 1907:551f.); S71 Cruel uncle; T110 Unusual marriage; W181 Jealousy.

In PM96 in this volume a girl is also abandoned. No matter the culture, wealth increases an individual's desirability! Why did the polar bear let himself be killed? Perhaps because he could never really become part of Eskimo society, even by marriage, because the kin ties that under normal circumstances accrue from marriage were negated by the animosity of the rich man and his sons.

PM30. The First Eskimo Drum

A village of Uŋŋaluk̲likmiut people lived somewhere the other side of Kotzebue [around Shismaref?]. A man and his wife lived a little ways away from this village. These two had always lived there. He hunted. One time while he was out hunting he saw a shadow on top of him. He looked up and saw an eagle. He didn't know what to do, so he grabbed his bow and arrow and got ready. When it got close he shot it where the wing joins the body. Then he ran to the side and pretty soon he saw that the eagle had fallen behind him. He looked and it was dead. He skinned it and dried up the skin. He put it away on top of the ik̲igut. He started hunting again and bringing home food.

One time he went walking again and got far away from the house. He saw a shadow on the sun and looked up to see two boys walking in the air. He couldn't do anything, so he started waiting. They got close and stopped in front of him, but didn't touch the ground. They said that they had come to get him. They said that again and then said, "Our mother's heart is funny." The man couldn't do anything, so he went with them. The boys took his hands and took him up into the air traveling with them. They went around and finally came to a little hole. They went through and saw a house. The man heard a sound like a clock ticking. He listened and it was from the house.

He got near and kept hearing the sound. The boys took him in. He saw a woman and her heart was beating. That was the sound that he had heard. She said, "When my son never returned home I thought about him too much. I worried about him and that's why my heart got funny." The man thought, "Maybe that eagle I killed was her son."

So he said: "One time when I was walking I saw something towards the sun. I saw an eagle and tried to save myself. I shot and killed it. I skinned it and put the skin on top of my iḳigut. I didn't try to kill him first. The eagle went towards me when I didn't know and I had to kill it." The woman started being glad saying, "I expected my son to come home any time. I have found out that he will never come home again, but I am glad to know what happened." She told the man: "When you go home, if you ever visit another village, take the eagle skin along with you. When you get to the village have the people meet. When they close the meeting in the evening go out and put the skin on top of a pole near the house where they meet." She also told him before he left, "Make a drum so that it will sound like my heart. Take it to the meeting."

The two boys took him out through the hole, went around and around, and took him down to the place where they had met him. They left him there and he went home. A few days later he took his wife to Unŋaluḳlikmiut. He took the eagle skin along. When they arrived they invited people from there and from other villages to meet. They started coming. He made a drum that sounded almost like that woman's heart. They had a meeting all day, ate, and were happy. Towards evening, when they went out to sleep, the man put the skin on top of a pole. He went to bed and slept.

In early morning he heard the pole making a lot of noise. He waited and kept hearing it. It sounded like cracking. He went out and looked at the pole and the eagle skin wasn't there. The boy that was an eagle had become himself again and gone home to his mother. The drum was of thin wood, thinner than plywood. Since that day they have made Eskimo drums that sounded like that drum. THE END.

I heard this from Frank Burns.

A2824 Origin of drum; B211.3 Speaking bird; B455.3 Helpful eagle; D352.2 Transformation: eagle to man; E1 Person come to life; F56 Sky window (West Hudson Bay—Boas 1901:339; Central—Boas 1888:599; Labrador—Hawkes 1916:153; Greenland—Holm 1912:80; Rasmussen 1921:III, 165, 170; Rink 1875:468); F62.1 Birds carry person to upper world; F163.3 House in other world; F559.7 Remarkable heart; H1385 Quest for lost persons; J130 Wisdom (knowledge) acquired from animals; P251.6.1 Three brothers; R13.3 Abduction by eagle.

This story is widespread in northern Alaska, being known from Rasmussen 1932: 9–16 (Colville River), 17–33 (King Island); Curtis

1930:168–77 (Kotzebue), 197–98 (Noatak); Ostermann 1952: 38–42 (Colville River), 255–59 (King Island).

PM31. THE MAN WHO BROKE THE POLAR BEAR'S LAW

In Point Hope lived a man and his wife with no children. The man always chased polar bears. Every time he went hunting he caught and killed one. He always ran real fast so that he beat the other men and got to the polar bear first. They went hunting again and all the men started chasing a polar bear. This man was ahead, but he couldn't catch the polar bear. Finally he noticed that he couldn't see the mountains. He was far out on the ice. He kept running and the polar bear turned to face him. It was going to jump on him, but he dodged to one side. They kept sparring with each other. Finally the polar bear stood up in front of the man. They were apart now. The polar bear wiped its forehead with its left paw. Then it took the cover off its head. It was a young boy. He was hot and sweating. He opened his skin as far as his chest. The man saw that he had all kinds of beads on his neck. The polar bear said, "You are hard to get. All these years I have killed men, taking their beads and putting them on this string around my neck. Finally my string became full. I have killed a lot of men. This is the first time I didn't kill a man." The man said, "All these years I've been killing polar bears and this is the first time I didn't get one."

When they talked it got dark. The polar bear said, "Let's stay overnight here. You won't be cold." The man went to sleep on the polar bear's stomach and he wasn't cold. When they woke the polar bear said, "It's time for you to turn back home." When the man turned back the polar bear stopped him and said, "If you ever reach home don't let your wife touch you for three days. Don't let her get close to you." This was the law from the polar bear. They both started home.

When the man reached home he told his wife, "You're not supposed to touch me for three days. I'll sleep on the floor." They went to bed and he slept on the floor close to his wife. She didn't touch him for three days and two nights. On the last night, close to morning, he woke up and his wife was lying along his back. When he saw that he told her, "This was the last night. Something will happen to me." After they woke up he expected all day that something was going to happen. Towards evening he started breaking out in sores all over his body. When they went to bed a lot of water was coming out from his sores and wetting his kaichik (caribou-skin mattress). His wife changed it and continued changing it every time it got wet. All night she did that. He wet a lot of skins.

For a whole year he was that way, wetting his bed and his wife changing it. In the springtime he was still that way, and when the ice started breaking up his wife left him. He couldn't eat and he kept on being wet. The people went out to their summer camps and left him in Point Hope alone. All summer there was nobody to help him. He got real skinny with his bones showing, but he couldn't die. Once when he woke up he saw a little woman in his house. She gave him water and a little meat to eat. She started feeding him a little at a time. He didn't know where she came from.

Finally she began to give him more food and water and his eyes began moving around. He was getting stronger. She gave him more every day. He started sitting up when he got his strength back. Finally he started getting fat and the sores started getting better, clearing up from his head first. They all cleared up. He started walking around inside the house. The little woman kept feeding him. One time he went out and walked around the house and came back in. He noticed that the little woman was gone and he didn't know how she had gone out. He didn't see her go out, but she was gone.

He got fat and was as strong as he was before he got sick. He started packing wood and getting water. In the fall when it started getting cold the people that had gone to camp started coming back to Point Hope. When the umaypaks came he always sat by his door. One evening he was sitting there with one arm inside his parka and the other hand outside with a mitten on it, and he saw a boat coming. When it got to the beach, a man and a woman got out and put their things down. He recognized his wife with another man. He started walking down because he wanted to see his wife.

He got close and the couple recognized him as the one the woman had left. The other man bent down to get a stick and walked towards the man with his arm inside the parka. They walked towards each other. They got close and the man who had been sick said, "I didn't come to fight. I came to see my wife." The other man was going to hit him, but he got ahold of the stick with his mittened hand and broke it. He took his other arm out of his parka and said, "I didn't come to kill. I came to see my wife. I haven't seen her for a long time." The other man tried to hit him with the rest of the stick, so he grabbed it and killed him. The woman started coming up to meet her first husband. He said, "I didn't come to kill, but to see you. You both wanted to fight, so I'll kill you." He hit her and killed her too. After that the man lived alone and didn't get married again. THE END.

Ahsitjuk Kilyikvuk, a Point Hope man, used to tell this story.

B15.1 Animal unusual as to his head; B211.2.3 Speaking bear; C110 Tabu: sexual intercourse; C940 Sickness or weakness from breaking tabu (Greenland—Rink 1875:375); F660 Person of remarkable skill; N821.1 Help from little woman; W126 Disobedience.

PM32. THE UGRUK WOMAN

There were people living on the coast by Shismaref someplace. Farther over lived a man and a wife with their son. Farther over still lived a grandmother and her granddaughter. The boy always brought home lots when he hunted. His mother would work on the meat when he came home. She got tired of working and looked for a daughter-in-law. She brought a girl home, but the son didn't want to get married. The girl would sleep with the parents and the son slept alone in his own house just across the way. When she slept in the boy's house, she never showed up again. This happened often. The woman would bring home girls and started letting them sleep in the boy's house, but the girls would sit by the door and the boy wouldn't do anything, so they would leave. The mother got real tired of working by herself.

One winter the boy went out hunting, but he couldn't find ugruks and seals close by so he went farther down the coast with his kayak. He saw a house and stopped and got out. He went close and went inside the stormshed. He looked inside and saw a woman sewing. He went inside and started going close to the woman sewing seal skins. She kept moving. Finally he tried to get her, but she kept walking around. He forgot how shy he was at home. He really wanted to touch her, but she got away. Finally he got bashful and gave up. He walked out, got in his kayak, and went home. He was unhappy and his parents found out why. Every time he went out he came home without any animals. His mother gave him food, but he didn't want to eat. After awhile he went to bed and lay there never going out hunting. He got skinny and didn't want to eat.

His mother went out and went to the grandmother that lived farther over. She went in and the grandmother asked, "What's wrong?" The woman told her that her son hadn't eaten since he came home that time from hunting. The grandmother said, "He must have seen something or something must have happened to him while he was hunting. My granddaughter can try to find out what he is thinking. She can travel fast. I want some new clothes for her before she goes." The woman made a parka and took it and some clothes over. The granddaughter just put the parka on. The grandmother said, "You can wait here while my granddaughter goes."

The grandmother took her jaws off for her granddaughter's sled. She took a piece of duck down and put it on her [the girl's] head and then let her go. She told the woman to wait there, for it wouldn't be long. The granddaughter traveled and soon saw a house. When she went in the stormshed she saw a woman sewing seal skin. She went in and grabbed the woman and put the parka on her. The woman couldn't move. The parka was made with fur outside and fur inside so it was real stiff. The granddaughter took her out and put her on the jaw sled and went towards home. When they got there and went inside there was blood all over the floor from the grandmother who took her jaw off. She and the boy's mother were waiting. The grandmother asked for another parka and clothes for the woman. The boy's mother went home and got them. They let the woman put them on and the woman got her strength back.

When she got better they took her to the boy who couldn't move anymore. They told the boy, "We have brought you that woman you saw. She is here." He tried to open his eyes, but they were real heavy. Finally he opened them and asked for water. They gave it to him and gave him a little food at a time so that he could get his strength back. The woman started helping him. He married her and she fed him until he got strong. They moved into the boy's house and started living together. The boy started calling that granddaughter "sister." He started hunting again and bringing home food.

One time when he was going out his wife told him not to kill females. When he couldn't find anything to shoot he went farther along the beach and a female ugruk started bothering him. He didn't want to kill, but she got in his way so he shot her. He pulled it home with a string. He got close and saw his wife. She said, "I told you not to get a female. I'm going to kill you." He came up with the ugruk, getting real close, and she kept saying the same thing. She tore her parka down her chest and started scratching her chest. Her hands turned to ugruk flippers. She kept scratching. He didn't pay attention. He kept bringing the ugruk up. The granddaughter told the woman not to bother her husband, but the woman wouldn't listen. Finally when he got too close the granddaughter told her "brother" to run away.

He left the ugruk and started running out on the ocean ice. The woman followed and he ran way down. She still followed, crying, "I didn't want you to get a female and I'm going to kill you." He kept running with his wife behind. He ran for days and finally saw a house way up on the land. He ran towards it. He went inside the stormshed and looked into the house. He saw a large main room and a smaller room on each side. He went in and sat down in the main room, but things there didn't look neat. He went to one of the side rooms, but things there didn't look neat either, so he went to the third room and sat down there where things were neat.

While he sat there he heard someone coming. It was a woman with a bucket of berries. She said, "After he sat down in my room he sat down in the second room and then he went to the third room and he sat there." Another woman came and went to the second room. Later a young girl came and went to the boy. They were all sisters. The first was the oldest, the second the next oldest, and the girl that came to him the youngest. He stayed with her. The eldest sister was a mean woman and every time the youngest girl went someplace the boy suddenly couldn't move. The eldest sister somehow made him so he could not move. When the young girl came back she would work on him and make him so he could move.

While he was there he heard his wife's voice getting closer. The young girl said: "If she catches you here you won't live. So you might as well start running again. There is a hill farther over there and if you go on top you will see a house below. Be sure to go there. If you go through the door there is a polar-bear head by the bottom of the ladder. Step right on top, if not he will eat you. There is a brown bear's head near the inner door. Do the same thing." He went out and his wife was close. He ran and went up the hill and saw the house. He went to it and went down the ladder and saw the polar-bear head. It had no hair on top because the people had stepped on it too much. He stepped on the right place and passed. He did the same with the brown bear.

Inside he saw an old couple. The old man said to his wife, "Get some akuktuk" [Eskimo ice cream made with seal or caribou fat and berries]. She got some in a wooden bowl and put it in front of the boy. He stuck his finger in and licked it off. He was going to have seconds, but there was none left. The old woman brought another bowl and the same thing happened. He started hearing his wife's voice. She got closer, saying the same things that she had before. She got to the door and went in. Pretty soon her voice got far and they heard the sound of chewing. He was safe. The polar bear ate that ugruk. She was so mad she didn't watch her step.

He stayed for a few days and one morning asked the woman if he could go out. She said, "Sure. You can go to that first house that you were at. The girls there are our daughters, and you can marry the youngest. The eldest is just like a witch; she bosses the family too much." The old man gave him a bow and arrow and a hunting outfit.

He went to the house and stayed with the young girl. He started hunting caribou. His wife went with him because he didn't know how to use a bow and arrow. She showed him how. They came home and the boy was going out alone the next day. He saw some caribou and killed some. He told one of the female caribou, "Go see how my parents are." The caribou went.

The young girl went and got her dogs. That polar bear and brown bear were her dogs. The caribou wasn't away long when the boy started hearing a noise in the air. His "sister" was already there in the jaw sled. They got in their sled, leaving only the eldest sister. They went with the bears for dogs, but they were too slow, so they changed to the jaw sled and got home fast. They traveled back and forth to visit. That first wife of the boy's was an ugruk and she was real jealous of females. THE END.

I got this story from Maria Stalker.

B15 Animals with unusual limbs or members; B575.1 Wild animals kept as dogs (Central—Boas 1888:599; Greenland—Rasmussen 1921:I, 318,

363; Rink 1875:248); B601.18 Marriage to seal (Greenland—Rink 1875: 127); B651.8 Marriage to seal in human form; C841 Tabu: killing certain animals; C901.1 Tabu: imposed by certain person; D127.1 Transformation: man to seal (MacKenzie River—Jenness 1924:84; Central— Boas 1888:621; Cape York—Rasmussen 1921:III, 100; Greenland—Rink 1875:222, 224, 450, 469); D327.2 Transformation: seal to man (Greenland—Rink 1875:456); D681 Gradual transformation; D992.4.1 Magic jaw (human); D1110 Magic conveyances; D1520 Magic object affords miraculous transportation; D1440 Magic object gives miraculous power over animals; D1711 Magician; D2072 Magic paralysis; F1041.1.13 Death (illness) from shame; K730 Victim trapped; K1626 Would-be killer killed; K2212 Treacherous sister; L111.4.1 Orphan hero(ine) lives with grandmother; N825.3 Help from old woman (Greenland—Rasmussen 1921:II, 162); P252 Sisters; Q211.8 Punishment for desire to murder (Smith Sound—Kroeber 1899:177; Greenland—Holm 1912:47; Rink 1875:157, 222, 469); R227.2 Husband flees from animal wife; T311.1 Man averse to marriage. Shares motifs with PM23 in this volume.

PM33. THE JEALOUS HUSBAND

Some people lived down at the coast. Farther over lived a man and his wife. When the man went out hunting he didn't like to let his wife go visit people. He put her in the house and poked sticks in the ground all around her so she couldn't move. That's how jealousy is. When he went out he always locked the door with wood. They had a little baby. Every time he was going to go he still put sticks around his wife so she couldn't move. She stayed there with the baby inside her parka on her stomach. He locked the door so she couldn't go out.

One time, as soon as he had gone, she heard the door on the storm-shed breaking. There was a noise for awhile and a woman came in. She took the sticks off and told her: "You get ready before your husband comes home. Work on a seal skin. Then put your baby on your back and get that skin and go out to meet your husband when he comes home in the kayak. Put that seal skin in the water and get on top of it. It will take you across the ocean. If you land on the other side, when you get to the beach follow the trail to the right. If you walk over you'll find a house. Go in and stay awhile. There will be a man in that house. If he gets tired of your staying there he will get fresh with you and try to get you. When he does, run to the right again, along the beach. If he follows you there are two trees standing on a hill close to the beach. Climb up to the top of one tree, way on top. The man will come and cut the tree down. When it is going to fall, jump to the other. They are close together. When he cuts the first tree kick it real hard as it falls and say, 'Please, tree, hit that man with your branches.' If the tree kills him you can walk to the hill." Then the woman went out.

The first woman started getting the seal skin ready. She went in and out of the house and then she saw the kayak coming. When her husband got close he said, "You, little woman, you'll never live." He was jealous because she went out. She went in and worked some more. When her husband came closer she went to the beach and went to one side of where her husband was going to land. She got on the seal skin and took off. She traveled for a few days through the water, finally landing on the beach. The seal skin never got wet. She didn't forget and took the right trail. She walked until she saw a house. She got close and heard no sound, so she went in. She looked and saw only a man's things inside. She stayed there. Pretty soon she heard somebody coming and a man came in. When he got to the doorway he said, "I'm going to have somebody to talk to." He was glad there was a stranger. He asked if she had eaten and they started eating.

The man went hunting every day. He always brought wood home. When he was going to cut the wood he told her to go out. She saw a big rock on the floor. It was scarred on top like somebody worked on it all the time. The man also always said, "Don't go look at the house behind this house." There were things like buried houses there. One time when he went hunting she started to think, "I wonder why he doesn't want me to see those houses up there." She went up there and opened one house. She saw a dead woman. When she went home she didn't say anything.

One time when he brought wood home and sent her out she thought, "I wonder what he is making." She found a hole to peek through and saw the man chopping the wood between his knees. When she looked closer she saw that the point of his penis was flint and he was working the wood with it. That's why he killed all those women when he used them.

When they slept she slept on the floor and the man slept on the bed. One time when they went to bed she only pretended to sleep. She heard the man working again. She looked and saw him working between his legs again. He said to his penis, "Every time I have a helper you don't stay still." She found out he was sharpening it. A few days after he sharpened it he said to her, "I want to use a woman. I haven't used one for a long time." She went up to his bed and said, "Don't make a fool of me; use me quick." She got in his bed and lay on her back with her feet on the wall and her hands on her chest. He came to her and started to put his penis in. She shoved him up into the air with her hands and jumped from the bed. He landed on the bed and the flint point of his penis got stuck in the wood of the bed.

She got dressed, put her baby on her back, and went out. He called to her, but she wouldn't listen. She started running, really running. She went up the hill and saw two trees close together. She turned around and saw the man running after her. As she climbed the tree she heard the man say, "If I catch you I'll kill you." The man got under the tree and started chopping it with his penis. He kept cutting and finally the tree started shaking. It really shook. The woman said, "Please, tree, kill that man down there with your branches." She jumped to the other tree and kicked the first one real hard. It fell and killed the man. The branches poked him.

She watched and he didn't move, so she got down and walked along the hill. She walked and farther over behind the hill on a flat she saw two women picking berries. She went to them and they took her home. When they went to the house the woman said, "Let us take your baby inside. You wait out here for awhile. It won't take long." She gave them the baby. While she waited she heard them laughing inside. One woman came out and said she could come in. It was a big house and in the middle of the floor was a dug-out square pit. You could sit in it with you legs hanging down. A boy was sitting on the edge. The people of the house said to her, "When you pack your baby you have a hard time so we let him get big." The big boy sitting there was her son. They had blown into his mouth and made him big. They stayed there with those people for a few years.

One day the father of the women started building a boat. When he finished it he told the woman, "You should go see your husband. Leave your boy with him." They put meat in the boat and all of the people went. After they traveled for a ways they came to the beach in front of the house. They landed and went up. They saw a real old man. It was the woman's husband. He had gotten old real fast. The woman said, "I have come here to leave the boy with you. The boy that went with me will stay with you." So they put the meat down, gave it to the old man, and left the boy. They went on, taking the wife with them. Those people were brown bears. That's why they never got old. The woman stayed with them. THE END.

Frieda Goodwin told me this story.

B435.4 Helpful bear; D56 Magic change in person's age; D313.3 Transformation: bear to man (MacKenzie River—Jenness 1924:54; Greenland—Rasmussen 1921:I,134; 1921:II,11; 1921:III,52, 86; Rink 1875: 196); D801 Ownership of magic object; D1110 Magic conveyances; D1520.5.3 Magic transportation by seal skin (Bering Strait—Nelson 1899:512); D2060 Death or bodily injury by magic; F547.3.6 Extraordinary penis cuts down trees; K500 Escape from death or danger by deception; K1626 Would-be-killers killed; N820 Human helpers; Q210 Crimes punished; Q411.6 Death as punishment for murder; R210 Escapes; S62 Cruel husband; T81 Death from love; T257 Jealous husband; T320 Escape from undesired lover; W181 Jealousy.

A similar motif, the flint penis, is found in PM152 in this volume and, perhaps, in Lucier 1953:218–22 (Buckland). That's how jealousy is! Why was the son brought back to his father? Possibly because the wife wished to go off with the bears.

PM34. UUSKHIILHAK

A man and his wife had two daughters. They all stayed alone. Nobody with them. The daughters always walked outdoors together and when they walk farther their father tells them, "If you find a baby don't take it home." One time when they went out walking again they parted from each other. When they parted the oldest girl found a baby, so she put it in her parka and took it home. When the oldest girl took the baby home her father told her, "I always told you not to take babies home, but you took it home so you can have it for your child." Her father told her she can watch it.

The oldest girl starts taking care of the baby and the baby starts getting big, and one moonlit night she goes out with the baby and while they were walking she looked up and saw a man with a sled going through the air. He went down and went to the girl and told her he had come to get her. When that man told her this she went over to tell her parents. When she asked them they let her go with that man. The girl got inside the sled and they went around and started going up. While they're going up they went in through a hole in the sky, went farther up and then they stopped. When they stopped this man said he was going to drink water and left the girl alone in the sled. She stayed there for awhile and a woman came and told the girl they should change clothes, but the girl didn't want to change. But that woman tried to take the girl's clothes off, and took them off. When the woman took the girl's clothes off she also took the baby and went to the sled.

The girl couldn't move when she put the woman's clothes on. When the girl put the woman's parka on she got weak and became a beetle. She started going and when she saw caribou she went close to them because she wanted them to step on her, but they always went beside her. Then she saw another bunch of caribou and went towards them and finally one of them stepped on her and she became a woman without any clothes. When the caribou stepped on her she didn't know what to do because she had no clothes. She looked around but couldn't find that man, so she picked some grasses to cover herself and finally she made a little hut of grasses and stayed in there. After she made that little hut she tried to sleep, but couldn't, so she looked out and saw a real fresh fawn caribou (dead) and got up and started working it. She worked on it and then ate.

She started living better after she ate. Every evening after she worked that fawn, dead caribou started staying beside her, but she didn't know who put them there. She started making clothes out of those caribou and thought about her baby and started making clothes for him, mukluks for him when she can't forget him.

That man who put caribou by her was named Uuskhiilhak. When he went to his home town a lot of boys came over to see what kind of girl he got for a wife (the woman who stole the parka). The boys said, "That woman is just like the girls around here. She's not different." That woman works and Uuskhiilhak hunts and always brings food home every time he hunts. Uuskhiilhak went hunting again and when he hunted he saw the little hut, but didn't know really what it was, so one time he went over. When he got close he looked in and recognized the girl he took. They both recognized each other. Before he did anything else he went home. When he went home he stayed with that woman again and one time he said, "How come you stink so?" This woman said, "I work too much and sweat; that's why I smell." Uuskhiilhak put his wife in his lap and started playing with her hair. Before, every time they had gone to bed, the woman would face Uuskhiilhak and sleep. She didn't like to turn her back on him.

Finally she went to sleep in his lap and Uuskhiilhak opened up her hair and saw lots of beetles together moving on the back of her neck. He put her hair back. He started gathering some wood. He built a fire there and took his wife up. When it got burning good, flaming high, he threw his wife on the fire.

He went to get the girl. He took her home and the boys in the village came over to see her. When they saw her she was pretty, not like the first woman Uuskhiilhak had taken home. They started living there. She started making mukluks for her boy and let him put them on. They went often to see their parents, visiting back and forth. THE END.

I heard this from Frank Burns who heard it from Jack Henry.

C740 Tabu: doing deed or mercy of courtesy; C901.1 Tabu imposed by certain person; C930 Loss of fortune for breaking tabu; D184.1 Transformation: man to beetle; D382 Transformation: hymenoptera to person; D447.1.2 Transformation: human hair to insect; D665.1 Transformation of rival in love to be rid of him; D1110 Magic conveyances; D1532 Magic object bears person aloft; F10 Journey to upperworld; F56 Sky window (West Hudson Bay—Boas 1901:339; Central—Boas 1888:599; Labrador—Hawkes 1916:153; Greenland—Holm 1912:80; Rasmussen 1921:III,165, 170; Rink 1875:468); F511 Person unusual as to his head; H63 Recognition of other transformed persons; K955 Murder by burning; K1810 Deception by disguise; N820 Human helpers; P252 Sisters; Q210 Crimes punished; Q261 Treachery punished (MacKenzie River—Jenness 1924:87; West Hudson Bay—Boas 1907: 551f.); Q411 Death as punishment; S112 Burning to death. Similar to Curtis 1930:199–200 (Noatak) and EH5 in this volume.

If you disobey your parents trouble will follow.

PM35. MAKLUKIK AND THE UGLY DUCK

There was a village somewhere, not by the ocean. In it lived a man and his wife and their boy, who was a good hunter. One time when the boy went hunting he never came home. His father looked for him, but he couldn't find him, so he and his wife started living alone. One night when the father went to toilet he heard a baby crying close by. He went over and found a small baby. He picked it up and took it

into his wife. He told her, "I found our son." They started calling the baby "son" and raising him. After a few years the boy grew up and started playing outside alone. He grew tall and started helping his parents.

One day two strange boys came and stayed with them. When they came in the evening one of them said, "A man told us to come here. He told us to get an ugly duck skin from his youngest brother. That's why we came." The boy started hunting ducks. It was summertime. When he got ducks they were all real nice looking; there were no funny ones. All summer he looked for an ugly duck. When he took ducks (tiŋmak) home they always looked good. He gave up because he couldn't find an ugly duck. He didn't go out anymore but just laid in bed. He got skinny and finally couldn't move. His father went out into the village to get some old men. He always took them home to question them about that ugly kind of duck, but no one could tell him about it. No one knew.

A few nights later a real old man came in that the father hadn't questioned. He started telling about the time he walked all over hunting ducks when he was young. One time he had gone way far over to some high rocky mountains. He was walking under them when he saw what he thought was an ugly duck on top, but he couldn't climb up there. It was a real steep place between two mountains. When the old man went out the boy tried to open his eyes. Finally he did and called to his mother that he wanted some water and a little piece of meat. From that time on he ate and drank a little more each day and gained a little weight. Finally he started eating a lot of food. He got stronger and stayed outside again and ate without help.

When he got his strength back he started planning to go to that mountain. He let his father go get that old man again and had the old man tell him about the rocky mountains where the duck stayed. His mother got him ready. A few days later the boy left. He would stop to sleep at night and then go again in the morning. He went on that way and finally got to a rocky mountain like the one the old man described. He got close and saw two mountains with a deep gully between them. He looked toward the top of the mountain, but he couldn't see anything.

He started up the gully and went until he saw a big rock. He stopped and looked around. He saw something from the top of the mountain coming down the gully towards him, so he hid in the big rock. He looked but he couldn't see what was coming. He heard the noise of it sliding. He looked again and saw part of whatever it was, but he couldn't completely make it out. The noise got closer and he got his bow and arrow ready. Before he looked again he shot his bow and arrow towards the thing coming, and then really hid under the rock. Pretty soon something fell just beside him making a lot of noise. He tried to look at it, but he could not see it good. He turned around and then looked again, but his eyes were kind of funny. Finally he saw an ugly kind of duck.

He skinned it, dried up the skin, and started home with it. He traveled during the day and stopped to sleep during the night. Finally he reached home and his parents put the skin on top of the ikigut. That boy's name is Maklukik. When Maklukik went home with that funny duck skin he and his parents stayed until falltime and the two strange boys came again and asked for the funny duck skin. They said again that the man who sent the two strange boys wants his youngest brother to send him the funny duck. Maklukik is that man's youngest brother.

The two strange boys took Maklukik and a few other boys of the village with them to take the funny duck skin back to Maklukik's brother. The two boys told the rest of the boys not to break any trees on the way. Before they went they set up a tree in the place from which they left. As they are going two of the boys asked each other, "I wonder why they don't want us to cut any trees?" These two boys cut a tree on the way. After awhile the others missed the boys who had cut the trees.

The two strange boys took Maklukik and the rest of the boys through a hole in the sky, and after they went through they saw a village farther over. Maklukik and the others went over to the village.

The two boys who cut the tree and were thus left behind found out when they woke up that they were in a dark place. They didn't know which way to go. They started saying to each other that they would be strangers to other people.

When Maklukik took the funny duck skin to his brother, his brother tried to look at it, but it was too shiny so he had to turn his head. Finally after awhile he could see it. They had a meeting for Maklukik and the rest of the boys. When they closed the meeting Maklukik's brother asked him what he wanted. Maklukik said, "I want a woman that I can't see good, just like that skin, a shiny girl." Maklukik and the boys started for home. On the way they stopped by the tree that they had stood up. While they were there two boys that had gotten lost brought some strange boys from under the ground and met them. All the boys went home together. The two boys that were lost hadn't known how to get home so they had looked for people, and that's how they had found those boys under the ground. After they got home and stayed for awhile the strangers from under the ground went back.

The brother started looking for the girl that Maklukik had asked for. He couldn't find one. When he gave up he lay in bed and got skinny just like Maklukik had before. Finally an old man came in and told him that once when he was young and out walking he had seen girls by a river who were so shiny he couldn't look at them. The brother was home alone when the old man came in. After the old man told him that, the brother ate and drank and got his strength back. He asked the old man again where the girls really were. The old man told him and the brother went to that river.

He saw what he thought were three girls swimming in the water, but they were so shiny he couldn't see them good. He looked for their clothes and tried to see the girls. Finally he could make them out, so he grabbed one set of clothes. The three came up and two dressed and went away. He tried to see the third, but she was too shiny. Finally he could make out that she was a girl. He let her put her clothes on and took her home. He wrapped her up like Maklukik had wrapped the skin and waited for some strangers to take her down to Maklukik's village. They did and when Maklukik received her he tried to see her, but he couldn't. Finally his eyes got good and he could see her. They got married. THE END.

Frank Burns told me this story.

B30 Mythical birds; C518 Tabu: cutting down tree; C901.1 Tabu imposed by certain person; C950 Person carried to other world for breaking tabu; D361.1 The Swan Maidens; F574 Luminous person; F1041.1.13 Death (illness) from shame; H506 Test of resourcefulness; H934 Relative assigns tasks; H1150 Tasks: stealing, capturing, or slaying; H1331.1 Quest for marvelous bird; H1381.3 Quest for unknown woman; J151 Wisdom acquired from old person; J1050 Attention to warnings; K1335 Seduction (or wooing) by stealing clothes of bathing girl; N825.2 Help from old man; P251 Brothers; Q115 Reward any boon that may be asked. Similar to Rasmussen 1932:89–95; Ostermann 1952:204–8 and, in terms of the exchange between two men, PM64 in this volume.

The importance of kin bonds and the shame of not being able to fulfill a kinsman's request are emphasized. The Swan Maiden motif is very widespread and, in the Eskimo area, has been extensively studied by Kleivan (1962), who offers many references. Though she does not believe Rasmussen's Noatak version (similar to the one recorded here) is a proper variant, she included it in her analysis.

PM36. The Dog Woman

There were people at Point Barrow. Among them was a man and his wife and their son, who always hunted and got food. When the son was working outdoors cutting the meat he always saw a female dog passing by and he would throw her meat. She always took it away rather than eat it there. The dog always passed when he cut meat and then went up towards the hills. One time he went hunting towards the mountains. He walked all day until he saw a house. He stood outside for awhile, but he heard no noise, so he went in. He saw a woman in the house with six kids, two of them were human boys, two of them brown bears, and two of them polar bears. The woman told him to stay, so they got married.

One evening the woman said to the kids, "The tirichik is ready to go out from the ground. If it does Point Barrow won't have any people. It's up to you if you kids want to fight that tirichik." The kids went out to fight that tirichik while he was in the ground and killed it there. After they killed the tirichik the mother wanted the children to go away. She sent the polar bears to the ocean, the brown bears to the land, and the two boys to Point Barrow.

Later she and her husband went to his parents in Point Barrow. When he went out hunting on the ice he always found a bunch of dead seals in a pile. The two polar bears got them for him. They hunted for him. The two boys got married and started living in Point Barrow. That woman was the female dog that the man always gave food to. She became a woman when he went up to her house. She wanted to marry him so her kids could help him because he had helped her and her children by giving them food. She had those kids while she was a dog. The two of them lived in Point Barrow after that. THE END.

I have forgotten who told me, maybe Carl Stalker.

B10 Mythical beasts and hybrids; B350 Grateful animals; B631 Human offspring from marriage to animal; B632 Animal offspring from marriage to animal (MacKenzie River—Jenness 1924:80; Central—Boas 1888:637; Cumberland Sound—Boas 1901:167, 226; Greenland—Holm 1912:56, 82; Rasmussen 1921:I, 363; 1921:II, 200; Rink 1875:413, 465); B651.4 Marriage to dog in human form; D300 Transformation: animal to person (Greenland—Rasmussen 1921:III, 205; Rink 1875:450); Q40 Kindness rewarded; W11 Generosity.

PM37. THE MAN WHO BORROWED AN ULIMUN

Some people lived down at the coast. Among them was a rich man with an ulimun. He always wanted people to use it. He always used it himself when he worked. Once one man went to borrow the ulimun because the rich man had always said that if people wanted to use it they should just come and get it. After he used it he heard that the rich man was going up to the karigi, so he went up too. All the people went up. The rich man got out his Eskimo drum and played it. He started pointing with a drumstick to men saying, "I wonder if this man ever got my ulimun?" He pointed in turn to all of the men. Finally he got to the man that had borrowed the ulimun. That man thought of the ulimun and how he had put it on top of something out by his house. He told the rich man that he had borrowed it and had forgotten to bring it back. After he said that he tried to get up. Suddenly he became a bull caribou. His parents tried to take him out of the karigi. He got out and walked away. He went away because he was a caribou. THE END.

Frank Burns told this.

D114.1.6 Transformation: man to caribou (MacKenzie River—Jenness 1924:56); D1711 Magician; P150 Rich man.

PM38. The Boy Who Hunted with His Hand

Somewhere between Wales and Shismaref lived people, including a grandmother and her grandson. Every time he was out the grandson always kept one hand inside his parka. They always saw him with his hand inside his parka. One time an old woman came over to see them and said to the boy, "Boys don't look good when they have one hand inside their parka. Why don't you put your other hand out?" The grandmother said, "He's always like that when he puts on his parka."

When he got bigger the boy started going farther from home. He still walked with his hand inside his parka. One time he saw some ptarmigan and he took his hand out. He put it up in the air and said, "Aahahak." The ptarmigan heard the voice and looked at him. When they saw his hand they fell down and died. He went over and gathered them up. He looked at their noses and saw blood. They had gotten nosebleeds and died. He took them home to his grandmother and they started getting ptarmigan.

He started walking again and saw an arctic hare (ukaliksugruk). When he got close he put his hand in the air and said, "Aahahak." When he went over to the hare and looked at it, it was dead and it had blood on its nose. That was how he killed it. He took it home. Every time he went out he'd come home with all kinds of animals. When they looked at his hand they would die. He even killed brown bears. That grandmother and her grandson got rich. His hand, the one he hid, had a hole in it. That is why he hid it. Every time animals saw that hand they had to die. They always die. The End.

I heard this story from Wanda Stalker.

D2061.2.3 Murder by pointing (Greenland—Rasmussen 1921:III; 114, 240, 246); F515 Person unusual as to his hands; L111.4.1 Orphan hero lives with grandmother.

PM39. The People Who Didn't Know How to Have Babies

A King Islander (Uukiivakmiut) and his son went out hunting on the ice. They were drifted and never came home. When they drifted they were on the ice all winter. They couldn't get to land. In the spring the ice started to break up and they were drifted way down.

They found a tree that had a big root. They got on the tree and drifted through the water with the swift current. When the ice goes out the current is very fast. That big tree was from the Kobuk River. They drifted in the water for a long time.

One morning when they woke up they found that the tree was on the beach. They got down and started walking along the beach. They saw a village, went there, and entered the first house. An old man and his wife living there welcomed them and invited them to stay in their home. They were real nice old people and the man and his son stayed there. The old woman was pregnant. One night they were sleeping, but the boy's father had trouble sleeping. When he woke up he saw the old man get up from his bed and get something from the top of the shelf. It was a real long piece of flint and the old man started sharpening it. When he finished he put it back in its place.

The boy's father asked the man why he sharpened the flint. The old man answered, "When the women in this village are pregnant they cut open their stomach and let them have the baby. If they don't cut the woman the right way the woman dies. That's why there's not many people in this village." The visitor said, "If you want me to show you how a woman should have a baby I could. In my village women have babies before we have to cut their stomach." When the old woman started labor the stranger started working on her like they did in his village. He got her ready and she had her baby before they had to cut her stomach. After she had the baby the old couple thanked the stranger.

The stranger heard that the rich man's daughter that wasn't married was pregnant. "If the women of this village want to learn I can show them how to let a woman have a baby. If the rich man's daughter is going to have a baby I'll take a few women with me so they can learn." The old couple told the rich man that the stranger wanted to help his daughter if she is going to have a baby. The rich man can gather some of the women and the stranger will show them.

After the rich man heard about this his daughter went into labor. They went to get the stranger and he went up. He let the people of the village get their women and all of the women went there. He started showing them when the rich man's daughter had her baby.

After he showed them they started having babies like that in the village and soon there was lots of kids. The people thanked him. After awhile the old man planned to take him home. The village was someplace by Point Lay. The old man and his eldest son took the stranger and his boy with his boat. They passed by Point Hope. They didn't want to stop there because Point Hope men were mean. They got as far as Kivalina and the old man left them there. He told them to go right straight ahead to their home. They traveled and got home. THE END.

This is as far as I heard this story from Carl Stalker.

J151 Wisdom from old person; J1919 Fatal disregard of anatomy; Q40 Kindness rewarded; T584.3 Caesarean operation upon a woman at childbirth as a custom; W27 Gratitude.

PM40. WHEN KAIVAKLIICHY MARRIED HIS GRANDDAUGHTER

There were people living on the coast some place to the south of Kotzebue. Among them were three boys and a younger sister living with their grandfather. Their mother and father had died and the grandfather took care of the four. The three brothers were fast runners, and when people hunted polar bear the three always ran fast and got the polar bear. The young girl didn't want to get married; she liked being single. Her grandfather told her to marry, but she didn't want to. The grandfather got sick and died. The brothers buried him and put his tool box (ḳuksik) beside him. His tool box was made of a hollowed-out log and had a cover.

After they buried him they continued living in the village. The young girl still didn't get married. One time when the water was real calm they started seeing something black coming from way down the coast. When it got closer they found out it was a kayak. It was a young boy with nice clothes. He put his kayak up and they saw that he had beads (naakun) on his forehead. When he got to the village he stayed with the three brothers and the girl.

The girl got married to the young boy because he was a stranger from some place. The young boy always lay with his wife in the morning. When the people said, "There's a polar bear," he still would remain lying with his wife. One time when the people said, "There's a polar bear outdoors," his wife told him to go out. He put his clothes on and went out. He got to the stormshed and started coughing. He kept coughing and then stopped. His wife went out and he was lying flat on the floor. He was dead. When the girl got close she recognized her grandfather. His kayak had changed back to his tool box. That grandfather had become a young man and gone to get married to his granddaughter because she didn't want to get married. After he died again the girl got married right away. That old man's name was Kaivakliichy. THE END.

Ralph Gallahorn told this story.

D56 Magic change in person's age; D450 Transformation: object to another object; D658 Transformation to seduce; E605 Reincarnation in another human form; K1310 Seduction by disguise or substitution; P253.0.3 Three brothers and one sister; P291 Grandfather; Q321 Laziness punished; T311 Woman averse to marriage; T410 Incest.

Marriage is important in north Alaskan Eskimo society because the kinship network of both the individual and the family is thus extended. However, if an individual marries within the kin group, as in this story, the resulting incestuous arrangement does not extend the kinship network. Thus this story presents a balance between two themes—a girl who does not want to marry and a marriage that is unacceptable in societal terms. The death of the prime mover in the dilemma is inevitable, though an additional, more rational (in Eskimo terms) explanation is adduced for the grandfather's death, namely that he failed to follow the accepted norms of behavior concerning daily living. In any case, the desired outcome was achieved because the girl entered into a socially approved marriage.

PM41. THE MAN WHO WANTED HEADS

There were people living at the coast including a grandmother and her grandson and a rich man with kids. The grandmother and her grandson lived in the boy's father's house. When the grandson got big he noticed hunting outfits on the wall. The rich man had some people to get the grandson because the rich man wanted to see him. He told the grandson, "I want to eat polar bear's head. There is a polar bear way out on the ice, so far you can barely see the mountains." After the grandson heard that the rich man wanted a polar-bear head he left early in the morning with a braided rawhide lasso (niauk). He ran, then walked, then ran.

Finally, when he looked back he could barely see the mountains, so he started watching carefully. He went on and then he saw a polar bear's eyes and nose. When he saw the head he threw the niauk over it and jerked the polar bear's head off. He started home with the head. When he got there he took it to the rich man. After that rich man asked for the head he didn't eat it.

After a few days the rich man had the grandson come over again. When he came in the rich man said: "I want to eat another head, a person's head this time. Beyond those mountains way over there that we can barely see are some more mountains. If you get close to them you'll hear a noise. That is where you'll get that head." The grandson went home and his grandmother told him that the rich man had sent his father away and that was why he never came home. The rich man had asked for a head and the boy's father had gone hunting it and never returned. She said, "Your father went over to those mountains beyond those that we can see. Then he turned back and between the two groups of mountains they killed him."

The grandson went and passed the first group of mountains and got to the area between the mountains. He was walking along the beach. He heard a noise in the flat between the mountains. He went a little farther and then walked up. He saw a lot of people sitting about a great campfire. While he was watching them they grabbed a man, took his head off, and ate it. They they saw him and all started crying, "For my head, for my head." He started running back and they chased him crying, "For my head, for my head."

He kept running and finally got to the first mountains. He looked back and some of the men following him were falling down. He ran and they continued to fall. More of them fell, and when he passed the mountains only one of them was left, crying as he ran, "I want to eat that head." The grandson kept running. The other man followed, but he couldn't get close. When they got to the village the grandson ran into the rich man's house. Before the other man got to the door he fell down. When he fell the grandson took his head off and let the rich man's wife cook it. When it was done he took it to the rich man and made him eat it. He said, "You eat it. That's how you killed my father." The rich man ate it even though he didn't want to. When he finished the grandson said, "That's how you killed my father." The rich man died soon after that. Those hunting things that the grandson had seen were his father's. THE END.

Austin Thomas told this story.

F560 Unusual manner of life; G670 Occasional cannibalism, deliberate; H900 Tasks imposed; H1154.0.1 Task: bringing head of animal; L111.4.1 Orphan hero lives with grandmother; P150 Rich man; P233.6 Son avenges father; Q211 Murder punished (Cumberland Sound—Boas 1901:168; Greenland—Rasmussen 1921:III, 76, 111, 294); Q261 Treachery punished (MacKenzie River—Jenness 1924:87; West Hudson Bay—Boas 1907:551f.).

In PM6 and PM19, respectively, a man's head and a dog's head are cooked and fed to wrong-doers. Antagonism between rich and poor is relatively rare in these stories.

PM42. Aakikmak

In Diomede there are two brothers and one married sister (the youngest child) whose husband's father is still living. The middle brother is married and has children. The oldest brother is married too, but he had no children. Each of these people, these two brothers and their sister, lived in separate houses. The sister had a baby, and when she had her baby the middle brother's youngest boy hears that his aunt's baby boy looked different from all the other kids. When he heard about it he went over to see the baby, and his aunt, the baby's mother, tells him, "You can see that baby when he gets big." The baby's neck is different, it stretches from the base of his head to the outside of his shoulders instead of curving in a thin column between his shoulders.

When the sister heard that her husband didn't come home she suffered, suffered so much she died. Her baby goes to live with her husband's father, the baby's grandfather. The baby is named Aakikmak. Aakikmak and his grandfather start living in the sister's house. Aakikmak starts trying to breastfeed from his grandfather and does it so much that finally there is milk coming from the grandfather's nipples. Aakikmak starts growing big from his grandfather's milk. The middle brother always liked Aakikmak and also sends clothes over to him when his mother died. The middle brother's youngest son wanted to see Aakikmak and one time this youngest son never came home.

Aakikmak starts crawling on the floor, going far when he crawls. He was still drinking from his grandfather's nipples. Later he starts walking. When he walks he goes out to the stormshed and later when he got bigger he went outside the stormshed sideways. He started going out in the evening when the people were sleeping;

when nobody's out he starts staying out. When he stays out at nights his grandfather went up to the karigi in the evening when the people met.

One evening Aakiḳmak was out and his grandfather at the karigi; when his grandfather came home that evening he had tears in his eyes, so Aakiḳmak asked him what was wrong, and the grandfather said that if Aakiḳmak didn't go up to the karigi tomorrow his oldest uncle, the one without any kids, was going to kill him. After his grandfather told him this Aakiḳmak said, "Don't worry. They're not going to do anything to us, Grandfather." They slept that night and next day Aakiḳmak and his grandfather went up to the karigi together.

When they went up to the karigi and went in through the storm-shed Aakiḳmak went in sideways; he's too big in the neck region to go in frontways. When they went in the inside door Aakiḳmak pushed his grandfather over into the room (over a partition at the base of the doorway). He pushed himself in the door with his hand lifting him up over the partition and in sideways again. When he went in he looked around and thought to himself after seeing a lot of men in there, "This man is my uncle." He sat in front of his uncle with his back towards his uncle. After he sat down in front of his uncle, his uncle saw how big he was from the back and didn't say anything.

His uncle told Aakiḳmak that he can go out hunting now. They, Aakiḳmak and his oldest uncle, went home together from the karigi and early in the morning, after a few days, he went hunting by himself. He came home in the afternoon of the same day he went hunting with five wolves. When he took the wolves home he gave them to his younger uncle (middle brother) who liked him. The oldest uncle heard that Aakiḳmak got five wolves and so he told his wife to go ask for a ruff for him. His wife was kind of lazy, but she went to the middle brother and he gave her a whole wolf skin.

Aakiḳmak went hunting again the next morning after he had gotten the five wolves and again returned in the afternoon with five wolverines. Again he gave these to his younger uncle, and when the oldest heard about the five wolverines he sent his wife over to the middle brother, and when she went in the middle brother asked her what she wanted. She said, "Your oldest brother wants a piece of wolverine." The middle brother gave her a whole skin.

After Aakiḳmak brought the wolverines home they stayed in their place, and when summer came Aakiḳmak asked his younger uncle to take a walk with him. They went walking and after walking a little while they came to a little hill and went up the hill and looked around and saw four brown bears. Aakiḵmak told his uncle, "You wait here. I'll go hunt those brown bears." The uncle waited while Aakiḵmak went close to the brown bears. The brown bears saw him and ran towards him. When they got close to him he hit one with his hand and the bear fell down and rolled over. Same thing happened with the other three bears. Then he laughed, "Ha, ha, lots of fun." He kept hitting them with his hand, every time one came close. He had a lot of fun with them. Finally they didn't bother him anymore and he talked to them and took them over to his youngest uncle who was waiting on the hill. They took them home and tied them on poles.

Aakiḵmak let his youngest uncle make him a sled, and after he finished Aakiḵmak planned to go with some of his cousins. When they went they used the brown bears as dogs. They kept going, sometimes really fast, but the bears never had to run. They saw a village and got close and the villagers said, "There are strangers coming," and started running towards them. When they got close and stopped the villagers said, "They've got brown bears for dogs." They were scared and stood looking at them. The brown bears took the sled on to a house where they stopped. Aakiḵmak tied the bears to poles.

They went inside and the man of the house said, "Why did you come?" Aakiḵmak answered, "We are looking for my father and my cousin who are lost." The man said, "The one that took your father and cousin is real tough. He is an aŋatquq. He has an eagle and a tirichik." Aakiḵmak started spinning, standing on the floor. When he stopped he started laughing and said, "Lots of fun. Diomeders should have that man to spill their slop buckets for them."

Aakiḵmak and his cousins stayed there, slept, and then left. Aakiḵmak took one young boy from among that man's sons to show him the way. The sled had a house on it. Aakiḵmak told the boy to tell the brown bears which way to go and the brown bears would take them. Aakiḵmak stayed inside the house. They went and the boy stayed in the front showing the brown bears the way. The bears went the direction he pointed.

Towards evening they saw a village. When the villagers saw strangers they came running. They got close and then stopped, saying, "They have brown bears for dogs." The brown bears took

Aakiḳmak and his cousins to a house where he tied them up. When they went inside they found an old man with kids. The old man asked, "Why did you come?" Aakiḳmak said that he was looking for his father and cousin that had gotten lost. The old man replied, "The one that got them is an aŋatquq. He has a tirichik and an eagle." When Aakiḳmak heard that, he said, "Lots of fun," and he spun on the floor saying, "Diomeders should have that man to spill their slop buckets for them." They stayed there and ate. Then people came to get them saying, "The man-who-always-kills-people wants you."

They went up to the karigi with the people of the house. Aakiḳmak looked around and saw one man sitting there that he thought was the man-who-always-killed-people. There was a curtain on the side of the karigi. That man asked, "Why did you come?" Aakiḳmak repeated that he was looking for his father and his cousin. The man-who-always-killed-people got kind of mad. Aakiḳmak got up and started spinning. Every time he stopped he would laugh and say, "I'm going to have a lot of fun." Then he said, "It would be good if Diomeders had that man to take the slops out." The man-who-always-killed-people called for his eagle. The eagle put his claws inside the window and started looking for Aakiḳmak. At first Aakiḳmak pretended he was hiding, and then pretty soon he grabbed the eagle's legs with both hands and started pulling him through the window. The eagle's bones cracked. When Aakiḳmak pulled him in the eagle was dead. Aakiḳmak threw the eagle to the man-who-always-killed-people.

The man called his tirichik, but it never showed up, so he gave himself up to Aakiḳmak saying, "You can do anything you want to me." Aakiḳmak took him out and took him to a house where he let him stay alone. Aakiḳmak would visit him and when he did the man-who-always-killed-people would start crying. He stayed there alone while his wife lived in their house. They stayed for a few days and the man-who-always-killed-people had to stay alone. After a couple days Aakiḳmak went to see the man-who-always-killed-people and told him that they were going to go back home and take him along, but that they were going to leave his wife. Aakiḳmak took him to his wife and said, "We are going to leave here." The man-who-always-killed-people started crying. Aakiḳmak let the woman go out because he didn't want the man-who-always-killed-people to know he was really going to take her along. He was going to hide her and take her too.

When Aakiḵmak left he took a girl from the man he had stayed with. These were Selawik people. They started off towards home and when they got to the first village they stopped at the same house. When they went in the man of the house said to the man-who-always-killed-people, "So you followed them too, eh." He tried to make fun of the man-who-always-killed-people. These people are from Buckland. The man-who-always-killed-people said, "I am going to Diomede and spill their slops out." They left Buckland and Aakiḵmak took a girl from the house where they stayed for his cousin's wife. The Selawik girl was for Aakiḵmak.

When they went home he gave the man-who-always-killed-people's wife to his grandfather. The man-who-always-killed-people stayed with Aakiḵmak. In the morning he would go out and spill the Diomeders' slops, every house. Aakiḵmak let him have good clothes and everything he needed when he worked like that. Aakiḵmak's grandfather got old and died. Aakiḵmak let the man-who-always-killed-people take his wife back. Aakiḵmak always took his wife and his cousin's wife to Buckland and Selawik to visit, but they lived in the Diomedes. Aakiḵmak was not an aŋatquq, but he was a strong man. THE END.

This is as far as I had heard this story from Daniel Walton.

B455.3 Helpful eagle; B575.1 Wild animals kept as dogs (Central–Boas 1888:599; Greenland–Rasmussen 1921:I; 318, 363; Rink 1875: 248); B877 Giant mythical animals; D1711 Magician; D1717.1 Magic power of monster child; F546.6 Milk in man's breast; F1041.1.2 Death from grief for death of lover or relative; H1385 Quest for lost persons; L100 Unpromising hero; N820 Human helpers; P253.0.2 One sister and two brothers; Q211 Murder punished (Cumberland Sound–Boas 1901: 168; Greenland–Rasmussen 1921: III, 76, 111, 294); S71 Cruel uncle; T611.2.1 Child miraculously suckled by his grandfather; W10 Kindness.

PM43. TUAKIKPAKAKTUK

In Siberia (Kutlik) lived some people, including a grandmother and her grandson. When the grandmother was about to die she told her grandson: "When I die bury me up there close to the house. After you bury me come and see my grave every summer. If the summer is good there will be something by my box. Plants will grow from my limbs. If the plants grow big, store them away because people might like them." When she died he buried her as she had wished. In the springtime when the greens were coming up he visited her grave. After things were really growing he found some plants there. He picked them and stored them away. People found out about them and started burning them. That was old-timer's tobacco, really strong. That is where tobacco (tuakikpak) came from. After that the boy was nicknamed Tuakikpakaktuk. He started planting tobacco when the people wanted it and spread the dried leaves all over. His real name (or perhaps his son's name) was Kukarii.

Tuakikpakaktuk was partners with a man from Shismaref. In addition to Tuakikpakaktuk's partner, a grandmother and her grandson lived in Shismaref. The grandson always saw men coming home from hunting carrying white and red foxes. When he got big he stayed out to watch the men as they came in. One time he asked his grandmother, "How come those people bring white and red foxes home? How do they get them?" She answered: "They always go out and cut a tree. They hollow out the inside and put some bait in there. When the fox smells it he comes in one side. They put a snare near the bait and when the fox tries to eat he gets caught. (This type of trap is called siisak.)" The grandson and the grandmother decided to make that kind of trap. The grandmother showed him how and the grandson worked on it most of the night. After he finished he went to sleep.

He woke early in the morning and left to set the trap. Then he went home and went to bed. He wanted to see the trap real badly, so he left early again the next morning. When he got close to the trap he saw a tail sticking out the end, so he said, "Maybe a red or a white fox." He went over and took the trap off and found a dark fox with white lines down the back (napuhuutlik). He took it home and his grandmother skinned it. She dried it up and put it away.

Every year Tuakikpakaktuk's partner, who lived alone way farther up from the village, came down to the village and took some men from there to go by dog team to Tuakikpakaktuk's grandmother's grave where there was some tobacco. Tuakikpakaktuk's partner heard that the grandson had gotten a napuhuutlik. When he heard that he went down to the boy, after he had returned from Siberia, and asked him for the skin. The grandmother and the grandson didn't want to sell it, so Tuakikpakaktuk's partner grabbed the grandson and tied his hands behind his back. He built a fire and sat the boy by it so that it burned his back. As the boy's back burned he scraped the skin off with a sharp stick until he could see the bones. After that he let the boy go inside to his grandmother. When the boy went in his grandmother saw him. She wet her hands from her mouth and rubbed his burns. Then she put him to bed where he stayed.

After awhile the grandmother gathered some old clothes, put them in a grave box, and took them up to the graveyard. She buried them. Her grandson was still in bed. She cried up there all day and then went home. Tuakikpakaktuk's partner went back to the grandmother's house and went in. He said, "I might as well kill that boy instead of just burning him." She said, "He's up there in the graveyard." When she said that Tuakikpakaktuk's partner went out and went home.

Tuakikpakaktuk's partner decided to go to Siberia again. He came to Shismaref and got some men. A young boy went into the grandmother and grandson and said, "I want to help you. I'll hide the boy in the sled. He should take that napuhuutlik skin with him. I'll hide him from the man that's trying to kill him." When they went the boy put the grandson in the sled and took him with the other teams. The grandson put the skin in under his parka. Whenever they stopped the boy watched over the grandson. They spent one night, and after they went again in the morning they reached Tuakikpakaktuk's house.

The Siberian villagers didn't go into Tuakikpakaktuk's house very often. In the evening the young boy took the grandson to Tuakikpakaktuk when there was nobody around. The grandson took the skin along. When they went in Tuakikpakaktuk was home alone. The grandson took the fox skin out of his parka and showed it to Tuakikpakaktuk. He put it in front of Tuakikpakaktuk. Tuakikpakaktuk kept rubbing it because it was the first time he had seen that kind. The grandson said, "Your partner wanted it, but my grandmother and I didn't want to give it to him. When he didn't get it he burned my back." He took his parka off and showed Tuakikpakaktuk. Tuakikpakatuk felt so sorry he even had tears in his eyes. He said, "My partner shouldn't have done that."

When his partner came in he didn't welcome him. He sent him out and broke the partnership. He made a partnership with the grandson because they were both orphans. As the young boy left to take the grandson home Tuakikpakaktuk said, "When you reach home try and burn that man the same way. See how he likes it." After they got home and the grandson's wounds healed up he went up to that man, built a fire, tied his hands behind him, and burned him. As the man burned the grandson kept scraping the skin off. Finally the man died from his burns. THE END.

I heard this story from Frank Burns. When Frank Burns' father was a young boy those villagers came from Siberia and they and the Shismaref people came to Sheshalik in skin boats. Frank Burns' father saw the boy who was burned. He took his parka off and showed his back to the people and Frank Burns' father saw a big scar on his back. The boy that was burned was named Shuktii. This is a real true story, not a play story.

A2611.2.2 Tobacco from grave of woman; A2691.2 Origin of tobacco; J151 Wisdom (knowledge) from old person; K500 Escape from death or danger by deception; K640 Escape by help of confederate; K955 Murder by burning; K1626 Would-be killers killed; L111.4.1 Orphan hero lives with grandmother; L111.4.4 Mistreated orphan hero (West Hudson Bay—Boas 1901:309; Ungava—Turner 1894:265; Central—Boas 1888:630; Cumberland Sound—Boas 1901:188; Greenland—Rasmussen 1921:I, 123, 230, 238; 1921:II, 34, 38; 1921:III, 90, 295); N820 Human helpers; P310 Friendship; Q210 Crimes punished; Q261 Treachery punished (MacKenzie River—Jenness 1924:87; West Hudson Bay—Boas 1907:551f.); Q411 Death as punishment; S112 Burning to death; W10 Kindness. Similar to Spencer 1959:464 (Point Barrow); in Lucier 1953: 228 (Buckland), a boy is tortured by fire to get a skin.

Story includes description of how to make a foxtrap of a type made in Noatak in historic times. Tobacco was an important item in the extensive precontact trading between the inhabitants of eastern Siberia and northern Alaska. Spencer (1959:462–64) presents data on tobacco acquisition and use by north Alaskan Eskimos.

PM44. THE BOY WHO BECAME AN ARCTIC TERN

A grandmother and a grandson lived in a village with other people. One evening they stayed home. The boy went out to toilet. It was moonlight. A woman came from he knew not where and stood by him. She said, "I have come to get you for my husband." The boy said, "My grandmother always told me not to get married while I was young." Then the woman said, "Try to look down." The grandson looked down and he had left his grandmother way below already. That woman had taken him up in the air.

Since he couldn't go back he followed the woman. They came to a house and went in. The woman's parents and her three brothers were there. The woman married the boy and he started living there. He started getting cranky because he didn't hunt and wanted to. When he got real cranky he told his wife he was going out hunting. His father-in-law told him, "Don't reach those hills up there. If you do I don't think you'll come back."

When the boy went outside he could see the hills far up there. He went hunting and got caribou from the flat. When he went hunting one time he couldn't find caribou close by, so he went up into the hills. He got one caribou and started back, but he couldn't find his way home. When he couldn't find his way home it got foggy. He kept walking all day and towards evening the fog started lifting. When the fog lifted he saw his house close by. He went into the house and his father-in-law said, "So our son came home."

After a few days he went out hunting again. He couldn't find caribou close by, so he went back to the hills. He got caribou there and he started home again. While he was walking he got lost and couldn't find his way home. He looked back and saw something just like a big black rock wall coming towards him, so he started running. After awhile he looked back again and saw that it was getting closer and was beginning to close around him, so he really ran. The black rock wall started closing up until there was just enough room to run out. It looked like he might not make it out, so he put his mouth inside the shoulder of his parka and called, "Grandma, could I go home?" And she answered again, "Maybe you'll come home, grandson." He ran with all his strength and he made it through the opening. When he got out he looked back and saw nothing, no rock, just the flat. He saw his house a little ways and went over. His wife was waiting for him outside. When they went in his father-in-law said, "Our son came home again." They didn't expect him to come home after he went to the hills.

He went out hunting again and the youngest brother went along. When he heard that they were going to the ocean his father-in-law told them, "Don't get a spotted seal. If you get one you won't come home." They both had sleds and put kayaks on the sleds. They got to open water and started using their kayaks. They found a large round ice floe and the grandson said to his brother-in-law, "You go this way and I'll go that way." They parted and went around the ice floe. The grandson met a spotted seal. It started bothering him. So finally he killed it with his spear.

Suddenly he blacked out. When he recovered from being blacked out he heard a noise like somebody in pain. He was in a house and a voice said, "If you take that spear out from the wounded one maybe you'll go home." He looked around and saw a man. Then he went over to that noise like somebody in pain and found a young boy laying with a spear, with the harpoon line still attached, stuck in his back. He took the spear out and the young boy stopped suffering. The man said: "All your things are outside. Your kayak and your sled are ready to go. Go the way that your sled points and your sled will take you. You will travel through the ice. If you can't use your sled and your kayak anymore leave them and walk through the ice. If you get to open water you'll cross it some way. There will be fishes there. Don't eat from them no matter how hungry you are. After you pass you'll find some more fishes in the water. Don't eat from them either. If you pass by those you'll get to a third bunch of fishes. You can eat from those."

After the man told him all this the boy went out and saw his kayak and sled all ready. He put his sled towline over his shoulders and went. He kept going and when the ice got broken up he used his kayak, sometimes dragging it through the ice. When the ice got too big to drag the kayak he left it and started walking. He walked until he came to the open water. He didn't know how to cross it. It was so far he couldn't see the other side. He didn't know what to do and he walked around for awhile. Then he thought of his magic charm (añ-yuk) and he took it off and then pretended to put it back on again. He became a miṭkutaylyuk (arctic tern) and flew around for awhile.

He learned to fly and then went into the air and started flying over the open water. Close by he saw a lot of fishes, but he thought of what the man had said, so he passed them by. He came to some more and passed them too. He was hungry, but he didn't eat. When he got to the third fishes he ate from them and then flew across the water. He kept flying until he saw ice, where he landed and became a man. He walked until the going got slow, then he changed into a bird again. He flew until he saw a house close by. He landed and became a man.

When he got close he saw that it was his house. His wife was outside waiting and they went in. His father-in-law said, "Our son came back again." He stayed there and in a few days his brothers-in-law said, "Of all these times you have been away maybe you have a story for us, how you've hunted or where you've been, or what you did while you were away." They kept bothering him, and finally he got tired of them. He told them, "Build an aaluyuk. When you finish it fill it with water and I will tell you the story of when I was gone."

The brothers made an aaluyuk, finished it, and filled it with water. The boy said, "If I become some kind of animal in that water and you boys don't want me to stay here anymore, don't turn the plate upside down. If you still want me, turn it upside down." Then he began telling them the story about the time he shot the spotted seal. He became a mitkutaylyuk in the house and started showing how he crossed the open water. He flew around the house and the brothers watched him. He said, "That's how I flew over that open water." While he was flying he got close to the water-filled plate and suddenly flew into it. The brothers turned it over right away, but it was too late. When he went through the water he started home to his grandmother. When he got there his grandmother was dead. The house had fallen into the ground. That boy is still a mitkutaylyuk now. THE END.

Wanda Stalker told me this story.

C221.1.3 Tabu: eating fish; C610 The one forbidden place; C841 Tabu: killing certain animals; C901.1 Tabu imposed by certain person; D150 Transformation: man to bird (Greenland—Rasmussen 1921:II, 14; Rink 1875:148, 287, 327); D327.2 Transformation: seal to man (Greenland—Rink 1875:456); D350 Transformation: bird to man; D1170 Magic utensils and implements; D1392.1 Amulet saves one from death (Greenland—Rasmussen 1921:I, 187; 1921:III, 114, 211, 216; Rink 1875:168); D2135 Magic air journey (MacKenzie River—Jenness 1924:40; Greenland—Rasmussen 1921:I, 87); L111.4.1 Orphan hero lives with grandmother; N825.3.3 Help from grandmother; P253.0.3 Three brothers and one sister; R10 Abduction. Similar to Spencer 1959:436–38 (Point Barrow). Both PM23 and PM32 in this volume include a taboo against killing female seals. In Curtis 1930:235–37 (Selawik) a boy calls on his grandmother for aid.

PM45. The Two Who Became Aġruks

Some people lived down at the coast, including a grandmother and her grandson. The grandson always took his grandmother's potty out, every evening and every morning. One time in the evening he didn't come back for a long time, so the grandmother went out to look for him. Towards morning, when the aġruks [the two beams of light cast by the sun when it first reappears above the horizon in late December] came out, the grandmother looked for her grandson.

It was getting bright and she looked towards the sun and saw her grandson doing an Eskimo dance. He was real lively because he was so happy about the reappearance of the aġruks. The grandmother thought, "What should I do? Should I try to scare or surprise him?" She went over behind the boy, who was real happy, and scared him from the back. The grandson didn't know what to do. He started running and then flying towards the aġruks. Then the grandmother didn't know what to do, so she followed him, flying too. The grandson landed in the sky and became a star. The grandmother stopped below him and become a smaller star. When the aġruks come up the grandmother and grandson always move towards them and become aġruks. When the aġruks go down they go back to being stars. THE END.

Frank Burns told me this.

A761 Ascent to stars (Cumberland Sound—Boas 1901:174); D293 Transformation: man to star; D450 Transformation: object to another object; L111.4.1 Orphan hero lives with grandmother.

PM46. The Woman Who Played Football Alone

There were some people living in a village located on both sides of a river. Farther over lived a grandmother and her grandson, and on the other side of the section of the village, on their side of the river, stood a house alone. When the villagers went down to the river from the houses on both sides to play football a woman would come out of this house which stood alone and go down to the riverbank in front of it. She would play ball there alone as long as the men played football. When the men quit she would go back in the house. When the people went over to visit her house they never came out.

When the men went down to play football the grandson always came out to watch. He always saw that woman playing ball by herself while the men played football. He noticed that she always quit and went in when the men did. Once he said to his grandmother, "I wonder what kind of house that woman has." The grandmother said, "People always go over and see her if they want to, but once they go inside they never come out. You can see if you want to." The grandson went over to the woman when she was playing ball by the riverbank. When he got close the woman went into the house. He went by the door and looked around. He couldn't understand what kind of house she lived in.

He went into the stormshed and when he got there he smelled something that really stunk from inside the house. When he got to the door he saw the woman with her back turned towards him holding the ball in her hands. When he went in he tried to see her face from behind, but she'd move it to the side whenever he looked over her shoulder. He got close, but he still couldn't see her face. He got ahold of her and tried to turn her around, but she was really strong and he still couldn't see her face. Finally he could see her cheek, and by moving from side to side behind her as she turned her head he could see more and more of her face. She started getting weak. Then he could see half her face. She got weaker. Finally he saw her face and she got real weak. He looked at her and saw only one big eye with no nose between. The woman got really weak and just stood still. The grandson said, "Well, I'm going out for awhile."

He went out and started walking, but he couldn't find the way. He followed a narrow trail and he couldn't find the way out to his house, so he kept going for awhile. Finally he thought to himself, "If I can't go out I might as well turn back." He turned back and followed the narrow trail. He got to the house and started inside to the woman. When he got to the door he looked around inside the house. On the left by the corner he saw some old human bones. A little farther on were some bones with a little meat on them. On the right by the door he saw a person alive but unconscious and breathing real slowly. He said to the woman, "What are those bones to you?" She answered, "They are my grandmother's bones, all of them." Then the grandson said, "How can you live in this house? Let's go over to my grandmother and stay with her."

She didn't say anything, so they went over and went in. His grandmother said, "No matter how people look when they like each other they get together." She put the food on the floor and let them eat. That woman couldn't put the ball away; she kept it under her arm. While she was eating she forgot and dropped it. After they finished eating she said to the grandson, "You should make a place for my ball so I can put it there." The grandson made a place and she put the ball there. The grandson and the woman got together and got married. When the men of the village started playing football again the woman got her ball, went out, and played alone with it even though she was married. Every time the men went out to play football she'd go out and play with her ball. THE END.

Wanda Stalker told this.

D2089.9 Trail magically closed; F512.1.1 Person with one eye in center of forehead; F560 Unusual manner of life; G670 Occasional cannibalism, deliberate; L111.4.1 Orphan hero lives with grandmother; T10 Falling in love.

I am not sure about the function of the ball in this story, unless it represents security for a woman who apparently had no kin except a grandmother who lived beyond society.

PM47. How People Got Fire

On a river lived a man, his wife, and one son. Farther up the river is a village. The son always hears that there is a man someplace with fire (iknikkutiilik). People of the village farther upriver always went to that man with fire to get fire, but they never came home. The son thinks to himself, "I wonder how they go to get fire."

The son has an uncle in the village. His uncle had kids. The son went over to his uncle and stayed with him and tried to find out where that man with fire is. He keeps asking people where the man with fire is, but nobody can tell him because the people who went to get fire never returned. The son still keeps asking the older people where the man with fire stays, but they don't know. One time the son starts talking with a really old man, and the really old man tells him that man with fire is way over some place real far. The old man showed him the trail to reach the man with fire.

When the son found out about the trail he left in falltime along this trail. He traveled all fall and all winter. He'd stop and then go.

He traveled more in summer, and the next fall and the next winter he traveled. He'd stop and then go. And a second summer he traveled and got close to the place the old man told him about, but he couldn't see it. Three years he traveled, and after three years, in the summer, he began to recognize the place the old man told him about. He traveled that summer and came to a river and went down to the beach.

When he went down to the beach he looked around and thinks that according to what the old man told him, the man with fire is across the river. He looked around and saw big rocks in a line far apart in the river, going across the river. So the son thinks, "Maybe if I can take long steps I can make it across." After he saw the rocks he jumped from one rock to another, and this way went across.

After he went across he walked up towards a hill. On the way he saw some old bows and arrows that belonged to the men who had tried to get fire before. He kept walking up to the top of the hill. When he got on top he saw another hill far off, and in a valley between the hill where he stood and the other hill was a house. He saw a man go out from the house, so the son hid on the hill. When that man went out from the house he looked around. The son was hiding. Then the son thought to himself, "I won't get to that house if I stay a boy," so he used his amulet hanging around his neck and became a squirrel.

When he became a squirrel he went between niggerheads and while he's going he thinks to himself, "I wonder how far I've gone." So he puts his head up to look. He saw that that man had gone out from the house again and was looking around, so the squirrel put his head down again. That man went back inside the house after looking around. The squirrel got close to the house. When that man went in the squirrel started going between the niggerheads again. And then that man went out again and looked around; then he went back in again. The squirrel stopped and thought to himself, "I'm not going down to that house as a squirrel," so he used his amulet again and became a piece of duck down.

When he became a piece of duck down the wind wouldn't come right away, so he stayed where he was. Soon the wind came and blew him through the air. The wind blew him everywhere all over; pretty soon he landed in front of the house. When he landed in front of the house and the man in the house never came out, he used his amulet once more and became a boy again. That man still didn't go out, so the son waited outside for awhile. He never heard a noise, so he went up to the window and opened it. When he opened the window and looked down he saw the man sitting by the inside door facing the stormshed door. He had fire in his lap.

The boy looking down through the window wonders to himself about why his parents gave him two little dolls he has inside his parka. He takes them out and stands them up in the window. The two dolls start dancing around in the window, dancing around real lively all over. That man who was sitting with fire in his lap knows the two dolls are up there and says, "Go ahead dance, dance real lively." The son went to the door while the dolls were dancing and went in. When he went in he saw the man with fire looking up towards the window at the dolls dancing.

While the man was looking at the dolls in the window the son took the fire from his lap and ran out with it. He kept running to the hill and down the hill. When he got close to the rocks on which he had crossed he looked back and saw that man running after him. That man said, "You think you'll live? I'll kill you if I catch you." The son jumped the rocks across the river again. When the son went across he looked back and saw the man had stopped because he couldn't jump the rocks. That man said, "You share that fire with other people since I can't get it back."

The son started going home. He went home after three years, same as it had taken him to get there, and it was fall when he got home. When he reached his uncle's village he went to his uncle's house and shared the fire with him. He then went home to his parents. That's how they start having fire. That boy took the fire home. THE END.

That's how far I heard this story from John Adams, who heard it from Barrow and brought it to the Noatagmiut.

A1415 Theft of fire (Ungava—Turner 1894:340); A1415.0.2 Original fire property of one person: D117 Transformation: man to rodent; D200 Transformation: man to object; D275 Transformation: man to feather; D801 Ownership of magic object; D1268 Magic statue, doll (Bering Strait—Nelson 1899:494); H960 Tasks performed through cleverness or intelligence; H1150 Tasks: stealing, capturing, or slaying. H1220 Quest voluntarily undertaken; J151 Wisdom (knowledge) from old person; K311 Thief in disguise; K311.6 Thief takes form of animal; K341 Owner's interest distracted while goods are stolen; K832.7 Dupe induced to look about: theft accomplished; N825.2 Help from old man.

In some ways this story is similar to EH6 in this volume.

PM48. Kutliruk

A man woke up on top of a little hill. It was sunshiny. The sun was so hot that he was weak and couldn't move. Towards evening, when the sun went down and the ground got damp, he felt better. The man's leaves were dry and the evening damp made him lively. The man was kutliruk (a little plant with cotton inside the stem and flowers). The End.

I heard this story from Frank Burns.

PM49. The Cotton Grass

There was a young boy staying somewhere. One morning he went out walking. He saw a woman dressed in a pretty parka with a pretty white ruff and long black-striped mukluks. She was singing and dancing. The boy didn't try to get close; he just watched her. She sang: "These, these are my clothes / my new clothes not used before / my new clothes not used before / my clothes, aanii, aanii." When she finished her song she brought her hands from above her head down through the air. The boy looked around and when he looked back at the girl's place he didn't see her. Instead in her place he saw a niggerhead [sedge tussock]. The wind was blowing the cotton grass. The End.

Ralph Gallahorn told me this story.

I do not believe that the point of this tale lies in the possible transformation of a woman into cotton grass. Rather, on one level, the story is a comment on the tricky quality of vision under certain lighting conditions in the arctic (cf. Stefansson 1951:72–73) and, on another level, a further example of a natural world without sharp boundaries between man and beast or man and plant.

PM50. The Old Woman Fools the Rich Man's Son

There were some people somewhere, including a rich man, his wife, and their son. The son always went hunting and got lots of animals. His mother got tired of working so she brought home a girl for a daughter-in-law, but her son didn't want to get married. Two old women lived farther over in a house. One of them had some seal oil in a little bag that she kept by her bed. She took it out and rubbed the seal oil all over her face and body. She spread it all over herself. This was in winter. The old woman made herself pretty with the seal oil.

When the other old woman went to sleep in the evening this old woman went out. It was moonlight. She walked to the rich man's house. The rich man's son was out and the old woman walked close by him. The rich man's son looked up and it was the first time he had seen this woman. He kept looking at her. She got close and they met. He took her inside and they got married.

When he hunted the woman always worked for him, and all the rich man's wife had to do now was sew. That old woman worked real hard. One time when she was working she asked her husband, "Can I take those two old women a piece of meat?" He said, "Go ahead, it's yours." She took a piece of meat over and just put it in the stormshed so that the other old woman wouldn't find out about her.

Another time she asked her husband the same thing and he said, "Don't ask me, just take the meat over." She took a big piece and put it in the stormshed. That old woman couldn't make mukluks for her husband because she worked on meat too much. One time she started a pair of mukluks, but she couldn't see the eye of the needle no matter how hard she looked. Finally she finished a pair of mukluks.

One time she seemed sick and her husband asked, "What's wrong?"

She answered, "When I was with my brother I always packed too much when they got meat from way over. One time I hurt my back." Once when the man went hunting in the spring he couldn't find caribou close by. A little bird (naḵuktukruk, "black feathers on top of the head") started landing close to him. Soon it landed in front of him. It was a female bird. It took its hood off and said, "You don't know you have a wife with one of the old women. You never thought of her as one of those little old women in your village." After she told him that he started feeling sad. He put his head down and got bashful. The bird put its hood back on and flew away.

The man started home before he got caribou. When he got home he was different. He didn't want to eat and he couldn't say anything. He finally told his wife, "You should go home to your friend, that old woman. I found out you're an old woman too." He sent her away and the woman went back home to the other old woman. In the stormshed was a lot of food that she had brought. She became an old woman again. The rich man's son didn't like to marry those young girls, but he did after this. He had been fooled by that old woman. THE END.

I heard this story from Wanda Stalker.

B131 Bird of truth; B211.3 Speaking bird; B451 Helpful bird, Passeriformes; D56 Magic change in person's age; D658 Tranformation to seduce; J130 Wisdom (knowledge) acquired from animals; J1050 Attention to warnings; P150 Rich man; T311.1 Man averse to marriage.

Note that here, as in other stories, a bird or animal speaks by "taking its hood off."

PM51. MISSANIK

On King Island was a man and his kayak. When the ice started breaking up he was drifted. The ice was funny and the water too swift for him to get back. After a few days adrift he was getting skinny because he had nothing to eat. When he didn't know what to do he got down inside his kayak and lay there. He got weak. While he was inside the kayak drifting he began hitting something under him. He stuck his head out and saw land. He was on a beach. He got out and tried to put his kayak up. He kept pushing it from the back trying to put it on top of some grasses. He kept pushing, he was so weak, and finally he got it to the grasses. He lay down in the sunshine and looked around, noticing some white flowers growing there. He ran his hand through the sand and when he looked at it the sand was full of beads. They had fallen off from the flowers. This is somewhere way down south where the current is real swift.

The man fell asleep. When he woke up he heard people talking. From just beside him he heard two boys saying, "Poor thing, we should take him home. He needs help." The two boys tied him and started packing him on their backs. When one got tired the other would take over. They took him to a house and when they went in he saw a man and his wife. The two boys' mother gave him a piece of meat and a little water. They fed him a little at a time, but more every day. He got his strength back.

When he got healthy he went out hunting. The people he was staying with were real nice people who had moved off from a bad village. There were just a few people living in this place. When the man was strong enough to start hunting the old man told him, "Maybe you can try to go home now. I will show you which way to go." It was spring. The man got his kayak ready. He took two handfuls of beads with him. When he was ready to go the old man asked, "Why are you going to take those beads?" And the man answered, "They are so pretty I want to take a few home." The old man said, "People don't care about beads around here, there are so many." Then he said. "Go straight through the swift water all the way. Go all summer. After it freezes up go to people and stay there all winter, but don't get married if you reach that village. You won't go home."

The man traveled with his kayak and when winter came he got to the village that the old man told him about. He went to a house and stayed there all winter. He gave the man one bead to stay there. In the summer he went with his kayak again. After he had paddled all summer he reached King Island. This man's name was Missanik. THE END.

John Adams (Agnuruk) told me this story.

C110 Tabu: sexual intercourse; C901.1 Tabu imposed by certain person; F815 Extraordinary plants; J1050 Attention to warnings; N825.2 Help from old man; P251 Brothers. A fuller version of this tale is found in

Rasmussen 1932:121–32 (Point Hope) and Ostermann 1952:216–22 (Point Hope). The land to the south where beads are plentiful may refer to the country of the white man.

PM52. NAUUK

A man and his wife and their son, Nauuk, were living at Point Hope. At Point Hope people were cutting up a dead whale that they had found. Nauuk's mother and father went along too. His mother had real long breasts. His father had a funny kind of fingernail. The people cutting the whale got tired and went to sleep. In the early morning, while they slept, Noatagmiut came for war. They killed the Point Hope people, but Nauuk and his mother ran away while the men were fighting. They ran towards Point Hope.

Nauuk's mother looked back and saw some Noatagmiut coming after her. Nauuk had a belt made of a loon's head and neck. His mother put him down and said, "The Noatagmiut will hit you like this," and poked him with the loon bill. She put him on her back again and started running. When she saw the Noatagmiut coming closer she couldn't run. Her breasts were hitting her knees. She put them over her shoulder, but they kept falling. As the Noatagmiut started catching up to her, she put Nauuk down and he ran ahead of her.

When Nauuk looked back the Noatagmiut had caught his mother and thrown her in the air. The men waited below with their spears to kill her. Nauuk kept running and when he looked back he saw his mother in the air again. He saw a man running after him. When the Noatagmiut got close he said, "I've got no son. Let me take you home." But Nauuk was so scared he kept running. Finally he could see Point Hope a little way and the man kept following. When Nauuk got to Point Hope the people asked, "Where is your mother?" Nauuk said, "They threw her in the air and killed her on their spears." A few days later the Point Hope people went to look for the boat that had never come home. They got there and found the Noatagmiut had cut the bodies to pieces. They looked and found Nauuk's father's funny finger, so they knew he had been killed too.

Other people raised Nauuk and he got big. He thought of his mother and father who had been killed by the Noatagmiut. He let the men make him a bow and two bags of arrows. The women fixed his mukluks. He said, "I can't forget my mother and father." He took off towards Sheshalik. When he got there he stayed behind Sheshalik and watched the people at Nuvuvruk.

The people started going home in the fall. The Noatagmiut started going through Kaypisuanik [one of the Noatak delta distributaries—which flow away from the main stream]. He followed them. Every time they stopped he stopped, because he didn't want them to see him. When the Noatagmiut put up their skin tents and built a big fire, an old man and his wife with their own boat would put their tent up farther away from other people. They did this every time. One evening Nauuk went to them. When he got inside they asked, "Where did you come from?" He said, "When I was a little boy the Noatagmiut threw my mother in the air and speared her. A man ran after me and said, 'I am looking for a son.' I am looking for that man." The old man said, "I was the one who ran after you. Because we have no kids I wanted you for a son. I felt sorry for you."

In the evening the Noatagmiut men always made a fire and stayed around it while the women stayed in the tents. While Nauuk and the old man talked he told the old man and his wife that he wanted to start a war. He said, "You old people stay behind the way you are now. Put your tent up farther away." So one evening when the Noatagmiut put up their tents again Nauuk stayed with the old people. The Noatagmiut men built a big fire and Nauuk went over to them, and when he got behind them a young man stood up to warm his back. He looked tough, so Nauuk took an arrow and shot him in the chest.

Then Nauuk kept jumping through the fire and landing on the other side, killing the men as they tried to run away. He killed all the men. Then he went to the women in the tents and started hitting them. The women were so excited they got in the boats and started paddling on the land. They thought they were on the water. He killed all the women and children so there was nobody left but the two old people.

Nauuk went back to them and took them upriver to their wintering place. He stayed with them for awhile and hunted. He brought them a lot of caribou. The old woman dried them up. When winter came he told them he was going home. He said, "If you happen to go to Sheshalik again and put up your tent, I'll be back. Dry up a round ugruk bladder and hang it by your door so that I will know your tent." Then Nauuk went back to Point Hope.

Summertime came and the Point Hope boat went to Sheshalik. Nauuk was bringing some muktuk to the old people. When they landed at Nuvuvruk he looked for their tent. Finding it apart from the other people, he went in and gave them some muktuk. THE END.

Edna Hunnicutt told me this story.

F546 Remarkable breast; F552.1.3 Extraordinary fingernails (Greenland—Holm 1912:87; Rasmussen 1921:III, 79); F660 Person of remarkable skill; H79 Recognition by physical attributes; H80 Identification by tokens; L111.4 Orphan hero; N825.2 Help from old man; P233.6 Son avenges father; Q40 Kindness rewarded; Q411.6 Death as punishment for murder.

The action in this story is emphasized by two graphic literary touches: hitting Nauuk with the loon's bill to represent the pain of spears and the fear of the women that made them try to paddle on land.

PM53. The Grandson Who Killed Men-who-always-killed-people

(This is the same story that Edna told but longer.)

A grandmother and her grandson were living between Uḳaliḳsuk and Siiuksiinaichik. They were living on flounders and ptarmigan. When the boy got big he and his grandmother would take walks. She'd get a heavy stick and put it on his back and let him take it home. Every day she walked with him and let him carry a heavy stick home. This way he became strong.

Once the grandson asked his grandmother, "What are those things in the willows that always move?" She answered, "Caribou." He then asked, "How do they always hunt them?" And she answered, "With bows and arrows." The boy got bigger and started hunting caribou. The first time he hunted he got one caribou and brought it home to his grandmother. After that they always had caribou meat. He'd cut them up and take them home and his grandmother would dry them. After awhile he started carrying whole caribou home. They built iḳiguts for the meat and didn't have to eat flounders anymore.

Once the boy asked his grandmother, "Are we staying alone, Grandmother? Are there no people close by?" She told him that there were people in Uḳaliḳsuk and said: "When that man-who-always-killed-people killed your father I took you away. Your uncle lives down there. He has three boys and a girl. They live in a place under a mountain on a flat, and across the river lives the man-who-always-kills-people and the other people." After he heard that the grandson couldn't stay away. He wanted to see his uncle and the man-who-always-killed-people.

He went and took his grandmother with him. When his grandmother got tired they would stop for the night. The boy would get a caribou, they would eat, and then go to sleep. It was summer and they were walking. Finally they reached Uḳaliḳsuk. His grandmother showed him where his uncle's house was and they went down.

When they went in the people recognized his grandmother. The three boys found out about their cousin. They stayed overnight, but the grandmother couldn't stand kids around, so the next day they built a little house. After a few days the grandson wanted to go hunting because he had always hunted. He took his youngest cousin, and when they saw caribou he said to him, "You wait here. I'll go down to those caribou." The grandson went down and his cousin kept watching him. Then he could not see him and the caribou started falling. Pretty soon all the caribou were down from the place where they had been standing and the grandson stood up.

They went home and a man came to them and asked, "Did you get caribou today?" The grandson answered, "Of course I got caribou today." Then the man said, "How come you talk rough like that to me?" He went off and pretty soon someone came and said, "That man-who-always-kills-people wants you." The grandson answered, "I'll be up there in awhile."

His four cousins wanted to help him. The girl wanted to help the most. She got her ulu, sharpened it, and hid it in her sleeve. They went up to the karigi and the grandson said to his cousins, "If he is tough and I can't fight him, you guys will help me, but maybe I won't need help." They went into the karigi and the grandson looked around. He saw the man-who-always-kills-people, who was tough looking. He and his cousins sat down. The man-who-always-kills-people said, "You shouldn't talk rough to me. I wouldn't have sent people after you."

The grandson started talking rough again, trying to make him mad. The grandson thought of his father, that the man-who-always-kills-people had killed him. The man-who-always-kills-people got up from his seat. As he did the grandson looked around and saw a sharp, blood-covered bone on the floor. The grandson got up, too, and they met in the middle of the floor. The grandson got ahold of the man who-always-kills-people by the shoulders and pulled him up and down. Finally the man-who-always-kills-people's bones started cracking. Then the grandson put him on the floor; his bones were broken. The grandson said to him: "I heard you killed my father. I'd kill you, but I want to break your bones again. Heal up and I'll come back and break your bones again. You've been treating people rough so you'll pay for it."

The grandson and his cousins went home. A few days later the grandson asked a man, "How's the man-who-always-kills-people?" And the man answered, "He is better. He'll live." The grandson hunted again with his young cousin. After they got caribou they went home. He asked a man again, "How's the man-who-always-kills-people?" And the man answered, "He can go out now." When the grandson heard about that he went across and shook the man-who-always-killed-people again, breaking his bones. He said, "Try to heal up. You killed my father like that. If I hear you've healed up I'll come do it again." After that the grandson went out hunting. In a few weeks he asked how the man-who-always-killed-people was and he heard he could walk, so he went up and broke his bones again. This time the man-who-always-killed-people died from his broken bones.

After they buried the man-who-always-killed-people they lived there without anybody bothering them. After awhile the grandson decided to take a walk to find people. His youngest cousin went with him. They started walking. They would stop for a night and then walk again. In the spring when the brown bears go out they saw four brown bears. The grandson told his cousin to stay where he was for awhile while he went down. The brown bears saw the grandson and ran towards him. The cousin watched him walking along, and then suddenly he couldn't see him anymore. The brown bears couldn't see him either, so they walked away. The grandson got up and his cousin went down to him and asked, "Where have you been hiding? What did you do?" The grandson answered: "You see this small lake here? I jumped in there when they were coming after me. That's why they never saw me. I became a nunukruk̠ (a small bug that swims real fast on the surface of the water)."

They went on and reached a village with people. They went into the first house and saw a girl, her brother, and her parents. The man said, "I'm sorry to see you come because we have a man-who-always-kills-people here." While they were talking someone called and wanted them in the karigi. They all went up and the grandson saw an old man sitting by the door with his head down. The man-who-always-killed-people was talking. The grandson got up, went over to him, and shook him like he had done to that other man-who-always-killed-people. He broke his bones and left him on the floor. He told the people in the karigi, "If you guys have something on your mind, or this man has killed your friends, come down and hit him while his bones are broken." All of them went down and started poking the man-who-always-killed-people. When they left him he was dead. After they had gone back to their places the old man stood up and said: "You should have come earlier. A few days ago that man killed my son. When strangers came he would take one boy from this village and kill him too. That's how that man-who-always-killed-people was to everybody." They buried the man-who-always-killed-people and the grandson and his cousin went back to the first house they had come to. They stayed overnight and then left.

They walked to another village where the whole thing happened over again and the grandson killed the man-who-always-killed-people. Then they went to another village where the man-who-always-killed-people always swam a race with strangers in the river. He challenged the grandson. They started running, and when they got to the water the grandson started swimming with the man-who-always-killed-people behind him. The grandson became that bug again and swam across. The man-who-always-killed-people couldn't see him, so he kept swimming. There was a long log on the edge of the other shore. The bug went up on the shore and then became the grandson again. He grabbed the man-who-always-killed-people and hit him on the log where that man-who-always-killed-people used to kill strangers. That's how he killed the fourth man-who-always-killed-people.

From there he and his cousin turned back towards home. They had gone as far as Sakvaaluk. The grandson said that if he had heard Kotzebue had a man-who-always-killed-people he would have gone there, but Kotzebue had none so he turned back and went home. When they got home he got his cousin a wife from the second village they had gone to and he got one from the first village. They used to visit back and forth. THE END.

Frank Burns told me this.

D180 Transformation: man to insect; H1562 Test of strength; J652.4 Warnings against certain people; K1626 Would-be killers killed; L111. 4.1 Orphan hero lives with grandmother; P233.6 Son avenges father; P253.0.2 Three brothers and one sister; P293 Uncle; Q211 Murder punished (Cumberland Sound—Boas 1901:168; Greenland—Rasmussen 1921:III, 76, 111, 294); Q411.6 Death as punishment for murder; Q450.1.1 Torture as punishment for murder; S118 Murder by cutting. Similar to EH3 and EH7 in this volume.

PM54. THE MULGI

A grandmother and her grandson lived at a place with a lake close by. When the boy was old enough to stay out by himself his grandmother got sick and died. The boy was lonesome, so he walked out towards the lake. When he got close he saw a mulgi (loon) on the water. When he got to the shore the mulgi came towards him. He watched it. When it got close it dived. He looked for it but it never came up. He watched for a long time, but he never saw it again. Maybe that mulgi was his grandmother. THE END.

I heard this from Frank Burns.

D150 Transformation: man to bird (Greenland–Rasmussen 1921:II, 14; Rink 1875:148, 287, 327); L111.4.1 Orphan hero lives with grandmother.

Motif D150 may not actually apply.

PM55. THE BIG-MOUTH PEOPLE

There were people at the coast. They always hunted on the ice. Farther over there was a house where some people lived who always worked outdoors, but never went over to visit other people. The people from the village always came over to visit, but they couldn't see these other people because they went in before the visitors came close. When the people went out to hunt on the open water the people from the house alone would go out and hunt too. The villagers would come over to see them, but they would go farther over so that they couldn't be seen. These people were quiet people. They weren't mean and didn't fight. They just didn't like to see people.

When the villagers were in the karigi they started talking. They thought that they should invite the strange people to the karigi. Two men went over to get them. They went through the stormshed and in the door. The people in the house lay facing the wall because they didn't want the men to see their faces. The two men said, "We have come to invite you to the karigi." The father of the house said, "We'll come up to the karigi." The two men went back to the karigi. The people started playing their drums. They played them real fast and loud. Pretty soon they stopped the drums and they heard somebody outside. They started the drums again even faster.

A man and his wife came in wearing pretty clothes, fancy parkas with big wolf ruffs. The two started dancing. When the man got to one end of the floor he said, "Akahha, you people that invited us, you must be surprised to see us." He went back to the other end of the floor and said the same thing. These two people had big mouths reaching as far as their ears. After they danced their kids came through the door and started dancing with them. When they quit the villagers put out food and everybody started eating. The big-mouthed people ate with them. The father said, "We were always bashful because of our big mouths. We didn't like to stay with people. From now on we will stay with you." Since that time that they met those villagers, the big-mouth people stayed with them and met them in the karigi. The big-mouthed people were quiet people. They were wolves. THE END.

Putumie Norton (James Norton's father) told this story to me.

D313.2 Transformation: wolf to man (MacKenzie River—Jenness 1924: 74); F544.0.1.1 Remarkably large mouth.
    Note the physical and social isolation of those who feel (with reason) they differ from the norm.

PM56. THE BLIND BOY AND THE MULGI

A woman and her son lived at Sealing Point. The boy always hunted and brought home lots of things. His mother always worked hard when he came home. She got tired of working. She started cooking for her son before he came home. She cooked her pee with some meat in it. When her son came home she set the food in front of him and he started eating. He smelled the food, but he ate it anyway. His eyes started getting blurry; then he couldn't see anymore.

All winter he couldn't see. One day during the winter a polar bear came to their window, put his arm inside, and started searching for people. The son said, "Give me my bow and arrow." His mother brought it and aimed it for him. She aimed it under the polar bear's arm. When the boy shot he heard a noise and knew he had hit the polar bear. His mother said, "You didn't hit it. You hit the window frame. That polar bear got away." His mother went out and saw the polar bear dead. She didn't tell her son, but cut it up and put it away. When she cooked it her son could always smell the good food, but she never fed him. She ate it alone.

In the springtime after the boy got the polar bear he got tired of staying home and started walking toward Napuksuk [a tower made of four poles for looking out at the ocean]. He knew the trail so he walked along. When he turned back he walked away from the ocean through the first beach towards a little lake. When he got close he started to hear a mulgi. He stopped, leaned on his stick, and listened.

He understood the mulgi to say, "Come on, ahhh, come on." It stopped and he thought to himself, "Maybe it wants me to come up," so he started walking towards the mulgi. He got to the lake and stood close to the water. The mulgi came up and said, "If I could help you to see I would. Get on my back." The man got on his back and the mulgi dived in the water with him. They stayed down for a long time.

When the man had a hard time breathing it brought him up. The mulgi told the man to open his eyes and the man did, but he couldn't see. The mulgi took the man down a second time. When the mulgi came up it asked, "How are your eyes?" And the man answered, "A little blurry, but I can see light." They dived again and when they came up the man could see, but not clearly. When they had gone under and come up a fourth time the mulgi asked, "How are your eyes?" The man opened them, looked, and they were good. He looked around to the places that he used to go. He could see.

The mulgi told him, "Your mother made you so that you couldn't see. She cooked and put her pee in the food. After you ate it you couldn't see." When the man went home he was mad. He hit his mother and killed her. THE END.

Carl Stalker used to tell this story.

B211.3 Speaking bird; B450 Helpful birds; B516 Sight restored by animal (Central—Boas 1888:626; Cumberland Sound—Boas 1901:169; Smith Sound—Kroeber 1899:169; Greenland—Holm 1912:31; Rasmussen 1921:I, 312; 1921:III, 203; Rink 1875:100); D2060 Death or bodily injury by magic; F952 Blindness miraculously cured; K333.1 The deceived blind man; K2210 Treacherous relatives; Q210 Crimes punished; Q261 Treachery punished (MacKenzie River—Jenness 1924:87; West Hudson Bay—Boas 1907:551f.); Q411 Death as punishment; S12.1 Cruel mother blinds son (Greenland—Holm 1912:31; Rasmussen 1921:I,

312; 1921:III, 201; Rink 1875:99). Similar to Keithahn 1958:76–79 (Seward Peninsula), Lucier 1958:96–98 (Noatak), and to several versions current at Point Barrow (Spencer 1959:396–97; Spencer and Carter 1954).

PM57. The Jade House

There were people living on the Kobuk River between Kiana and Noorvik. A young rich man and his wife lived there. They had their first baby, a boy. In a year or so the wife got pregnant again and died in labor. The rich man took all the household things to the grave so that the house was empty except for the little boy. When the man had taken everything up to the grave he went up and lay by his wife's side. He stayed there, got skinny, and died.

The little boy stayed in the house with no bedding or food. The other people of the village didn't want to go in and help him. He cried all the time. All winter the boy stayed in that house, hungry and with no bedding. After awhile he started going out and eating the crumbs left after the other people had eaten. All spring he ate other people's leavings. In summertime when they started fishing he went to people and ate from where they cut fish. He got stronger when it was warm.

In the falltime he still had no place to stay. He heard about people in Tuklumaruk, below Noorvik. He went to them, but they wouldn't let him stay with them. He found a place under a tree and stayed there. In the evenings he would cry.

One evening he sat with his head down, lonesome, cold, and hungry. Finally he lifted his head and looked out. Straight ahead of him he saw a house he hadn't seen before. He went over. When he got close a boy about his same age came out. The boy had no arm on one side. He said, "Let's go in," and took the boy in to his parents. He saw a lot of food. He looked around and saw the other boy's clothing hanging there, parkas with no arm on one side. The man of the house said: "We know that you have been suffering and having a hard time. This boy with no arm is your young brother, the one that killed your mother. If you eat things from here you are going to become invisible like us, but if you go from here and walk farther down you will find your grandmother and cousin. They are at Ahsiraanik (a mountain above Noorvik towards the Selawik side). If you go down there a boy will run towards you."

The boy went out from there and followed the trail that the man had told him about. When he got to the trees a boy came running to meet him. He was a small boy like him and when the boy got close he said, "Let's go live with my grandmother up there." They went into the house. He started eating. When he found out that he and the boy were cousins he stayed with them.

When the boys got big the grandmother said, "You boys should build a better house. You should build a jade house." She ate all day, just kept eating. They slept and in the morning she got them ready to go. She said, "Got get some jade so that you can make your house. When you get on the sled and go, don't open your eyes until you land." They went, using her jaws for a sled. They got on the jaw sled, closed their eyes, and left.

When they landed they opened their eyes and found they were on Jade Mountain [north of the Kobuk River]. They loaded up their sled, closed their eyes, and ended up at home. They went back to Jade Mountain again. While they were loading their sled this time the jade man found out that they were there. They got in the sled and went home, never going back. They made a jade house. When the grandmother got old she died. Before she died she said, "If you plan to leave the house break it down because people might fight over it." The boys lived there awhile and then decided to move downriver. They broke up the house and went downriver where they built a new house. This one was not of jade. The End.

I heard this story from Daniel Walton.

D992.4.1 Magic jaw; D1520 Magic object affords miraculous transportation; D2121.2 Magic journey with eyes closed (Bering Strait—Nelson 1899:511; MacKenzie River—Jenness 1924:52; Central—Boas 1888:629; Smith Sound—Kroeber 1899:171; Greenland—Rasmussen 1921:II, 14; 1921:III, 103, 124, 257; Rink 1875:147, 196, 219); E421.1 Invisible ghosts; F516 Person unusual as to his arms; F770 Extraordinary buildings and furnishings; F1041.1.2 Death from grief for death of lover or relative; L111.4 Orphan hero; P295 Cousins; T211.9.2.1 Grieving man goes to die where his wife's corpse lies; T580 Childbirth. The jade house also appears in Lucier 1958:111–15 (Noatak) and Giddings 1961:108–10 (Kobuk River).

The distribution of this tale is not surprising since the only known source of jade in northern Alaska lies on the northern edge of the middle Kobuk Valley.

PM58. THE PITMIK

There were people at Cape Prince of Wales. Among them was a grandmother and her grandson. The grandson was old enough to hunt. He always saw men go out hunting and bringing different kinds of animals home, including foxes. He asked his grandmother, "How do they get white and red foxes?" His grandmother said, "They always make a pit deep enough for a fox to fall in so that it can't climb out. If you are going to make one don't put it where there is a trail where people might step. Put it farther away."

The grandson made a trap and every time he went to see it he got wolves. After he got ten his grandmother wanted him to make his trap a little differently. He changed it and got another kind of animal than wolves. Every time he fixed it a little differently he caught a different kind of animal. Finally he caught all the different kinds of animals that walk. When he got enough he made an ikigut and put the animals on top. He moved his trap down to the ocean and started getting all kinds of sea animals. He brought them up to the ikigut.

The last time he went to see the trap he saw a pair of legs with black-and-white mukluks sticking out of it. He saw that it was a girl. He took her out of the trap and took her home. He waited until she got healthy and then married her. The grandson became a rich man from his catch. When he got to be middle-aged he died. That kind of trap is called a pitmik. That trap is like that. It lets people get rich and then they die when they get middle-aged. Another man took that grandson's place and married the woman. He hunted with the trap and got rich. When he was middle-aged he died. Another man married that woman and the same thing happened. THE END.

Jack Henry told this.

D801 Ownership of magic object; D1170 Magic utensils and implements (trap); D1417 Magic object imprisons persons; J151 Wisdom (knowledge) acquired from old person; K730 Victim trapped; L111.4.1 Orphan hero lives with grandmother; N440 Valuable secrets learned;

N825.3.3 Help from grandmother; P150 Rich man; Q272 Avarice punished. A similar trap appears in PM144 in this volume.

Paul only laughed when I asked why the grandson didn't catch ten girls! He could not explain exactly how the trap worked in the ocean. The story points out the dangers of unusual success, especially when magical means apparently were employed. That skill be rewarded was acceptable in Noatak Eskimo society, but too great a reward (or too easy an accomplishment) set an individual apart and engendered jealousy. Thus one should be a good hunter by following all the societal rules, but not a great hunter by using magic.

PM59. THE RAVEN

A man lived alone by a river right under the edge of a low hill. Farther down the river also under the edge of a hill was a village, and upriver from the man was another. It took him a whole day to walk up there. A rich man with his daughter lived in the upriver village. She didn't want to get married. Men came from different villages to marry her, but she turned them all down.

The man who was living alone saw people would go right to other houses and talk to the people inside. He liked to talk, but there was nobody to talk to. He started thinking to himself and finally picked up some willow leaves and some grasses from outside his place. He started working them and made a headband. He picked a couple more leaves, thought again, thinking that what he believed might come true, and he pretended that those two leaves were spring caribou skins for blankets. He thought again and made a leaf into a wolverine shape. He pretended that it was real good wolverine skin and when he finished it he hung it up on the wall. He made real fancy mukluks with wolverine tops with leaves, and when he finished them he hung them up too. He also made a parka out of leaves. He worked all night making wolf skins and everything else he could think of.

Finally he got sleepy, went to bed, and slept a little. He woke early in the morning and looked at the things he had hung up. They were exactly the things he had thought of, including a new parka, a beaded headband, and so forth. He put his new clothes on and went up to the village where the rich man's daughter lived. Just before it got dark he saw the village. He waited for dark.

He knew where the rich man's house was and went there. As he stood in front of the stormshed he saw a woman come out. She looked at him and went back in. She came back out right away. The man had brought the wolverine skin along with him. The woman invited him to go into the house. When he got in he took out the wolverine skin in front of the rich man and took off his beaded headband. When he put the wolverine skin and the beaded headband in front of the rich man, the rich man looked at them and told his daughter, "You better give him something to eat. Other people don't bring up good skins and things."

Finally the man got married to the rich man's daughter. He lived with them for a little while, perhaps one or two weeks. While they were staying with the rich man's family he told his wife, "I have a place down the river." He told her that he was going to take her there. They started walking and it took them all day to walk down. Finally the man stopped and told his wife, "There's my house down there." She tried to see the house but she couldn't. She could only see a little hump where the man pointed.

They walked to the house. They went through the door and slid down into the stormshed. They went inside and the woman saw nothing in the house. She thought to herself, "This is no place to live." There was nothing in the house and it was all dirty. They had some fish ḳuk to eat, and then the woman took the man's two spring skins, wrapped them around herself, and went to sleep. When she woke up she knew that the man had worked all night, that he'd never gone to sleep. She looked around and saw all kinds of things inside the house, including wolf skins, wolverine skins, and all kinds of food. The floor in the house was clean and she felt happy. They lived there all their lives. They stayed rich and never went hungry. That man was a tulugak, a raven. THE END.

I heard this from Frank Burns.

B652 Marriage to bird in human form; D350 Transformation: bird to man; D2105.3 Rubbish magically becomes food and clothing; P150 Rich man; T311 Woman averse to marriage.

PM60. THE WOLF MAN

A rich man and his daughter lived in a village somewhere. She didn't like to get married. Finally she went out someplace. While she was walking, a long ways from home, she saw a single house with a long pole outside in front. She went in. There was nobody there, but there was some food. When she looked around she saw no woman's clothes, no woman's things.

She stayed for awhile and she heard somebody coming. A young man came in wearing a squirrel parka with a good wolf ruff. He looked like a rich young man. He asked, "Did you have something to eat?" She answered, "No," and he said, "Let's have something to eat." He was a kind young man. He said, "I'm glad I'll have some company with me. I am always alone." After they ate he let her stay with him, and finally asked her to be his wife.

They lived together for awhile. The man liked to go out hunting and he went every day. When he left he would tell his wife, "Have something to eat any time you want. Don't do any hard work. Just eat." She started getting fat. The man hunted every day and when he got home he would look at his wife. He knew she was getting fat.

Once when she was home alone she went outside to look and she saw a raven right on top of the pole. After that it always stayed there. When her husband left again she went out and saw the raven on the pole. It started talking to her saying, "Maybe sometime your husband will eat you. Maybe tomorrow or sometime soon. If he goes hunting tomorrow you climb up the pole." The next morning when her husband left the woman waited, and just before it got dark she climbed up the pole. She stayed up there.

Her husband came home and went into the house. He saw nobody there, so he came out and looked around. He went by the pole looking around for his wife, but he never tried to look up. He couldn't find her. She stayed on the pole while the young man went back and forth looking for her. Finally he went into the house and shortly a wolf came out, snarling and looking around. Finally the wolf left, going straight away. She watched for awhile and then came down and started going back to her village. When she got home to her parents she got a husband in no time. THE END.

Jack Henry told this story.

B211.3.6 Speaking raven; B451.5 Helpful raven; B651 Marriage to beast in human form; D113.1 Transformation: man to wolf; J130 Wisdom (knowledge) acquired from animals; J1050 Attention to warnings;

K640 Escape with help of confederate; P150 Rich man; R227.1 Wife flees animal husband; T311 Woman averse to marriage. In PM66 in this volume a boy is fattened for eating.

PM61. The Bird That Killed

There were people living in a village at the coast, including a man and his wife. When they had a child it was always a boy. When the boy got old enough to hunt he would go out in his kayak and never come back. This always happened. It happened to two or three boys. Then they had another boy. When he was old enough to hunt he always saw bows and arrows hanging in the house. His father never used them and finally the boy asked him, "Who do all those bows and arrows belong to?" The father answered, "Your brothers. When they went out to hunt in their kayaks they never came back." The boy started hunting on the land and finally he wanted to go out in a kayak. One day he went out. At first he paddled right along the beach, then he went straight out to sea. He went way out and finally saw a rock bluff in the water. He got close and looked, but there was no place to land. He went all around it and found no place to land.

He heard a bird on top of the bluff. It came down and landed on the bow of his kayak. The bird looked at him, then flew to him and landed in his mouth. The boy tried to breathe, but he couldn't. Finally he tried to get something out of his stomach. He had medicine with some kind of leaves from the ground in his stomach. He tried to spit and finally spit the bird and all out. The bird landed upside down on the water, dead. After he killed it he picked it up and started home. When he got there he took the bird to his parents and told his father, "Maybe this bird killed all my brothers out there. When I got to the bluff down there the bird came down, stuck in my mouth, and gave me a bad time. It almost crippled my lips, see how they are." The boy wouldn't have come home if he hadn't had that medicine. The father took the bird and started beating it until he smashed it to pieces. The boy's lips got worse and after awhile he died. If his father hadn't got mad at the bird maybe the boy would have lived. The End.

I have forgotten from whom I heard this, but perhaps from Charles Stalker (Kutrun).

B16.3 Devastating birds; D2089.3 Animals magically stricken dead; H1161.1 Task: killing murderous bird; J552 Intemperate pugnacity.

Apparently this story is a warning against excessive anger and aggression, no matter the provocation.

PM62. The Kikvik

There were quite a few people living in a village on a river, including a grandmother and her grandson. There was also a rich man who was always interested in Eskimo stories. The rich man had people come to the karigi and told them to tell stories. Everybody came, and when someone had no story to tell the rich man always told him to go out. Every night they went to the karigi and told stories. The grandson always went too. When it was his turn he had no story, and so he had to go out.

One night the grandson went to the karigi again and had to leave. He asked his grandmother if she had no stories. He liked to listen to those stories and didn't want to leave. His grandmother said she had none. The next day the grandson went up to the karigi again to hear stories. He had to leave again, so he asked his grandmother again if she had no stories, and she replied that she had none. He said, "I know that rich man will make me go out again if I have no stories. I like to listen." This happened a third time.

Finally his grandmother told him, "Follow the river and you'll find your uncle up there. Maybe he will give you some stories." She showed him the trail saying, "Follow the river and you will see a trail going up inside the trees. After you pass the trees you will see a low hill and on the end is your uncle's place."

After his grandmother showed him the way the boy left and followed the river. He found the trail through the trees, and after he passed them saw a low hill. He went to the end and found the place where his uncle lived. There was a hole in the hill, which was the door to the house. There was nobody outside, so he opened the door and went in. His uncle was sitting in there. The boy stopped by the door and his uncle asked, "What can I do for you?" The grandson said, "My grandmother told me to come over here and get some stories." His uncle said, "Come over here; I'll tell you some stories."

By the uncle was a piece of wood like the one the women used to cut mukluks on (kikvik). The uncle said, "Kneel down close to the kikvik and I'll do the same thing on the other side. Start looking down and I'll do the same." They both knelt down and the grandson looked at the kikvik. He saw a village right there in the kikvik. From a house a man came out and went into the willows. The man saw a rabbit and got it. He went to the house, opened the door, and threw the rabbit in. Just then the grandson heard something right by him. He heard something drop. He looked back and saw a rabbit someone had thrown in.

He looked at the kikvik again and saw a man from another house go out and hunt. The man killed a caribou, took the hindquarter off, and started home. When he reached home he opened the door and threw the hindquarter in. The grandson heard something by him, looked, and there was the caribou meat. His uncle said, "That's all there is. Here. I'll give you this kikvik. If you get back to your grandmother you try it and see how it works."

The grandson got home and told his grandmother, "Let's try the kikvik my uncle gave me for my story." They knelt down with the kikvik between them and started looking at it. The same thing happened; they got a rabbit and some caribou meat. He and his grandmother started to use the kikvik for stories. They didn't go to the karigi anymore but looked at the kikvik instead. Finally everybody heard about it, heard that they had something in their house. The grandson didn't tell people about it, but they heard anyway. They asked the grandson to take the kikvik to other houses and the same things happened there. When they needed some kind of animal they would use the kikvik and have it in the house.

Finally the rich man heard about the kikvik. He asked the grandson to go to the karigi and listen to some stories. The grandson took the kikvik and sat down with the people. The rich man said, "Come on, ilaypuruk (poor boy), tell some stories." The grandson said, "I'm not going to tell stories while you stay over there. Come over here and I'll tell you some stories." He set the kikvik between them. He and the rich man looked and the same thing happened. The rabbit and the caribou quarter dropped by the rich man. Then the grandson said, "That's all my stories," and took the kikvik home. The grandson started using the kikvik after that. When he wanted something he would think of it and it would come. They started getting rich. They filled their caches and their house. They had so much they had no place to put things. When the grandson got rich he married the rich man's daughter. THE END.

Frank Glover told me this story.

D801 Ownership of magic object; D1170 Magic utensils and implements; D1472 Food and drink from magic object; H1220 Quest voluntarily undertaken; L111.4.1 Orphan hero lives with grandmother; N820 Human helpers; P150 Rich man; P293 Uncle.

When the grandson had no stories to tell he was unable to take part in the social activities of the *karigi*, and therefore had to leave.

PM63. A KING ISLAND MAN TELLS THE TRUTH

(I have forgotten some of the beginning of this story.)

This story took place in King Island. After the men came home from hunting with kayaks and by walking they would tell stories of what they did. One man told what he did while he was hunting. He had gone alone, and when he told his story the other men didn't believe him. Every time he hunted and then returned he'd try to tell stories, but the other men wouldn't believe him.

One time he went out in his kayak thinking that he might see some walrus. He paddled for awhile and finally he saw something floating out there. He thought it might be a dead walrus or something. When he saw it, it was lying on top of the water. When he got somewhat closer the animal looked up and he saw that it had long ears. Then it lay back in the water again. He started paddling his kayak backwards because he didn't recognize the animal. Then he thought that if he went back to King Island the men in the karigi wouldn't believe him if he told what he saw. He started towards it again. He got close and again the animal looked up. It saw the man in the kayak and stood up right on top of the water. It started walking towards the man, then it started running towards him, faster and faster.

When it got real close he took his walrus spear with the attached buoy and speared it. He tipped over his kayak on purpose. The man felt the animal hit his kayak, then he couldn't hear it anymore. He turned his kayak right side up with his paddle. The animal had dived and he saw his buoy not too far away. Then the animal came up, looked around, and saw the man again. It got up on top of the water and started running after him. He took his killing spear (tukpuk), poked it in the neck, and turned his kayak over again. He felt the animal touch his kayak again. When he came up with his paddle he saw the buoy closer than the last time. He started following it, and when the animal came up it was weak.

The animal stopped, and so did the man because he didn't want to get close. The animal stopped moving and the man thought, "Maybe I killed him." It was dead. After he killed the animal he decided to take it home because he knew the men wouldn't believe him if he left it. When he got to the place where they used to leave their kayaks he tried to pull the animal up, but it was too heavy. He could just move the head. Finally he took the head off and set it up on top of a big rock. The animal had real long sharp teeth, just like a shark's. The man went up to the karigi and started telling his story. Everyone saw the head, so from now on they believed him when he told about his hunting trips. The End.

I have forgotten, but maybe Charles Stalker told me this story.

G308 Sea Monster.

PM64. The Trading Partners

(I have forgotten the beginning and the end of this story.)
There was a family living down at the coast. The family included an old couple and their kids, who had children. One son had a partner somewhere inland far enough away, so that it took a day to walk up there. The son and his partner traded all the time. The inland man brought the son animals, and the son took the inland man seals and other coastal animals. One time the son told his partner, "I want to have all kinds of fur animals. Lay the skins on the ground clear from your house to mine." The inland man started hunting for fur animals. He skinned and dried them. Finally he thought that he had enough to reach the coast. He tried one day, laying the skins down end to end, and reached his partner's house. His partner got all those furs for himself.

Then the son asked the inland man, "What do you want?" His partner thought for awhile and finally said, "I want lots of beads. Lay them on the ground clear up to my place." The coastal man thought for quite awhile. He didn't know where to find that many beads. Finally he started looking. He went here and there, but he couldn't find many. He kept looking all summer and finally it got to be fall. He thought that he couldn't find enough beads, so he got sad and quit looking.

One day he went to the beach to the point where the high waves washed up, dug out a sitting place, and sat down there. He was sad and he didn't eat or drink. He thought that he would sit there until he died. His wife came to see him and sometimes his parents came too, to try to help him, but he didn't eat or drink and finally he started getting skinny.

One night he was sitting there. He was real weak and couldn't even hardly move. He was looking out to sea in the darkness. He saw something like lightning way out at sea. His wife wasn't looking after him anymore. He noticed that the lightning was getting closer as he watched. Finally he knew that it was a boat coming straight towards him. It hit the beach right in front of him. People came to him and asked, "Why are you sitting here?" He told the story of how his partner wanted beads and he couldn't find enough. The people said, "We have brought you some beads in the boat." They unloaded the boat. It was almost full of all kinds of beads. Then the people went back out to sea.

When his family woke up the next morning they went down to look at him to see if he was still alive. He said, "I would like a little water and a little food." He was thin and weak. After a few days he got his strength back and could sit a little straighter. They fed him until he got strong. He took the beads to his house. One day he tried to see if there were enough beads to reach his partner, and there were. His partner gathered the beads and took them home. THE END.

Ralph Gallahorn (Aŋnuyak) used to tell this story.

F1041.1.13 Death (illness) from shame; H900 Tasks imposed; H920 Assigners of tasks; N820 Human helpers. PM35 in this volume also involves two individuals fulfilling each other's request.

PM65. PAALUK AND THE FEAST

There was a village at Tuklumaruk, a place six or seven miles above Selawik. A grandmother and her grandson lived there. The villagers had a karigi. In the fall, after freezeup, when the ice got good and solid, they decided to have a kivauk (feast) with some people from Kotzebue. The grandson was getting big. Two strangers (also called "kivauks") came and everybody went up to the karigi to listen to what they had to say. The two strangers had counting sticks (aiyupak) with signs giving a message from a partner in their village to his Tuklumaruk partner. The grandson went up to the karigi too, and they listened to the strangers. The first kivauk said that a Kotzebue man (he gives the name) says such and such to a Tuklumaruk man. Then the second kivauk repeated the messages, and when he was almost done he said, "That grandson should go down to our village. He is invited. Somebody sends for him." After the kivauks gave the messages everybody went home, and the grandson told his grandmother, "I was one who was called down."

People started getting ready. They went to the karigi every night and made plans. One night after they went out a young man came over to the grandson and said, "Lucky, I'm going to have mittens. Luckier than you ilaypuruk." The grandson didn't say anything. The next day they all went up to the karigi again to get ready. The young man said to the grandson, "Lucky, I'm going to have a kaichik, luckier than you." The grandson did not say anything.

One day while they were getting ready the grandson went home and told his grandmother, "We're going to leave tomorrow morning." The grandmother told him: "You had a father before and he had two dogs. I'll show you the trail and you go upriver. When you see a sandbar go to the edge of it and you'll see the same trail going through some willows. Pass them and you'll find a low hill with gravel at the base. If you think that's the place, start calling. After you call, start going back along the same trail. Run as fast as you can. Try to get to the river. As soon as you jump on the ice your dogs will stop right on the edge of the river. They won't bother you after that. Go back up and get them ready to go. They will have harnesses and a sled. Bring them home."

The grandson went up the trail as she had shown him and got to the place. It was just like she had said. There was a hole in the gravel under the hill. He called and ran back as fast as he could. Something chased him. He got to the river, jumped on the ice, and the noise stopped. He looked back and saw two brown bears lying down and looking at him. Their ears went down, so he knew they didn't want to bother him. He went back up to them. They were already harnessed and the sled was already hooked up. He went to the sled and told them to go, and they took him home to his grandmother's house. He tied them to their old poles when he got home.

His grandmother didn't come out to see him, so finally he went inside. He saw her weeping with her nose running. She was feeling sorry about him because she thought those two brown bears might bite him and he would never come home. He said, "Don't worry about me, grandmother. I have two brown bears out there." She went out and saw the two brown bears tied to the poles. She started kissing them on the nose saying, "These are my son's dogs." She was kind of surprised to see them. She went back into the house and told the boy: "Grandson, you should have some food to take along. Your father's two caches are on the hill a little ways from here. If you look around you will see the door. You can open it and see what's in there. You can open the other one and see what's in there too."

The grandson went up the hill and when he got on top he looked around. He saw a door, opened it up, and found a lot of dried fish. He took some out and closed the cache. He looked around and saw another door. He opened it and found all kinds of dried meat. He took some out and closed that cache. After he took the stuff home he loaded the sled with food.

The next morning the akpatuks [the people going down in response to invitation] left. The grandmother and grandson had two good dogs, so they tied all the rest of the sleds behind theirs. The grandson told the young man that had been bothering him, "Tie your sled behind mine." They finally got down to Tikiraayukgruk (a sandspit in Kobuk Lake about fifteen miles from Kotzebue) and stopped there. The two kivauks started going home to Kotzebue leaving the akpatuks. After awhile the two kivauks got to Kotzebue (Kikiktakrumun) where there was a rich man. This rich man had sent for the grandson.

The rich man had a good runner who used to go meet the akpatuks when they came from different villages for a feast. The runner didn't want to go meet the grandson. The rich man looked for somebody else, but nobody wanted to go. When he couldn't find anybody he finally thought of one young man who was so weak that when they had games he always fell down when anybody just touched him. This young man was called Paaluk because he fell down when he ran. The rich man said to Paaluk, "I wish you could meet my friend's son. Take this little piece of meat and give it to him." The young man said he would go. The kivauks started going back to where the grandson and the rest of the people waited, taking a little meat with them. Paaluk went too. On the way Paaluk always fell down and he was left behind. Finally the kivauks got to Tikiraayukgruk and met the akpatuks. They stood in two rows facing each other and the kivauks said, "Here's meat from your friends in Kotzebue. You can come get it." Finally it was Paaluk's turn and he said, "Here's your piece of meat from your friend, that rich man, to you, grandmother and grandson." He tried to take it over to them, but fell down again.

They got ready to go back to Kotzebue and the grandmother said to Paaluk, "Put on my old mukluks now. When you get to the karigi and start going in you can take them off." They started to race back, and when they ran Paaluk fell all the time. Finally he started getting better and started passing some of the other kivauks. Finally he felt really good and passed all of them except three. Two of the men ahead of him were running together. They were talking and Paaluk heard one of them say, "Who's that guy close to us now? He's going to pass us." The other said, "It might be Paaluk." The first said, "It couldn't be Paaluk." And the other replied, "But it might be Paaluk." He passed them and they recognized him. Then he saw one man way in front running all alone. Paaluk ran faster and faster and caught the best Kotzebue runner. It was the rich man's runner who had gone to meet somebody else.

When he got close to Kotzebue everybody was waiting. They saw one man way in front of everybody else. Paaluk heard them talking. Somebody asked, "Who's that runner way in front?" Somebody else said, "It might be Paaluk." And a third person said, "It couldn't be Paaluk." Then they recognized Paaluk. Paaluk got there and went into the karigi. He took off the old mukluks before he went in. The old people were waiting inside. They asked, "You came back before you got all the way up there?" He answered, "I got up there too." They waited for a little while and the good runner came in. The old people asked him, "Did he get up there too?" He answered, "Yes, he was up there. Naami, too bad. I used to be a good runner before, but now I'm not as fast as somebody else who can run."

Everybody got in and came to the karigi. They started meeting in the karigi and everybody had a good time. The grandmother and the grandson were invited to the rich man's place and they stayed there because the grandson's father was the rich man's friend before he died. They had a good time and gave everything to each other. The inland people gave meat to the Kotzebue people and the Kotzebue people gave different kinds of sea animals to them. Finally they finished the feast and went home. THE END.

I was told this story by Frank Glover.

B575.1 Wild animals kept as dogs (Central—Boas 1888:599; Greenland —Rasmussen 1921:I, 318, 363; Rink 1875:248); D810 Ownership of magic object: a gift; D1065.2 Magic shoes; F681 Marvelous runner; J151 Wisdom (knowledge) acquired from old person; L111.4.1 Orphan hero lives with grandmother; N825.3.3 Help from grandmother; P150 Rich man.

The Messenger Feast is also part of PM127 and PM140 in this volume. This story incorporates a considerable amount of detail concerning the Messenger Feast.

PM66. THE POLAR BEAR FIGHTS THE BROWN BEAR

A mother and her son were living alone down at the coast. The son always saw brown-bear claws hanging on the wall by his mother's bed. He was a good hunter. One day he went way out on the ice to hunt, but he couldn't find anything. Finally he saw a house on the ice. He went to it because it was on his way. When he got close there was no one around outside, so he went in. When he got inside he saw no men's things, only women's.

While he was there somebody came outside. A big fat woman came in. She asked, "Did you have something to eat already?" He answered, "No, I haven't eaten anything." She was kind and asked him to marry her, and he did. The woman went out and hunted every day. In the morning before she left she would tell her husband, "Stay home and eat anything you want. You don't have to hunt. Stay and eat." After awhile the boy started getting fat.

One time the woman came home late and looked at him from the doorway for awhile. Then she came in and they had something to eat. After that whenever the woman came home, she'd look at the boy for awhile. One time a little woman came from somewhere while the big woman was out hunting and told the boy, "Your wife is going to eat you now because you are fat. That's why she tells you to do nothing but eat to get you fat. You better not eat too much now and exercise after she goes. Try to get thin again." The little woman left.

The big woman came home again and looked at him, but did nothing. A few days later the little woman came in after the big woman left and said, "Maybe your wife will eat you tomorrow. If she doesn't and goes out hunting again, you'd better leave. Try to get home." The next morning the big woman left again and the boy started home. He went along walking, then running, and sometimes looking back to see if his wife followed. Finally he saw her following. She was a big polar bear. He ran as fast as he could, but the polar bear was faster.

Soon he could hear her right behind him. He swung his arms behind him and then looked back. He'd cut the ice and there was a wide strip of open water. He saw his wife on the other side. He kept running. She crossed the water and followed. He swung his arm again. When he looked back he saw his wife on the other side of an even wider stretch of open water. He never stopped running. Finally he saw a big black spot in front of him. It was a big brown bear. His wife was getting close behind. He passed the brown bear and it met the polar bear. They started fighting. They fought for quite awhile and when he looked back the polar bear was down and the brown bear was still standing up. The brown bear was his mother. The little woman was a fly, smaller than a nahviivuk [house fly]. THE END.

Jack Henry told this story.

B435.4 Helpful bear; B615.7 Marriage to bear in human form (MacKenzie River—Jenness 1924:76; Central—Boas 1888:638f.; Smith Sound—Kroeber 1899:176; Greenland—Holm 1912:82); D113.2 Transformation: man to bear (Kodiak—Golder 1907:297; 1909:10; Bering Strait—Nelson 1899:493; West Hudson Bay—Boas 1901:326; Cumberland Sound—Boas 1901:251f.; Cape York—Rasmussen 1921:III, 124, 211, 297; Greenland—Rasmussen 1921:I, 184; 1921:II, 96, 184; Rink 1875:193); D382 Transformation: hymenoptera to person; D615.4 Men transformed to animals fight; J652.4 Warnings against certain peoples; K640 Escape by help of confederate; K1626 Would-be killers killed; K1810 Deception by disguise; N821.1 Help from little woman; Q211.8 Punishment for desire to murder (Cumberland Sound—Boas 1901:62; Smith Sound—Kroeber 1899:177; Greenland—Holm 1912:47; Rink 1875:157, 222); Q411 Death as punishment; R153.4 Mother rescues son; R227.2 Husband flees from animal wife; T110 Unusual marriage.

Paul says that in stories inland bears are always stronger than polar bears. The translator gave two instances of which he had heard where brown bears killed polar bears.

PM67. The Short Boy

In King Island, or Little Diomede, lived an old couple who had two sons. One son is a real young man, but grown up tall, and the other son, the younger, did not grow much; he is short. One day, while they were living together in the village, other people from the village killed their father. After their father was killed their mother was real worried. Finally she died from worry (sadness) and the two brothers lived all alone in their home.

The younger brother hunts on the ice and finally gets a polar bear and is taking it home. When he gets close to the village on his way home he heard somebody behind him with a bow and arrows. He heard the string being "cocked," so he fell down and the arrow passed over him and struck in the ice right in front of him. He crawled on the ice and looked back at the man behind him, and another arrow went over his head. While he was looking back the younger brother said to the man, "You want to fight with me?" The man said, "No, I lost the fight already." The little younger brother said to him, "Bring my polar bear up to my place." The man was [too] lazy to bring the polar bear, so the younger brother said, "If you don't bring my polar bear to my place I'll kill you myself." The younger brother walked back to the man. The younger brother had a killing spear, so he killed the man and left him lying where he fell on the ice. He left the two arrows where they were stuck, too, and then went home, but never told his elder brother about killing the man.

After he went home he stayed for the night and still never said anything about the dead man. He and his elder brother slept and early in the morning somebody (a man) came into their house and told them, "We missed somebody yesterday. He never came back from hunting." The younger brother said to the man, "You people can't find him around this village. He's down on the ice. I killed him. I never started fighting with him; he started, so I killed him." The man went out.

That morning after talking to the man, the people of the village

264

went down to the ice to look for the missing man. They found him there dead, just the way the younger brother told them. There was a big spear still in the dead man and the two arrows in the same place where they were left. The people buried him. That man the younger brother killed was the same man who had killed the two brothers' father.

The two brothers lived there for quite awhile. A visitor came from the village, a young lady, and the elder brother asked her, "What can we do for you?" The young lady said, "My father told me to come over to be a bride for your younger brother." The elder brother said to her, "I don't know." She went out and went home. After a few days she came in again. The elder brother said, "What can we do for you?" She answered the same thing she had before. At first the elder brother said, "I don't know," but finally he said, "It's all right." The younger brother married her. The young lady had told the elder brother, "My father wants your younger brother in place of his son." That man that was killed on the ice was the woman's brother that had killed the boys' father and tried to kill the younger brother. That's why her father wanted him in place of his son.

They lived together with her parents for awhile. One time a man came in from the village and told the younger brother, "That man that was going to (supposed to) marry your wife is mad. He wants to kill you." The father-in-law said, "It's too bad for him. My son-in-law is real tough." The man who sent the message was real tough too. The messenger went out and told the other man what the father-in-law had said, but that didn't stop the man. He still wanted to fight and was already in the place where they were supposed to fight, where everybody could watch them. Finally the younger brother came up to fight him. They faced each other. The man had a bow and arrow, but the younger brother did not. He didn't want anything to get in his way, so he had only his father's old knife and spear.

They started fighting and got close together. The man grabbed the spear away from the younger brother and broke it. The younger brother got mad, took his knife out, and jumped behind the man. The man tried to face him, but the younger brother stayed behind him so the man couldn't see him. Finally the younger brother stabbed him from behind and killed him. Then he said, "If anybody feels sorry about this man, now is the time to fight me if they want to." No one did and everyone went home. The younger brother's mother had been picking berries just before the younger brother was born and a dwarf had come along and slept with her, and that's why she had this small boy. THE END.

Ralph Gallahorn used to tell this story.

F451 Dwarfs; F1041.1.2 Death from grief for death of lover or relative; J652.4 Warnings against certain people; K1626 Would-be killers killed; L111.4 Orphan hero; P233.6 Son avenges father; P251 Brothers; Q211 Murder punished (Cumberland Sound—Boas 1901:168; Greenland— Rasmussen 1921:III, 76, 111, 294); Q411.6 Death as punishment for murder; T81.7 Wife dies on hearing of lover's or husband's death.

Though not stated directly, the idea that dwarfs are stronger and swifter than normal men is implicit in this story.

PM68. AHPAKINYA

There was a man from Point Hope named Ahpakinya. Ahpakinya lived with his parents before he got married. After he got married he and his wife lived together in another house. He was a good hunter. At whaling time he got two whales and then quit and they started staying home.

While they were living there he was once drifted on the ice early in the winter. After he floated out people waited for him all winter, but he never came back. That spring his wife married again. People started talking to her saying, "We hope your new husband is a good hunter like Ahpakinya. We hope he's just the same."

Later that same spring, just before the ice went out, Ahpakinya came home at night and went into his parents' house. They recognized him. He was skinny and dirty, so they cleaned him up. They kept him hidden and told nobody else that he was back.

Finally they had no more meat in their house or cold storage. Ahpakinya's cold storage had been full when he had drifted out. His mother went over to her former daughter-in-law's house and asked through the window, "Does Ahpakinya's cold storage have any more meat? My husband is hungry. He wants some whale meat." Her former daughter-in-law came out and went to the cold storage. She got a piece of meat and gave it to Ahpakinya's mother.

Ahpakinya began to get stronger. When they had no more meat again his mother went over and asked for some more. Her former

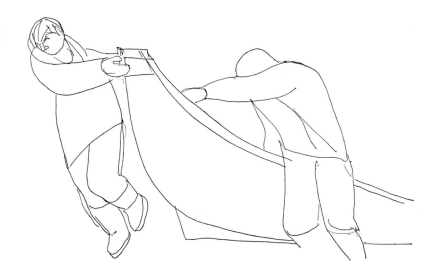

daughter-in-law gave her some again. She still did not know that Ahpakinya was home. Her mother-in-law would say, "'Ahpakinya's father is hungry for whale meat." Finally Ahpakinya could walk around inside the house.

Everybody was whaling. When the season was over it was time to start the celebration. The people began to get together. They still didn't know Ahpakinya was home. After everyone else had gone over to the celebration, Ahpakinya and his parents went over, Ahpakinya walking between them. When they got close they heard somebody say, "That looks like Ahpakinya's shape." One of the old people said, "Ahpakinya couldn't have lived this long. He is already lost." When the three got there the people recognized Ahpakinya.

He and his parents sat down with the rest of the people. The Ahvariki began (whale flipper; also the celebration where they eat whale flippers). A woman cut a little piece of flipper for someone. She would call for him saying, "You did something to me once, but I forgive you." This continued with the women cutting the flipper and giving it out. While they were celebrating they had dances. Then they quit and started home. Ahpakinya didn't try to take his wife back. He started living with his parents. THE END.

I heard this story from Calvin Barger. [Herbert Onalik, who was translating this day, heard it from Kunuk, a Point Hope man. Herbert commented that Paul told it almost the same way.]

H79 Recognition by physical attributes; W11 Generosity.

PM69. The Man Who Lost His Wives

In Point Hope there was a man that always got married and always lost his wives. He came back in the falltime before freeze-up from the Kukpuk, where he had gone to hunt caribou with his skin boat. The villagers heard him crying from a long way off. He came home alone, saying, "I can't help it. I've lost my wife." After he lost his first wife he lived alone for awhile and then got married again. This happened three times. Every time he went up the Kukpuk he lost his wife.

One summer he got married again to the only daughter of a couple who also had three sons. In early summer he and his wife went up the Kukpuk to hunt caribou for summer skins and dried meat. In the fall they got ready to go back to Point Hope. Just before they left the man said to his wife, "There is a lake up there that I always go and see just before I leave." He wanted her to come along.

When they got to the lake it looked nice and calm, but the woman saw that right around the edge of the lake the water shook a little though there was no wind. There were some willows along the edge of the water and from them was hanging the front quarter of a caribou that had dried up in the sun. The man took it from the willows, took it over to the water, and sunk it in about half way. Then he pulled it up. There was no meat at all left, just bone. Worms had eaten it up. He showed it to his wife and told her, "That is how they are going to eat you, just like that."

She started getting scared. She couldn't help it. Then she said, "What's that thing over there? Try to see it." He looked and she took off running. He was a good runner and he caught her. He took her back and threw her in. In no time her clothes floated up from the water. He went back to the boat and started down the river.

When he got close to Point Hope he started crying again like he had before. He said, "I loved her all right." When he got to Point Hope his wife's three brothers went to the boat and started unloading it. They took everything ashore. He stayed with his brothers-in-law and their parents.

Next spring, while they were in the house, they heard something from in the sky. It was something singing. It got closer and finally they knew it was a woman singing. She got real close to the window and sang, "My husband threw me in the lake and the worms ate me in the lake." She called to her mother and said, "Mother, my husband threw me in the lake and the worms ate me in the lake." Her husband looked up and then tried to run away. The three brothers grabbed him and tore him into pieces. That woman was coming home, but her brothers spoiled it. If they hadn't killed the man she would have come back. She never returned. THE END.

I heard this story from Makan. Iŋnuyyuk Swan used to tell this story, but a little differently. Her version had a hole in the ground with worms in it.

K950 Treacherous murder; P253.0.3 Three brothers and one sister; Q211 Murder punished (Cumberland Sound—Boas 1901:168; Greenland—Rasmussen 1921:III, 76, 111, 294); Q411.6 Death as punishment for murder; S62 Cruel husband. Similar to Lucier 1958:100–1 (Noatak), Ostermann 1942:69–70, and EH9 in this volume.

Paul notes a third version that I did not collect.

PM70. THE AŊATQUQ BECOMES A ROCK

In Shismaref lived people and among them lived one aŋatquq. One day the aŋatquq walked out from the village to a hill, which he climbed. There he met another man. When they met the aŋatquq asked, "Are you an aŋatquq too?" The other man answered, "Yes, I'm an aŋatquq." The Shismaref aŋatquq asked him, "Did you become a rock?" The other man answered, "Yes." After they talked about the rock they both said, "We're aŋatquqs."

The Shismaref aŋatquq went back to Shismaref and the other man left to go to his home. They both got their Eskimo drums and met again on top of the same hill. They sat facing each other and started playing their drums, and they both took their walrus tusks out. When they worked on the walrus tusk the other man became a walrus tusk through his aŋatquq and the Shismaref aŋatquq became a rock.

The other man became a man again after he was a walrus tusk for awhile, but the Shismaref aŋatquq that had become a rock couldn't become a person again; he just stayed a rock. The other man got tired, so he blew on the rock and it started burning. The rock burned for awhile and then stopped. It was still a rock. The rock got cold, and when the other man got tired of it he put his Eskimo drum on top of the rock (the Shismaref aŋatquq) and left it there and then went home that evening. He stayed home overnight and early the next morning went back to see the Shismaref aŋatquq. When he went up he found the Shismaref aŋatquq still a rock. The rock is still on top of the hill near Shismaref. THE END.

Frank Burns told this story.

D200 Transformation: man to object; D231 Transformation: man to stone (Bering Strait—Nelson 1899:505; MacKenzie River—Jenness 1924:84; Cumberland Sound—Boas 1901:172; Labrador—Hawkes 1916: 159; Smith Sound—Kroeber 1899:172; Greenland—Rasmussen 1921:III, 159, 194); D1711 Magician; D1719.1 Contest in magic (Greenland—Rasmussen 1921:II, 334; Thalbitzer 1904:7).

The obvious explanation for this story is that of a contest of magic powers. However, a secondary element may be the ambivalence in Eskimo society surrounding shamanism; an aŋatquq used his powers casually to become a rock and was unable to regain human form. Involvement with supernatural powers does include some risks.

PM71. INYUHUYUK

There were people at the coast. Among them were a man and his wife and their son, called Inyuhuyuk, who always hunted. When the boys in that village played football the son never played, but just watched them. One time while he watched he saw a girl playing football with the boys. She had her parka on inside out. She went after the ball and the boys couldn't catch her. The boy walked down, but instead of playing football he got ahold of the girl and took her home. They got married. The girl had big upper teeth (tuluvak).

The boy's mother used to work real hard, but when her son got married she quit working. The girl worked for them, serving food and all. The boy and his wife stayed for a few years and had two boys. When the girl worked on seals and ugruks she always licked her hands because she liked the oil so much.

One time the old man was up at the karigi making a spear, and his son was up there too. The girl was cooking at home. She was cooking with seal oil and the old woman saw her lick her hands again. As she went out to her cooking the old woman said behind her back, "Even though she's not a polar bear, she always licks her hands when she cooks with oil." The girl heard her. She didn't like what her mother-in-law said, so she got her two boys and left.

Through the window of the karigi somebody said, "Inyuhuyuk's wife left." Inyuhuyuk took his spear and ran out after his wife and kids. They ran towards the ocean and he followed their trail. When they were not too far away and he could see them, he looked at their tracks and saw that they had become those of polar bears. Towards evening the polar bears stopped and waited for him. When he got to them they made a cave in some high-drifted snow and stayed over-night. He went to bed in the middle of them, so he didn't get cold.

Early in the morning they left again and Inyuhuyuk followed. In the evening they stopped and made a cave. The next day they went again. Towards evening they saw some tracks going towards the land. There were so many tracks that the trail was wide and hard. When they got to the tracks they stopped at one side and stayed overnight. Early in the morning Inyuhuyuk heard somebody walking

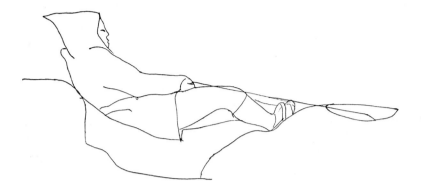

by. The steps passed and his wife said, "That's my brother." After that another man came by. It was her second brother, and her third brother passed soon after. She said, "They are going down to hunt seals."

When no more men came they left the cave and walked towards the hills. When they got close they found some houses and they went into one. An old man and old woman were there, Inyuhuyuk's wife's mother and father. The old people really liked their daughter's kids. The old man thought that his sons might do something to his son-in-law, so he hid him. He took a house pole off and hid him behind it so that he could see out. Towards evening the three brothers came home and smelled something different. Their father scolded them saying, "That's your brother-in-law," so they quit smelling and accepted him. The three brothers liked their nephews. Inyuhuyuk's wife's boyfriend before she left the village wanted to hunt with her husband, so he calls through the window one morning. The boyfriend was jealous of Inyuhuyuk, and if he didn't get a seal before him he was going to kill him. The old man answered, "Yes, we'll go hunting."

He told his son-in-law: "If you and the other man go down you will run. When you get to a hole jump through it. Try to find a bug (kumarak: always eats seals right away when they are left in the water) in the water, and if you do grab it and throw it out of the hole.

Then get on top of the ice. That other man will start running after you, so run as fast as you can towards home."

The two went down to the ice and when they got to the hole they both jumped in. The boy found a bug, threw it up, and got out of the water. He saw a seal lying there. The bug became a seal. As he put the seal on his back the other man came from the water with a seal, and they both started running towards the village. The boy got home first and went into the house. The other man didn't follow him.

In a few days someone called through the window again saying, "Inyuhuyuk, that same man and you should see who can stay under the water longer." The old man said, "Yes, we'll be down there." Then the man went away from the window. The old man told his son-in-law: "Put my old parka on. When we used to have these games I would always win them all. You two will sit on the ocean bottom side by side. When there is no more air put your mouth inside your parka while the other man doesn't know about it and breathe two times. If he gets tired try to beat him to the hole and get out first. When you get on top of the ice run home as fast as you can."

The two started off, went to a hole in the ice, dived in, and sat on the bottom for a long time. When Inyuhuyuk ran out of air he breathed two times in his parka and got better. After they had stayed for awhile the other man got tired and started to go up. Inyuhuyuk moved quickly, beat him out of the hole, and started running home. The other man ran after him, but didn't catch him.

After a few days somebody called through the window again. They said that the other man wanted Inyuhuyuk again. He wanted to see who could slide down first from a hill. The old man answered, "Yes, we'll be up there," and the man ran away. The old man told his son-in-law: "Put my old parka on. They never beat me when I was young and we had sliding contests. When you start to slide, if it looks like he is going to beat you push with your feet two times."

They went to the top of the hill and started sliding down on their stomachs. The other man started leading, so Inyuhuyuk pushed with his feet and went ahead. He got to the finish line first, got up, and ran home. The other man chased him, but he never caught him. When Inyuhuyuk came in his father-in-law said, "Those are all his tricks. That's all he knows."

Inyuhuyuk stayed with them. Those people were polar bears. After that they visited back and forth with Inyuhuyuk's parents. When the girl found out that Inyuhuyuk never played football with the other boys, she became a girl and went down so that he would see her. THE END.

Daniel Walton used to tell this story.

B651.7 Marriage to bear in human form (MacKenzie River—Jenness 1924:80; Central—Boas 1888:638f.; Smith Sound—Kroeber 1899:176; Greenland—Holm 1912:82); D113.2 Transformation: man to bear (Kodiak—Golder 1907:297; 1909:10; Bering Strait—Nelson 1899:493; West Hudson Bay—Boas 1901:326; Cumberland Sound—Boas 1901: 251f.; Cape York—Rasmussen 1921:III, 124, 211, 297; Greenland— Rasmussen 1921:I, 184; 1921:II, 96, 184; Rink 1875:193); D410 Transformation: one animal to another; D682.3.1 Animals in human form retain animal food and habits (Central—Boas 1888:217; Smith Sound— Kroeber 1899:173; Greenland—Rasmussen 1921:III, 73; Rink 1875: 456); D810 Magic object a gift; D1050 Magic clothes; F513 Person unusual as to his mouth; H48 Animal in human form recognized; H911 Tasks assigned at suggestion of jealous rival; H1385 Quest for lost persons; H1543 Contest in remaining under water; H1563 Test of skill; J151 Wisdom (knowledge) from old person; K11 Race won by deception; P253.0.3 Three brothers and one sister; S551 Cruel mother-in-law; T110 Unusual marriage; W154 Ingratitude. Similar to Spencer 1959: 419–25 (Point Barrow).

PM72. THE EAGLES

A young man and his wife lived on a river. They stayed there for a few years and had two boys. After a few years the two boys started playing out. They always stayed out together when they got big. One day when they were out they somehow got separated and the elder brother got lost. His parents looked all over for him, but they couldn't find him. His father looked all over for the boy and finally gave up. When he gave up looking for his eldest boy he got in bed and wouldn't eat, even though his wife would tell him that the boy would come back sometime. He started getting skinny and finally got real skinny. His wife tried to help him, but he told her he didn't need help.

One day she went out and started walking away from their house. She tried to follow the birds, any kind of bird she saw, but the birds flew away. When she saw a woodpecker (tuyuk) she started follow-

ing it. The woodpecker flew around and finally flew straight to the
flats. The woman followed the woodpecker to the flats, leaving her
husband and youngest boy at home. She walked through the flats and
went up to a hill. The river went around the hill, and when she got
on top she saw a house on one side of the river. Across from it were
a few other houses.

She went to the first house, where she stayed outside and listened.
She heard the people inside singing and beating a drum. When they
quit they would always laugh. They were having a lot of fun in there.
When she went to the door it was open a crack. She stood outside and
looked in. The people sang, and when they quit began laughing again.
She looked in and saw a kind of old woman with her chin in her
hands, watching her. She tried to hide by the door. The old woman
said to somebody in the house, "I always told you not to take kids
home. See that poor woman who is looking for her kid."

The woman went in and saw her little boy sitting on the floor.
There were also two boys and their mother, the old woman. The boys
were playing drums and the little boy was dancing. When they quit
they would laugh at him. The woman recognized her boy and stayed
there. A rather old man, the woman's husband, came in. He said,
"I was across the river with my younger brother for awhile." He took
the woman across to meet his younger brother. When they came back
the old man wanted to take her home. She took her boy along. Those
two boys that played the drums liked kids so much that they took
them from other villages. When they got tired of them they always
took them home, but the woman had come looking for her son before
they got tired of him. The old man told the woman and her boy to
get on his back. He told her to close her eyes and she did. They went,
and when they landed she got down before she opened them. She
opened her eyes and there was nobody there except her son. They
went home.

Before he had taken them home the old man had told the woman
that sometime they were going to come get her. When the woman
went inside the house she told her husband that she had brought
their son home. The skinny man opened his eyes and saw his son
close by. After awhile he asked for a little water. His wife gave him
water and a little food. She fed him. He got fat and started sitting up.
He got his health back. When he started walking outdoors the old

man came and got them. They stayed with the old man for awhile and when they wanted to go home he took them back. They visited back and forth. That old man, his younger brother, his wife, and their two sons were all eagles. THE END.

I heard this from Carl Stalker.

D352.2 Transformation: eagle to man; D2121.2 Magic journey with closed eyes (Bering Strait—Nelson 1899:511; MacKenzie River—Jenness 1924:52; Central—Boas 1888:629; Smith Sound—Kroeber 1899:171; Greenland—Rasmussen 1921:II, 14; 1921:III, 103, 124, 257; Rink 1875:147, 196, 219); F1041.9.1.1 Man keeps to his bed, mourning over lost son; H1385 Quest for lost persons; P251 Brothers; R13.3 Abduction by eagle.

The woodpecker referred to is probably *Dendrocopos pubescens nelsoni* (Nelson's downy woodpecker) which is called *tuyuk* by the Nunamiut (Irving 1960:85). One wonders why this bird is specifically mentioned in the story, as woodpeckers are unimportant in north Alaskan folklore.

PM73. THE BOY WHO BECAME AN EAGLE

There were people living at a river where it flowed into the sea. Among them was a man and his wife, and staying with them was their nephew, whose father had died. When the nephew got bigger the wife started after him. She was really after him and he was caught so he started using her behind his uncle. When his uncle stayed out hunting he always stayed home. One time his uncle caught them, but he said nothing because he knew it wasn't the boy's fault, but his wife's.

When the people needed wood they always went upriver to where there were trees. One time the uncle told the boy that they should go upriver and cut a rotten tree, hollow out the inside, and make a poke for seal oil out of it. He took his nephew upriver in a kayak and they started cutting a rotten tree. People never had made pokes like that before, but that's what he told his nephew they were doing.

He cut a real big tree and carved it out inside with enough room for his nephew to fit in there. When they had almost finished he told his nephew to go inside and work on it a little bit more. They had made a cover before that, and after the nephew went in the uncle covered it up and put something around the top so that the tree wouldn't leak. He made the log roll down to the river and set it free, so that his nephew floated downstream.

The log got to the ocean, and because the wind was from the east it began drifting out. So the nephew traveled as the waves took him along. He stayed in the ocean until he got skinny. He was thirsty and hungry. Finally it felt like he had bumped the bottom and the log stopped. He tried to kick the lid off, and when he got it off he went out and found he was on the beach. The sun was quite hot. He crawled up a ways and then stayed there. He was too weak to stand.

While he was there he saw somebody coming along the beach. It was a man who got closer and then came to him. The man looked at him and felt real sorry because he was so skinny and couldn't move. He said, "I left my parka not too far down the beach. I am going to get it." When he came back he told the boy to get on his back. While he was trying to get on the man's back an eagle came from the sky, and they both got on the eagle's back. The eagle took off toward the sky.

After traveling for awhile the eagle went in through a hole in the sky. The eagle became a young girl. The man and the nephew went into a house and the man said, "I have two daughters; one became that eagle." He told the girls, "Clean him up, bathe him, and feed him. You have no brothers." After they cleaned him up and put him in bed, they started feeding him every day. He got fat and started walking around. When he got strong the man said to his daughters, "He's strong enough to find food now. You won't have to hunt anymore. Your younger brother will hunt for you now."

They let him put the father's eagle parka on. The girls became eagles and showed him how to fly. They held his wings and took him up. After they took him way up they dropped him. He started twisting and turning any old way because he couldn't fly. When he got close to the ground they took him up again. They did that all day and soon he could fly a little bit. Towards evening he could fly pretty well, so they took him home. He started flying alone after that.

One day after he had come home the father put his eagle skin on and went out hunting. He came home towards evening carrying a man. He told the boy, "Eagles eat all kinds of animals, but when we feel like eating something different I bring home a person." The boy saw a little house farther over from theirs and the man told him, "When we are going to eat a man we always go over to that house to feast. You can stay here. You don't eat people like us." He stayed home. The two girls and their father went over.

The boy started hunting and bringing home food. One time the father told him that if he went out hunting not to bother people. He started flying and he flew over some villages. One time while he was flying he saw a kayak going up a river. When he got close he recognized his uncle, so he went down and landed by the kayak. He told his uncle that he remembered when he had sent him out to sea in the log.

After he talked to his uncle he took him, still in his kayak, up in the air. When they got way up he dropped him. His uncle fell and kept falling, and when he got close to the ground his nephew grabbed him, took him up, and dropped him again. When he dropped his uncle the third time he did not pick him up, so the man hit the ground and died. After this the father was different. At first he wouldn't even talk to the boy. Then he told him, "I told you not to bother people." He knew that the boy had been playing with his uncle. He told him again, "Don't make fun of or play with people." After the boy played with his uncle he never played with or made fun of people again. THE END.

This is as far as I heard this story from Frieda Goodwin.

B455.3 Helpful eagle; B552 Man carried by bird; C830 Unclassified tabu; C901.1 Tabu imposed by certain person; D152.2 Transformation: man to eagle (Kodiak—Golder 1903:94); D531 Transformation by putting on skin (Kodiak—Golder 1903:95; Bering Strait—Nelson 1899:468; Central—Boas 1888:617; Cumberland Sound—Boas 1901:181; Greenland—Rasmussen 1921:I, 364; 1921:II, 13; 1921:III, 75, 143, 262; Rink 1875:146); D1532.1 Magic flying skin; F56 Sky window (West Hudson Bay—Boas 1901:339; Central—Boas 1888:599; Labrador—Hawkes 1916: 153; Greenland—Holm 1912:80; Rasmussen 1921:III, 165, 170; Rink 1875:468); F62.1 Birds carry person to upperworld; F163.3 House in other world; J130 Wisdom (knowledge) from animals; P252 Sisters; Q210 Crimes punished; Q411 Death as punishment; S71 Cruel uncle; S143.1 Child abandoned in hollow tree; T257 Jealous husband; T421.1 Aunt seduces nephew. Similar to EH14 and PM5 in this volume.

PM74. Nahkunuk

A man, his wife, and their one daughter lived behind Kassituk (a shallow place between real Sheshalik and Nuvuvruk) down at Sheshalik. Their daughter always walked around the beach. In the fall when it started freezing she started walking north along the beach. She saw a little hump in the sand on the edge of the water. It was a nahkunuk [a marine gastropod]. When people eat that snail they always take a little white piece off and throw it first. If people eat that piece they get cross-eyed right then (when a person is cross-eyed he is nahkunuk).

She took the nahkunuk home and stored it in her bed. She said nothing to her parents. That same fall her parents talked to each other saying, "Our daughter has company now at night." They found out somebody was getting in their daughter at night. When the daughter went out the mother looked for something in her bed. She saw the nahkunuk there and put it back where she found it.

One day the nahkunuk told the daughter, "If I become a person right here in the bed your parents won't believe it, but if I go away and come back a real live man they will believe me." One day the nahkunuk left. He was gone a whole year. The next summer on a real nice calm day the three saw something way out at sea. When it got close to them it was a kayak with a young man. He landed right by them and stayed with them.

That fall another young man came from the north to visit. When the man from the north stopped there he said, "I came over here to wrestle with that other young man because he is taking my woman." Nahkunuk said, "I have never wrestled before. I don't know how." The stranger said, "I want to wrestle anyway." They went down to the sand. They stood facing each other and started wrestling. The stranger tried to throw nahkunuk two times, but nahkunuk told him, "Let me try to throw you." He threw him in the water on the other side of the sand bar. Then nahkunuk said, "If you want to try again next time I'll throw you a little farther out." The stranger gave up and went home. THE END.

I have forgotten who told this story.

B659 Marriage to other animals in human form; D398.1 Transformation: marine gastropod to person; D658 Transformation to seduce.

PM75. Tuuvaŋnuvuŋa

There was a village on the coast, maybe around Shismaref somewhere. A grandmother and her grandson lived there. The grandson was old enough to walk around the village. He saw someone working with aŋatquq so he knew how to do it. One night after his grandmother was asleep he started working the way aŋatquqs do. He made a little Eskimo drum so that he could carry it inside his parka. Sometimes while someone is aŋatquq(ing) he will fall down unconscious. They call him niksiiktuk then.

After the grandson learned about aŋatquqs he always carried the Eskimo drum when he played out with other kids When there was nobody around he'd try it, just like the aŋatquqs did. He didn't really do anything, but just acted like them. One day he tried again. He tried to become niksiiktuk, and he did it right there. He didn't know what he was doing. When he finally came to he felt like he had a rope on his feet.

While he was hanging there he heard someone talking behind him. He heard a man say, "I wonder what that boy's name is. Go ask him what his name is." A man came over, but the boy didn't say anything so the man went back. The first man asked what his name was again, but when the other man came over the boy didn't answer. The third time the first man said, "We'll eat him this time if he doesn't say his name." The other man came over and asked and the boy said, "My name is Tuuvaŋnuvuŋa."

The first man told two other men, "Go and take him down. Let him see what we can do here." The two men took him down and then started getting ready. They got a ṭuk, a fish spear, an ice scoop, and a bag. They started walking around inside the house. The one with the ṭuk jabbed it into the floor. He cracked the ice. He kept ṭuking on the floor, bailing out the ice with a scoop. He finally made a hole and the water came in. He held the fish spear and looked through the hole. He used his fish spear and got quite a few fish of different kinds.

Then he quit and put the fish in a bag and the ice back in the hole.

The two men walked around the house in the opposite direction that they had before and went back to their places. The man said, "If you are going home you can take the ṭuk, the ice scoop, the fish spear, and the bag. You can try them in your home." When he got home he and his grandmother tried them. They did the same thing in their house and got all the fish they needed. THE END.

Putumie Norton told this.

D810 Magic object a gift; D1170 Magic utensils and implements; D1444.1 Magic object catches fish; D1472 Food and drink from magic object; D1711 Magician; D1720 Acquisition of magic powers (Greenland—Rasmussen 1921:II, 222; 1921:III, 111; Rink 1875:461); D1733.5 Magic power from swooning (Greenland—Rink 1875:400); L111.4.1 Orphan hero lives with grandmother; N820 Human helpers. In PM144 a boy uses a magic gaff to bring objects through the floor of a house.

Here, attempting to become an *aŋatquq* has its benefits. In the Canadian arctic, where snow houses were built on the sea ice, fishing through the house floor was conceivably possible, though I know of no references to same. North Alaskan Eskimos occasionally built shelters or set tents on the ice, usually during the period they were hunting whales, but did not engage in fishing as described here.

PM76. THE MOUNTAIN CALLED AIYASSIRUK

The Aiyassirrukmiut (way down below Unalakleet) people lived in a village on the coast. One family lived in the mountains above the village. Sometimes the village or that one family would run out of food. The father in that one family was an aŋatquq. Once they had nothing to eat and their cache was empty. After his kids had gone to sleep the father went down to visit the village through his aŋatquq. He went down right straight through the mountains between his house and the village.

When he got to the village he went to a house of a rich man which had a long pole in front. He landed on top of the pole and started listening to the people inside. Someone said, "We should have something to eat before we go to bed." Finally a woman went out with an aaluyuk. She went to the cache and went inside. The cache was in the ground and had a ladder down to it. After she worked inside she set the platter up through the hole so that she could get out. The aŋatquq swooped down and picked up some meat before the woman could come up. The aŋatquq was a white owl (ukpik).

He went straight home through the mountains again. When he got home he put the meat in his cache and flew back again along the same trail. He landed on the pole and listened. The woman was inside and someone said to her, "How come your platter is not full?" She replied, "I filled it real full. I don't know why some is gone." Someone else said, "We won't have enough to eat with just what is here."

The woman went out to get some more meat. She went into the cache and the same thing happened. The aŋatquq took the meat home through the mountains and then went back. He landed on the pole again. When he got there the woman was inside. Someone asked what had happened to the meat and they started quarreling. That family had an aŋatquq too. He started looking for the meat. He said, "There is a white owl sitting on top of the pole. Maybe he took the meat from us."

He went after the owl with his aŋatquq and caught him. He tied him with his aŋatquq and started bringing him inside the house, but the owl stopped by the pole in the middle of the stormshed and the aŋatquq inside had lost him. He started looking for him again and saw him in the stormshed. He wound a rope around the owl with his aŋatquq and pulled him through the hallway to the trapdoor up into the house. The owl stopped again, just below the door. Then the owl grabbed somebody from the house with his aŋatquq to take his place. The person was tied in the ropes. The owl watched him.

Two men with two spears above the door in the house started spearing the man through the trapdoor as the owl watched. They thought it was the owl. After they killed the man the owl went home through the mountain and went to sleep. The next morning he and his wife awoke. He asked her, "Is there anything left in our cache?" His wife answered, "No, there's nothing left." He asked again and got the same answer. Finally she went to check. When she opened the cache door it was full of two different kinds of meat. They ate all they wanted.

In the afternoon, after they ate, two young men came up from the village. They started talking, saying, "Last night one of us never woke up. We don't know why." The aŋatquq said, "I don't know either why he never woke up." The two men went back home. That's why they call the mountain Aiyassiruk (going through) because that aŋatquq went through. THE END.

Charles Stalker told me this story.

D152.3 Transformation: man to owl; D1711 Magician; D1719.1 Contest in magic (Greenland—Rasmussen 1921:II, 334; Thalbitzer 1904:7); D2121 Magic air journey (MacKenzie River—Jenness 1924:40; Greenland—Rasmussen 1921:I, 87); K311 Thief in disguise; K311.6 Thief takes form of animal; K520 Death escaped through disguise, shamming, or substitution; K527 Escape by substituting another person; Q211.8 Punishment for desire to murder (Smith Sound—Kroeber 1899:177; Greenland—Holm 1912:47; Rink 1875:157, 222). In PM136 in this volume a substitute is murdered.

PM77. PUUYUUVAYLUK

There was a village at the coast. An old couple lived there with their son and his wife. His wife got pregnant. Just before the baby was born he made a little ebrulik for her to have her baby in. She moved into the little ebrulik just before she had her baby. She had a baby boy, but it was different from regular boys. It had a different shape. She stayed in the ebrulik three days[3] after the boy was born.

While she was waiting she decided she didn't want to keep the baby because he had a big open belly in the belly-button area. She had a nalak (white seal skin) so she sewed the hole in the boy's stomach with the nalak. After she sewed it up she thought again, "I don't want to keep him." So she laid him away from her to freeze to death. She got chilly herself, but the boy didn't die.

On the fourth day she went home to her husband. She never showed the boy to the people, not even to her husband. When she worked around the house or outside she covered the boy up with bedding. One day she told her husband, "While I work around don't try to see the baby." While she was working outside one day she left the boy inside. Her husband was inside with the boy, but his mother was out. She heard a baby cry from inside while she was working. She went straight in to see what happened. There she saw her husband lying on the floor with his tongue lying outside his mouth. He was already

---

[3] Although Paul Monroe says that the mother stayed in the ebrulik for three days, Edna Hunnicutt mentions several times that four days is the length of time a woman must stay away from the main house upon the birth of a male child.

choked. She started digging on the floor right beside her husband. She buried him under the floor inside the house. Nobody knew what happened to her husband. Then she started carrying the boy on her back.

One morning when she was working outside she had the boy on her back. She saw other kids outside playing and heard them say, "We've never seen that woman's boy. She keeps it a secret." When the woman heard them she took the baby out from off her back and told him, "Those kids said they want to see you." After she said that the baby started crying. One of the kids playing dropped dead. The same thing happened like with the father, the kid's tongue was out and he was choked.

Finally the woman started feeling sorry about the way her boy acted. She didn't want to stay in the village anymore. She got ready to move. She took her boy along with her and left. On her way when she felt tired she lay down to rest and sleep. She traveled for a long time that way. One day she saw a good-size house on the way. She looked at it. There was nobody around, so she went into the storm-shed, which was big. There she saw cut caribou meat, cut into halves, all stacked around the walls of the stormshed. She looked around and then went inside the house.

When she went in she saw nothing but men's things, no woman's things. During the night while she was staying there somebody came in. She saw a man coming home. When he went in he asked her, "Did you have anything to eat yet?" She answered, "No." He said, "We should have something to eat. I'm glad I'll have some company with me." So she started staying with him.

While they were living there her husband took out a piece of meat and threw it outside when they heard something coming that would stop outside. Every morning she heard this something come and every morning her husband threw out a piece of meat. That man didn't do much hunting after he married that woman. One morning she told her husband, "Don't try to see my baby." While she was working outside one day she heard the boy cry from inside, so she went straight in and found her husband lying dead just like her first husband, tongue lying out. He was already choked.

After the boy killed his stepfather she threw meat out every morning when she heard the rattling noise outside the house. Then they had no meat left in the stormshed because there is nobody to hunt for them. Once early in the morning she heard the rattling noise outside, but she had nothing to throw out and didn't know what was making that noise. She told her boy, "That thing outside wants to see you." The boy went out and she heard the boy and thing making noise outside for just a little while. Then she heard the boy cry again. She went out to see what had happened. There she saw a tirichik dead.

After the boy killed the tirichik they moved again to another place. While they were traveling and had stopped for the night the boy started talking to her. He said, "Next time if we get to some village or to a person you let people see me. Don't be bashful about me." They kept traveling and finally got to a little village. They started staying with a family. The elder son in this family had a boy the same size as the woman's boy. That woman got married again to one of the younger sons in that family. The two kids started calling each other "cousin."

While they were living there the two boys started playing outside by the house. They never went around with other kids but always played together. They got bigger (after people saw the boy he began to grow). The family didn't know the boy's name. One morning the grandfather asked the boy, "I wonder what your name is." The boy looked back at him and said, "My name is Puuyuuvayluk (puuyuuak is crab). That's me."

One morning while they were playing out one of the other kids tried to fight with Puuyuuvayluk's cousin. While they were fighting Puuyuuvayluk got mad and killed one of the other kids. They quit fighting and went home. He and his cousin got to be young men. They hunted and went around together. They never got anything, so finally Puuyuuvayluk hunted alone. He came home with one eagle. They skinned it and he used it for his parka.

After he got the eagle, he, his cousin, and his uncle started making a boat. When they finished they all went out on the ocean to hunt in the morning. Just before afternoon they came home with a big load of walrus. When they got to the beach Puuyuuvayluk said, "Mauramik, we wanted to see that thing all right. That's why we stayed out that long." It wasn't afternoon yet when they came home.

One morning Puuyuuvayluk started putting on his parka. He wanted to fly with it. He took off, stayed out a little while, and came home with a young woman. She was to be his wife, so he married her. They hunted out at sea again and whenever they returned Puuyuuvayluk always said the same thing, "We wanted to see that mauraa all right, but we never saw it."

One morning Puuyuuvayluk got ready to go out alone with the eagle skin. When he got ready he decided to take his cousin along. They went off flying for awhile. Finally they saw a lake with a low hill by it. When they saw the lake the water was kind of muddy. Puuyuuvayluk told his cousin, "You better watch me from the top of the hill. I want to go down and see what I can see in that water."

When Puuyuuvayluk got down the cousin didn't see Puuyuuvayluk anymore because he had dived into the water. He stayed under the water for a little while and finally came back up. He went to his cousin and told him, "I got that mauraa that I used to want to see when we were out hunting." The mauraa, the one he killed, was a tirichik (they call it "mauraa" in Shismaref). They didn't take it home, but left it there.

After Puuyuuvayluk had stayed home for a little while he got ready to go again. He wanted to take his cousin and his wife. They loaded up the boat with all kinds of meat and then went right along the beach. After a few days they saw a village on the coast. Puuyuuvayluk asked his wife, "Do you recognize this place?" His wife looked and said, "It looks like my home." When they got to the village Puuyuuvayluk said, "Show me where your house is, so that we can land in front." She showed him and they landed in front of her parents' house. Puuyuuvayluk said, "Go up and see your parents. I'll stay here for a little while."

She went up. When she got in the house her father recognized her and said, "You came home." She said, "Yes, I came home." He asked, "You have a husband now?" And she answered, "Yes." Her father was real happy. He was a rich man. He sent someone down to get his son-in-law. Puuyuuvayluk went up and into the house. The father saw his son-in-law for the first time. He was a man all right, but a little different from other men in the village in shape. The father had his daughter in his lap.

They started unloading the boat. After they finished they lived with Puuyuuvayluk's wife's parents for awhile. That same summer the rich man and his son went out to hunt walrus. Every time they

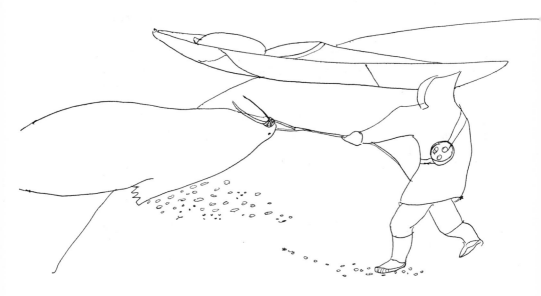

came home with nothing. One morning when they were getting ready
to go out Puuyuuvayluk asked if he could go with them. His father-
in-law said, "Yes, you can go." They went out quite a ways and saw
a bunch of walrus. They went after them, but didn't get any. They
looked around and saw some more walrus. On the way towards them
Puuyuuvayluk saw a tree with roots on it floating in the water. He
picked it up and put it in the boat. The others thought, "I wonder
what he's going to use that tree for."

Puuyuuvayluk got in front of the boat to try to get a walrus from
the second bunch. When the walrus got close he picked up the tree
and aimed it at them. He threw it and killed a few. They picked up
the walrus and took them home. Puuyuuvayluk told his brothers-in-
law and his father-in-law, "Divide up the meat with the other houses.
Let everybody have some." They did and Puuyuuvayluk told them,
"There's more someplace. If we hunt maybe we'll get more."

As long as they were there Puuyuuvayluk hunted for his mother-
and father-in-law. Every time he went out he brought a boatload
home. Finally Puuyuuvayluk felt like going home. They left and
reached his home. When Puuyuuvayluk had flown around with the
eagle skin he had gotten his wife from King Island. She was out picking berries. After they got home they visited back and forth to King

Island. Puuyuuvayluk probably lived somewhere around Shismaref or Wales. The End.

Ralph Gallahorn told me this story.

B877 Giant mythical animals; C310 Tabu: looking at certain person or thing; C901.1 Tabu imposed by certain person; C920 Death for breaking tabu (MacKenzie River—Jenness 1924:51, 58; Central—Boas 1888:600; Greenland—Rasmussen 1921:II, 341; Rink 1875:341); D152.2 Transformation: man to eagle (Kodiak—Golder 1903:94); D531 Transformation by putting on skin (Kodiak—Golder 1903:95; Bering Strait—Nelson 1899:468; Central—Boas 1888:617; Cumberland Sound—Boas 1901: 181; Greenland—Rasmussen 1921:I, 364; 1921:II, 13; 1921:III, 75, 143, 262; Rink 1875:146); D1717.1 Magic power of monster child; D2060 Death or bodily injury by magic; F529 Other monstrous persons; F610 Remarkably strong man; P295 Cousins. EH14, PM5, and PM73 in this volume also feature people who learn to fly with eagle skins; in PM108 death follows if someone looks at a boy.

In most of these stories an individual who causes death is punished, but here the boy was not at fault when people died from seeing him after being told not to look.

PM78. The Black People

A man and his wife and their one daughter lived alone somewhere. Their daughter was out working when she saw a big black spot far away coming along the ground toward her. When it got close she saw that it was a man with a sled. Both the man and sled were completely black. He came up to the house, stopped, and said to her, "I have come to get you." He was all black, even his face. The daughter said, "Well, I've got to go tell my parents first." She went in and the man followed her.

He stood by the door and told her father, "I have come after your daughter." The father said, "I am not going to let my daughter go with a black person like you." The stranger got a little angry and stamped on the floor with his right foot. The house tilted sideways a little. The father said to his daughter, "Daughter, you should go with that man. He won't be good to us if you don't go." She got ready and left the house before the stranger. Before the man went out he stamped with his left foot on the floor and the house straightened up again. He went out, put the daughter in the sled, and started pushing it by himself because he had no dogs.

After they went for a little while they saw a house right ahead of them. It was the man's house. They stopped and went in. Everything inside was black and his parents were black too. While they were there the daughter started feeling lonesome and mad because they didn't have much in the house. After they were there for awhile somebody came outside and then started into the house. The daughter saw a woman just like herself, not black. The strange woman said to the family, "I have come to get this woman here. She won't be gone long."

They went out and over to the woman's house, which was a little ways away. Everything inside the house was nice, just like at the daughter's home. While they were there the black man's father came in and said, "I want to let you go now. You should not stay with us. You are better off going away." He started getting her ready to go. He cut four little pieces of meat for her to eat on the way. He got her four sled deer and said, "These sled deer of yours will take you to your uncle."

She started off. Sometimes she went fast and sometimes slow. During the night she saw a house again and the four deer stopped right outside. She went in and saw people. They let her eat. While she was there, before they went to bed, the black mother came in. She had a half fish in her hand. She said to the daughter, "Daughter-in-law, why are you trying to go away from us?" As soon as she said that the people in the house grabbed her, cut her into pieces, and threw her outside. The daughter slept there and when she woke up she found out it was her uncle's house.

Her uncle got her ready to go again. He said, "Your sled deer will take you to another uncle of yours." She left again. Her sled deer ate as they traveled if they were hungry. She ate from the four pieces of meat from the black man's father. In the afternoon she saw a house again and stopped outside. The people inside were almost the same as the last house she had visited. Just before they went to bed the black mother came in again, said the same thing, and was torn to pieces again.

The next morning her uncle got her ready to go to yet another uncle's house. At this third house the same thing happened again. When her third uncle got her ready to go he didn't say anything to her; he didn't say that she would get to another uncle. When she got ready, she left. She traveled all day and all night for several days. Finally she saw a little house, outside of which the sled deer stopped.

There was nobody outside so she went in and saw a little old woman. The old woman didn't say, "Let's have something to eat." She said, "It's good to have a stranger. You can stay with me now for a long time."

Every day the old woman worked on braided sinew (ivalu). Finally she had a big bag full. One morning she said to the daughter, "Maybe it's about time to let you down from here. Your parents miss you and they're sad." The daughter used to see a cover in the floor of the house. The old woman opened the cover, and as she lifted it the daughter heard noise from not too far below. She heard people saying, "Moon, moon, give us life." The old woman tied the daughter with sinew around her waist, after putting new clothes on her, and let her down through the cover.

She went down for a long time. She couldn't see the ground at first, but then she started seeing it. There was nobody around. She saw only four old poles in the ground. Just before she landed she stopped right above the four poles and didn't go down anymore. She finally turned into a spider (nigrarruk). The young man's family were fish (almost like dtalik [burbot], but fish that live in the ocean [kayuluich]). I don't know what the uncles were. The four sled deer had taken her to the moon. She never reached her parents. THE END.

I heard this from Peter Carfield from Noorvik.

D181 Transformation: man to spider; D370 Transformation: fish to people; D2080 Magic used against property; D2135 Magic air journey (MacKenzie River—Jenness 1924:40; Greenland—Rasmussen 1921:I, 87); F16 Visit to land of moon (Central—Boas 1888:598; Greenland—Rasmussen 1921:II, 30; Rink 1875:440); F51.1.1 Spiderweb sky-rope; F60 Transportation to or from upperworld; F527.5 Black man; N820 Human helpers; N825.3 Help from old woman (Greenland—Rasmussen 1921:II, 162); P293 Uncle; R10 Abduction; R210 Escape.

Reindeer utilized to pull sleds were not introduced from Siberia into Alaska until the late 1800s; hence this is either a Siberian folktale, an Alaskan folktale with the addition of an introduced element, or a post-1890 creation.

PM79. THE BABY WITH THE BIG MOUTH

In Kotzebue lived a rich man and his family. He had a daughter. There was another family with a daughter and her husband. This daughter and her husband had a baby boy. One day this family started making akutuk. After they finished eating the akutuk they forgot to put some on the baby's lips (that was the law—putting some on the baby's lips). That same night after they forgot to put akutuk on the baby's lips they went to sleep. They slept that night, and while they were sleeping the daughter's mother started hearing a sound like somebody eating beside the daughter and her husband. The old woman looked over and saw the baby eating his mother. The baby had a big mouth that stretched from ear to ear. The baby had already eaten his father when he started eating his mother.

The old couple put their clothes on trying to make no noise. They didn't want the baby to hear them. As soon as they put their clothes on they went out and started waking up all the people in the village, telling them what had happened. After they told the people to leave the village they all went out towards the lagoon and crossed it to the other side. After they crossed the rich man said, "I forgot my knife in our house." He wanted two young men to go back and get his knife. So he called them and said, "If somebody goes to get my knife he will have my daughter for his wife."

So everybody wanted to go. The rich man called the grandson first to try. The grandson listened for awhile, but was scared to go back. He said, "I'll try." So he went back across the lagoon and into the village. When he got close to the house he saw the baby go out from his house crawling. He (the baby) went into other houses and came back out right away. The baby got close to the rich man's house and the grandson thought to himself, "If that baby is getting close to the rich man's house I'll go down to the house and go in first." When the baby got close to the house the grandson ran down to the house, went in, and searched for the knife.

Just when he found it, just before he went into the stormshed, he was in the hallway between the house and stormshed and knew he'd meet the baby there, so he felt the ceiling and found a rafter he could hang on. So he lifted himself up and the baby went by under him. After the baby went inside the rich man's house the grandson went out and started running towards the lagoon as fast as he could. He looked back and the baby was following him. He ran and ran, but whenever he looked back the baby was getting closer and closer. The grandson heard the rich man's voice saying, "Hurry, hurry! He's gaining on you."

Just before the baby caught him the grandson crossed the creek mouth on two long trees that had been set up as a bridge. As soon as the grandson was across the people on the other side pulled the two trees apart. The baby was still on the trees and so he fell in the water. The sheefish started eating him from all sides. That's why sheefish have a little hump under their jaw; the baby is in that hump. After the baby was killed everybody went back to his house. The grandson married the rich man's daughter because he had his knife. THE END.

Abraham Lincoln told this story. They used to have games in the public house in Kotzebue and before the last bell rang somebody would tell a story. He would quit when the last bell rang and that's what happened here.

A2320 Origin of animal characteristic: head; C740 Tabu: doing deed of mercy or courtesy; C920 Death for breaking tabu (MacKenzie River —Jenness 1924:51, 58; Central—Boas 1888:600; Greenland—Rasmussen 1921:II, 341; Rink 1875:341); F513 Person unusual as to his mouth; G670 Occasional cannibalism, deliberate; H331 Suitor contest; H960 Tasks performed through cleverness or intelligence; P150 Rich man; Q210 Crimes punished; Q411 Death as punishment; Q415.9 Punishment: being eaten by fish. Similar to Curtis 1930:259–60 (Kotzebue) and Ostermann 1952:164–65 (Colville River).

Undoubtedly, the knife mentioned was a metal knife, traded from Siberia, that had great value in aboriginal times. This story also suggests oral aggression. I have included motifs Q210 and Q411 because breaking a taboo is a crime in Eskimo social terms and death followed as a consequence.

PM80. THE POOR BOY KILLS THE BROWN BEAR

A poor boy lived in a village at the mouth of a river. A rich man and his son also lived there. When hunters went upriver in their kayaks they would never come home. The rich man's son and the poor boy were good friends. One day the rich man's son went upriver with his kayak and he never came home. The poor boy felt sorry about his good friend, so after awhile he went over to the rich man and asked him, "Do you have an old kayak that I can use?" The rich man said, "Yes, I have an old kayak out here."

The poor boy borrowed it and took it to the river. It was the first time he had ever used a kayak, and when he tried it he kept tipping over. Finally he learned how to use it and started upriver. When he saw some leaves or something floating on the river he would take his spear and spear it saying, "Maybe you are the one that killed my friend and the rest of the men." Then he saw some ducks and got some. He put them in his kayak and kept going. He was still mad. Then he saw a seal and killed it. He cut it in half and set it inside his kayak.

He kept going until he saw a good-sized trail going straight up through the trees. He landed there, pulled his kayak up, and started up the trail. After awhile he saw a little house right on the edge of the trail. He stood outside, but saw nobody, so he went in. There was nobody inside. He thought, "Well, I'd better bring some seal meat, those ducks, and my gear up to this house." He did so.

After he stayed for a little while he started to hear someone coming from outside the house. The person came in through the stormshed and then the poor boy saw the top of his head coming up through the trapdoor. The person came up as far as the bottom of his nose and said, "If you don't give me anything I will eat you." The poor boy took one of his ducks and threw it to the man. The man went down in the stormshed, ate it, and came up again. He said the same thing and the poor boy threw him another duck. This went on until the poor boy had no more ducks. The man came up again, halfway now. The poor boy threw him half of a seal and the man went down and ate it. When he came again the poor boy threw him the other half.

Now this poor boy had nothing left except his hunting gear. He got ready with his spear and when the stranger came up again, saying the same thing, the poor boy speared him in the middle of his chest and said, "Here's your meat now." The man fell down and then went out from the house. The poor boy followed behind. The man started up the trail with the spear in his chest. Following him the poor boy saw a village on a flat. He looked around and saw a little house on the edge of the village.

When he went in he saw two little women inside. He picked up a piece of wood and knocked them both down. He was still mad. He hid one of the old women and took her place. He lay down and put the other old woman facing towards the wall behind him. Someone came in and said, "We'll pay you something. Our hunter is hurt now." The poor boy said, "We were smoked up from our fire. I don't know about my friend. Maybe she isn't well. I'll try to go up and help him myself."

The poor boy followed the man up. Before he went in he told the man, "Tell them to turn the lamps off. Let the room get dark and I will try to help him." When he went inside the house the room was dark. There were some people in there. He heard the man he had speared being really sick on the floor. He felt the man and found his spear. He followed the spear to its head and pulled it out. Then he took his knife, stabbed the man, and killed him.

He went out and straight down to his kayak. When he ran the people came out of the house and chased him. When he got to his kayak he jumped in and went out in the river. The people followed along the river's edge. They were really mad. When they got to the willows they grabbed them and pulled them up saying, "That's what we'll do to you if we catch you." The poor boy picked up his spear and threw it in front of them saying, "That's what I'll do to you." Finally the people went away. Those people were brown bears. After that when people from the poor boy's village went out to hunt they always came home. THE END.

I heard this story from Ralph Gallahorn.

D313.3 Transformation: bear to man (MacKenzie River—Jenness 1924: 54; Greenland—Rasmussen 1921:I, 134; 1921:II, 11; 1921:III, 58, 86); H1220 Quest voluntarily undertaken; H1385 Quest for lost persons; K500 Escape from death or danger by deception; K914.3 Slaying under cover of darkness; K1626 Would-be killers killed; N825.3 Help from old woman (Greenland—Rasmussen 1921:II, 162); P150 Rich man; P310 Friendship; Q211:8 Punishment for desire to murder (Cumberland Sound—Boas 1901:62; Smith Sound—Koeber 1899:177; Greenland—Holm 1912:47; Rink 1875:157, 222); Q411.6 Death as punishment for murder. Similar to Curtis 1930:258–59 (Kotzebue) and Spencer 1959: 388–91 (Point Barrow). In PM19 in this volume a poor boy also kayaks upriver in search of a lost rich boy.

PM81. The Boy Who Ate the Bird Eggs

A poor boy lived alone. He had no grandmother or anything. While he was walking around outside he found some bird eggs. There were quite a few. He picked them up in his hands. The mother bird was flying around by him, not making any noise. Finally she said to him, "Ahgilii, give me back my kids." The poor boy said to her, "I'll have these eggs. I'll have them yet." The bird said, "No, you won't have enough food with these few little eggs. Maybe someday you will have more food coming to you." The poor boy took the eggs home anyway. He cooked them and ate them. After that he started getting a bellyache and died. THE END.

Ralph Gallahorn told this.

B211.3 Speaking bird; J585 Caution in eating; Q212 Theft punished; Q411 Death as punishment; T617 Boy raised in ignorance of world.
    Edna Hunnicutt (p. 47) mentions that a long time ago people died from eating eggs.

PM82. THE WOLF MAN

A man lived with his daughter and son down at Sealing Point. They had a cache outside their house. One day the man forgot to bring his potty in just before he went to bed. That same night when he wanted to pee he felt for his chamber and found nothing, so he put his mukluks on his feet and his parka on and went out to pee. While he was peeing he looked back over his shoulder and saw a man sitting under the iḳigut. He had long ears and was listening to and looking at him. The man who was peeing couldn't move. He wanted to go in, but he couldn't move. He fell down and tried to crawl in, but still couldn't make it.

He tried to get up to the window so he could call to his son and daughter. It was getting towards morning and his daughter woke up and started going out. She didn't know her father was gone. Just before she went out the man sitting under the iḳigut got up and walked towards Irgissugruk (a mountain with a flat top behind Sealing Point). After he started towards there the daughter came out and chased him away. He was scared of her. After the long-eared man left, her father could walk again. The long-eared man was a wolf. THE END.

Charlie Stalker told me this story.

D313.2 Transformation: wolf to man (Mackenzie River—Jenness 1924: 76); D2072 Magic paralysis; F542.1 Long ears.

PM83. THE WALES WOMAN

There was a widow living down at Wales. The people had a meeting in the karigi. They took the widow over to the bluff on the point of Cape Prince of Wales and threw her down. They didn't know what had happened to her, but they thought she was lost for good. A few years later the people who had thrown her down, one by one, didn't return home from hunting.

In the same village lived two brothers, one of whom had a son. After the boy was born his father went out hunting in his boat with a crew of men. He never returned. He must have been one of the men who threw that widow down. The boy's uncle liked him, so he raised him and took care of his mother.

When the boy got to be a young man he used to walk out of the village. One day he went over to the bluff where they had thrown the woman down. He looked around and saw a door in the bluff. When he went to it someone from inside opened it for him. He went in and saw a middle-aged woman. There were also a lot of men inside the house. The woman was sewing right by the door and there was a whale bone by her side. One of the men got up, walked toward the woman, and grabbed the whale rib. He said to the woman, "This woman keeps us in here," and hit her on the head. The woman didn't pay any attention to him. She wasn't hurt, but kept on sewing as if the man hadn't hit her.

After the young man saw that he went home. He didn't talk about it. One day he went back over to the bluff to see what was going on. He looked around and finally saw a big hole in the bluff. He looked at it more closely and saw something like a boat in there. He went in and it was a boat. It was a man in the boat who talked to him saying, "This is my boat. You better take all of these aŋatquq tools (aññuluk) out of the boat and take them home. You have an uncle. Let him make you a boat and after he finishes put these aññuluk in it the same way that they are here." That man was the boy's father.

The boy took the aŋatquq tools home. His uncle came in and sat by him. He sniffed him for awhile and then said, "You smell like my brother smelled." The boy told him, "I would like to have a boat. You should make me one." His uncle liked him, so he got some wood and worked it making a boat. When he finished the boy took the aŋatquq tools and tied them in it the way they were in his father's boat. He started hunting with the boat and helped his mother and uncle by getting a lot of meat. THE END.

This is as far as I heard this story from Jack Henry.

D1555 Underground passage magically opens; D1711 Magician (implied); D1814.1 Advice from magician; D1841.5 Invulnerability against weapons; E400 Ghosts and revenants, miscellaneous; F560 Unusual manner of life; L111.4 Orphan hero; P251 Brothers; P293 Uncle; Q211 Murder punished (Cumberland Sound—Boas 1901:168; Greenland—Rasmussen 1921:III, 76, 111, 294); R45 Captivity in mound (cave, hollow hill).

PM84. AŊNASUVINIK

In Point Hope there was a man named Aŋnasuvinik. He had a wife who had a younger brother. The younger brother was small. Aŋnasuvinik always beat up his wife. When he did he always picked on his wife's younger brother too. Aŋnasuvinik and the other people used to go with boats to hunt caribou. One time when they stopped where they hunted caribou the other people, who were some brothers, went one way and Aŋnasuvinik, his wife, and her younger brother went another way. They'd hunt caribou all summer and dry them up.

When they got ready to go back to Point Hope they'd pack the meat to the boat on the beach. Aŋnasuvinik made a bow and arrow for his brother-in-law. One time when they started bringing some meat to the beach they saw some ptarmigan and Aŋnasuvinik started shooting with his bow and arrow. His brother-in-law wanted to shoot too, but Aŋnasuvinik grabbed him and put him behind his back because he wanted to kill them all himself. Behind Aŋnasuvinik, his brother-in-law took out his two arrows, shot him in the back, and killed him.

The wife and her brother went home to Point Hope. The brothers that went out hunting started home after that. One time they stopped and put their boat on the beach and the youngest brother started to walk up to Aŋnasuvinik's hunting place. He wanted to toilet, so he walked a little farther down. He stopped to toilet, and while he was sitting he looked around. He saw two mukluks showing above the ground. When he went there and dug he found Aŋnasuvinik dead.

He went over to the rest of his brothers and told them he had found Aŋnasuvinik. The other brothers went up and the eldest said, "He asked for it. He treated his wife and brother-in-law badly, and that's what he was going to get when his brother-in-law got big." They took the arrows from Aŋnasuvinik's back and the eldest brother put them away.

When they got to Point Hope they went to their house and were going to sleep when all of a sudden somebody took their window off and tore it up. Every night somebody took their window off. Finally one time when the people went up to the karigi the eldest brother took up the arrows that had killed Aŋnasuvinik. He went to the door and threw them on the floor saying, "These are the arrows that killed Aŋnasuvinik." Then he went out. Aŋnasuvinik's brother-in-law got up from the crowd, ran out the door, and never showed up again. The people had thought that the brothers had killed Aŋnasuvinik. That's why they had taken the window off. Aŋnasuvinik's sister was the one who took the window off.

When she found out it wasn't them she put a new window back every morning to try to repay them. When they found out about Aŋnasuvinik's brother-in-law, Aŋnasuvinik's sister forgave the brothers. The people in the karigi said that it was Aŋnasuvinik's fault because he bossed his wife and brother-in-law too much. THE END.

Carl Stalker told me this story.

J50 Wisdom (knowledge) acquired from observation; P251 Brothers; Q280 Unkindness punished; Q411 Death as punishment; S0 Cruel relatives-in-law; S62 Cruel Husband.

Undoubtedly, Aŋnasuvinik deserved to be punished for his cruelty, but apparently murder was too drastic a solution as the murderer fled the village.

PM85. THE BIRD WHO TOLD

A man and his wife lived by some running water. They had two boys. When the younger brother was old enough to play out the father didn't come home one time. His wife started raising the boys. Towards spring, when the birds came, the boys would follow them when they landed outside the house. One bird couldn't go away from there. He always followed them around making a lot of noise. One time when the bird was hollering again the two brothers heard it sing about their father. It said, "Ahchuliichuliichuliiliihi, ahchuliichuliichuliiliihi. Your father got married to Pissiksuklik's daughter. Ahyaagie. Mayaagi." They went home to their mother and told her what the bird said about their father. She asked where the bird was. Then she went over and the bird sang the song again. She found out that her husband had married another woman. She stayed there for awhile with her kids and then they all went to look for her husband. They became wolves, and when they found him they tore him apart. THE END.

I have forgotten who told me this story.

B131.3 Bird betrays woman's (man's) infidelity; B211.3 Speaking bird; D113.1 Transformation: man to wolf; H1385 Quest for lost persons; J130 Wisdom (knowledge) acquired from animals; Q241 Adultery punished; Q411 Death as punishment; T481 Adultery (MacKenzie River—Jenness 1924:87; West Hudson Bay—Boas 1901:223). A longer version of this particular folktale is widespread in northern Alaska, being known from Nelson 1899:407–10 (Norton Sound); Lucier 1953:217–18 (Buckland); Curtis 1930:261–62 (Selawik); Ostermann 1952:185–87 (Noatak); Lucier 1958:94–96 (Noatak); and Ostermann 1942:95–99 (MacKenzie River).

PM86. GETTING THE ROCK FROM CAPE THOMPSON

A man and his son-in-law lived in Point Hope. They stayed there through the fall and then planned to go towards Kivalina way to set nets for belugas. When they got to where they were going to set their net they found that they had no rock for the ends. The son-in-law decided that he would get a rock from Cape Thompson, where the birds always nest. He was going to get them through his aŋatquq.

When he went his father-in-law started watching him through his aŋatquq. The son-in-law went to the highest cliffs to get the rocks and got a big one from on top. When he turned back he went along the beach close to the water. When he got close to the net both he and the rock fell in the water. The other man watched to see if his son-in-law would come up any place, but for a long time he didn't.

Then the man saw a head come up from the water not too far out from the beach. Then the son-in-law stood up halfway in the water and the other man saw that he had a rope around his shoulders. The son-in-law was walking backwards towards the beach pulling the rock with a rope. When the rock got close to the beach the other man saw that the rope was tied around the middle. The rock had a place for the rope. The son-in-law fell with the rock because he wanted to work on it in the water with his aŋatquq. After that they used the rock for their net. THE END.

This is as far as I heard this story from Carl Stalker.

D1711 Magician; D2136.1 Rocks moved by magic (Greenland—Rink 1875:258).

PM87. THE MAN WHO SET TRAPS

Down at Cape Blossom (Iglugrak, beavers used to build their houses there and that's why they call it Iglugrak) there lived a man and his wife. The man used to hunt caribou in spring and winter behind Iglugrak. He was waiting behind Iglugrak, sitting on a hump where he used to sit and wait for caribou. While he was waiting he saw caribou coming. He got ready to shoot, and all of a sudden he didn't know what he was doing, like he had passed out.

When he woke up he was lying down just under a hill in the flat. When he woke up he sat up and looked around. He saw running water. He got up and started walking toward the running water and saw a house a little farther away, and he walked to the house and when he got close he went to the door, stayed there a few minutes, and then went inside, where he found an old man, his wife, and their daughter. When he went in the old man said, "I'm glad we're going to have somebody with us." So the old man gave the man his daughter.

So the man stayed with them, and one morning when he woke up he heard his father-in-law talking. He heard the old man say, "I want to eat the kind of ptarmigan that has its two legs joined together. I want my son-in-law to go out and hunt that kind." He told his son-in-law, "There's ptarmigan like that on the other side of the hill."

When the man went up the hill he saw the ptarmigan and the ptarmigan saw him. The man thought, "I'm not going to reach him as a man." So he used his amulet and became a squirrel and started going through inside the snow. He thought to himself, "I wonder how far I am." So he lifted his head through the snow and saw the ptarmigan's neck. The ptarmigan was looking around. It was a big ptarmigan. So the man who had become a squirrel went inside the snow and kept going through the snow. He thought to himself again, "I wonder how far I am?" So he dug up through the snow and found himself underneath that big ptarmigan.

The ptarmigan didn't know the man was under him, so the man took his bow and arrow and shot the big ptarmigan, which fell down in the snow.

The man changed back from his squirrel disguise and became a man again. There was a lot of wind from the wings of the big ptarmigan. He waited until the wind from the wings stopped and then went up. When he got up he looked around and saw the big ptarmigan dead. He didn't take the ptarmigan home because it was too big. He went home without the ptarmigan.

When he went home his father-in-law was lying down singing a song. When the son-in-law came in he sat up and said, "So my son-in-law came home." The son-in-law said, "I got the big ptarmigan." The father-in-law said, "Let it stay up there; I don't want it."

The man stayed home a few days after he shot the ptarmigan, and then his father-in-law said, "I want to eat fish. I haven't checked my traps in a long time. They're just in that running river there." When the man went down to the traps there was high water covered with ice, so he saw just a few poles standing up. When he went down to the traps he walked to the traps, but the ice was thin and there were bubbles in it. He was scared to go closer to the traps, but he started walking to the traps even though the ice was thin. He got to the first pole and started following the poles and went to the mouth of the traps. When he got to the mouth of the traps the ice started breaking up and he started falling down. Then he stopped falling. When he fell down he opened his eyes and found that he was in a ditch.

When he looked up he saw an open hole above him. He didn't know how to go up, so he stayed there. While he was there he thought of his bow and arrow. His bow had a braided string on it, so he took the string off, took the braids out, and then had a long string. He tied the strings together, tied one end to the arrow, and threw it up through the hole. His arrow got stuck and he pulled at it, and when it wouldn't come loose he climbed the string. When he climbed out he took his bow and arrow and went home. He didn't take any fish because that was really the old man's trap for people.

When he got close to the house he heard his father-in-law singing. And when he quit singing he always said, "My son-in-law is going to find what he's looking for." His son-in-law went into the house. The ptarmigan, too, was really that old man's trap for people, but the man got both of them. When the son-in-law was out in the evenings he thought he recognized his real home in the flat. That old man was going to send the man home, and so one time when he woke up he found himself in Kiipaluk, near his home. THE END.

This is as far as I heard this story from William Trueblood from Kotzebue. They call him Trueblood because he used to spit up blood.

B872 Giant bird; D117 Transformation: man to rodent; D2121 Magic journey (Greenland—Rasmussen 1921:I, 219); H900 Tasks imposed; H931 Tasks assigned in order to get rid of hero; H1150 Tasks: stealing, capturing, or slaying; J1100 Cleverness; K730 Victim trapped; K800 Killing or maiming by deception; K2210 Treacherous relatives; P261 Father-in-law; R10 Abduction. The giant ptarmigan appears in Ostermann 1952:246–51 (King Island) and Rasmussen 1932:224–25 (Kotzebue). In Rasmussen's version the killing of the giant ptarmigan is just one incident in a long story. In PM47 in this volume a man also changes into a squirrel.

PM88. SELAWIK AND BUCKLAND WARS

In Selawik lived a man, his son, and the son's wife. The man had no wife. His son always went hunting for caribou. In springtime the son went out camping alone. He stayed away all summer, so his father started using his son's wife. The son hunted all summer and in the fall went home. When the son went home into his house his wife told him, "I'm not good anymore. Your father's been using me." So the son went next door into his elder brother's house.

He stayed there with his elder brother all winter. In spring he took off to Buckland because Selawik and Buckland people always had war and he wanted to get killed. He hunted all spring and summer and in the fall got to Buckland. Towards evening he got close to the village and heard a noise. The Buckland people were playing football. When he got closer the people saw him and started running towards him while he was walking towards them. When they got closer he pulled his parka halfway off and covered his face with it and stopped. He was ready to get killed. He thought they would kill him, but when two boys reached him they picked him up and carried him to a house.

When they went into the house he saw two old people, a man and his wife, and there was a girl with them. The two boys who had picked him up took him to their mother and father, the old man and old woman. The girl there was their sister. He told them, "I came to get killed, but you took me home." The old man said, "Those two boys took you home because they want you for a husband for my daughter so you can marry her." So he got married to the girl and stayed with them.

Those Buckland people used to kill anybody who came, but they didn't kill him because the other people were scared of that old man and his sons. The son and his new wife went to Selawik in falltime to see the son's elder brother. When they reached Selawik they stopped at his elder brother's house. The Selawik people and Buckland people quit having wars because the Selawik boy had gotten a Buckland girl for a wife. They were friendly after that. THE END.

I have forgotten who told me this.

P253.0.2 One sister and two brothers; S11 Cruel father; T481 Adultery (MacKenzie River—Jenness 1924:87; West Hudson Bay—Boas 1901: 223); W11.5 Generosity toward enemy.

In a sense both the father and wife were punished for their adultery because the son withdrew himself as a provider.

PM89. THE WOMAN WHO PLAY DIED

In Cape Prince of Wales there lived a man, his wife, and their two young boys. When the two boys got big (about eight or nine) they started playing out. Their mother got sick. When she got sick she died in a few days. Her husband buried her. Her husband always went up to see the grave. Three days after she died he went up to see her grave and the woman wasn't there. When she wasn't in the grave her husband started raising the boys and they got big.

Springtime came and he still watched his boys. When the ice went out they saw a boat coming toward them from the point. The boat reached their place and the two boys went down to meet the boat.

When they got close they saw a man with his hair cut straight all around his face (like somebody had cut it with a bowl on his head). The two boys helped the people in the boat. When they went home they told their father, "That man we saw down there looks like our mother."

When the boys talked about that man, their father told them to go get the man and invite him to dinner, so they did. They took the man home and he stood by the door. He was wearing men's clothes, but had a funny haircut. The man standing by the door got hot, so the father told him to take his parka off and the man said, "When I go to people's, I don't take my parka off." When he didn't want to take his parka off the father got close to him and grabbed him and took the parka off.

When the father took the man's parka off he saw real white skin, like nalak, wound around his upper body. The man had breasts. He was his wife. The father said, "That time you died I shouldn't have buried you. I should have killed you." So the father took a knife and stabbed the man who was really his wife. That time when she got sick she was playing sick and she play died, because she wanted to run away from her husband. THE END.

Wanda Stalker told this story.

E586.2 Dead returns third day after burial (Labrador—Hawkes 1916: 153); H79 Recognition by physical attributes; K1837 Disguise of woman in man's clothing; K1860 Deception by feigned death; K2213 Treacherous wife; P251 Brothers; Q261 Treachery punished (MacKenzie River—Jenness 1924:87; West Hudson Bay—Boas 1907:551f.); Q411 Death as punishment.

PM90. The Boy Who Married a Dwarf

In Point Barrow, a little farther up from the village proper, lived a man and his wife. They had a son who always hunted for them. In summertime when the son was hunting he got a caribou and was going to work it when he saw two men in the willows. The two men came out from the willows and went to the son and said, "We hear you are a fast runner."

The two men were dwarfs who came to invite the son to their village. The son followed the two dwarfs who were running. While they were running they reached a house. The two dwarfs thought they would leave the son far behind, but he was just a little behind. In the house were the dwarfs' parents and their sister. The two dwarfs had gone to get the son for a husband for their sister because she didn't like to marry a dwarf.

After the son stayed overnight the dwarfs took him up to their uncle. They let him visit with their uncle. When they went up to see their uncle the two dwarfs and the son went to the karigi for a meeting. The uncle let the son sit close to the wall. While he was sitting here he heard an arrow come toward him. Somebody had shot toward him. When he heard the arrow he jumped to one side. When the son jumped he saw the arrow stick in the wall where he had been sitting. It just missed him.

The two dwarfs' uncle had gone by the door and shot at the son; he thought he would kill him. When the uncle didn't kill the son he said, "I'm not going to worry about you. Nothing will kill you when you're hunting." The uncle said, "When I'm out hunting I never miss any kind of animals. This is the first time I've ever missed with my bow and arrow."

After they stayed in the karigi a little while they went back to the home of the dwarfs' parents. They stayed with the dwarfs' parents a few days, and then the son took his wife back to his parents because he was worried about them. The son and his wife stayed with his parents for a few days after they got there. When the son went hunting he always took his wife along so that she could pack some meat. His wife always packed a whole caribou on her back and took it home. She was really strong.

One time when they were hunting on the beach they saw a man come out from the ice. This man from the ice had come to see his niece's husband. It was the girl's uncle who came from across the ocean. After the man saw his niece and her husband he went away. The son and his wife had a baby boy. When he got big he was a tough-looking boy. After they had stayed with the son's parents they went back to the wife's parents. They would visit back and forth. THE END.

Daniel Walton used to tell this story.

F451 Dwarfs; T110 Unusual marriage.

PM91. THE UMUKS

A man and his wife lived with their son in Point Hope. There also lived there another man and wife, with their son, who were not close relatives to the first. Both named their sons after grandparents who had died. The parents showed the boys that they should call each other umuk. This means that the first boy is named after his father's father and the second boy after the first boy's father's mother. Also, the grandmother and the grandfather called each other umuk. These boys played together.

One time when they went to the beach other kids were playing over aways, but these two always played alone. It was fall and the beach had thin ice. They didn't notice when the other kids left. After awhile they saw men standing close to them. It was three brothers. They got ahold of one boy and threw him in the water through the ice. They gave the other boy a ṭuk, and every time the boy in the water tried to come to the beach they said, "Push your umuk down." And he pushed the boy farther out with the ṭuk. He cried because he didn't want to push the boy out, but they told him to. They let him do it several times, and finally the other boy froze in the water. The three brothers left.

Crying, the boy went home. His parents asked him what was wrong. He said, "Those men wanted to ṭuk my umuk, so I kept pushing him in the water and he froze." When he told them, they and the other boy's parents went down with him to find the boy. They found him frozen in the water. THE END.

This is as far as I heard this story from Carl Stalker.

K958 Murder by drowning; K2200 Villains and traitors; P251.6.1 Three brothers; S131 Murder by drowning (Central—Boas 1888:637; Labrador —Hawkes 1916:152; Greenland—Holm 1912:56; Rasmussen 1921:I, 363; 1921:III, 200).

An unusual relationship through naming is described.

PM92. THE POLAR-BEAR WOMAN

A man and his wife lived in a village on the beach close to Shismaref. A rich man also lived in the village. They had a karigi. The first man had an unmarried elder brother. The man and his wife stayed there for a few years and died, leaving the elder brother alone in the house. In the evening he'd go up to the karigi and stay there until everybody left to go home. He went there every night. One night when he went home the house seemed different. There was meat cooked for him, even though there was nobody there. Every night when he went home from the karigi after that he'd find cooked food and a cleaned house.

One evening when the woman brought food for the men at the karigi the elder brother saw a plate held up by the hands through the katak (entrance passage) and then it was placed in front of him as he sat by the door. Every evening when the woman brought the food the elder brother would see the plate and arms holding it for him. The rich man saw the plate and looked at the arms. They were fat arms.

One evening when the arms brought food up the rich man ran and grabbed them. The arms pulled him down through the door. They make lots of noise for awhile, and then there was silence. Later the rich man said, "Airii," and then there was no more noise, so the people went down to the door. They saw the rich man there dead with his head cracked open. The rich man had sons.

When they went home from the karigi the elder brother saw a woman in his house. He got married to her. The woman was real tall, had a big nose, and her teeth showed. She was a polar bear. She had seen that elder brother was quiet, so she had planned to get married to him.

Because the woman had brought food to him in the karigi and then killed the rich man, the rich man's sons wanted to fight the elder brother. The woman told them not to pick on him because they could not win. The elder brother and his wife went to the karigi. He fought the boys and killed them all, leaving only their mother. He was strong but quiet. When her boys were killed the mother started crying. She cried and cried and finally started making noise like a wolf. The woman that was a polar bear was working in the house one day when she saw a wolf was going to jump on her. She knew it, so she turned around and grabbed it and killed it on the sharp rocks of the stove.

The elder brother and his wife had a baby boy. One time when he got big he started walking through the beach. He met two boys who were the polar bear's brothers. They invited their cousin to their house, but he didn't want to go alone. He went home and got his parents, and they went and visited his mother's parents, who were also polar bears. They stayed down there for awhile, and when the two boys were going out to hunt the elder brother would put his father-in-law's parka on and go with them.

One morning the elder brother was going down to a hole that they used to go in and hunt. Just when he stuck his head in the hole a walrus came up. It stuck its tusk in his back and killed him. The elder brother's wife and their son stayed with her parents for awhile and then went back home. The boy got big and started hitting and killing walrus. He had a real long rope. He put all the walrus he killed on it and pulled them home with his kayak. The second time he went out he killed a lot of walrus. He tied them to a rope and was going back home when the walrus' dog came from the back, grabbed the boy, and killed him. THE END.

This is as far as I heard this story from Daniel Walton.

B10 Mythical beasts and hybrids; B615.7 Marriage to bear in human form (MacKenzie River—Jenness 1924:76; Central—Boas 1907:638f.; Smith Sound—Kroeber 1899:176; Greenland—Holm 1912:82); D113.1 Transformation: man to wolf; D113.2 Transformation: man to bear (Kodiak—Golder 1907:297; 1909:10; Bering Strait—Nelson 1899:493; West Hudson Bay—Boas 1901:326; Cumberland Sound—Boas 1901: 251f.; Cape York—Rasmussen 1921:III, 124, 211, 297; Greenland—Rasmussen 1921:I, 184; 1921:II, 96, 184; Rink 1875:193); D531 Transformation by putting on skin (Kodiak—Golder 1903:95; Bering Strait—Nelson 1899:468; Central—Boas 1899:617; Cumberland Sound—Boas 1901:181; Greenland—Rasmussen 1921:I, 364; 1921:II, 13; 1921:III, 75, 143, 262; Rink 1875:146); F513 Person unusual as to his mouth; J514 One should not be too greedy; N831.1 Mysterious housekeeper (Kodiak—Golder 1903:88; West Hudson Bay—Boas 1901:223); P150

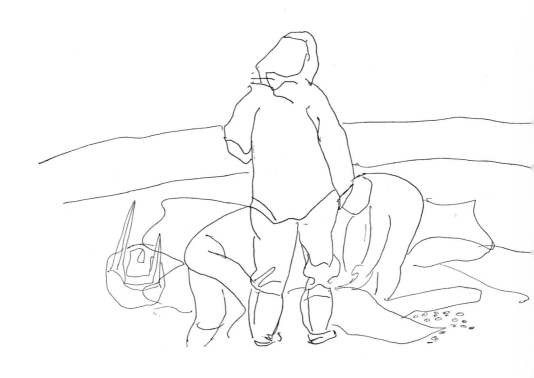

Rich man; T110 Unusual marriage. A fascinating description of the walrus dog can be found in Jenness (1952:9).

PM93. The Puppy Who Became a Boy

An old man and his wife with no kids lived in Point Hope. The old man always went out hunting but he never got anything. One time when he did not go out he started walking along the beach. He saw a just-born puppy lying there frozen. It was real pretty, so he took it home and put it on the floor by the door. Toward evening the puppy started melting and making noise. They stayed awake for a few more hours and the puppy started moving around, so they went to sleep. The next morning it was walking around. They fed it and tried to let it grow.

The puppy got big and one morning when they woke up they missed it, but by the door they saw a little baby. They were so excited that they wanted to reach the baby quickly. They both jumped out of bed and ran down, but the baby became a puppy. It stayed a puppy for awhile and then one morning they missed it again. They saw a little boy sitting by the door. One of them went down and grabbed the little boy. The puppy became a boy and stayed a boy.

The boy got big and the old man made a play whaleboat. After he put everything in it he put it by the door. One morning they woke up and heard a noise in the stormshed. The boy got in the play boat and went out. He saw a whale in the stormshed, so he took a spear from the boat and killed it. They worked on it. When the boy got big he started hunting and got a lot of food for those old people. THE END. This is as far as I heard this story; I have forgotten from where.

C757 Tabu: doing things too hastily; D341 Transformation: dog to person; D1121 Magic boat (Kodiak—Golder 1909:17; Bering Strait—Nelson 1899:500; MacKenzie River—Jenness 1924:41; Central—Boas 1888:628; Cumberland Sound—Boas 1901:181; Smith Sound—Kroeber 1899:171; Greenland—Holm 1912:43; Rasmussen 1921:III, 102, 294; Rink 1875:154, 300, 417).

I have included C757 because in a number of these tales doing something too hastily has bad consequences. Having a son to provide for them is the fulfillment of an old couple's dream.

PM94. THE MEAN GRANDDAUGHTER

In a village lived a rich man and his son and a grandmother and her granddaughter. The rich man's son got sick, so the rich man told somebody to go over and tell the grandmother and granddaughter. Somebody went over and told them, "The rich man's son is sick." The granddaughter said: "Yes, I will go over and try to help him. Get him ready. Lay him on the floor and put a piece of log under his head for a pillow. Then turn the lights off."

When they were just about ready the granddaughter started over. When she went in the room was dark. There were people around inside the house. She heard the rich man's son in the middle of the floor. She felt and found him lying there with a log for a pillow. She told everybody in the house to start singing, and they did. While they were singing she called out again, "Sing louder and maybe I'll try to help him this time." Everybody started singing louder. She took out her big ulu and cut the rich man's son's head off.

She went out and home to her grandmother. She told her, "Grandmother, let's run away from this village. If anybody knows how that young man died they'll do something to us." They got ready and left. While they were on the way the granddaughter said, "Let the trail behind us get stormy." The trail behind them got real stormy, but their way was nice and clear. They kept going until late in the afternoon. They got to a creek and went upstream until finally they got to some open water. The granddaughter got some water from the open place, and when she did she saw a lot of beads on the bottom. She picked up a few and went back to her grandmother. She told her, "Grandmother, maybe we're still too close to that village. We'd better get started again and go farther." They went off again.

After they had been on their way for awhile they stopped again and camped. The granddaughter made a house. She was a good hunter and hunted caribou. When she got caribou she took all the parts home. They had a big cache outside. She took out all the lower leg bones, cut them in half, and stood them in a circle around the house. She put three bones upright in the ground behind the house but inside the circle. She said, "That's how far I'll go if I have to go back."

One morning the granddaughter walked up a little ways and she saw three young men. When they saw her one came over, leaving two behind. They thought that she looked like a rich girl because she had beads on her forehead. The granddaughter and the man started talking. The man said, "A rich man sent us looking for a grandmother and granddaughter." The granddaughter said: "I don't know about that. I saw some smoke down there a little while ago when I got there. Maybe those two live down there. I'd better go down and check. If they are there I'll let you know. I'll wave my hand and you can come down." She went down to her place.

When she got there she climbed on top of the house and said through the window to her grandmother, "Grandmother, try to throw your spear up through the window. Act like you're trying to kill me." The grandmother stuck her spear up and the girl waved to the three young men. They ran down. When they got close they stepped on the three bones she had stood up and the bones cut their feet. They started to work on their feet, and while they did the granddaughter shot them with her bow and arrows. The End.

Kenneth Flood told me this story.

D2141 Storm produced by magic (West Hudson Bay—Boas 1901:321; Central—Boas 1888:584, 622; Cumberland Sound—Boas 1901:164; Greenland—Rasmussen 1921:I, 367; 1921:II, 170; 1921:III, 158, 270; Rink 1875:223, 375, 450, 469); K730 Victim trapped; K824 Sham doctor kills his patients; K914.3 Slaying under cover of darkness; L111.4.1 Orphan hero(ine) lives with grandmother; P150 Rich man. The sharpened caribou-leg bonetrap appears in Lucier 1958:111–15 (Noatak) in conjunction with a jade house.

One of the rare cases where treacherous murder goes unpunished.

PM95. The Big Woman

A grandmother and a granddaughter lived alone along a creek. They had nothing but fish to eat. One day the grandmother got sick. She got worse and worse and knew that she was going to die, so she told her granddaughter: "If I die here don't try to stay alone. Go upstream from our place, and when you get to the end of the stream go along the slope under the hills. While you are walking you will see a small bluff. There are some wolves there that will try to chase you. Don't try to run from them, but just stay where you are. Then they will quit chasing you and leave you alone. If they don't get you, continue in the same direction. You will see a big lake on your way. Go on the right side, and when you get on top of the hill you will see a village. There might be some people there if they haven't left."

The grandmother started looking for something behind her and finally brought out her old belt. There were some wood shavings hanging on it. She gave it to her granddaughter and told her, "If you happen to have a hard time while you are on your way, use these shavings." Finally the grandmother died.

Since her grandmother told her not to stay in the house alone the granddaughter started upstream the way she had been told. She went along the slope of the hill beyond the end of the creek and saw a little bluff, from which the wolves came after her. She didn't move and the wolves went away. She kept going and saw a big lake. She went on the right side of the top of a high hill, where she saw a village below. She looked at it and saw nobody there. Right by the edge of the village she saw a house standing alone.

She went down to it and started going in. There was a middle-aged couple inside. While she was there their son came home. The middle-aged woman started telling her a story: "There is a big stout woman around here someplace. When she comes to the village she takes all the men and women out hunting with her and tells them what to do for her. She is mean. I want to keep you for my daughter-in-law, but I'm afraid of that big woman."

After she said that the young man went out and got some caribou. When he returned the middle-aged woman said: "You can have my son for your husband. When some of the women started getting mean to the fat woman she went down to the edge of the lake on a little high spot and fought them. She killed some of them. When she comes back to the village you try to be nice to her. She always comes around to visit us. If she comes you get ready for her. Get some dried meat from the caribou's belly and give it to her. Every time she comes do the same. When your husband comes home with meat cut off the belly piece and put some sand on top of it to dry it. The big woman likes it that way."

The next time her husband came home the girl fixed some dried meat. One day her mother-in-law said, "It might be any time now that the villagers and that big woman come home." The next morning they saw a big crowd of people coming. And the old people said, "They are coming home from hunting." The girl saw the big woman way in back, coming last with a big sled and a big load of meat that the men had gotten and the other women had worked. All the villagers went home to their houses and the big woman went to her house.

The girl took the meat that she had dried over to the big woman. The big woman thanked her saying, "That's the kind I like to eat when I first come home." She started eating it without using an ulu, but just chewing the whole thing. The girl went home to her husband. The same day, when it was almost bedtime, the big woman came in. The girl and her husband went to bed. The big woman went to bed with the girl's husband, lying right between them. The girl couldn't go to sleep because she felt sorry for her husband and she started to get mad. Her mother-in-law told her not to get mad all right, but she did anyway. Finally she started pushing the big woman with her elbow. The big woman put on her clothes and went out.

After she went out the girl and her husband slept. The big woman didn't come back, but when they awoke someone called in, "The big woman wants to see that girl." Her father-in-law started giving her a bath. Then her mother-in-law gave her a real soft spring-skin parka. After the girl put it on she took out her belt with the wood shavings and put it on. Then she went out. She saw the big woman by the lake on a little high spot, so she walked down. Everybody was watching. When she got there they grabbed each other to fight. The daughter-in-law saw something like a hole in the high spot and thought maybe that that was the place where the big woman was going to try to kill her. The big woman threw her, but the girl landed on the other side of the hole. While they were fighting the girl started sweating and told the big woman, "Let me try to throw you once. You aren't going to try to throw me in that hole all the time."

She thought of the shavings on her belt. She grabbed the big woman and threw her in the center of the hole where she dropped out of sight. In that hole were the same wolves that the girl had seen by the cliff. They grabbed the big woman, tore her to pieces, and ate her. After the girl killed the woman her husband walked over to her and took her home. The people didn't feel sorry about that big woman. The girl lived there after that and everybody had peace. That granddaughter and grandmother must have been from that village before. THE END.

I heard this story from Frieda Goodwin.

D810 Ownership of magic object: a gift; D956 Magic stick of wood; D1777 Magic results from power of thought; J151 Wisdom (knowledge) from old person; J624.5 Warnings against certain peoples; K929 Murder by strategy; L111.4.1 Orphan hero(ine) lives with grandmother; N825.3.3 Help from grandmother; Q211.8 Punishment for desire to murder (Cumberland Sound—Boas 1901:62; Smith Sound—Kroeber 1899:177; Greenland—Holm 1912:47; Rink 1875:157, 222); Q411 Death as punishment.

PM96. THE GIRL WHO WAS LEFT ALONE

In a village somewhere lived a rich man with three sons and one daughter. One of the sons had a wife. The daughter didn't want to get married. Her father told her to get married, but she said no.

Finally her father said to everyone in the village, "Pack up and get ready to go from here to someplace else." He asked one of the aŋat- quqs to make his daughter go to sleep.

They started getting ready to take everything away from the vil- lage. The rich man got ready too. The eldest son's wife started feeling sorry about her sister-in-law because they were going to leave her sleeping in the house. They cleaned everything out of the house and cache. The eldest son's wife started getting some stuff ready to leave her sister-in-law. She hid a needle, some sinew, and an ulu inside the house so that if her sister-in-law looked for them she could find them. The eldest son's wife put her old clothes outside and covered them up with a little dirt. She got an old poke with a little seal oil in it and put it under the steps of the cache, so that if her sister-in-law went into the cache she'd step on it.

While the girl was sleeping everyone left and went away. Finally she woke up and looked around inside the house. There was nothing there. She went out and looked around the village, but she found nobody there. She started to look for food. She went to the cache and found it empty, but while she was looking she stepped on the old poke. She picked it up and took it in the house. She had already found the sewing equipment and the old clothes. She started to make mukluks (pukruk) from the old poke.

After she finished she stayed for a little while. She put out a few snares and once in awhile got a few ptarmigan to eat. Finally after the snow melted she started walking away from the village. She camped a few times and finally got to a river. She camped there and then started upstream. When she saw some fish in the river she thought that she should stay in that place a little while and catch some fish. She stopped and made a little ebrulik. She started getting fish.

One morning while she was there she went up towards the land when she came out of the house. In a little ways she found a freshly killed caribou. She looked around and saw nobody, so she worked on the caribou. She dried it up and took the skin and ivalu. In a few days she found another caribou in the same place. She worked on it too. One day a young man came. She invited him to have dried fish with her. They ate and the young man said to her, "I killed those caribou just behind you. I was trying to help you because you were all alone here."

After they ate the young man said to her, "My father likes to eat dried fish too." When he was getting ready to go she gave him some dried fish. She stayed alone for a few days and then the young man said, "I came to take you home." The woman said nothing for a little while. She knew that she had nobody to help her, so she followed him. They reached the young man's family and the woman became the young man's wife.

The young man had two unmarried brothers. The family lived alone at that place. Her mother-in-law worked on clothes for the girl while she just worked on food. One day she started thinking of her sister-in-law who had left those things for her. She started making a fancy parka. After she finished, her husband wanted to travel because he thought he might see a village. He took his two brothers, his wife, and the parka. His wife wanted to give it to her sister-in-law if she found her.

They traveled and finally saw a village, outside of which they stopped. Her husband told her, "You should go to the village. You might find your parents there." She went over and, when she got there, recognized her parents and went into their house. She went straight to her sister-in-law and gave her the parka. Her father recognized her and wanted to embrace her, but she tried to stay by her sister-in-law.

In a little while she heard growling outside. She went out and saw that they had killed a wolf right outside the house. It was one of her brothers-in-law. She went to where they had stopped and went away with two wolves. She became a wolf. THE END.

I have forgotten who told me this story.

B651.6 Marriage to wolf in human form (MacKenzie River—Jenness 1924:38); D113.1 Transformation: man to wolf; D1711 Magician; N820 Human helpers; P150 Rich man; P251.6.1 Three brothers; P253. 0.3 Three brothers and one sister; P264 Sister-in-law; Q40 Kindness repaid; S11 Cruel father; S301 Children abandoned; T311 Woman averse to marriage; W10 Kindness; W27 Gratitude. In PM29 in this volume a girl was abandoned.

If the daughter would not marry and add a provider to the family, as well as extending the kinship ties of the family's members, then she was a burden.

PM97. THE PORCUPINE

A man and his wife lived in Point Hope with their daughter. After the daughter grew up and got to be a young woman she became real lazy. She stayed in bed all the time. She was so lazy that her mother even had to feed her. In the summertime everybody moved out to the hunting camp. Her father got ready to go. They left the girl in the house. During the fall the couple came back. When they got to the house their daughter was gone. They saw porcupine tracks going away from the house. That girl was a porcupine. THE END.

Carl Stalker told this story.

D117 Transformation: man to rodent; Q321 Laziness punished; S301 Children abandoned; W111 Laziness.

PM98. HUNTING ELEPHANTS

A man was out hunting in the summertime. He camped by a creek for overnight. He saw an elephant [kiiligvuk, mammoth] coming from upstream, closely followed by a dog with its mouth up to its ears. Following them were two men. When they saw the man they went over to him and said, "You better come with us. Maybe that dog has killed that elephant already." They went and found the dog with a dead elephant just a little ways away.

As they started cutting it the two men said, "We should have some meat from this elephant." They told the man to get some wood from the lake close by. He went down and got some dry wood. He came back and tried to make a fire, but the dry wood wouldn't burn. One of the two men went over to get some wood himself. He picked some willows from in the water and went back. He made a fire with the wet willows. They started cooking some meat over the fire. After they ate, the two gave the man a piece of meat from the elephant and told him, "If you go home store this meat in your cache. If someday you and your wife have nothing to eat, cut some of it off, leaving a little in the cache, and eat the rest."

After they told him that the man went back to his camp. During the falltime he went home to his wife and told her what the men had said. He stored the meat in his cache. They lived through the winter and in the spring they started to get low on food. They had nothing much to eat, so they cut a piece off the elephant meat, leaving a little in the cache. They ate the meat. When they got hungry again they went in the cache and found the piece of elephant meat as big as it was before, so they did the same thing again. Those two men were living under the ground, just like there are people in the air. That's why they used wet wood and hunted elephants. The End.

Frank Burns told this story. In Noah's time the elephants didn't want to go into the ark because they were too stout. That's why they went underground.

B15.1 Animal unusual as to his head; B877 Giant mythical animals; D1652.1.9 Inexhaustible meat; F80.1 Physical features of underworld. Similar to Giddings 1961:71–73 (Kobuk River); Ingstad 1954:277 (Anaktuvuk Pass); Gubser 1965:33 (Anaktuvuk Pass); Ostermann 1952:151–53 (Colville River); and Rasmussen 1932:68–72 (Colville River).

The bones of mammoths and other extinct animals frequently wash from the banks of the rivers in northern Alaska. Thus the Noatak Eskimo assumption that mammoths live underground is reasonable, though I'm not sure about the Eskimo explanation of how they got there! Nordman (in Ostermann 1952:152) offers two explanations for Eskimo stories about mammoth hunting: racial memory of the time when the Eskimos' ancestors actually hunted mammoths, or the finding of entire frozen mammoths by aboriginal Eskimos. In view of the several thousands of years since the mammoth disappeared from Alaska, the first explanation seems doubtful. Nor have any entire or partially fleshed mammoths been found, so far as we know. The description of mammoths may have come from Siberia, where such remains have been located, or early white travelers to northern Alaska may have described the mammoth, whose bones the Eskimo knew.

PM99. The Girl Who Disappeared

Three brothers and their young sister lived in a village. They had no parents. The youngest brother was young too, while the older two were young men. When the three brothers went out hunting the young girl stayed alone in the house and worked. She never visited other people. While they were living there her brother sometimes went to the karigi in the evening and stayed for awhile. When they came home they always found her inside the house cleaning up and working.

One night when they went to the karigi again she started scrubbing the floor. While she did she saw a rope hanging inside the house from the window. She stopped scrubbing and started thinking, "Maybe they want me to tie myself up with that rope." She tied it around her waist. After she did she went up through the window.

In awhile the brothers came home from the karigi. They didn't see her in the house, but just saw the scrubbing water on the floor. They started talking, "Maybe our sister went out to visit people." It got late, so they went to sleep. When they woke she still wasn't home. That same morning they looked around the village, but they didn't find her. They started to miss her, so they got a young woman from the village to take her place and work for them. She was a good worker too.

One time they went to the karigi for the evening. When they got back to the house they heard a noise from above. Someone said, "Down there is my brothers' house. I wish I could stay with them and have a good time with them." The brothers heard that. In a little while they heard their sister say the same thing, but from closer. The third time she said the same words from just above the window.

Finally they saw her feet through the window. The elder and the younger brother wanted to grab her. They made no noise, and finally when she was halfway in, the elder brother grabbed her around the waist. As soon as he did the girl disappeared like the snap of a finger. She was gone for good. After they lost her the younger brother said, "Maybe if I'd grabbed her after she had gotten to the floor she'd be home." The elder brother had grabbed her too soon, and that's why they lost her. THE END.

Jimmy Hawley told this story.

C757 Tabu: doing thing too soon; F10 Journey to upperworld; F51 Sky rope; P253.0.3 Three brothers and one sister; R10 Abduction.
   Again, the danger of being too hasty.

PM100. ULULIINAH

A man and his wife and their baby boy lived on a river. The mother of one of them lived with them. The man and the wife would go hunting together while the mother took care of the boy. One day after they went out hunting the baby started crying. The mother tried to stop him, but he kept crying. She started to sing, "Ululiinah crying, Ululiinah crying." The third time she called loudly, "Ululiinah crying," someone started coming outside. A big stout woman came in and told the woman, "Let me put him in my parka and take him out. I will bring him back."

The big woman took him out and while they were gone Ululiinah's parents came home from hunting and asked the mother, "Where's Ululiinah?" She said, "A woman took him out. She told me she'd bring him right back, but she never returned." The boy's parents started looking for him. They looked around for a long time, but they never found him. The big woman took Ululiinah home. She let him play out, but she tied him with a rope from inside.

One day Ululiinah saw two people close to a hill and he started singing, "One of them / with bow and arrow / one of them / with pretty parka." While he was singing the woman asked him from inside, "What are you doing?" Ululiinah said, "There is a seagull and a raven fighting each other up there." She didn't come out.

The two people started looking for the singer. They started seeing something on the side of the hill. It was a child and they recognized their son. They got close and watched him for a little while. Ululiinah didn't know they were there. Finally the father went down. When he saw Ululiinah was tied with a rope he took it off and tied it to a rock. They took Ululiinah home. THE END.

I have forgotten where I heard this story.

H1385 Quest for lost persons; K500 Escape from death or danger by deception; K640 Escape by help of confederate; R10 Abduction; R153.1 Parents rescue son. Similar to Curtis 1930:190–91 (Kotzebue); Lucier 1958:98–99 (Noatak); and Ostermann 1942:80–83 (MacKenzie River).

PM101. THE BOY WHOSE SNOWSHOES MADE HIM RICH

In a village on a river lived a grandmother and her grandson and a rich man and his daughter. When the grandmother went to sleep her grandson started making snowshoes. When he finished he went to bed and slept. After he woke he worked around the place for a little while. Then he said to himself, "I better go upstream and take my snowshoes along." He went, passing a creek coming into the main stream and then going on upriver, until he decided to go over to the creek through the willows. He put on his snowshoes. When he got to the creek he took his snowshoes off and walked down the creek to home.

After he got home he and his grandmother did a little work and then went to bed. The next morning the grandson said, "I better go see my snares." He went up the same trail without using his snowshoes. When he went through the willows he found ptarmigan caught in his snowshoe tracks. He needed no snares. He tried to get them without putting his snowshoes on, but he couldn't, so he put them on and got the ptarmigan. He went back to his grandmother.

Whenever the grandson went out somewhere and got to a place where nobody was going to be walking by, he put his snowshoes on, used them for a little while, and took them off again. The next day when he went over to look, his tracks had caught all kinds of animals that had crossed his trail, just in his snowshoe tracks. He lived that way.

He started getting rich from the snowshoes and made his own cache outside his house. One day the rich man gave him his daughter for a wife. The grandson and his wife lived there for awhile. Finally the grandson told her to come with him when he went out hunting. They walked for quite aways until they got to a low hill. He told his wife, "You stay here while I go over the hill. Don't go anyplace." He put his snowshoes on and went over the low hill. While he was on the other side he heard his wife making noise, so he started back. His wife was snared in his tracks. He took her out and told her, "I told you not to move. If I didn't hear you, you would be dead." They went home. Finally the grandson became rich like his father-in-law. THE END.

Frank Burns told me this story.

C610 Tabu: the one forbidden place; C901.1 Tabu imposed by certain person; D801 Ownership of magic object; D1065.3 Magic snowshoes; D1445 Magic object kills animals; L111.4.1 Orphan hero lives with grandmother; P150 Rich man.

PM102. SIITAKUUYUK

There was a man named Siitakuuyuk. A brown bear raised Sii-takuuyuk. Siitakuuyuk went up to Point Barrow and stayed up there. Every time a Point Barrow man went hunting he didn't come home. So Siitakuuyuk started walking out by himself to a big lake behind Barrow. He walked around the lake, and farther up on a point he saw a man sitting, his back toward Siitakuuyuk. This man who was sitting said to Siitakuuyuk, "I saw you first." Siitakuuyuk said, "No, I saw you first. Your back was turned toward me." So they started quarreling. This man was sitting on top of a rock that looked big. Then the man said, "Let's run a race." The man sitting on the rock had carried, by pack, the rock from a mountain so he could sit on it and wait for people. He was the one who killed the men that went hunting and never returned.

The man asked Siitakuuyuk which way he wanted to race. On one side from the point where the rock was placed were lots of small hills and on the other side was a flat. So Siitakuuyuk chose the hilly side so that when they're running he can go through the hills and then onto the flat. That way he can win. They were going to run in a circle, going opposite directions, and come back to the rock where the man was sitting. So they started and Siitakuuyuk jumped from hill to hill, and when he got about halfway he heard the man make a noise on the other side, in the flat, and so Siitakuuyuk answered him with a sound and kept jumping the hills. When he got to the flat he never saw the man pass him. He ran through the flat and the man ran on the other side, the hilly side. Siitakuuyuk heard him make a noise and answered it. Siitakuuyuk could tell he was ahead of the man, so he ran even faster back to point where the rock was.

The man, who got there last, saw Siitakuuyuk there already. He took out a dagger of walrus ivory sharpened to a point on both ends and threw it at Siitakuuyuk. He missed and the dagger went right through the middle of the niggerheads. That's how sharp it was. The dagger had blood on it. That's what he used to kill the other men. Siitakuuyuk ran after the dagger, grabbed it, and pretended to throw it at that man who jumped up. Then Siitakuuyuk really threw the dagger and hit the man.

The man knew he wouldn't live. He was hit bad. So he told Siitakuuyuk, "If I die, take my head off and put it on top of that rock and my body on the ground. If people come around and hunt tell them to put one arrow on the rock because I like to shoot." Then he told Siitakuuyuk, "I've got a family. My wife is going to expect me home and I have two sons too young to hunt. So you go tell them I'm not coming home." The man's head is still on that rock. No animal ever touched that head.

So Siitakuuyuk went home after he buried the man's body. He stayed in Point Barrow for awhile and then started looking for the man's family. Before the man had died he told Siitakuuyuk that his family lived in the hills behind Barrow and not to go to them from the front but to come up from behind. So Siitakuuyuk did as the man told him and stayed with the family awhile. He told them that he had killed the man, but that the man had started the fight first. Then Siitakuuyuk got married to the man's wife. The man's sons started planning to kill their stepfather. Their mother told them not to try because Siitakuuyuk was tough and would kill them.

When the two boys got old enough to hunt, Siitakuuyuk went back to Point Barrow. The Barrow people always went hunting down the coast. Some men never came home when they went hunting down at the coast. So Siitakuuyuk went down to the coast and saw an iceberg with two sides and an open, but ice-covered, path between the sides. So Siitakuuyuk went between the sides of the iceberg, carrying his kayak, and said, "Aaklaa" ("I wish this path was good for something"). He passed through the iceberg with his kayak (carrying it) and farther up came to a flat piece of float ice on which he saw people. The people were moving around.

When he got close to those people he thought to himself, "Some people never come home from hunting. I wonder if that's them." So he went slow, watching those people, but he didn't go to them right away. When he got even closer to the ice he wondered where people went because there was nobody around. So he watched close around him to see what would happen, and all of a sudden under his kayak came a polar bear with its mouth open. So Siitakuuyuk jumped from his kayak onto the ice and the polar bear kept trying to get him from under the ice. So he walked on the ice and the polar bear followed him under the ice. He jumped to a real thick part of the ice and the polar bear got on top of the ice, trying to get Siitakuuyuk. Siitakuuyuk started jumping over the polar bear and then ran between its legs. He kept doing this for a long time.

Then Siitakuuyuk started running towards that iceberg he saw when he was coming. He started running between the two sides and the polar bear was still running after him. Siitakuuyuk ran out farther on the ice, after going between the sides, and the polar bear got caught between the two sides. When the polar bear got stuck, Siitakuuyuk ran around the side of the iceberg, came up on the polar bear from behind, and killed it with his spear.

Siitakuuyuk didn't cut the polar bear after he killed it, but went home instead. When he got home he told the people at Point Barrow to take their sleds and go down to that polar bear. It was the biggest and he was going to share it. It was a six-legged polar bear. When a hunting man came from Barrow the polar bear always put his six legs out so they would think there were people down there. He let his legs move. So the Barrow people went to cut that polar bear and they all had loads coming home. That's what never let the hunters come home. After Siitakuuyuk killed the polar bear, people who went out hunting always came home.

After that polar bear was killed the Barrow people stayed in their village all winter. Springtime came and Siitakuuyuk knew that some people never came home when they went up to the lake with their kayaks. So when Siitakuuyuk went into the karigi he told the people he should go up to the lake and see what's there. If he finds anything he'll come back and tell the people. Siitakuuyuk went up to the lake with his kayak and paddled along it. He saw a big fish coming after him, so he paddled real fast. The big fish was fast, but Siitakuuyuk was faster. He could see that big fish going under the water, just like a shishauk.

He paddled to a shallow place and started bringing his kayak up the beach. When he got there he jumped out. The fish started coming through the mud and after he got out of the water was stuck there. Siitakuuyuk killed it. The fish was as big as a beluga and looked like one, but the bones looked like the biggest whale they ever caught at Barrow. Those bones are still at Point Barrow, where Daniel Walton saw them. Siitakuuyuk was tough; that's why he killed these animals. The Point Barrow people started coming home from hunting after that and they still do.

(This is as far as I heard this story one time, perhaps from Daniel Walton. Another time I heard some more.)

Siitakuuyuk lived in Point Barrow and had a family. His eldest son's hands were real big. When the boys played football the eldest son never joined in, but just watched. Farther up from Point Barrow lived the Ligligmiut at the mouth of the Colville River. One man there always sent for Siitakuuyuk's eldest son, but the latter never went up. Siitakuuyuk's eldest son was married. His wife was short, had a hook nose, talked a lot, and was friendly.

When the Point Barrow people went up to Liglig, Siitakuuyuk and his family went too. They went by boat, having to portage across some places. They would stop at night. When they reached Liglig, the man who always asked for Siitakuuyuk's eldest son asked if he were coming, and the Barrow people said yes. The man asked again and the Barrow people said, "You'll find out about him from his wife. She is friendly and talks too much."

Siitakuuyuk and the rest of them got there. The man invited Sii-takuuyuk's eldest son to his house, but the latter said, "When we go someplace we stay together." Then the man talked to Siitakuuyuk's eldest son's wife about him. After they settled down and put up their tents they were invited up to the karigi. Everybody went up.

When they went in Siitakuuyuk's eldest son looked around and saw a ball hanging from a string by the window, ready for the kicking game. The man who had asked for him stood up and said, "I want to play with you in the karigi. That's why I always sent for you but you never came. Now that you're here I want to play with you." Siitakuuyuk's eldest son said, "I never played before so I don't know how to play, but I'll try." The man who asked for him went down, jumped, and tried to kick the ball, but he couldn't. He told the other to try. The eldest son said, "I never did it before, but I'll try." He tried but missed. The man who had asked for him said, "Keep trying. Maybe you'll kick it." When he tried again he didn't kick the ball, but went completely through the window.

After he went back in through the door the other man got mad and wanted to kill him. Siitakuuyuk's father said, "We don't know how tough my grandson is because he never plays with kids. I think his hands are not only big, but tough too, so why pick on him?" Some people went out from the karigi. The man who always asked got his bow and arrow ready. When Siitakuuyuk's eldest son went out he saw that the other man was ready. The other man told him to get his bow and arrow. He did and when he was ready he went down.

They started shooting at each other. Siitakuuyuk's eldest son had brought only two arrows. The man who always asked kept shooting, but Siitakuuyuk's eldest son dodged the arrows. He started sweating. When he was sweating lots he took out his first arrow. He aimed it and shot, but missed. He took out his last arrow, and after he shot saw that the man was falling down. The man hadn't seen the arrow when it was shot and that's why he got hit. He was dead. Point Barrow people went home. The man who got killed had a number of kids. After they got to Point Barrow, Siitakuuyuk started thinking about those small kids and how hungry they might be. He went back and raised them. When they got big Siitakuuyuk went back to Point Barrow. THE END.

This is as far as I heard this story from Daniel Walton.

B15.6.3.1 Six-legged quadruped; B61 Leviathan; F514 Person unusual as to his nose; F515 Person unusual as to his hands; J1110 Clever persons; K950 Treacherous murder; K1626 Would-be killers killed; P281 Stepfather; Q211 Murder punished (Cumberland Sound—Boas 1901: 168; Greenland—Rasmussen 1921:III, 76, 111, 294); Q411.6 Death as punishment for murder; S139.2.2.2 Head of slain enemy set on rock; W10 Kindness; Z200 Heroes.

A string of adventures held together by a common hero. More about Siitakuuyuk can be found in PM131 in this volume.

PM103. Kavaachuuk and Taamautayluk

In Kotzebue, down by the present army base, lived a man with his wife and kids. Farther up was another house with a man, his wife, and kids. This first man was named Kavaachuuk. The second man farther over was named Taamautayluk. Kavaachuuk's wife always filled a big poke in summertime with dried salmon in seal oil. Kavaachuuk always left this in the house when he went to the coast in winter. So in spring his kids always had this to eat. In spring when he came back from the coast to Kotzebue he missed the poke. It wasn't in the house. Every time the men played football Kavaachuuk was real clumsy. He fell whenever everybody touched him. When he couldn't find the poke he looked for it and found it in Taamautayluk's iḳigut. When he found it he took it home.

After Kavaachuuk took his poke home Taamautayluk sent one of the men over to Kavaachuuk to tell him, "I want to have war over that poke." Taamautayluk had said, "We'll be shooting each other with bow and arrows." So Kavaachuuk started building a sled. Kavaachuuk knew that he was clumsy and would get killed, so he was building the sled so they could put him in it and take him to bury him. When Kavaachuuk finished the sled he sent a message to Taamautayluk that he was ready to fight. So Kavaachuuk got ready, putting his long parka of caribou on. The sleeves were short (about two inches below the shoulder).

Kavaachuuk took his sled and met Taamautayluk where they were going to fight. Kavaachuuk stopped close to Taamautayluk. Kavaachuuk and Taamautayluk kept shooting at each other and their arrow bags were empty before they killed each other. After they finished all their arrows they walked past each other, touching shoulders as they passed, and went to pick up their arrows. Again they started shooting at each other. Kavaachuuk finally wounded Taamautayluk and they quit fighting.

After Kavaachuuk wounded Taamautayluk, he told him, "Don't eat berries from the ground." He made a law for Taamautayluk not to eat berries. Kavaachuuk wasn't really clumsy. He pretended he was when playing football. Taamautayluk was resting after he was wounded and finally his wound healed up. When Taamautayluk healed he started hollering to his wife that he wanted berries, even if Kavaachuuk said he couldn't eat any. Finally his wife got tired of hearing him ask so she gave him some berries, half a poke of salmon-berries. She put it in front of him and Taamautayluk ate all he wanted. When he got full he quit eating berries, and soon his wound started opening again. His wound got real big and killed him. THE END.

Paul Green (Agnik) told me this story.

C225 Tabu: eating certain fruit; C901.1 Tabu imposed by certain person; C920 Death for breaking tabu (MacKenzie River—Jenness 1924:51, 58; Central—Boas 1888:600; Greenland—Rasmussen 1921:II, 341; Rink 1875:341); J1050 Attention to warnings; Q212 Theft punished; Q411 Death as punishment.

PM104. THE NIŊYUK

There was a piece of wood in a river. The wood was called niŋyuk (cottonwood), a kind they don't burn around here. It was drifting in the river going downstream. The niŋyuk stopped in front of people. When it got to the bank in front of people it started going up to visit the people. When the niŋyuk went into a house in the village (on the river a little up from the coast) he saw a grandmother and her grand-daughter. The niŋyuk became a boy when it went into the house. The grandmother and granddaughter saw the boy come in wearing real nice clothes. He looked like a rich boy. The granddaughter started "aftering" this boy, and in a few days they got married.

The boy stayed over night with his wife and next day went up to the karigi. When he went inside to the karigi he took his parka off and the people commented on him as a strong-looking, nice-looking boy. The boy started staying with these people for a few days.

Farther over in the village lived a grandmother and her grandson. One night the grandson came home looking real sad. He went to bed he was so sad. And the next morning the grandson didn't get out of bed, so his grandmother asked him, "Why are you so sad?" The grandson was lying with his face towards the wall. He said, "That boy who came took the girl I wanted to marry." His grandmother said to him, "Don't feel so sad about it. We'll go up to the karigi and you two can wrestle about it."

So they went to the karigi and the two started wrestling. The grandson and boy got hold of each other and started wrestling. They kept on wrestling, and finally the grandson threw the boy to the floor. The grandson was on top of the boy on the floor. When they both got up the people saw a piece of bark on the floor. They started wrestling again, and again the boy was under the grandson on the floor. When they got up once more the people saw a bigger piece of bark on the floor where the boy had been lying. A third time they started wrestling and a third time the grandson threw the boy on the floor, and when the boy hit the floor he became a niŋyuk again.

The grandson got bashful when the boy became a piece of wood. He got so bashful he left the village, taking another boy with him. The grandson and the other boy started walking through [along] the bank when they went. They didn't go too far, just down to the coast. They saw a house and went in. There was a family in the house. So the two boys stayed overnight in that house.

In the early morning, when the grandson went out to toilet, he looked around and saw a house farther down on the beach. While he was looking at that house farther down he saw a girl come out and start playing ball. He went back into the house where he'd stayed and asked the family about who lived in that house farther down. They told him a grandmother and her granddaughter. The father of the family told the grandson, "When people go to that grandmother and granddaughter they never come out."

So the grandson told the boy he had taken with him, "I'm going down to visit for awhile. I'll be back. You wait here." While the granddaughter was playing ball the grandson walked down, and when he got close she went into the house. When the grandson went into the house he saw by the inside door, by the katak, a live killer whale, the whole thing [agluchurak: killer whale]. He stepped over the killer whale and went in, where he saw the grandmother and granddaughter in the house.

He stayed there awhile and started to go out. He could not find his way out. When he couldn't find his way out he turned back into the stormshed and saw the killer whale. He looked for a stick, found one, and hit the killer whale with it, killing it. Then the grandson went in to the grandmother and granddaughter again and stayed there for awhile. Then the granddaughter went out and came back in crying. And the grandson left again, and this time found his way out and went back to the house where he'd spent the night. When he went back to the house he got the other boy and they both started back to their home village. When they went home they started living like they did before. THE END.

This is as far as I heard this story from Ralph Gallahorn.

D431.3.1 Transformation: bark to person; D956 Magic stick of wood; D1445 Magic object kills animals; L111.4.1 Orphan hero lives with grandmother.

PM105. THE SELAWIK-INDIAN WAR

The Selawik people always stayed in camp. In fall when the ground got hard the men went to have war. When they got on top of a hill they met some men coming from some other place to have war with them. The strangers were Indians. They got in two rows facing each other. The Selawik people had one man who was tough and a good shooter on each end of their line. The two started shooting at the Indians and killing them. When they had war in the old days and they knew people were good shooters, they always put them at the end of the Indian line; they they could keep shooting and finish the rest.

The Selawik people killed Indians until there was just one left. They kept shooting him, but he couldn't die. They hit him in the head, but he didn't die. Finally they cut his head off, but his head kept talking. The head said to the Selawik people, "You are letting me suffer from pain. Spear one of my toes. My heart is in my toe." After they speared one of his toes they took his mukluk off and found the heart still beating. They kept spearing it and finally killed the man. THE END.

I have forgotten, but maybe Tinuk, Agnes Anaktok's brother, told me this story.

D783 Vital head; F559.7 Remarkable heart; P552 Battle formations; Z311 Achilles' heel. The "heart in a toe" motif also occurs in Rasmussen 1932:121–32 (Point Hope); Ostermann 1952:216–22 (Point Hope); and PM108 in this volume.

PM106. Kunuyuk

Two brothers lived in Point Hope. The eldest was named Kunuyuk and the youngest Kavisik (fish scales). They always went to Point Lay and stayed by the bird cliffs for awhile. After that they went up to the mountains and hunted caribou and siksikpuks. The brothers had wives and the younger brother had a son. In the fall after they hunted siksikpuks and caribou they went back to Point Hope. They stayed there for the winter and in the spring went back to camp.

They had their traps set for siksikpuks and in the fall when they planned to go back to Point Hope again they went up to close the traps. These traps were baited with a big rock above the siksikpuk's hole to fall on the siksikpuk when it came out. They both went, each to his own traps, but when they came back to camp the younger brother said he hadn't taken his off. The next day the younger brother went to see his traps. He looked at them all, and when he got to the last trap he saw something shiny in it. When he got close something made him walk real fast, pulling him towards the trap. When he got close he saw a real big hole under the rock. He thought to himself, "Maybe I'll try to go in quickly."

He went in and saw a lot of siksikpuks. The elder brother and the younger brother's wife stayed home overnight. When the boy didn't return the elder brother got worried and started checking his traps. He saw his younger brother sitting outside the last trap hole. When he got close the younger brother turned and looked at him. Then the younger brother made a noise like a siksikpuk and went in the hole.

The elder brother went to the hole and called inside saying, "Kavisik, you come out." The boy called from inside, "I'm not coming out. I have teeth like a siksikpuk already." All day the elder brother tried to get the boy to come out, but he wouldn't. The elder brother got tired of waiting and went.

The younger brother really liked his son. The next day the elder brother took his sister-in-law and his nephew over to the trap. When they got close the younger brother was sitting outside with his back towards them. He turned and looked at them, made a noise like a siksikpuk, and went inside. The elder brother went to the hole and said, "Come out. I've brought your boy, the one you like. Come out and see him." The younger brother said, "I can't. I have teeth like a siksikpuk already."

All day the elder brother called, but he wouldn't come out, not even to see his son. They got tired and went home. The same thing happened the next day. The elder brother tried for a few days, and then one day he got tired of waiting so he went back to camp. He decided to leave for Point Hope.

The next morning they packed their things in their boat and when they were ready to go got in. Just then they heard a voice behind them saying, "Wait for me, wait for me." It was the younger brother's voice. The elder brother told his sister-in-law, "Don't turn back and look at him or you will become invisible." They started off. The younger brother got close, still saying, "Wait for me, wait for me." The elder brother kept telling his sister-in-law not to look back. Finally the younger brother (his soul) flew over the boat. He was crying. He went on and they never saw him again.

They went home to Point Hope. The younger brother's son got old enough to hunt. One summer the elder brother left towards Point Barrow, walking along the beach. He never went to houses when he came to them, but just watched people from far off. Finally he got to a bigger village named Iviruluk. He stayed around there for quite awhile, but never went into the village. He just watched, not letting people know he was there. After a few days he turned back to Point Hope.

He stayed in Point Hope all winter and the next summer he planned to go to Iviruluk again. He took along his nephew. He had been using another man's wife. She was a fast runner. Her husband told her to go with the elder brother. They left and soon reached Iviruluk. Iviruluk had a karigi made out of rock. The elder brother said, "When we go down to the village follow me closely. I am going straight to that rock karigi so follow me in." They got close to Iviruluk and the villagers found out that strangers were coming and ran towards them. The three started running toward the karigi. They met the people, passed them, and went in the karigi.

The door slammed shut and the elder brother turned around to find that he and his wife were there but the nephew was gone. They were locked in and couldn't get out. They had no water and nothing to eat. They noticed a kind of bright spot in the ceiling that they thought might be a hole. That same night, after the people went to sleep, the nephew was out by the door, but he couldn't get in. He tried for a few nights and then he didn't come back anymore. They began to get hungry and thirsty.

One night a woman's voice called through the hole saying, "Are you still alive?" They answered, "Yes, we are still alive." The woman said, "I'll put food and water through the hole. Tomorrow our chief is going to burn this karigi. His name is Tutalluk."

The next morning they started hearing people through the opening. The people threw fire through the open place and then some fat so that the fire burned hot quickly. The two started getting warm. The elder brother said to his wife, "Do you know anything we can do?" She said, "No," but started to vomit something up. She did, and something came out. The woman had magic like a wet spring fog. The thing she vomited broke like a rock and the fog put out the fire.

The man on top who had started the karigi burning said when he heard that noise, "Gee, Kunuyuk's stomach burned and it burst." The woman came that night and told them, "Tomorrow Tutalluk is going to let the karigi fall in. I will try to pull you up if I can." She put a rope down and Kunuyuk let the woman go up first. After she was up the two women pulled him up. The woman took them home and when they went into her house they saw her husband. He was Kunuyuk's cousin. They didn't even let them stay the night, but got them ready and let them go home. As they went Kunuyuk told his cousin, "Leave your house and build a new one farther away from these people."

Kunuyuk and his wife went home to Point Hope without finding out what happened to his nephew. When they got to Point Hope, Kunuyuk's first wife told the woman that Kunuyuk had been with, "After you had lots of fun you came home." The woman said, "Yes, I had lots of fun when they put the fire in the karigi and I was sweating." The husband of the woman was with Kukuyuk's first wife and was beating her up because he thought his wife wouldn't come back.

After the winter passed Kunuyuk planned to go to Iviruluk again to fight the people. He asked the Point Hope men to go with him, and the men came out one by one from their houses to join him. Finally the last man came out with no mittens. It was a poor boy. When he came out Kunuyuk said, "Why are you going with us? You won't help." The poor boy said, "I really want to go." They gave him spears and a bow and arrow and went.

When they got to Iviruluk it was moonlight. Kunuyuk told the men, "Don't bother that house farther over." He told the poor boy to go to one house that had a light. They thought that someone in there was trying to have a baby. The poor boy went there and peeped through the window. He saw three young boys sleeping, so he shot them with his bow and arrow. Those boys were tough and if anybody came to kill the people they were supposed to run out and kill them. The house of Kunuyuk's cousin was left alone. After they had war Kunuyuk's cousin, Kunuyuk, and the rest of the men went home. THE END. This is as far as I heard this story from Daniel Walton.

C310 Tabu: looking at certain person or thing; D117 Transformation: man to rodent; D681 Gradual transformation; D1412 Magic object pulls persons into it; D2143.3 Fog produced by magic (Greenland—Rasmussen 1921:I, 109; Rink 1875:451); J1050 Attention to warnings; K640 Escape with help of confederate; K1626 Would-be killers killed; N820 Human helpers; P251 Brothers; P251.6.1 Three brothers; Q211.8 Punishment for desire to murder (Cumberland Sound—Boas 1901:62; Smith Sound—Kroeber 1899:177; Greenland—Holm 1912:47; Rink 1875:157, 222); Q411 Death as punishment; R210 Escapes; T257 Jealous wife or husband.

PM107. AHVRALUKE

A grandmother and her grandson and a rich man lived in a village. The people always stayed in the karigi. The grandson always went there too. The rich man would say, "Ahvraluke, dance first." But Ahvraluke never danced when the rich man told him. When he went home he told his grandmother that the rich man had asked him to dance, but that he didn't. One evening he and his grandmother went up to the karigi. His grandmother started singing, so Ahvraluke went down and started to dance. Ahvraluke danced, his grandmother sang, and pretty soon the people heard a noise outside. It got close and ice filled the karigi and started killing people. The rich man told them to stop, but they kept on. Later, after everybody was killed, the grandmother and grandson became some kind of seashell and were drifted. THE END.
Wanda Stalker told me this story.

D233 Transformation: man to shell (Greenland—Rasmussen 1921:I, 114); D904 Magic ice (Bering Strait—Nelson 1899:516); L111.4.1 Orphan hero lives with grandmother; P150 Rich man.

PM108. The Boy Who Always Ate Frozen Food

A grandmother and her grandson lived on a river. The grandson had a puppy. The grandmother fed the grandson with ptarmigan when he was small. He got big quickly and started hunting caribou. The dog always went with him. When he got older he asked his grandmother, "Are we staying alone? Are there any people nearby?" His grandmother answered: "You see that hill on the flats. There are people under it. We used to live there, but I brought you up here. In that village there is a rich man with a daughter. That rich man always eats ptarmigan because he likes them."

The grandson planned to go there. His grandmother told him to hunt ptarmigan first to take along to that rich man. He hunted ptarmigan, filled his bag, and went home. Early in the morning he started off. When he was leaving his grandmother said, "You have another grandmother down there. She lives in a house farther off from the rest. You can stay with her."

The boy went, walking and running. Towards evening he got close to the village. When it got dark he went to the house that his grandmother had told him about. He went in and saw an old woman. She found out that he was her grandson and let him stay there. He said, "I came in because my grandmother told me about this house."

The rich man found out about the stranger in the village and invited him to visit. The grandson went in and the rich man asked, "Do you have any ptarmigan with you?" The grandson said, "I took only a few." The grandson went to get the ptarmigan, and when he brought them back the rich man asked, "How much do you want for them? Take some stuff from the iḳigut if you want." The grandson said that he didn't want anything for them, so the rich man offered him a reindeer for a sled saying, "This is a real fine reindeer. If you want it you'll find it over at the corral." The grandson said, "Yes, I'll try it."

When he got the reindeer he went home with it and started using it to go places. His grandmother always told him not to go to the hills far up there. One time he went with the reindeer, taking his dog alone. He went up to a mountain, down to a river, and then farther over. The reindeer didn't want to go and the dog didn't want to go either, but he made them. He saw a trail like an otter trail going through the snow. He followed it, but the dog and reindeer were real slow. Farther on he found a house and went in.

He saw nothing, so he sat down and waited for awhile. Soon he heard someone coming. A head started coming up through the floor. When it got up as far as the eyes it stopped. The grandson said, "Come, little brother, I won't do anything to you. I have come to get you." The head came farther up. It was a young boy with no clothes. His mouth was so big it went from ear to ear. The grandson put him inside his parka and took him for his brother.

When they went into his house the grandson put him to bed. The boy stayed there and the grandmother cooked ptarmigan for him. She tried to feed him, but the boy said that he couldn't eat cooked ptarmigan. The grandmother asked him, "What do you always eat?" He answered, "I always eat frozen ptarmigan," and he started eating them.

They raised the boy. The grandson would take him along when he went caribou hunting with his reindeer. One time the boy said, "I want to try to shoot some caribou." The grandson put him down from inside his parka and the boy went off so swiftly that the grandson didn't know he had gone. The caribou started falling down. The boy came back and the grandson put him in his parka again.

One evening when they went to bed the grandson thought to himself, "I wonder how that boy looks now." The grandmother had made a bib that covered the boy up to his nose so that people couldn't see his mouth. The grandson opened the bib while the boy was sleeping. He saw that his mouth still went clear to his ear. When they woke up the boy said, "Did you see my mouth?" And the grandson answered, "No, I never."

They planned to go to the village again. The grandson took his grandmother and the boy along. He hunted ptarmigan to take with them. When he got there he took them over to the rich man and the rich man gave him his daughter. They got married. The grandmother made clothes for the boy. The rich man's son took the grandson and the boy over to the corral to see the reindeer. When they were over there they saw the reindeer.

The rich man's son and the other men liked the boy, so they started playing with him. One man touched his bib and opened it so that they saw his big mouth. The boy got bashful, and before the grandson knew what had happened he had killed the man. When the grandson found out, the boy ran away, so the grandson followed him. The boy went inside a house and killed another man. As he came out the door the grandson grabbed him and started holding him. He kept holding him and finally got tired. The boy tried to get away to kill more men.

When the grandson got really tired he called his dog. The dog came and got ahold of the boy's leg. The grandson wanted to kill the boy before he killed more people. He tore the boy's arm off and his head off, but they always went back on. That's why the grandson got tired. The dog had ahold of the boy on his toe and he kept biting it. Finally the boy got weak, fell to the ground, and couldn't move. His heart was in his toe and the dog had bitten it. The grandson couldn't kill him, but the dog did. THE END.

I have forgotten who told this story.

C610 Tabu: the one forbidden place; D1717.1 Magic power of monster child; D2060 Death or bodily injury by magic; F513 Person unusual as to his mouth; F559.7 Remarkable heart; L111.4.1 Orphan hero lives with grandmother; L161.1 Marriage of poor boy and rich girl; P150 Rich man; W11 Generosity; Z311 Achilles' heel. Rasmussen 1932:121–32 (Point Hope), Ostermann 1952:216–22 (Point Hope), and PM105 in this volume also feature the heart in the toe.

In PM77 a boy who was death to look upon was not punished because he was not really at fault; here the boy pays with his life, possibly because he is slightly more aggressive. The presence of reindeer indicates Siberian influence.

PM109. THE CARIBOU MAN

A man and his wife lived alone. He always hunted caribou and they had meat all the time. In the wintertime they put snares all along the water running from open springs to catch caribou. After a few years they had a baby boy. One time when the boy was big enough to play out his father went to hunt caribou and found a few. When he saw them he didn't try to kill them, but followed them from behind. When they stopped to eat he sat close and watched them. When they went to sleep he went to sleep too.

One time when they went to sleep the man who was sitting close by was going to sleep too, when one of the caribou got up. It came to him, put its nose to the ground, and opened its hood. It was a middle-aged female. The caribou gave the man a pair of mukluks because she knew his mukluk bottoms were torn. She said, "You can wear these if you go walking," and so he put them on.

When the caribou went again the man followed from behind. Pretty soon he started walking like a caribou, and so he went around with them. One time the caribou that had talked to him said, "If we stop and are going to eat you think of what you'd like to eat and it will come so that you can eat it." When he was digging in the snow he thought of what he'd like to eat and that food was there.

The caribou came to him again and said, "The wolves always bother us. And when one of us is slow they catch him and eat him. We are going to test you and see if you are slow." The caribou started running fast and the man tried to run like them, but he started falling. He kept falling when they were running so when they stopped the caribou said, "Next time they start running, put your head up and look at the sky. Then you'll learn how to run like us." When the caribou started running again he looked up to the clouds. He started running better and caught up with them. Then the wolves started running after the caribou and they ran, scattering all over. He followed the caribou that talked to him. The wolves didn't catch them.

One time when he was walking he got caught in one of his own snares and couldn't come out. After awhile a boy came. When he got close he got his spear ready to kill the caribou. The caribou recognized his son so he took his hood off and said, "When you were a small boy I followed the caribou far and that's why I never came home. Take the snare off and take my parka off." The boy did and then led his father home. When he went into the house it was so smelly he couldn't stand it. He couldn't eat the food that he used to. He didn't sleep with his wife, but another place in the same house. His lips were big, just like a caribou's lips. Because the man couldn't eat human food he got skinny and died. THE END.

Frank Burns told me this story.

B211.2.2 Speaking caribou; B443 Helpful wild beasts, ungulate; D114. 1.6 Transformation: man to caribou (MacKenzie River—Jenness 1924: 56); D682 Partial transformation; D1777 Magic results from power of thought (MacKenzie River—Jenness 1924:64); F513 Person unusual as to his mouth; J130 Wisdom (knowledge) acquired from animals; K730

Victim trapped; U135 Longing for accustomed food and living. Similar
to Keithahn 1958:90–96 (Seward Peninsula); Gubser 1965:327–30
(Anaktuvuk Pass), and EH2 in this volume.

PM110. AHKIYYINNI

A man lived close to Ķuvañik (a river flowing into the Utukok
River). They always had Eskimo dances of different kinds there.
Finally that man, who was named Ahkiyyinni, died. They buried him
on top of a hill and when people went downriver they could see his
grave. One time, after a few years, a boat came down from upriver.
When they got close to the grave one man started to shout, "Ahkiyyinni, up there, dance." Ahkiyyinni's grave started standing up and
he showed as just a skeleton. He started dancing. He took his shoulder
blade and lower arm bone and played them like a drum. He started
singing: "Ahkiyyinni, Ahkiyyinni, Ahkiyyinni. With my shoulder
blade and my arm bone I'm playing my drum. How should I dance?
How should I dance? Ahhohoy."

As he said the last word the boat started rocking a little. Ahkiyyinni
sang the song again and the boat rocked more. The people told him
not to sing anymore. Ahkiyyinni sang the song a third time anyway.
That boat rocked a lot and then tipped over. The people drowned.
THE END.

My mother told me this story. I asked for stories lots of times, so
she told me this one.

D2060 Death or bodily injury by magic; E230 Return from dead to
inflict punishment. The same story is found in Keithahn 1958:31–33
(Seward Peninsula).
Making fun of the dead is dangerous.

PM111. THE IKLUKĶINIK

On a small hill under Ignitkallik (the big mountain behind Sealing
Point) lived some people. In the summertime people saw some boats
coming. They met the strangers when they got to the shore. The
strangers unpacked their boats and started staying there. There were

some young boys and young girls with them. One of the young boys from the village got married to one of the visiting girls.

In the fall the strangers started going with their boats. The boy decided to go with them. After they went for awhile they got to the ice. The boat went under the ice and the boy went with it. Just when he ran out of breath they came up. The boy breathed real hard because he had thought that he wouldn't make it. The boat started going again. The boy saw some ice farther ahead that was wide. He thought, "I can't make it." So he got out of the boat and was left behind. He started home and when he got there he found out that the strange people were iklukkinik, a kind of small fish that can come alive after it's frozen. THE END.

Frank Glover told me this story.

B654 Marriage to fish in human form; D370 Transformation: fish to person.

PM112. THE MAN WHO LIKED TO HAVE HIS BACK SCRATCHED

A man and his wife lived in Point Hope. When the man hunted he didn't bring home much. One day when it was real nice he started walking towards the mountains. When he got to a little hill he stood on top and watched. He saw smoke coming towards him from the ground. When it got close to him he saw that it was a caribou. The caribou hid behind him. Another smoke came along real fast, and when it got close he saw that it was a wolf. It came to the man and asked, "Where's that caribou I was following?" The man said, "It just passed by." So the wolf started going again.

After it went, the caribou came out and thanked the man, saying, "If you weren't here that wolf would have killed me." He kept thanking the man and finally asked him, "What do you wish? Do you want to be an aŋatquq? Do you want to be rich? Or do you always want to get things like the other men when you hunt? What do you want?" The man thought for awhile and then said, "When I go home from hunting I want to get close to the stove and have my wife scratch my back for me." The caribou said, "I'll only let you wish for one of the three things that I said," but the man kept wishing for the other. Finally the caribou gave up and left.

The man walked for awhile and didn't get anything, so he went home. After he came in his wife brought him a little food which she had gotten from other people. After he ate he went to the stove and let his back get warm. When it started to get itchy he called his wife to come and scratch his back. She scratched for awhile and then stopped.

He told her to keep scratching, but she said that his skin was getting red. He told her to scratch anyway, so she did for a long time. Then she told him she was cutting his back with her nails. But he said to keep scratching. Finally his skin came off because she had scratched him so much, but he still wanted her to scratch his back. She kept doing it and finally he asked, "Where is a kumiġun (a scraper for hides)?" She found one and started to scratch his back with it. She told him his bones were showing, but he told her to keep scratching. Pretty soon he got weak and fell on the floor. He died. THE END.

I heard this story from Carl Stalker.

B211.2.2 Speaking caribou; B211.2.4 Speaking wolf; B341 Helpful animal's injunctions disobeyed; B360 Animals grateful for rescue from peril of death; D1720.1 Man given power of wishing (Greenland—Holm 1912:25; Rink 1875:453); D2063.4 Magic scratching; J200 Choices; Q115 Reward: any boon that may be asked.

The danger is desiring something other than the offered reward.

PM113. THE BALL THAT CAUGHT MEN

I can't remember the first part of this story.

Some people lived down at the coast, including a rich man, his son, and a grandmother and her grandson. When the grandson started playing out he always saw an old grave on top of a hill. When the men went out from the village to hunt seals they never came home. One time the rich man's son didn't come home. He had liked the grandson and always walked with him.

One time when the grandson went up to see the old grave again he walked a little farther and saw a house. He went in and saw a man who said: "There is something down in the ocean that never lets the men come home. There is an ugruk that always gets close to the kayak. When the men try to kill it the ugruk goes far off and they follow it across the ocean. That's why they don't return."

After the grandson heard this he went home and went to the rich man and asked him for a kayak. He got the kayak and paddled out on the ocean. When he got out aways he saw the ugruk. It came close to the kayak. He wanted to kill it so he followed it. He couldn't catch it, so he kept following it. Pretty soon he ran up on a beach. The ugruk didn't come up anymore. He got out of the kayak. He saw a lot of kayaks there on the beach, some of which were real old ones. He got his kayak ready to go and then went up on the hill.

He got on top and looked around. He saw a big, pretty ball hanging from a pole. He wanted to touch it, so he went over and when he did he got stuck in the ball. While he was there a man came, took him from the ball, and took him home.

I missed some of the story about here.

The grandson got away and started running to his kayak. When he reached the ball he told it, "I'm your boss now. You can catch your first boss." He got to his kayak and paddled off. When he looked back the man was hanging from his own ball. The grandson closed his eyes and started paddling real fast. He didn't know anybody was behind him, but he yelled out, "Come on, let's see who'll reach home first." When he opened his eyes he saw a lot of kayaks behind him. The men that had never come home followed him and he took them home. They all stayed home for a few days and then the rich man let the grandson marry his daughter. That's how the grandson let the men come home that the ugruk had taken away. THE END.

Frieda Goodwin told me this story.

D1256 Magic ball; D1417 Magic object imprisons persons; H1385 Quest for lost persons; K1600 Deceiver falls into own trap; L111.4.1 Orphan hero lives with grandmother; L161.1 Marriage of poor boy and rich girl; P150 Rich man.

PM114. The Poor Boy Who Grabbed the Ball

There were some people on a river, including a rich man and his daughter. Across the river a grandmother and her grandson lived alone. The rich man had a pole with a ball on the top. He said that if somebody could get that ball he could get married to his daughter. The boys tried to climb the pole, but they couldn't get the ball. The grandson was friends with a boy across the river and they always played together. When nobody could get the ball the grandson started thinking about it. He started walking downriver in the evening. When he stopped he heard strangers coming from downstream. The strangers stopped for overnight while the grandson watched them. When they went to sleep he started painting their sleds with something so that they wouldn't go. Then he went home.

In the morning the strangers couldn't move their sleds because they were too heavy, so they went back to where they came from without their sleds. The grandson told his grandmother about the sleds. They wanted to make their house bigger, so they put their feet on the wall and started pushing. The house got big. They did the same in the stormshed. Then they got the sleds with skins and meat on them and put them inside the house and stormshed. Those strangers were ahtaliks (like zombies or ghosts).

In the evening the grandson started thinking, "I wonder if I can go up that pole." He went over to the other side of the river. He got under the pole and looked at it, but it looked too hard. He started climbing up anyway, little by little, and finally he reached the ball. He took it down and went home. In the morning when the rich man's daughter woke up she went out and looked at the pole. She saw that the ball was gone, so they started looking for it.

The grandson went to his friend across the river and told him that he had gotten the ball. He gave it to him and they went up to the karigi, where they sneaked it inside. The people started wondering who had taken it off from the pole. The grandson and his friend were sitting together. The people couldn't find out who had brought the ball in, so the rich man said, "This ball will know who took him down." When they turned the ball around it was a person's head. They set it on the floor and the rich man said, "Go to the boy that got you." It started towards the grandson and when the head got to him it had a real happy smile.

Thus the people found out who had gotten the ball. The rich man gave his daughter to the grandson. When the grandson left the karigi he took his new wife home with him. When she went inside the stormshed she saw lots of food. She liked the smell of the fat. The grandson took his wife's parents home with him and they lived there for awhile. When they went in the stormshed they smelled the caribou fat. The rich man took a piece and ate it. He had thought that the grandson was poor because they called him ilaypuruk. That grandson got rich. When the girl's parents were going home after they had stayed for awhile the grandson gave them half the meat and fat and some white spotted skins. He gave his friend some food and skins too, and let him get married. The End.

Frank Burns used to tell this story.

D488 Houses magically made larger (Greenland—Rink 1875:219); E200 Ghosts and other revenants; F501 Person consisting only of head; L111.4.1 Orphan hero lives with grandmother; L161.1 Marriage of poor boy and rich girl; P150 Rich man; P310 Friendship.

PM115. Why Shismaref and Diomede Quit Warring

On Diomede Island lived a man, his wife, and their boy. One time the boy went out to toilet in the morning. While he was peeing he heard something behind him. Without looking he grabbed behind him. He grabbed a girl's long braided hair. The girl took him away from Diomede Island, walking over the ice. They went through the hills behind Shismaref. The aŋatquqs in the village saw them and turned their heads toward the two going behind the hill. The boy found out that the girl was frozen. He was holding her by her hair and it wouldn't come off from his hands.

He took her down to the village. He went inside a house and found that the man and wife there were the girl's parents. He put the girl on the floor. He took his hands off her hair and started walking around her. When he got to her feet he would kick them. When he got to her head he would kick it. Pretty soon she started moving. The boy kept going around her and kicking her, and all of a sudden she got her breath. She sat up and started telling her parents that she had been looking all over for somebody to help her but nobody cared.

The girl had died and her parents had buried her up on the hill. Finally she had gone to the boy and he had saved her life. Her parents told him that she had died a year ago. When she died the aŋatquqs were working on her. The boy and girl got married. The Diomede and Shismaref people used to have war before, but now the two villages quit having war. The parents were glad the daughter was alive. They told the Shismaref people not to fight anymore. After awhile the boy took his wife to Diomede, and that's how the two villages made friends. THE END.

I have forgotten who told me this.

D1711 Magician; E1 Person comes to life; E10 Resuscitation by rough treatment. In PM144 in this volume resuscitation is accomplished by kicking.

Note the equation of death and being frozen.

PM116. THE GRANDMOTHER'S REVENGE

A grandmother and granddaughter lived in Cape Prince of Wales. The granddaughter was fairly big. There was a karigi where the men always went up in the evenings after hunting and played games. One time the men dragged the granddaughter up to the karigi. When they took her in all the boys used her. When they finished she crawled through the trapdoor and went home to her grandmother. She couldn't walk. When she went in her grandmother saw that she was all bloody. She got up from her bed and put the girl there.

After she cleaned her up and let her go to sleep the grandmother started walking up to the karigi herself. When she went in the door she got down on the floor on her knees and elbows. She put her little fingers in her mouth and started crawling around the karigi. As she went the young men would get behind her and crawl like she was. They kept coming down from the benches until there were a lot of them following her and she led them out. The boys who were playing games had taken their parkas off after they used the girl because they were hot. So they were bare chested. They followed the grand-mother out without shirts or parkas on. It was wintertime.

When the grandmother and the boys following went out from the karigi she took them through the river and through a trail leading to the mountains. Some of the boys were freezing on the way. It was cold. The mountain they were going to was called Talukuk. On the way more of those boys were frozen. When all the boys were frozen the grandmother went home alone to her granddaughter.

The granddaughter rested and when she got good, in summer, the grandmother's relatives took the grandmother and granddaughter away because if the boys' relatives found out what happened they would kill them. They took them in two boats. When they went they took them to Point Barrow. So Cape Prince of Wales and Point Barrow people became friends. THE END.

That's how far I heard this story from Carl Stalker.

D2060 Death or bodily injury by magic; L111.4.1 Orphan hero(ine) lives with grandmother; N825.3.3 Help from grandmother; Q244 Punishment for ravishing; Q411.7 Death as punishment for ravisher; T471 Rape. Also found in Keithahn 1958:80–83 (Seward Peninsula).

PM117. THE RAVEN AND THE WHALE

This is a real true story. A raven got married to a duck named Mitik (that's the kind of duck). These ducks, the raven's wife, and some other ducks started going, flying. When they took off the raven got tired because he was behind. These ducks were fast. So the raven called out to his wife, "You and your mother get together." So they did and the raven got on top of them to rest for awhile. So the other ducks were ahead of them.

The raven's wife and his mother-in-law got way behind the others. So the raven got off from their backs and they started leaving him again. When he got off their backs once more they left him behind and he got tired of being left and turned back. He started flying around.

When he turned back he was flying over the ocean and saw whales. When he saw those he went straight to them. When one whale opened its spout (suppuktukvik) the raven went inside to a house. He saw a real bright light when he went in, and he saw oil dripping. While he was in there a voice said, "Don't eat from that oil that's dripping. Eat from any other place, but not from that oil that's dripping." The raven didn't see anybody around, just heard the voices. He ate from any place. He couldn't go out even though he wanted to.

Soon he was short of food inside that whale. When he was out of food he started eating the oil that was dripping. He started finishing this oil. When there was just a little bit of oil left the light got real dim. When he ate all the oil it got dark inside. When the light went out the raven stayed for awhile. Then the whale hit the bottom. It kept hitting it and pretty soon the whale stopped.

When it stopped the raven heard a voice from outside. Soon the ribs were opened and he went out. There were people working on the whale. When the raven went out he went to the grass and cleaned himself up. He started walking down to the people. He asked them, "Did it have any stomach? If it didn't have any stomach or guts it's funny." The people looked inside and saw no stomach or guts, so they went before they got any muktuk. The oil that was dripping was from the whale's heart. The raven started gathering muktuk for himself. THE END.

Carl Stalker told this story.

B211.3.6 Speaking raven; B282.16 Marriage of raven with another bird; F911.2.1 Raven dwells within whale (Bering Strait—Nelson 1899:465); F912.2 Victim kills swallower from within by cutting (with bill); F982 Animals carry extra burden. Similar to Nelson 1899:462–67 (Bering Strait); Rasmussen 1932:172–74 (Utukok River); and Ostermann 1952: 24–25 (Northern Alaska), 172 (Utukok River).

PM118. THE RAVEN WHO ATE THE DOG SKIN

There were people somewhere. A raven got married to a woman there. The two stayed there. One time a man killed a fat dog to have the skin for his pants. He hung the skin outdoors to dry. The raven went over and started eating from the skin. He tore it up. When they went to the karigi the man that killed the dog had the men take their mukluks off because there were raven tracks around. They were getting close to the raven. The raven said, "Everybody has five toes." When they almost reached him the raven jumped up, got a little knife, and told the man, "Come on, let's poke each other with knives." THE END.

Carl Stalker told this.

B652 Marriage to bird in human form; D350 Transformation: bird to person; D682 Partial transformation; H48 Animal in human form recognized. Also found in Lucier 1958:102–3 (Noatak).

PM119. THE MAN WHO HUNG HIS NEPHEW

People, including a man and his nephew, were going up the Noatak River. When they got as far as the canyons they stopped. The nephew was big and could hunt alone. The man took a rope and went on top of the cliff. He tied the rope to his nephew's feet and hung him over the cliff, head down, where he left him. The man and the other people in his boat hunted caribou. In the fall they came downriver with their boat. When they got close to the cliff they saw the nephew still hanging there. When they got under the boy he fell and hit the water by the side of the boat. They watched and a walrus came up from the water. It made a hole in the boat and it sank. The people drowned. THE END.

I heard this story from Carl Stalker.

D127.4 Transformation: man to walrus (Greenland—Rasmussen 1921:I, 184; 1921:II, 96); K929.9 Murder by pushing off cliff; K2210 Treacherous relatives; P297 Nephew; Q211 Murder punished (Cumberland Sound—Boas 1901:168; Greenland—Rasmussen 1921:III, 76, 111, 294); Q411.6 Death as punishment for murder.

PM120. THE RABBIT

A rabbit had kids. She always played with them. One time she started singing a song for them. She sang: "These kids / their names / Auyaichak / Pikniktuvlu / Pikniktahavlu / Kilyumlu (sky) / Sunninikrumlu / Iiyakuatu raanuk (when the snow is so bright that rabbits can't see)." THE END.

My mother told me this story.

PM121. ḴUUKI

There was a tough man in Cape Prince of Wales. In Shismaref there was a boy who always practiced games with the rough men in the karigi. The boy's father said, "Maybe my son can beat that Cape Prince of Wales man. My son is tougher." The Cape Prince of Wales man's name was Ḵuuki. The boy's father said, "My son is tougher than Ḵuuki." Also in the karigi was a man from Shismaref who always boated with Ḵuuki. He said, "Ḵuuki is tough. When we are drifted out on the ocean he always brings us home. No man ever beats Ḵuuki. One time when our boat was stuck in the ice that was breaking up he took us out as if he were a flying duck. He always jumped from ice to ice with a rope, and when he got on top he pulled the boat out by himself. That's how tough Ḵuuki is."

I heard this part of the story from Ralph Gallahorn.

Some people from Diomede heard that Ḵuuki was tough. One summer a boat came to get him. The man that came wanted to kill Ḵuuki when he got back to Diomede. Ḵuuki got in the boat and went with him. When they got to the beach in Diomede the man that wanted to kill Ḵuuki got out of the boat with his spear. Ḵuuki took his spear and followed him to the top of a hill. Ḵuuki threw his spear away and took his knife that was pointed on both ends. The man tried to spear him while Ḵuuki tried to cut him with the knife. They kept fighting clear down the hill to the village. The other man reached his house and jumped over it. Ḵuuki jumped over it after him and got him with his knife. He killed him and then let the other Diomeders take him home.

I heard this part of the story from Daniel Walton.

Ḵuuki lived in Cape Prince of Wales. He had a wife and kids. They had a camp someplace behind the village where Ḵuuki kept his team of reindeer. He stayed away from the village so that the reindeer could feed. One time he lost his bull reindeer. Somebody else in the village had a herd of reindeer too. Ḵuuki went over and looked at the man's reindeer. He said to the man, "There's the one I lost. He's down in your herd." The other man said, "That's my bull." Ḵuuki said, "No, it's mine; I recognize it." The man said, "It's a wild one. If you can catch ahold of it you can take it home." Ḵuuki went down, jumped, and got ahold of the bull. He was going to move, but Ḵuuki got ahold of his legs, put the reindeer on his back, and went home. The other people didn't know how he did it.

A few years after that the man who stole the reindeer from Ḵuuki decided to go to Ḵuuki's place by dog team with some other men. Ḵuuki's cousin lived a little ways from Ḵuuki. The men took Ḵuuki's cousin's meat from his cache and everything from his house. They loaded on their sleds and then came towards Ḵuuki's place. Ḵuuki's kids told him, while he was cutting a piece of wood inside the house, "Some people are taking food away from your cousin's cache. There are lots of dog teams." Ḵuuki didn't do anything. The kids came in again and said, "People are taking our meat away from our iḵigut." He kept working. The kids came in again and said, "The people are leaving with heavily loaded sleds. They took all our meat and we have nothing to eat."

Ķuuki put his work down and went right out with no parka on. He saw the sleds far away and he ran after them. When he got close two men got down from the sleds with bow and arrows and aimed them at him. He kept running until he got real close, when he grabbed one of the men and broke his arrows. He got ahold of the other man too. He piled them on top of each other and then got on top of them. He called out to the dog teams, "Take the meat back. If you don't I'll kill you with my bare hands." He had no knife or anything. The people didn't want to get killed, so they returned the meat. THE END.

This is how far I heard this part from somebody, maybe Frank Burns.

F610 Remarkably strong man; Q212 Theft punished.
The presence of reindeer indicates that this story takes place after A.D. 1890 or is a Siberian story recast in a local setting.

PM122. THE MAN WHO HAD TWO WIVES

A man and his wife lived alone at the coast eating seal. Sometimes they would go up to where they could hunt caribou and dry up some meat. Finally they had two boys. When the father went out to hunt on the ice he always got ugruks and seals. The boys got big. One time their father went hunting and for the first time came home with an empty sled. Now he sometimes came home with one seal, sometimes with nothing. His wife thought, "I wonder why he can't get seals anymore."

When her husband went hunting again she left the boys home and walked along the beach. She came to a house. She hid and watched it. Soon a woman came out and looked at the ocean. A kayak came with an ugruk on it. The wife kept watching and when the kayak got close she recognized her husband bringing an ugruk to the second woman. The other woman went down to meet the man. The wife went home, not letting them see her. She started working like she had before, and soon her husband came home with nothing. She didn't mind, but kept working. She cooked for him and fed him.

The next day when her husband went out again she walked over to that other house. She went into the house and saw a big pot of seal oil boiling over the fire. She said to the other woman who was there, "What's that boiling in your pot?" The other woman got up, went over to the pot, and tried to see what was in it. The wife said, "Down there, it's down there. You can't see it." The woman got closer and the wife went behind her. She grabbed her legs and threw her in the boiling oil. Then she went home. She took her two boys and went off. Before she went she put her sewing board inside her parka. The three of them became brown bears. While they were traveling some men chased them and killed them. They started to skin the mother and when they cut her they found the sewing board in her breast. The End.

I first heard this story from Carl Stalker.

D113.2 Transformation: man to bear (Kodiak—Golder 1907:297; 1909: 10; Bering Strait—Nelson 1899:493; West Hudson Bay—Boas 1901:326; Cumberland Sound—Boas 1901:251f.; Cape York—Rasmussen 1921:III, 124, 211, 297; Greenland—Rasmussen 1921:I, 184; 1921:II, 96, 184; Rink 1875:193); H80 Identification by tokens; J50 Wisdom (knowledge) acquired from observation; K955.2 Murder by burning in hot oil; P251 Brothers; Q241 Adultery punished; Q411 Death as punishment; Q551.3.2 Punishment: transformation into animal; T481 Adultery (Mac-Kenzie River—Jenness 1924:87; West Hudson Bay—Boas 1901:223).

The woman who changes into a brown bear after learning of her husband's adultery, usually with the addition of the cutting board or some other wooden object, is a widespread motif in northern Alaska: Nelson 1899:467–70 (Norton Sound); Lucier 1953:217–18 (Buckland); Curtis 1930:261–62 (Selawik); Giddings 1961:67–69 (Kobuk River); Lucier 1958:94–96 (Noatak); Ostermann 1942:95–99 (Mac-Kenzie River). This motif is usually connected with the episode related in PM85 in this volume. In PM18 a woman is pushed into a boiling pot. I have assumed that the transformation into a brown bear was the penalty for murder, even though the murder might have been justified.

PM123. The Aŋatquq Fails

A Cape Prince of Wales aŋatquq had a boat. He and his crew went paddling out in it. So many killer whales came all around the boat that they couldn't move it. They didn't know what to do. The aŋatquq tried to use his aŋatquq, but it didn't work. The whales didn't go. Another man who was sad asked himself, "I wonder what my parents used to tell me long ago." After awhile he thought, "This is the way they taught me long ago." He asked for some mittens. He put them on and got down inside the boat. He put his arms up in the air and started talking to himself. Then he sat down and the killer whales started to go. Finally they couldn't see them anymore. People said that maybe he was praying. That is why the killer whales went away because he prayed instead of using aŋatquq. THE END.

Old Man Driggs (Iiluktuna) told me this story.

D1711 Magician; D1766.1 Magic results produced by prayer; V52 Miraculous power of prayer.

PM124. THE MAN WHO CHASED HIMSELF

A man and his wife lived at Sealing Point. They never went to Nuvuvruk with the other people, but wintered there trying to live on caribou. In the fall the man always hunted caribou and packed them down to Sealing Point, where his wife worked on them. One time he got some, but he didn't notice one dead one farther over. Finally he found it. It was a fat one and he cut it. When he took the caribou home in the morning he took a big piece of that fat caribou and fried it outdoors.

After he ate and his stomach was full he got sleepy. While he was sleeping a friend of his came from somewhere and saw him. He was sound asleep, so his friend got close to him and picked up a piece of burned wood. He put some marks on the sleeping man's chin [the charcoal marks resembled tattoos].

When the sleeping man woke up he was thirsty. He got up and went to a little lake to drink. When he put his head close to the water he saw a woman there in the water. She was real pretty. He got up and started running home to get his beddings and parka. He went in and got his things. As he started out his wife said, "What are you going to do?" He answered, "You're always jealous when I'm going someplace." He went out. He got to the lake and took his caribou parka off. When he looked in the lake he saw the woman again. He jumped in the lake. While he was in the water he tried to grab that woman, but he couldn't. After he stayed under the water for awhile he came up and wiped his face off. He couldn't find the woman. He looked in the water again and saw the woman, but her face was different. He went under the water a second time, but still couldn't find the woman. When he ran out of air he came up and started wiping his face. When he could see again he heard someone laughing real low. He turned around and saw that his friend was watching him. He got out of the lake and started chasing him. He kept chasing him until his friend got in a kayak and paddled off. Since he couldn't catch him he went home. THE END.

Kenneth Flood (Ḳuluuk) told me this story.

J1791.6 Diving for reflection of beautiful woman; J1791.7 Man does not recognize his own reflection in the water; P310 Friendship.
This is one of the rare humorous tales in this collection.

PM125. KIḲNALIK

A man named Kiḳnalik lived in some little lakes along Uḳaliḳsuk. He always strung a rope across the water and put some snares along it for ducks. He got lots, but after awhile he couldn't catch any. When he went to check his snares he found them disturbed, with a few feathers around, so he thought that maybe people were taking the ducks. He made a hiding place in the grasses behind his snares and

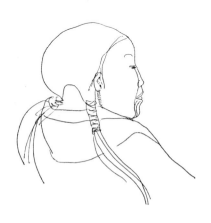

hid there to watch. Towards evening he saw two men coming from upriver. The snares had a few ducks. When the men came they went straight to the snares and took the ducks out. They put them in their bags. Kiknalik jumped up and started running after them. He put his parka on sideways and made a noise like "Ahvavavava (trying to sound like the devil). These two men are trying to take ducks from my snares."

They ran and he kept following. The two men went inside a house under a hill (the hill with a landing field [built after World War II] between Ukaliksuk and Sealing Point). When Kiknalik got close the door was open, so he peeked through and saw the two men lying on the floor. They were so scared that they fell to the floor as soon as they had gotten inside. They thought that the devil was after them.

While he was looking in, another man from inside the house took a drum and started playing it, trying to revive the two men. The man said, "If there is a devil behind those mountains let him come down." Kiknalik looked towards the mountains and saw a fire coming. He started running from the fire. He looked back and saw it behind him. While he was running it got close and his back got hot. He had on dog-skin mittens and a duck-skin parka. He took his mittens off and threw them, and pretty soon dogs started yelling from behind him. He looked back and the fire had stopped.

He kept running and when he looked back again the fire was coming closer, even though it was fighting with the dogs. When his back got warm again he took off his parka and threw it. He heard ducks quacking behind him. The fire stopped and then it came after him again. He saw a little house ahead of him. He opened the door and went in. He saw a little old woman. She took oil from her light and painted the door with it. They could hear the fire coming. It made a noise on top of the house and then they didn't hear it anymore. The old woman said, "You can go out now." He went out and looked around. He saw no fire, so he started home. THE END.

Edward Occut (Iyuk) told me this story.

D440 Transformation: object to animal; D444.10.2 Transformation: mitten to dog (Bering Strait—Nelson 1899:510); D672 Obstacle flight (MacKenzie River—Jenness 1924:79; Greenland—Rasmussen 1921:I, 106); D1711 Magician; G303.3.4.2.1 Devil as ball of fire; N825.3 Help from old woman (Greenland—Rasmussen 1921:II, 162); Q212 Theft punished; R271 Pursuit by fire. Similar to Keithahn 1958:15–17 (Seward Peninsula) and Curtis 1930:257–58 (Kotzebue). PM25 also features the obstacle flight.

The concept of the devil is, of course, postcontact in origin.

PM126. The Big Bird

A man and his wife lived alone. The wife always had a fire outside the house. One evening while she was at the fire she heard a big bird sing from above her. She said to her husband, who was in the house, "A bird made a noise from someplace above me." He said, "Let him holler so that he can clean your dirty skin pants." When she saw the bird flying toward her she went to the fireplace and hid in the smoke. Pretty soon a big bird came down and just missed her head. Her husband came out. He had gotten scared when he had heard the noise. He was so scared he was shivering. The End.

This is as far as I heard this story from Wanda Stalker.

PM127. Ilaypaaluk and Ilaypuruk

I didn't hear the first part of this story.

There were some people living on both sides of a river. They had two men go to other villages to invite them to come to a feast. When the men came home the people started welcoming the visitors. When the visitors got close to the village the two kivauks went out to meet them and then started reaching home. The akpatuks started running after them. All of the akpatuks dropped out except the two boys, one of whom was called Ilaypuruk and the other one of whom was called Ilaypaaluk.

They kept chasing after the one kivauk that did not drop out. The three ran towards the karigi. When the kivauk reached the karigi Ilaypaaluk pushed him down and passed him. Then Ilaypaaluk owned the karigi and they all had a meeting.

After they finished the feast the akpatuks and the villagers started having war inside the karigi. All the men were killed except Ilaypuruk and Ilaypaaluk and the kivauk who had almost won the race. Ilaypuruk and Ilaypaaluk tried to get the kivauk, but they couldn't kill him. They chased him out of the karigi and all over the village. They kept following him and when they got to the hole where the people got water the kivauk dived in. Ilaypuruk dived after him. Ilaypaaluk looked around and when he didn't see anything he jumped in too. They stayed underwater for awhile, and then the kivauk came up. Ilaypuruk and Ilaypalluk came up after him. The kivauk got tired and they caught him then. They killed him. THE END.

This is as far as I heard this story from Ralph Gallahorn.

The Messenger Feast is also mentioned in PM65 and PM140 in this volume.

PM128. THE PTARMIGAN

There was a village in one place and another village not too far over. The people stayed there during the winter. When one village ran out of food the people went over to the other village and asked for some, but they didn't have any food either. The people, in the springtime, come from the two villages to the Noatak River. There they found food. These people were ptarmigan and they started eating willows along the river. THE END.

I heard this story from Frank Burns.

PM129. MY COUSIN'S TIRICHIK

A man and a woman who were cousins lived together along the Kukpuk River. They went down to the coast and stayed for awhile. Then they went back up the Kukpuk with some other people. They made houses up there and stayed. People started coming and trying to kill them. They were so scared that they didn't go hunting. The man said to his cousin, "Do you know anything we can do?" She said, "No." Towards evening she said, "Don't look at the bank if you go out."

A few days later the man thought, "I wonder why my cousin told us never to look at that bank." He started walking up there. When he got on top he looked around. He saw two legs. He kept looking at them, but they were so long he couldn't see the ends. He went home and went inside. He said, "My cousin's tirichik," and fainted. His cousin revived him and he got better. No people bothered them after that because the tirichik ate any strangers. Those were the tirichik's legs. THE END.

Frank Burns told this story.

B877 Giant mythical animals; C315 Tabu: looking at certain object.

PM130. THE MAN WHO WAS SAVED BY A SALMON FIN

A man and his wife lived in a village on a river somewhere. When the man hunted he brought all kinds of animals home. One time when he hunted he got some sheep. It was in the fall and he got two rams. He brought the fat meat home and let his wife put it away in the cache. He told her, "When people are out of food give them a little piece from one of those sheep." The people had food all winter, but they got short in the springtime. When they were out the man asked his wife, "Where are those sheep we put away in case people ran out of food?" She answered, "They are gone already." She had eaten them herself without the man knowing. When they were out of food the husband got sick and lost weight because his wife had not saved the meat as he had told her.

When the people were going in springtime to their summer camps the wife left her husband in the house. He stayed there for a few days and then said, "I'm going to walk away from here while I can still move." After he went for awhile he came to a place where some people had stayed overnight. He looked for some food, but he found none from where the people had been. He went to where a dog had been tied, looked around, and finally found the bone from a fin of dried salmon. He ate it, bone and all. After his stomach got better he went again.

A little farther over he saw a camp with people and they let him stay with them. The people had a lot of food. He ate, gained weight, and got his health back. He started hunting again and bringing food home for the people. One time he got a wolf. Before he went back to camp he took the wolf to the place where he had eaten the salmon bone and left it there, saying, "I have returned what I found." He told the people about it when he went back to camp. He told them to go look at that place where the wolf was every time they had a

chance. After he told them that he found out that they were the people who had stayed overnight at that place before they moved up. The people went down and found the wolf at the dog's pole, so they took it home. A few days later when they went down to see the pole again they found a wolverine there. Every time the man went out hunting he took something by that dog's pole. Whenever he hunted he always gave meat to the people; he wanted to feed everybody. THE END.

This is as far as I heard this story from Carl Stalker.

F1041.1.13 Death (illness) from shame; J514 One should not be too greedy; S60 Cruel spouse; W11 Generosity.

   I have assumed that the man's weakness was from shame at the greed of his wife rather than just starvation.

PM131. MORE ABOUT SIITAKUUYUK

I didn't tell some of the story about Siitakuuyuk.

One time Siitakuuyuk's son went hunting back of Point Barrow. He came back with nothing. The next time he went out he also came back with nothing. The next time he went out he also came back with nothing. Finally Siitakuuyuk started thinking, "Why doesn't he bring something home? He always used to." The next time he went out

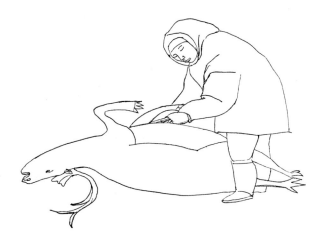

Siitakuuyuk followed him without letting him know. Siitakuuyuk's son saw some caribou. He shot and killed them all. He skinned them and then piled them together. Just before he finished he started running away.

Siitakuuyuk saw some men going after the caribou his son had killed. They were from Point Barrow. When he killed caribou the other men always took them, and that's why he never came home with anything. Siitakuuyuk went home. After his son came home with no caribou again all the men went up to the karigi. Siitakuuyuk went up too and told them not to bother his son when he was hunting. So they quit bothering him for awhile. But a few days later they started again.

One time when the boy was working on one caribou he got he saw them all around him. He ran away from the caribou. He saw a man hiding in front of him. Siitakuuyuk was holding his spear, so he ran towards the man who was hiding and when he got close speared him in the side. He put him up in the air, just like a speared salmon, and started twirling him around so that the people could see him. Then he threw the man on the ground dead. They quit bothering him after that. THE END.

I heard this from Daniel Walton.

J1050 Attention to warnings; Q212 Theft punished.
The rest of the Siitakuuyuk story is in PM102 in this volume.

PM132. The Boy Who Had Trouble Keeping His Wife

Some people lived on both sides of a river. They always got water from one place. A rich man lived on one side and a man, his wife, and their son on the other. Farther over on the same side as the man and his wife lived a grandmother and granddaughter. When the son hunted he always got caribou. When the granddaughter got big he started thinking about her. He couldn't say anything all day, so his mother asked him what was wrong. He said, "I've been thinking about that granddaughter over there. I wonder if she will marry me."

His mother went over to the grandmother and granddaughter and the old woman asked why she had come. She said, "I came to ask about your granddaughter. My son wants to get married to her." The old woman said, "The day before yesterday the rich man came to get her for his second wife." The mother went back home and told her son what had happened. The boy didn't say anything.

In the evening when it was moonlight the boy went across the river and stood by the rich man's house to see if the girl would come out. While he was standing there a little boy came and said, "My grandmother wants to see you." He went with the little boy and when they reached a small house they went in. The little boy's grandmother said, "I just wanted you to come here." He stayed for awhile, then went back to the rich man's house and stood by the door to see if the girl would come out.

While he was there the girl came out with a bucket. The boy got ahold of her and held her. When she didn't come in for a long time the rich man's other wife came out. She tried to get the girl away from the boy. The boy pushed her hard and hurt her, so she went in. The boy took the granddaughter home. The rich man didn't even go over and see them.

When springtime came and the ice went out they started down to Sheshalik. The rest of the people put up their tents farther down, while the son and granddaughter put their tent up at Nuvuvruk. One night when they went to bed, while they were sleeping, the boy woke up. Two men were coming along the beach by the water. They were talking and he listened. One said, "Cousin, let's go take that girl away from that man." The other man still wanted to go, so when they got close they came up to the tent. They pulled the woman out with no clothes.

The boy stayed there for awhile. Then he pulled on his pants and went out. The men were carrying the woman along the trail, one holding on to each arm. He ran after them and caught them. He got ahold of one man, twirled him around in the air, and threw him on the ground. He did the same to the other man and then took his wife home. The men didn't get up. He had killed them.

One night when his wife didn't come home the boy started looking for her. He thought of the rich man who had a conical house like an Indian's tent. He peeked through the door and saw his wife sleeping with the rich man. She was sound asleep, so he pulled her out and took her home. Another evening she didn't come home. He got mad and went over to the rich man's tent. She was sleeping there again. He saw a knife and stabbed the rich man in the stomach. After he took his wife home she never went away anymore.

A man at Sheshalik found out that the men were going to have a war after somebody killed the rich man. There were men in two lines facing each other. The man got ready, putting a gut parka and light slippers on. He went up to where they were in the two lines and got in the middle between the ends of the lines. He said, "You should have told me you were going to have war." Suddenly he was at the other end between the two lines. They didn't see him run. He said the same thing and suddenly he was back at the first end. He kept doing that. They watched him so much they quit fighting. They were afraid that if he got on one side he'd kill everybody on the other side. THE END.

This happened not long ago. I heard this story from Frank Burns.

F681 Marvelous runner; K950 Treacherous murder; L111.4.1 Orphan hero lives with grandmother; P150 Rich man; P552 Battle formations; T145.0.1 Polygyny.
   The conical tent may have been the Noatagmiut summer tent. In this tale marriage was arranged by a female relative.

PM133. THE INVISIBLE PEOPLE

At Cape Prince of Wales there was a river going into the ocean with houses around the mouth. The river went as far up as Tuluḳuk. Long ago Cape Prince of Wales had a lot of people on the flat along the river under the hill. The people went whale hunting, but they never saw any. There were always sandstorms at the village.

One time when the people came home again without whales a woman went out from her house. There was water in the river. She saw somebody going through the water with a sled. She started to follow it. When she got close she saw that there was a lot of whale muktuk on the sled, which was going towards Tulukuk.

Farther up the man reached a house. He called through the window, "Kringut." He kept calling the name, but nobody answered. He looked up and saw the woman behind him. He asked, "What did she say?" The woman answered, "She said that you should give me a piece of muktuk." He cut a big piece of muktuk and gave it to her. She put it inside her pants and started running home with it. She kept running and the piece of muktuk started getting smaller and smaller. When she reached her house and went in there was only a small piece left.

She cut it up and let everybody in Cape Prince of Wales have a small piece. After the people had had the muktuk, when they went out to get whales, they started to bring some home. The people up towards Tulukuk were invisible people. Cape Prince of Wales people could only see them sometimes. The Cape Prince of Wales people got no whales because the invisible people were hunting them. THE END.

This is as far as I heard this story from Carl Stalker.

D1981 Certain persons invisible.

PM134. NAULUKKACHIIYUK

A man named Naulukkachiiyuk lived on the Kobuk River. Naulukkachiiyuk and his youngest brother went hunting for siksikpuks in the summer. In the fall, when the ice came, they started back home. They found a lake where some beavers had been working. The beavers had made a dam at the outlet of the lake so that there would be water for the winter. Naulukkachiiyuk and his brother tried to make a hole so that the water would go downstream. While they were making the hole Naulukkachiiyuk looked up and saw Indians all over. He jumped in the water and started swimming.

Pretty soon he got to a bright place. It was the beaver's house. He went in and saw a beaver family. The house was real clean and dry.

There was cut wood in there. Naulukkachiiyuk looked around and saw a beaver with a funny face by the door. The father beaver told Naulukkachiiyuk, "If you get hungry you eat that beaver by the door." The funny-looking one said, "You're not going to eat me. Eat each other." He jumped in the water. That was a muskrat.

When the muskrat jumped in the water the father beaver said, "You can eat one of my kids." Naulukkachiiyuk got his knife and killed the oldest one. The rest of the beavers left one by one and the house got dark. Naulukkachiiyuk ate the beaver. He didn't want to go outside. After he finished the beaver he started eating his strings (mukluk ties). After he chewed them he ate his parka. Finally he got skinny.

One time when he woke up, after he had nothing to eat, the house was dripping. When he put his hands up he found out it was water. He tried to make a hole in the roof. He made a little one and then enlarged it. When he got out he looked through the hole. The sun was bright and there was water. It was spring. He went out and when his eyes got good he looked down to where he and his younger brother had tried to make a hole in the dam. He saw his younger brother hanging upside down. He felt sorry for him. He was weak, but he buried him and then went back home.

He started gaining weight. He stayed home during the summertime, occasionally hunting. In the fall, when the ground got hard, he got ready to leave. He went towards the Indian village. When he reached it he started looking at it. He didn't know how to kill all of the Indians. He wanted to kill them all at once. While the women were watching their nets he was watching them closely. The kids were playing in the sand and he heard them sing about him, "Naulukkachiiyuk, go inside a beaver's house." Naulukkachiiyuk kept watching. When they went to the karigi some people always stayed home. He got ready to burn the karigi if they all went in.

Finally after a whole year had passed a lot of people came from another village. Everybody went up to the karigi. After he watched everybody go in, Naulukkachiiyuk got ready. He took some wood up to the karigi. He closed the door with logs so that nobody could get out. He got some fat from the ikiguts. He went to the window and lit some willows that burn easily. He threw them in some fat so that the fire would really burn. After he started the karigi burning he told them, "It is Naulukkachiiyuk that is burning you." One of the men said, "I told you Naulukkachiiyuk wasn't dead. He went into that beaver's house." THE END.

I have forgotten who told me this.

B210 Speaking animals; B430 Helpful wild beasts; K955 Murder by burning; K1626 Would-be killers killed; P251 Brothers; Q211 Murder punished (Cumberland Sound—Boas 1901:168; Greenland—Rasmussen 1921:III, 76, 111, 294); Q411.6 Death as punishment for murder; R45 Captivity in mound (cave, hollow hill); W11 Generosity.

Apparently, beavers are very generous!

PM135. THE MAN FROM SIBERIA

On a beach in Siberia were a man, who was a reindeer herder, and his wife. They had two young boys. The man always had a spear with no point on it, just the wood sharpened to a point. When brown bear or any kind of animals tried to get him he would spear them. One time when he was watching the reindeer he started walking up the hill. When he got on top of the hill he looked around and saw people putting their stuff in a boat, getting ready to go. He started walking towards the people. He watched them, but didn't go over right away.

When they pushed the boat out he ran and jumped inside so they took him away. They came to a village where after a few days he got married to a woman. He stayed in this village which was on Big Diomede for awhile. There was wood on the beach from which he built a house for himself and his wife. They had two boys. One time some people were going out to camp. He watched until the boat got started, then ran and jumped in. The people took him away.

When they got to a beach he got down and went to the top of a hill he had left from the first time. When he got on top he saw his reindeer. There was somebody taking care of them. He went down and saw a boy at one end of the reindeer and then a minute later way over at the other end of the reindeer. In another minute the boy was back where he had first seen him. He went down and the boy wanted to kill him, but the man said, "You are my son." The boy didn't believe him at first, but he finally did.

The boy said, "Let's race to our house." The house was kind of far. They started and when the man got halfway the boy was at the house already. When the man got there another boy had his bow and arrow aimed at him. When that boy found out that it was his father he took him back up to the reindeer. The youngest boy got on top of the reindeer and jumped from the back of one to another. Finally he jumped on all of them. Then the elder boy got on top of the reindeer's horns and jumped from antler to antler. Finally he had jumped to all of them. They told their father to jump also. He got on top and jumped from back to back, but he didn't get far. When their father had left them, those boys used to exercise by jumping on the reindeer. I don't know how tough the two Big Diomede boys were. THE END.

Daniel Walton told me this story.

F660 Person of remarkable skill; F681 Marvelous runner; P251 Brothers.

PM136. AHLUYANIK

There was a man in Unalakleet named Ahluyanik who was an aŋatquq. Cape Prince of Wales people always picked on Ahluyanik with their aŋatquqs because he always tried to bother people with his aŋatquq. The other aŋatquqs took Ahluyanik's cousin away. Ahluyanik found out and started following them with his aŋatquq. He reached a house and went towards it. The door was open so he looked in and saw two men standing with spears, one on each side of the door. His cousin was by the door with his head down. The two men were trying to spear him.

Ahluyanik used his aŋatquq to put another man from the house in his cousin's place. He took his cousin away and the two men speared the other man. He took his cousin home and they slept all night. The people that took his cousin away said that one of their men didn't wake up the next morning. If they had known that he was their relative they wouldn't have speared him. Ahluyanik's aŋatquq was strong.

One time Ahluyanik took his dog when he went aŋatquqing. As he was going along he looked back and saw a dog just like his following them. He told his dog to go back to the other dog. His dog went back and the two dogs started fighting each other. They bit each other and Ahluyanik's dog killed the other one and then came back to Ahluyanik. The master of the dog that was killed didn't wake up. The Unalakleet aŋatquqs always tried to bother each other. THE END.

This is as far as I heard this story from John Adams.

D1711 Magician; D2060 Death or bodily injury by magic; H1385 Quest for lost persons; K527 Escape by substituting another person; K1626 Would-be killers killed; P295 Cousins; Q211.8 Punishment for desire to murder (Cumberland Sound—Boas 1901:62; Smith Sound—Kroeber 1899:177; Greenland—Holm 1912:47; Rink 1875:157, 222); Q411 Death as punishment. Murder of substituted person also part of PM76 in this volume.

PM137. The Boy Who Got Help From Nahguyyumin

A rich man, his son, a grandmother, and her grandson lived in a village. The grandson always played out, and when he did the rich man's son tore his clothes. When the grandson went home the grandmother sewed his parka. The next time the grandson went out the rich man's son tore his parka again. The grandson started walking towards the hills. He came to a house. When he saw the house he walked real softly and went up to the window. He peeped in and saw a man and a woman making love. He watched for awhile, then got down real quietly and went to the door. He made a noise and went in.

The man said, "After you saw us you came in." The grandson answered, "What were you doing?" They kept saying that. After awhile the man got less mad and asked the boy why he had come around. The grandson said, "That rich man's son always tears my clothes when I am outdoors. I felt funny and walked away." When the man found out that he said, "Go home. If you go to the karigi start singing as soon as you go in the door. Sing 'Mayulya, where did you come from? I came from up there, from Nahguyyumin.'" The two people that the grandson visited were brown bears. Before he went Nahguyyumin told him, "Make a seal poke out of carved wood. After you finish put it farther away from your house."

After that the grandson went home. The people went up to the karigi and he followed. He went to the door and sang that song. He added to the end, "Aŋnaha iiyaha." After he sang the song one bear started coming up from each side of him. They went into the karigi and looked for the boy that tore his clothes. One of the bears got ahold of the rich man's son and threw him to the other bear. They threw him back and forth until they killed him. Then they went out.

When the people went home from the karigi the grandson carved a piece of wood like a seal poke. He finished it and took it to a place where people never stepped. A few days later he went to see it and found just a place where a poke of oil had been. Maybe the two brown bears got it because the grandson got help from them. THE END.

This is as far as I heard this story from Benjamin Arnold.

B211.2.3 Speaking bear; B435.4 Helpful bear; D313.3 Transformation: bear to man (MacKenzie River—Jenness 1924:54; Greenland—Rasmussen 1921:I, 134; 1921:II, 11; 1921:III, 52, 86; Rink 1875:196); D450 Transformation: object to object; J130 Wisdom (knowledge) acquired from animals; L111.4.1 Orphan hero lives with grandmother; L111.4.4 Mistreated orphan hero (Central—Boas 1888:630; West Hudson Bay— Boas 1901:309; Ungava—Turner 1894:265; Cumberland Sound—Boas 1901:188; Greenland—Rasmussen 1921:I, 123, 230, 238; 1921:II, 34, 38; 1921:III, 90, 295; Rink 1875:93); P150 Rich man; Q280 Unkindness punished; Q411 Death as punishment. In PM23 in this volume a granddaughter claimed that the rich boy tore her parka.

PM138. THE MAN WHO COULDN'T TALK

Some people were trying to get shishauk with umaypaks. The belugas got close and a man speared one. The line tangled around his leg. The beluga was only wounded and when it ran off the man fell out of the boat. The beluga took him away and he stayed away all winter. Finally spring came and when the beluga came back the man was with him. He went back to his wife but he couldn't talk. He lived like he did before, but he never talked. He stayed with his wife all the following winter. In the spring the belugas came on the same day that they had come when he had been lost and on the same day they had come when he had returned. The man started talking that day. THE END.

I heard this story from Jack Stalker. Grace Baily's mother's stepfather went down from here to the coast. His name was Ahtaruk. He went hunting with an umaypak and got lots of beluga. There was just a little water with ice all over. Ahtaruk wanted to get more beluga. He tried and got caught with a rope and the beluga took him away. I heard that in Kikiktaruk [Paul said Greenland, but Floyd Wesley said somewhere beyond Herschel Island] when the men hunted beluga they got one with a man on a rope attached to the whale. When the beluga jumped they could hear the man make noise.

Maybe if they didn't kill the beluga it would have taken him back too. I have forgotten who told this story. This is a real true story.

D2020 Magic dumbness (Greenland–Rink 1875:154); D2025 Magic recovery of speech; F1088.3.2.1 Fisherman dragged through sea by beluga escapes.

If this incident actually did occur, the man's dumbness may have been psychological shock, rather than magical in origin.

PM139. Hunting Eggs

Two men lived with their wives in the Ipnuks (Ahvoutowruk) north of Kivalina. They each had a wife, but they changed them around. One time they went to the cliff to hunt akpahluruk eggs. They used a rope to gather the eggs. One man let the other down over the cliff. The man on the rope kept turning around in the air until he got to a ledge and stopped. The rope didn't go anymore, so the man on top threw the rope down.

The other man stayed on the ledge because he didn't know how to get up or down. He had no food or water, so he started to get skinny. He put his head down and thought to himself, "I'm going to die on these cliffs." Finally he looked up and saw a rope. He said, "How will I get up even if I tie myself in?" A voice from above said, "Tie yourself in the rope and I'll pull you up, but keep your eyes shut. Don't open them until you step on the ground."

The man tied himself in, closed his eyes, and somebody started pulling him up. When he got on top he sat for awhile and then opened his eyes. He was on top of the cliff. He looked around and saw nobody. By some running water in the hills he saw a brown bear going down. He thought maybe that brown bear had pulled him up. He looked around some more and saw a sharp rock with a place on it for a rope. It was about two inches wide. That man's kids are still using that rock to find eggs. The place where the rope goes is real smooth.

When the man went home to his wife she started feeding him and he got his health back. When springtime came he and the other man went to hunt eggs again. When they got there he let the other man down first. When the man reached the same ledge the man on top let the rope fall. The other man never came back. THE END.

This is as far as I heard this story from Carl Stalker.

B211.2.3 Speaking bear; B435.4 Helpful bear; K963 Rope cut and victim dropped; K1600 Deceiver falls into own trap; Q211.8 Punishment for desire to murder (Cumberland Sound—Boas 1901:62; Smith Sound—Kroeber 1899:177; Greenland—Holm 1912:47; Rink 1875:157, 222); Q411 Death as punishment; T141.2 Wives exchanged (Cumberland Sound—Boas 1901:223; Greenland—Holm 1912:75).

Perhaps jealousy is involved here, but not explicitly.

PM140. THE KUNUKSHRUT PEOPLE

The Naupaktomiut stayed around here someplace for the winter. While they were here two kivauks came. They invited them, and the Naupaktomiut went down the river. They went to Ḵuḵuksuukvik, a little hill by Killikmak. Then the kivauks took them to a lake by the ocean below Ḵuḵuksuukvik. The people had houses between the hill and the lake. When they gathered around the lake a funny-looking man started singing. After he sang the Naupaktomiut's bodies started getting weak. Those people were at Kunukshrut. After they got weak some Naupaktomiut, who weren't really aŋatquqs, helped them get better. Then they had a meeting. The Kunukshrut people gave them ahtaŋnuk (ugruk bottoms [for mukluks]) and seal oil and the Naupaktomiut gave back caribou and reindeer skins. After the meeting was over the Naupaktomiut went home.

When they got home they stayed the summer. The next winter they sent two kivauks to Kunukshrut to invite people. When the Kunukshrut reached the Naupaktomiut they started having a meeting again. The same funny-looking man started singing and the Naupaktomiut got weak. The Naupaktomiut, who weren't really aŋatquqs, made them better again. When the Kunukshrut left for home the Naupaktomiut gave them fox and other skins while the Kunukshrut returned seal ropes and seal oil. The Kunukshrut people were all kinds of animals that became people. The one that sang the song was a brown bear. The Naupaktomiut were really people. They were fooled by those animals. THE END.

This is as far as I heard this story from Ralph Gallahorn.

D300 Transformation: animal to person (Greenland—Rasmussen 1921: III, 205; Rink 1875:450); D313.3 Transformation: bear to person (MacKenzie River—Jenness 1924:54; Greenland—Rasmussen 1921:I, 134; 1921:III, 52, 86; Rink 1875:196); D1364.24 Music causes magic sleep (illness); D1711 Magician. The Messenger Feast is mentioned in PM65 and PM127 in this volume.

PM141. The Lost Men From King Island

Three men from King Island were drifted in their kayaks. It was foggy and they couldn't find their way home. They couldn't find any land. They tied their kayaks together when they wanted to sleep, but they didn't sleep much. One time they went towards a dark place, and after they got there their kayaks started touching sand. They looked up and saw an open place in a cliff. It was a cave with rocks and sand on the floor. They discovered the sand was beads. One man fixed a line to his spear and threw the spear on top of the cliff. When he tried to pull it down it was stuck, so he climbed up.

He told the other two to come up, but they would not, even though he said there were a lot of berries and greens growing up there. Finally when that man didn't come down the two in the kayaks started going through the cave. After awhile they saw a bright spot ahead of them. They came out to some open water. They paddled through it even though it was rough. And after a few days they got back to King Island. The man that went up on the cliff never came home. If those two had gone up they wouldn't have come home either. The End.

Jack Henry told this story.

F701 Land of plenty.
    The importance of beads in early historic Eskimo culture is emphasized by their mention in this story.

PM142. Three Brothers

Three brothers lived in Point Hope. When they went out whale hunting they used to take along their father, their brother-in-law, and a man who couldn't walk well. The eldest brother was named Kippiiak. One time in the fall, when the ice was way out, they went out in the boat and were drifted. When they saw the ice they put the boat on top and took the skins off. Five of them left, walking across the ice, leaving the man who couldn't walk well with half the boat skins. When they got to open water the brother-in-law wouldn't leave his father-in-law. He always swam across with a rope and when he got to the other side pulled his father-in-law across.

They split up, the three brothers going one way and the father and son-in-law going the other way. The three brothers had no food, but finally they found a small seal (pamrauk) that always stays on top of the ice. One of the brothers said, "The strongest one will eat it." Another said, "We should divide it and all have a share." The other two brothers grabbed that one and put out his eyes. He started running, but he couldn't see. When he came to open water he fell in and swam across. When he got to ice he got up and ran again.

The father was sitting on top of a little mound of ice. (I don't know what happened to his son-in-law.) The father had a rope. He was so skinny he couldn't move. When the ice got to the beach he tied the rope with his hands. He got up on the beach and kept walking along with the rope. He saw their house, so he went to the window and called inside, "I want water." His wife came out and gave him a drink. Then he walked in with his rope.

As he went through the doorway he saw his two sons sitting on the floor. They did not try to help him, but turned their backs to him instead. He sat by his wife and told her, "Invite all the other people to come over here." She did, and when everybody came in the father said, "All these years I tried to raise my boys. They never helped me. When I needed help they wouldn't help. For what did I raise them?" The brother who was blinded and the man who didn't walk good never came home. THE END.

Leonard Brown told this story.

K2210 Treacherous relatives; N820 Human helpers; P230 Parents and children; P251.6.1 Three brothers; P261 Father-in-law; Q2 Kind and unkind; W34 Loyalty; W154 Ingratitude.

Perfidy by blood kin is rare in Eskimo folktales, especially in contrast to the loyalty of kin by marriage.

PM143. The Brother With Good Ears

Three brothers lived in Point Hope. Their younger sister had a husband. The middle brother could always hear things real well when they were out hunting. The sister's husband always tried to beat her up. She had a little ulu on a string around her neck. One time when her husband tried to beat her she went away towards Point Barrow. Her brothers did not know she was gone. After she walked awhile she reached a house. The people there were gone, so she went in. Before she did she saw a lot of meat on the iḳiguts.

She stayed in the house and towards evening the people came back. It was four brothers, one of whom was real small, but he always followed the other three. The eldest brother married the girl. The young boy started staying home with the girl instead of following his brothers. When the brothers went out, the girl always sewed for them. One time when she was sewing the boy started pulling her sinew. She told him not to. He kept doing it all day. Finally she took the little ulu and pretended to strike him. He fell dead on the floor even though she never touched him. She didn't know what to do. She thought of the iḳigut so she carried him up there. There were a lot of skins and meat on top. She hid the boy inside the skins.

Towards evening the three brothers came home and when they didn't see their youngest brother they asked where he was. She said, "After you went he followed you. He hasn't returned." They looked for him, but they couldn't find him where they'd been hunting.

Springtime came and the snow started melting. The iḳiguts started melting and the brothers found blood dripping down from it. They searched up there and found their youngest brother. They asked the woman what had happened and she told them about when she had been sewing. They said, "You should have told us when it happened instead of letting us look for him." They got mad at her and planned to kill her. She started calling for her brothers. They said, "Do you think your brothers are going to hear you?" When she called, her brothers came because her middle brother had good ears and he heard her. The brothers started fighting each other and the girl's brothers killed the others. They took their sister home. The End.

I have forgotten, but maybe Carl Stalker told me this story.

D801 Ownership of magic object; D1170 Magic utensils and implements; D1827.2 Person hears call for aid from great distance; D2060 Death or bodily injury by magic; F641 Person of remarkable hearing; P251.6.1 Three brothers; P253.0.3 Three brothers and one sister; S62 Cruel husband; T320 Escape from undesired lover.

PM144. THE MAGIC AHĠUN

A grandmother and grandson lived among the Naupaktomiut. When the men came home from hunting they always brought home all different kinds of animals, including foxes. The grandson always watched them. Finally he asked his grandmother how they always caught foxes. She told him, "They always put deadfalls. If you do it like I tell you it'll be all right." She told him how to make a trap. The grandson didn't sleep much because he wanted to set his trap. He made one like his grandmother told him.

After he set it he left early the next morning to see it. When he got there he had caught a red fox. His grandmother told him, "If you get enough red foxes turn the trap a different way and you'll get different kinds of foxes." He turned it and when he went to see it next he had gotten a white fox. Every time he got enough of one kind he turned it and got a different kind.

Finally his grandmother told him to take the trap off, but he didn't do it. When he went to see it next the trap was real bright. When he got close he was drawn swiftly towards the trap. He tried to drag his feet and stop himself, but he couldn't. He saw a big open door. He became trapped in his own trap. Finally two boys came and took him out. They took him to a house and went in. He heard the people say, "Let that stranger see what you are going to do."

The boys got an ahġun (fish gaff) and pretended to put it through the door and gaff fish. They caught dried caribou meat. They did it again and pulled up a poke of seal oil. The next time they started to pull a woman up. When she came up halfway a man said, "If you like her pull her up. If you don't push her head down." They pushed the girl down. That's what they let the boy see. A man told the grandson, "When you go home you try. If you pull up a girl and you want her, pull her all the way. If you don't, push her back down."

They sent the grandson home to his grandmother. He made an ahġun and tried through the door. He pulled up meat and seal oil.

Then he put the ahġun through and hooked a girl. He pulled her up. The girl was stiff. He started walking around her, kicking her head and feet. Finally she caught her breath and started moving. When she got well the grandson married her. She had long mukluks and nice clothes.

They lived through the winter and in the spring he started making a boat. When he finished it he filled it with all kinds of meat. They started downstream. After awhile he asked his wife, "Don't you recognize any place?" He had seen a house farther down. The wife looked and said, "One time I lived someplace along here." They got close and she recognized the house. Behind it there was a grave. She said, "One time I was real sick and then I didn't know what happened. When I died they buried me in that grave." They went ashore and went to the house before they unloaded the boat. The grandson said, "You go in to your parents."

He went back of the house. He heard his wife's parents inside excited about their daughter. They were going to greet her, but she went out the back of the house right through the wall. The grandson grabbed her and held her for awhile. Then he said, "Try again." His wife said, "My father was making an arrow when I first went in." She went in again. Her parents were excited and were going to grab her, but she went through the back wall again. Her husband told her to go in again, saying, "Next time tell your father to stay still and not to try to grab you." She went in and told her father that. When she did not come out the grandson went in.

They were glad to have their daughter back because she had died a long time ago. After her parents settled down they started unloading the boat. They brought everything up. After they stayed for awhile the grandson made another ahġun and started pulling things up. He brought up a woman. He went around her kicking her until she became alive. Later he and his wife and the woman started downstream. After awhile he said to the new woman, "Don't you recognize this place?" She said, "Yes, I know this place. I was sick and then I didn't know what happened. That's my house."

They landed on the beach and went up to the house. The same thing happened that had happened at the first house. After the woman had come out through the back twice she stayed in. The grandson and his wife went in. The parents were glad to get their daughter back. They stayed for awhile and then the three started upstream. That man's wife was from Kimmikpuk (mouth of the Noatak). After they had stayed there for a few years they went up to the grandson's place. He didn't hunt for his grandmother because she had died. Those three went back and forth. THE END.

Ralph Gallahorn told me this story.

C757 Tabu: doing things too hastily; D801 Ownership of magic object; D1170 Magic utensils and implements; D1412 Magic objects pulls persons into it; D1472 Food and drink from magic object; E1 Person comes to life; E10 Resuscitation by rough treatment; K730 Victim trapped; L111.4.1 Orphan hero lives with grandmother; T145.0.1 Polygyny. In PM58 in this volume a magic trap is used; in PM75 a boy draws objects up from the house floor; in PM115 resuscitation is accomplished by kicking.

Again, the danger of doing something hastily is stressed.

PM145. THE MAN WITH THE SHORT PENIS

A man living in Point Hope had two wives. When he hunted he always brought things home. In the summertime he always moved towards Kivalina to hunt caribou. He took his two wives along to work the caribou he got. One time he got some caribou and packed them to his camp. He got tired and went to sleep while his wives started working the caribou meat. They started handing the meat up. Their husband was asleep. While they were working one asked the other, "Does your husband always do bad things to you?" She said, "No. Does he to you?" The first answered, "No."

They stopped what they were doing and went to where their husband was sleeping. They took his blanket and his pants off. When they looked they saw that his penis was real short. They started laughing at their husband. Finally he woke and heard them laughing. He got up and went over to them. He asked, "Why are you laughing?" One woman said, "This other woman cut the meat the wrong way. That's why." He knew that they were lying. He let them get wood and he piled it up high. He spilled oil all over it and lighted it. When the wood was really burning he threw both his wives in the fire. After a little while he jumped in too. THE END.

Carl Stalker used to tell this story.

F547.3 Extraordinary penis; J50 Wisdom (knowledge) acquired from observation; K955 Murder by burning; T145.0.1 Polygyny.

In Eskimo society, too, impugning one's manhood is not particularly safe! Perhaps the man's suicide was necessary because he overacted to his wives' teasing.

PM146. The Wolves and Wolverines

A man and his wife with no kids were living alone on a river. The man never stayed home but always went hunting. One day, though, he stayed home and started making some arrows, getting ready to go out again. That evening they heard someone walking outdoors. They didn't know any people were close. No one tried to come in; there was just somebody walking around. Finally a man from outdoors called for the wife to come out, but her husband didn't want her to. The man called again to the wife to come out. Her husband told her no. The man outdoors sounded like he was crying by the corner of the house. The house had two logs along the roof on the sides. The man outside kicked one of the logs and some dirt fell down. The husband started out. There was a noise like fighting outdoors. When it stopped the husband said to his wife, "Come out and see your husband." She went out and saw a wolf lying on the ground. The man and his wife were wolverines. When the husband went out hunting the wolf always changed into a man and came and used his wife. THE END.

I heard this story from Ralph Gallahorn.

D300 Transformation: animal to person (Greenland—Rasmussen 1921: III, 205; Rink 1875:450); D313.2 Transformation: wolf to man (Mac-Kenzie River—Jenness 1924:76); W181 Jealousy.

PM147. The Man Who Brought a Girl Back to Life

A man was walking in the wintertime when he came to some old houses. He went into one and looked for things. When he didn't find what he was looking for he went into the other houses, but he couldn't find anything he wanted. Finally he went to one and went in. He started searching around with his hands because the house was dark. He felt something hanging in the air, so he cut it down. He put it on the floor and started taking off some wolf and wolverine skins.

Pretty soon he found a body with a woman's parka on. He tried to warm her up, to make her alive. Finally the woman started getting kind of warm. He kept feeling her and his hand went to her belt. He moved his hand inside her pants and she made a sudden noise. He was scared, so he stopped. Then he tried again and got his hand farther down and the woman made a noise again. He got scared and stopped. This went on until finally the woman started breathing. She sat up and told the man that she had been sick and died. Her parents were rich, so they buried her in their house and left her. All the other people moved too. She was their youngest daughter.

When the two went out from the house they looked around for tracks. They found some heading one way so they followed them. They kept going and finally saw some houses. When they got to people a man and his wife recognized their daughter and found out she had a young man with her. She told them how he had brought her alive. The young man and the girl got married. THE END.

Papigluk, John Barger's uncle, told this story.

E1 Person comes to life; H79 Recognition by physical attributes.

PM148. THE BOYS WHO STOLE WOMEN

A man and his wife lived alone. He always hunted and brought caribou home. Once in the winter the man got some caribou and then came home. The next day his wife went up to pack some home. She didn't come back all day or night. Early the next morning the man went up to look for her. There was a caribou by her tracks. He saw that two men had taken her away. He followed their trail and after aways it looked like the woman had been jumping. Then there were no more tracks. The three had flown off. The man went home.

After that he often looked around for his wife. One time he got to a house. There was nobody around so he went in. He saw his wife lying between two men. The parents of those two men were there too. When he went in he took the beads off from his forehead and said, "I came to get my wife. I can pay with these beads." The father said to the man, "We're not short of beads. We have lots." Then the man took out his knife and offered it. The father looked at the knife for awhile and then said, "Yes, we really need those."

As the man was going out with his wife the father said, "Sometime my boys are coming to get your wife again. Get ready so they won't take her." After they got home they stayed all winter and the next summer. The next winter the man got ready because he knew that those boys were coming then. He put two men outside the door with spears, two more in the stormshed with spears, and two more in the inner doorway with spears.

A few days later they heard the boys coming. The two started making noise in the stormshed, but the men waiting for them with spears didn't make any noise. Soon a man's head started coming up through the doorway. The two men were waiting above with their spears. The man came up as far as his chest, looked around, and saw the woman. He hollered and made noise and then went away. The husband looked around and didn't see his wife. She had already gone. He went out and found that they had taken her again. The men who were going to spear them were stiff and the woman never came home again. THE END.

I heard this story from Ralph Gallahorn.

D2072 Magic paralysis; D2135 Magic air journey (MacKenzie River—Jenness 1924:40; Greenland—Rasmussen 1921:I, 87); H1385 Quest for lost persons; P251 Brothers; R10 Abduction; R133 Vanished wife rescued.

PM149. THE RICH MAN WHO BECAME A WEASEL

A rich man and a poor boy lived in a village. When the people went to the karigi the women brought the food up and the men are there. The poor boy went too. When they went out to go home the poor boy went out too. He saw a house with a bright light that he had never noticed before. He went in and found a young girl. He stayed there. In the morning the young girl said, "You can go home now."

That evening the people went up to the karigi again; the women brought food. Pretty soon a really pretty girl came in and put food in front of the poor boy. The rich man saw that girl. When the karigi was over the rich man said to the poor boy, "You go home to my wife and I'll go home to your wife." The poor boy said to the rich man, "Even if that young girl [the poor boy's wife] tells you to go out, don't go out."

Then the poor boy went home to the rich man's wife and stayed with her. Towards morning they expected the rich man to come home, but he didn't show up. He didn't come home for a long time. Then the poor boy and the rich man's wife who were living together saw a weasel (tiġġak) in the stormshed. It was the rich man. THE END.

I have forgotten who told me this story.

D124.1 Transformation: man to weasel, ermine (MacKenzie River—Jenness 1924:36); P150 Rich man; T141.2 Wives exchanged (Cumberland Sound—Boas 1901:223; Greenland—Holm 1912:75).

PM150. THE NAHVIIVUK

A man, his wife, and their son lived in Point Hope. Also living there was another man, his wife, and their daughter. The man with the daughter wanted the boy for his son-in-law, but the boy didn't want to marry the girl. The boy used to hunt and bring lots of food home. After a few days he got sick and was ready to die. When he was about dead a little old woman came in and said, "I know you want your son to live." The boy's mother said: "Yes, we want him to live if he can." The little old woman said, "I'll try to help him get better. That aŋatquq over there wanted your boy for his son-in-law and that's why he let him get sick. If people talk funny about my kids I always kill them too. I don't like people to talk about my children. When your son was hunting and got food he always gave half his share to my kids. When he got caribou in the hills he always brought my children half. He's been feeding them so I'll try to help him."

After the little old woman talked she suddenly disappeared. Pretty soon the boy, who hadn't even been able to open his eyes, opened them, looked around and said, "I want a drink of water." His mother gave him water and a little food. He started eating a little every day. He gained weight, sat up in bed, and felt happier. After he got better

he started walking around. The sickness went back to the aŋatquq and he died. The little old woman was a nahviivuk's mother. THE END.

I heard this from Edna Hunnicutt, who heard it from Jennie Mitchell. [Some of this story is missing. Edna, who was present when Paul was telling this story, heard it differently. The woman with a son didn't have a husband. When the boy got sick his mother sat by him with her head down waiting to see if he would die. She fell asleep and while she was sleeping heard a voice from the corner, something like a *nahviivuk*. When she opened her eyes she saw the little old woman in the corner.]

B483.1 Helpful fly; D382 Transformation: hymenoptera to person; D1711 Magician; D2060 Death or bodily injury by magic; N825.3 Help from old woman (Greenland—Rasmussen 1921:II, 162); Q211.8 Punishment for desire to murder (Cumberland Sound—Boas 1901:62; Smith Sound—Kroeber 1899:177; Greenland—Holm 1912:47; Rink 1875:157, 222); Q411 Death as punishment; T311 Man averse to marriage.

An alternate version is suggested by Edna Hunnicutt. During the summer, flies lay their eggs on fresh meat and the hatching maggots feed thereon.

PM151. THE NAATIGLUK

Down in Kotzebue, when they're going to have Christmas games in that old school building (when my wife Mary was still alive, a few years ago), people always waited for other people to come, and when they waited people would tell stories. This is a story I heard there.

In the ocean the dirt at the bottom started looking around and saw two villages. The dirt became a man. When the dirt became a man he was between the two villages he saw. They call that dirt "naatigluk." The naatigluk thought to himself, "I wonder which village I should go to." Then he went to one of the villages where there was a rich man. The rich man told the naatigluk, "You can stay with my wife."

This naatigluk went back to where he had been standing between the two villages. Then the naatigluk had a wife (maybe he made one out of dirt). So the naatigluk took his wife to the village he had visited before. When the naatigluk and his wife went to the village the rich man told the naatigluk, "You should go to my wife and I'll take yours." So that naatigluk and the rich man changed wives.

They stayed there and the rich man killed the naatigluk's wife, and when the naatigluk found out he went up to the rich man and let his (the naatigluk's) wife come alive. A few days later the rich man killed the naatigluk's wife again. Once more the naatigluk went up and let her become alive and then he took her back to his place between the two villages.

The naatigluk started making a sled. After the naatigluk finished the sled he put a rope on the sled and then tied it around his shoulders. Then he put his wife back of the sled holding on to the rail. They started going once more towards the same village.

When they got to the village the naatigluk started walking toward the rich man's house. He went inside to the rich man's house with his sled. First the naatigluk came in, then his sled, and when he got close to below the window the naatigluk started walking up through the air. He went out through the window. After he went out through the window the sled went up and behind it was the naatigluk's wife, going up through the window. The rich man, who was seeing the whole thing, jumped to the naatigluk's wife and grabbed her around her waist. The rich man was going to pull her down, but she didn't come down, so they kept going up, the rich man still holding the naatigluk's wife's waist, and finally they got so high the rich man got cold and fell. The naatigluk and his wife kept going up and then went up through a hole.

When they went through the hole the naatigluk saw a house close by. They went to that house, put their sled by the side of the house, and then went in. They saw a man when they went in who told them, "If you keep going you'll come to a house just like mine." So the naatigluk and his wife left this house and started traveling through the ice. The naatigluk and his wife came to a house just like the first house they went into and there was a sled outside just like their sled. Then they went into the house and there was nobody there. They saw a cover on the floor with a handle. The naatigluk opened it and saw the village where the rich man had lived under him. THE END.

This is as far as I heard this story because the bell for games rang. I heard it from Chester Downey (Siivik).

D430 Transformation: object to person; D1110 Magic conveyances; D1532 Magic object bears person aloft; F56 Sky window (West Hudson Bay—Boas 1901:339; Central—Boas 1888:599; Labrador—Hawkes 1916: 153; Greenland—Holm 1912:80; Rasmussen 1921:III, 165, 170; Rink 1875:468); F60 Transportation to or from upperworld; F163.3 House in otherworld; E1 Person comes to life; P150 Rich man; Q211 Murder punished (Cumberland Sound—Boas 1901:168; Greenland—Rasmussen 1921:III, 76, 111, 294); Q411.6 Death as punishment for murder; T141.2 Wives exchanged (Cumberland Sound—Boas 1901:223; Greenland—Holm 1912:75).

PM152. THE WOMAN WHO TRAVELED ALONE

A woman was traveling alone. After she went for awhile she came to a house with two ikiguts. She looked around, saw nobody, so she went in. There was nobody inside. While she was there a man came in. He was surprised to see her. He said, "Now I'm going to have somebody to talk to. Did you have something to eat already?" She said, "No." He said, "Eat, help yourself." She stayed with the man, sleeping on the floor. The man had raised a bed. The man would go out and when he came home the hair on his pants between his legs would be gone. She would patch the pants. The next day the same thing would happen. Every time she sewed his pants.

She started looking around and went over to the farthest ikigut. She saw some dead women piled on top. Their crotches were full of blood. So she found out about the man, but even though she knew, she kept patching the pants. One time she woke up in the night. She saw the man working between his legs. He said, "Every time I have a woman to help me you always want to boss me."

One evening he said to the woman, "I want to use a woman." The woman went up to his bed and got ready. She put her feet on the wall and her hands on her chest. She said, "Don't fool me. Finish quick." When he got on her she pushed him off and his flint penis stuck in the wood of the bed. The woman put her clothes on. The man told her to take them off, but she didn't listen. She went out and left.

She got to another house, went in, and found only a man's things. She got married to the man and he was real nice to her. One evening he said, "I'm expecting a woman. If she comes she is going to boss me around. I'm tired of her because she always beats me up." He got ready, making his wife a big ulu and sharpening it real well. He told her that if the other woman came through the door she should use her strength and kill her with the ulu.

They got ready and on the day the woman always came they heard her laugh outside, "Pikhihihihik." Then they heard her say, "You think you're going to live." She started laughing again. The woman stood by the door with her ulu. The other woman got close and started coming up through the door. When her head came up the woman hit her with the ulu on the back of the neck. That woman would come every year. The man was glad that his wife had killed her. THE END.

Edgar Foster, Kenneth Ashby's grandfather, told me this story.

F547.3 Extraordinary penis; S62 Cruel husband; T81 Death from love; T320 Escape from undesired lover. A flint penis is found in PM33 in this volume and, perhaps, Lucier 1953:218–22 (Buckland).

PM153. TUŊNALUK

A man from Point Hope always went up the Kukpuk for the winter. He stayed there eating fish. One spring he went back to Point Hope and in the fall he went upriver again. While he was up there he went to see his fish traps. He stayed late and then started home. When he got to his house he went inside and put a lamp. He had a room by the door. There was another room in the back of the house. He saw a woman with long mukluks lying in the other room.

He brought some frozen fish in to eat. When he was going to eat he threw a fish to the woman saying, "Here's your frozen fish." The fish came back to him, moving by itself. This happened a second time. He went over to the woman. He tried to shake her, but she was frozen real stiff. He tried to warm her up. He kept working on her and she started breathing. He knew the woman from Point Hope. She told him that she had been sick and then didn't know what happened to her. They stayed there talking and finally went to bed. The man was named Tuŋnaluk. They stayed together all night.

In the morning the woman said to the man, "We should go home to Point Hope." Tuŋnaluk said, "If you go to Point Hope the men will take you away from me." The woman said, "Nobody will take me away. I want to go home to Point Hope." She kept saying that. Finally she said, "If you don't go right now you won't have me." She told him that they were going to bury her three days after she had died. This morning was the third day and they were going up to check the house where she was lying. Tuŋnaluk got ahold of her because he didn't want her to go away. All of a sudden she popped, just like a clap of hands. Tuŋnaluk didn't know what he had done. He woke up and was real cold and shivering. He found he was outside in the stormshed. The woman left him by the door. He stayed alone after that. THE END.

Ralph Gallahorn told this story.

D2135.5 Object sent through air; E1 Person comes to life; J1050 Attention to warnings.

PM154. KAMIKSUVAK

A man and his wife with their two sons lived in a village at Beechy Point. After two or three years they had another son. When the baby grew up they made a bow and arrow for him and he learned how to shoot it. In the evening the villagers played football. The young boy always shot with his bow and arrow while they played football. One time while they were playing football it got stormy and the men started going home. The young boy was playing with his bow and arrow. His two brothers said to him, "There's a polar bear coming." They were just trying to scare him.

Then they left and the young boy started home. It got real stormy and he couldn't make it against the wind. He turned back and ran because he couldn't see anything. He got lost. He had caribou-fur pants with a hole in front because he was too small to take his pants down to toilet. He ran along the river for a long ways. He couldn't find his way home. When he got tired he dug a little place in the snow and went to sleep. When he woke he went again. People looked for him, but it was too stormy. When he got tired he slept again.

When he woke up he found that he was warm. After a little while the ground started shaking. He looked and saw a caribou covered with snow. He had gone to sleep on top of it. As he was hungry he looked around the caribou's place and found some caribou ahnuk and started eating it. His stomach got better. He stayed in the caribou's place because he didn't want the snow to cover what he was eating. Whenever he was hungry he ate some of the ahnuk. He stayed there all winter.

Then it started to get warm. It was springtime. Some time in the spring he went to an island where there was snow. He started digging and eating masu. He stayed there and ate greens when they grew. The ice started going so he couldn't get back to the ahnuk he had been eating. When the water got high he tied some willows together and sat on top of them. He went to sleep there.

When he woke up something was touching his hair. The water was very high and the ice was hitting the island. He went to sleep again and when he woke up the water was low. He thought of the caribou ahnuk again, and so he went over and found them. He picked them up and put them in water because they were dry. Towards falltime he started wondering if someone might not be living upriver. So he started walking up. When he got up aways he found a bank with some mud. He dug in it and made a place for himself where he went to sleep.

When he woke up it seemed like somebody was walking. A little while after he heard the noise somebody said, "Maybe I'm getting close to a boy now." Pretty soon someone started poking a knife through the hole to make it bigger. The boy could see the knife and the man's wrist when he poked in the hole. He grabbed the man's wrist and the knife fell. He picked up the knife and cut the man's hand off. So much blood came out that the man died. The boy made the hole bigger and put the man in there. After he hid him he cleaned up the blood. He said, "I've got a knife now." His clothes had gotten small, so he took the man's off and put them on. He went back in the cave with the man's body.

One time when he woke up he heard somebody stepping on top of him. A voice said, "Maybe I'm going to find that boy because there are tracks around here." The boy killed that man just like he did the first one and buried him in the hole. After a few days he thought to himself, "I wonder if there's anybody farther up." He started going again. His father had given him some beads for a headband when he was small. When the band didn't fit his head anymore he had a hole in his pants and tied them there. He walked and finally got to a little hill from where he could see. It was evening; he looked around and saw some bright lights. Farther over from those houses was a real dim light. After awhile some of the lights went out, but the dim light stayed on. He went down to that house. When he went inside he saw a man who said, "You shouldn't have come. Those people over there will kill you."

After they slept people came to get the boy. The man went up with him. They went up to the karigi. When they went in the boy saw an old man sitting there with no shirt. There were two boys sitting close to him. The old man asked him, "Did you ever hear about a boy that was lost?" The boy said, "I don't know about people." The old man said, "If you don't know about people that's the end of your life." And the boy wasn't even scared.

The old man called to his two boys and they stood up. Then he called the boy, who came in, and he stood up and faced the two boys. Those two were supposed to kill him. The old man told the two boys to question the boy first and ask him if he knew about any little boy that was lost. The boy said he didn't know any, but he told them how he had been lost and how he had lived as a small boy. Then he found the beads that were hanging on his pants. He took them off and gave them to the old man. The old man looked at them for a long time and then said, "My son came to me." He had put the beads on the boy's head himself. The boy's name was Kamiksuvak.

The old man said, "Kamiksuvak, come to my side." Kamiksuvak went to his father. When Kamiksuvak was born one of his toes was different. Thus he recognized his boy. He and his two older boys had searched for him when he was lost. He had thought about him so much that he had become a man-who-always-killed-people. The old man told his elder sons, "Take my son over to his mother." When the boy had gotten lost his mother had cried for him so much that she couldn't leave her bed. THE END.

Nellie Woods told me this story.

F517.1 Person unusual as to his feet; F1041.9.1.1 Man (woman) keeps to his bed, mourning over drowned (lost) son; H80 Recognition by tokens; P251.6.1 Three brothers; S301 Children abandoned; S350 Fate of abandoned child. Variant of PM21 in this volume.

PM155. AKTUK

Near Buckland, at the mouth of a stream going into the Kobuk, lived some Buckland people. This was a place called Inyuktuk (so called because the Selawik people killed the Buckland people there everytime they came to have war). The Selawik and Buckland people had war and the Buckland people killed the Selawik people. The Buckland people saw a man running away on top of the water. So one of the Buckland people asked, "Where did Aktuk go?" The people said, "He's running away on top of the water."

Then one man made a noise something like "Hiii." Aktuk started sinking into the water. Then the man made the same noise again and Aktuk had sunk as far as his waist into the water. The man kept hollering that noise and Aktuk sank out of sight. Aktuk stayed under the water a little while and when he came up he was a spotted seal. He went back in the water and never showed up again. THE END.

This is as far as I heard this story from Carl Stalker.

D127.1 Transformation: man to seal (MacKenzie River—Jenness 1924: 84; Central—Boas 1888:621; Cape York—Rasmussen 1921:III, 100; Greenland—Rink 1875:222, 224, 450, 469); D2125 Magic journey over water. Similar to Lucier 1953:229 (Buckland).

PM156. THE WOUNDED AHALIK

In Point Hope lived a man and his wife with no kids. The man always hunted, but he never got anything. The wife always went to get food from people before her husband came home and cooked it for him. One time the man went hunting down at the coast. He heard somebody hollering. The one that was hollering said, "Somebody come fix my wing if he wants to get rich, or to be an aŋatquq, or if he wants to be a good hunter." The man got close to the one that was hollering. It was an ahalik (old squaw duck).

The bird hopped around a circle of open water on the ocean. The man got the bird and tied its wing with sinew, splinting it with a piece of wood. That bird tried his wings and he could fly, so he went. A few days after this happened the man got food when he hunted. He started getting more after that. The man and his wife started getting rich after that. They had all the food and kinds of animals they wanted. THE END.

Ralph Gallahorn told me this story.

B211.3 Speaking bird; B390 Animal grateful for other kind acts; B450 Helpful birds; Q40 Kindness rewarded.

PM157. THE MAGIC HARNESS

I have no more stories. I know some parts, some middle parts, some ends, some beginnings. This is a story part:

There was a grandson who went to sleep. He started dreaming of a dog's harness. Before he woke up he tried to grab the stick part of the harness and he got it. When he woke he had a harness in his hands. When he woke up with the harness he started traveling with it. He flew through the air still holding the stick part of the harness. He hunted with that harness and he and his grandmother got lots of food with that harness.

The grandmother and grandson stayed in a village, and their village invited another village to their village. When the people from both villages got to a meeting place a boy from the other village, a poor boy too, got up and said, "I came to get the harness." He stamped his feet and said, "I came to get the harness." This poor boy from the other village knew the grandson had the harness, but the people of the grandson's village didn't know that the grandson had the harness. So the grandson said, "I don't have a harness." The other poor boy said, "I want to trade snowshoes for the harness."

So then the two boys traded and the poor boy from the other village told the grandson, "These snowshoes will take you where you want to go, even through the air if you want." So the grandson started using his snowshoes through the air and going someplace. One time when he was home he heard a voice calling for help, so he put his snowshoes on and started running. The grandson went where his snowshoes took him and soon he heard the voice from a cliff, and when he got to the cliff he saw a boy stuck with his feet inside the cliff. The grandson slapped the boy on the rump with his hand and the boy fell. When the boy came off, the grandson saw it was the poor boy from the other village with whom he had traded the harness. The poor boy got stuck in the cliff because he didn't follow where the harness took him. THE END.

I heard this from Pukik.

D801 Ownership of magic object; D1065.3 Magic snowshoes; D1110 Magic conveyances; D1520 Magic object affords miraculous transportation; L111.4.1 Orphan hero lives with grandmother; N820 Human helpers.

PM158. THUNDER AND LIGHTNING

A man and his wife lived behind Point Barrow. They had one boy and a little girl. They stayed there in the wintertime. The two kids grew up and started fighting with each other. One evening they really made noise and their parents couldn't go to sleep. They didn't stop making noise, so finally their father scolded them saying, "You should go play outdoors." The kids got quiet and went out because they didn't want their father to scold them. This was the first time he had ever scolded them.

When they got to the stormshed they lit a seal-oil lamp and took it and the seal skin out with them. They got inside the dried seal skin. When they had both sat down the seal skin took them up in the air. The burning oil in their lamp fell to the ground. When they touched the seal skin it made a noise. The Point Barrow people found oil somewhere [open pools of oil occur near Barrow]. It had dripped from that lamp. That noise is what we call thunder. When that fire falls we call that lightning. THE END.

I have forgotten who told me this.

A1141 Origin of lightning (Central—Boas 1888:600; Cumberland Sound—Boas 1901:175; Cape York—Rasmussen 1921:III, 61); A1142 Origin of thunder (Cumberland Sound—Boas 1901:175: Labrador—Hawkes 1916:153; Cape York—Rasmussen 1921:III, 62); D1520.5.3 Magic transportation by seal skin (Bering Strait—Nelson 1899:512); D1532 Magic object bears person aloft; P250 Brothers and sisters; Q306 Quarrelsomeness punished. Similar to Ingstad 1954:277 (Anaktuvuk Pass).

Eskimo parents very rarely scold their children, though older persons may occasionally tell children to be quiet.

PM159. KAHGRUK AND AHNIIGUTCHUK

When the people were going home from Nuvuvruk towards the Kobuk, the Noatak, Point Hope, and other places, a man from Point Hope said, "Let Kahgruk look at the hills for the last time." Kahgruk and his family stayed for a year and then Kahgruk died. Both that Point Hope man and Kahgruk were aŋatquqs.

Kahgruk's family decided to send a person to Point Hope. They killed a female dog and let it become a young girl through that aŋatquq. The man from Point Hope went out one evening to toilet before he went to bed. He saw a bright light in a house, so he went over. He peeked through the window and saw a young girl. That Point Hope man's name was Ahniigutchuk. Ahniigutchuk stayed all night with the girl. The Kobuk people had trapped Ahniigutchuk like in a fish trap. He never came home. They looked for him but never found him. In the springtime the Point Hope people found a man's bones and a dog's bones together on the beach. THE END.

Old Man Driggs told me this story.

D341 Transformation: dog to man; D1711 Magician; K730 Victim trapped; K800 Killing or maiming by deception; M341 Death prophesied.

PM160. TIĠUSINYA

A poor boy named Tiġusinya lived in Point Hope. The people there always had meetings in either a house or the karigi. The people always tried to let a man become an aŋatquq. One time Tiġusinya, who never went to those meetings, went up to one. The people were trying to make a man an aŋatquq. Tiġusinya hid behind a pole in the stormshed.

A man came in the stormshed while the people inside didn't know. The man put a mask of a wolf's head on. A woman from the house was going out to put something in the stormshed. She saw the man with the mask and thought it was the devil. The woman kept going back and forth. Finally the man went out and in a little while came back into the stormshed with a caribou skin. He spread it out on the floor and when a woman came out he beckoned to her. She came to the kaichik and they started doing bad things. When the man and woman left the stormshed Tiġusinya went out from his hiding place and went home. He went to bed.

The next day they started playing football. Towards evening people started lighting their seal-oil lamps. Tiġusinya met a man and said to him, "Did you get the devil?" The man said, "Yes." Tiġusinya asked, "Was it really a devil?" The man said, "Yes, it really was." Tiġusinya said, "Your devil is over there in that house that has a bright light." The man told the man that lived in the house with the bright light that Tiġusinya had seen him in the mask and knew all about it.

The man who wore the mask had the people gather together in a house. He invited Tiġusinya. When Tiġusinya went in there were a lot of people. A man who had a uŋnuk (seal spear) got up. Tiġusinya was sitting by the door. The man went all around the room pretending to spear people. He got close to Tiġusinya. He really was going to spear Tiġusinya, but the point of the spear fell off. He tried another time and the point came off again. He put the point back on, pointed the spear towards himself, and speared himself. He killed himself because he was so bashful. THE END.

I heard this story from Calvin Barger.

D1711 Magician; D1720 Acquisition of magic powers (Greenland—Rasmussen 1921:II, 222; 1921:III, 111; Rink 1875:461); G303 Devil; K1600 Deceiver falls into own trap; K1626 Would-be killers killed.

The devil, of course, is a recent introduction to Eskimo culture. In fact, the entire tale bespeaks of a morality more akin to our own than to that of the aboriginal Eskimo.

PM161. IMNALUKSUNIK

In Point Hope the women always went walking to go berry picking. There was a tall woman with a small husband. When the women went berry picking this tall woman always went with them. One time this tall woman went through the beach when she went berry picking. She saw tracks, but couldn't make out what kind of tracks they were. So this tall woman followed the tracks and came to a sand dune on the beach, where she saw a real skinny man lying. The man she saw had mukluks with holes in the bottom and he had tied the bottoms to the tops, and that's why he made funny tracks. This tall woman told this man, "Don't run away; I'm going home for awhile." Then she went home.

She came back with food. She started bringing food to him every day and finally he started gaining weight. When he got his health back he started walking around. One time this tall woman brought clothes for him. She brought her husband's clothes to him and let that man put them on. Before she had left home with her husband's clothes he had said to her, "If anybody tears up my clothes I'll tear up that person's clothes too." The tall woman took the clothes over and put them on the man. She took him to her home to visit.

When the Point Hope people came out to meet the two they ran towards them because they wanted to get ahold of the man. The woman said to them, "If anybody tears up my husband's clothes this man will tear that person's clothes." A small man was running behind the Point Hope people. He and the tall woman took the man home. The tall woman's husband was short, but the people were scared of him.

They let the man stay with them and he and the small man started hunting together. When he got seal the woman would cut them and show him how to do it too. The man showed the woman how to take the blubber off and how to put the skin in the ground to take the hair off for mukluk bottoms. They made nalak. He had her put skins in oil to take the hair off and showed them how to make seal rope. He made nets for seals and set them. He started getting seals.

When they went out to put the net he said to the short man, "You run way down to that piled ice. When you run out of breath stop and we'll make a hole there." They did that. Then the short man ran again, and where he stopped they made the other hole. After they set the net they started walking around on the ice to scare the seals. When they pulled up the net it had seals in it. They did that all day and every time they pulled up their net they got seals.

In the evening they went home, leaving the seals on the ice. In the morning the Point Hope men went seal hunting. They saw something black on the piled ice. They went over and found seals with no harpoon hole. That man showed them how to hunt seals with nets. The Point Hope people started inviting that man after that. The small man didn't go with him when he visited. In the summertime the man took the small man to his home. He was from King Island and his name was Imnaluksunik. THE END.

I have forgotten who told me this story.

J50 Wisdom (knowledge) acquired from observation; N820 Human helpers; Q40 Kindness rewarded; W10 Kindness; W27 Gratitude.
This tale offers an explanation of how the Point Hope people learned about seal hunting.

PM162. THE MAGIC STICK

Two brothers lived on Little Diomede (Inahlik). The eldest has a wife, but the younger was not ready to get married. The younger liked to run. His brother told him to get something from Big Diomede, saying, "Your sister-in-law will put a pot on the stove. After it's cooked she will set it on the table. If you are home by then you aren't too bad at running." As the sister-in-law put the food in the pot the boy got ready and left. After awhile the food boiled, and when the woman was thinking about putting it on a plate the young boy came in. He was a fast runner.

After a few years the Siberian people invited the villagers. The Diomeders and some of the other villagers went there in the wintertime. When they got there the head man of the Siberian village wanted the people to run a race. He said he had a prize for the winner, maybe a beaver or otter. There was a fast runner in the Siberian village too. When the Siberian head man found out that the Diomede boy ran fast too, he gave him some light mittens. He said that the boy and the Siberian runner would run together at first, separate at one place, and then meet farther over.

The people got ready to go from all over the village. They started running and the Diomede boy started pushing men. He kept passing until there were only a few ahead of him. Finally there was only one man ahead of him and he caught and passed him. He kept running and then he looked back and saw the last man he had passed far behind. He kept on running and he saw something ahead of him. He caught up and saw it was the last man he had passed. He didn't know how that man had gotten ahead of him.

He started running behind the man who was carrying a stick. The man said, "You can pass me." The Diomede boy said, "I can't." The man ran faster while the boy followed him. The man wanted to pass, but the boy didn't want to. They reached the halfway mark and turned back with the boy still following. The man carried the stick because it was magic and it took him along.

One time that man was drifted and could not reach home. A raven came to him and gave him a main wing feather. The raven told him: "You can make a stick for yourself. Put the feather inside the stick and hide it with red skin so that nobody will know it is there. That feather will take you along." That man reached his home. The raven had told him, "Somebody will take this stick away from you. If they do look for it. That person won't live." The Diomede boy ran with that man even though he had no magic, but the Siberian man won the race.

The Siberian man always took his stick with him. One time he lost it. He started looking for it in different villages. When he found it he took it back and the man that had stolen it died. When the Siberian man got old the Diomede boy had a race with him again. The boy said, "Maybe I can leave him now that he is old." They started racing. The boy would look back and the old man would be running just behind him with the stick across his back and under his arms. Every time the boy looked back the old man was just behind him. They reached the finish line together. THE END.

I heard this from Carl Stalker, who heard it from the Diomeders themselves.

B211.3.6 Speaking raven; B450 Helpful birds; D801 Ownership of magic object; D956 Magic stick; F681 Marvelous runner; J130 Wisdom (knowledge) acquired from animals; P251 Brothers; Q212 Theft punished; Q411 Death as punishment.

PM163. The Point Hope Man and the Dwarf

A man and his wife were living behind Point Hope under a mountain called Akmakruak. The man always hunted. He never stayed home because he liked to hunt. One time when he was walking he saw another man. When he met him it was a dwarf. The dwarf took his bow and arrow and aimed it at the Point Hope man. The man couldn't do anything else, so he started fighting with the dwarf. Finally he wounded the dwarf. The dwarf told the man that he had a wife and kids. He asked him to go tell them he had been killed. After the dwarf died the man buried him and then went to the dwarf's wife. He told her he didn't try to kill the dwarf first, but that the dwarf had started it. Then the Point Hope man went home. THE END.

Frank Burns told me this story.

F451 Dwarfs; W11.5 Generosity toward enemy.

PM164. The Uŋgaluk̇lik and Suttulik People Fight

In Uŋgaluk̇lik the people always hunted for wood. They went dogteaming to get the wood. When they were loading wood they saw a goose. It was winter. When they went home they told the people that they had seen a goose. One of them said, "We saw a goose. It's wintertime. I don't know how come the geese came so quick." Then the person fell down. The people from Suttulik, a village close to Uŋgaluk̇lik, had sent a goose through their aŋatquq. The one that fell on the floor was dead.

After a year the Uŋgaluk̇lik people decided to send an aŋatquq over to Suttulik. The Suttulik people were playing football when an ukpik landed by them. They saw that it had real red eyes, just like fire. The men got scared and started towards the karigi. The ukpik followed them. The people went inside the karigi and kept checking to see if the owl would come. Finally they said, "It just came in the stormshed." After it went in the stormshed a poor boy among the Suttulik people did some magic and the ukpik never went in the karigi. The poor boy saved that village. If he hadn't been there the

ukpik would have done something to the people. THE END.
I heard this from Carl Stalker.

D1711 Magician; K950 Treacherous murder.

PM165. Learning How to Make Love

A man and his wife had a small house with just enough room to sleep. When the people went into that house they always had to stand up because the house was so small that there was no place to sit. The man and his wife didn't know how to make love. When the man went out hunting his wife would always wait for him by the door. She would take her pants off. When the man came in he always licked her genitals instead of making love. One time when the husband went out a man came in to the woman. He said, "I'll show you." She said, "Yes." They got in bed and he showed her how to make love. When they finished the man said, "When your husband comes home you show him this." When her husband came home they went to bed and she started showing him. When they started they couldn't stop, so they got skinny and died. THE END.
Jimmy Hawley told me this story.

J1745 Absurd ignorance of sex; T81 Death from love.

PM166. Visiting the Siksikpuks

A man was out hunting. He reached a village. When he went into a house they started feeding him. He ate good food. One man in the house had a shoulder that always hurt. While the stranger was there the man had pain. The stranger left after he slept. The people that he visited were siksikpuks that became people. The man that always had pains had been trapped one time. He got out, but the wound from the trap caused him pain. After the stranger left he looked back and saw a siksikpuk hole instead of a house. THE END.
I heard this from Frank Burns.

D315 Transformation: rodent to man.

397

PM167. Kaalayhak

There were people in Kupaaluk, a place behind Point Hope. There were only a few people there. When the people walked they always saw an old house with tracks going in and out. Finally the Kupaaluk people ran out of food. They started talking about that old house, wondering what it was. They said, "We should go see what's over there." They went over to the old house and when they got close they started singing, "Kaalayhak, Kaalayhak, he get walrus, he get walrus, what part will he take for his food? What part will he take for his food?" They went to a window. When they quit singing they heard a voice make noise inside. Dried caribou meats tied together came out the window and after them a big poke of seal oil. Inside the house was a poor boy who lived alone. The people didn't know he had any food. The End.

Frank Burns used to tell this.

PM168. The Flounder and the Beluga

A flounder got married to a beluga. When the beluga went the flounder always put his stomach on his wife's back so he wouldn't come off. The beluga went to her hometown. The flounder stayed with the belugas for the winter. While he was there his brother-in-law said, "Somebody will come kill some of us again." When the flounder heard that his brother-in-law was expecting somebody the flounder had them make a place for him by the door. When they got ready they heard somebody coming. The beluga were scared, so they got by the back wall. Something with a hole in its face came in the door. The flounder jumped up and hit the face. The face made a noise and then went out. All the belugas went out to see. They saw a killer whale lying dead with blood on its forehead. Every year that killer whale would come and kill beluga. Nobody bothered the beluga after that and they thanked the flounder. The End.

I have forgotten who told me this.

A2493 Friendship between animals; K950 Treacherous murder; Q211 Murder punished (Cumberland Sound—Boas 1901:168; Greenland—Rasmussen 1921:III, 76, 111, 294); Q411.6 Death as punishment for murder; T110 Unusual marriage.

PM169. The Girl Who Married an Owl

There was a rich man with a daughter who didn't want to get married. Boys always went up to see her, but she didn't want to marry them. There was an owl (nipaluktuk) that became a man. He went to the village. The girl saw him; he had real nice clothes. She got married to him. They stayed with the rich man. One time he told his wife that he had a house farther away, so they started walking up to it. When they were going to stop for the night the man got caribou. They'd sleep and then go again.

One time the wife woke up and was cold. She looked around and her husband was gone. Her stomach felt funny. She got up and started looking for her husband. She saw a nipaluktuk on top of a little hill. The woman started vomiting. She vomited up a mouse. Then she started for home. The nipaluktuk had fooled her. He was feeding her mice instead of caribou. When the girl got home to her parents she got married to a boy from that village. The End.

Jack Henry used to tell this story.

B600.2 Animal husband provides characteristic animal food (MacKenzie River—Jenness 1924:52; Greenland—Thalbitzer 1904:6); B652 Marriage to bird in human form; D350 Transformation: bird to person; T311 Woman averse to marriage.

PM170. The Kaniuk

A caribou was walking. When it went across a little stream it saw a bullhead (kaniuk). The caribou put the kaniuk in his ear and took him away. It took him to the top of a hill and then dropped him there. It was real hot and the sun tried to dry the kaniuk up. The kaniuk was worried, so he sang, "On top of that hill there is a cloud, there is a cloud, there is a cloud." A little cloud came on top of the hill. It started getting bigger and then it started raining. When the rain started the kaniuk went through a little running water and got to his house. The End.

Maybe Edna Hunnicutt told me this story.

B211.11 Speaking fish.

PM171. How to Catch a Young Wife

In Sukmalairluk lived a man and his wife with a daughter who did not want to get married. Her father was rich. Both of her parents were old. One evening another old man said, "I wonder what kind of man that rich man's daughter is waiting for since she doesn't want to get married." His wife said, "She is waiting for you. She wants you for a husband." The man said, "Maybe she really is waiting for me." He started going after the rich man's daughter. He wouldn't let her sleep. She didn't want him. Sometimes she'd try to run away, but he'd always be in front of her. Finally she got tired of the old man bothering her so she got married to him. The old man now had two wives. THE END.

Makan, Grace Bailey's grandfather, told me this story.

P150 Rich man; T91.4 Age and youth in love; T145.0.1 Polygyny; T311 Woman averse to marriage.

PM172. The Head

There was a woman who had a son with no body, just a head (long ago boys and girls just had heads when they were around people, but when they were off alone they had a body too). When they had a karigi the head always went up. There was a girl who didn't want to get married in that village. When the head heard about her he went over to her house. She woke up and found the head sleeping with her. The head had long hair. The girl grabbed him by the hair, whirled him around, and threw him through the door. He didn't even make a noise.

After that the head kept trying to get that girl. She kept throwing him out of the door every night. He never made a noise when he landed in the stormshed. When she got tired she finally got married to the head. They stayed together and a few years later the village ran out of food. The head said to his wife, "I want everybody to go up to the karigi. When they go up I want you to bring two new caribou snares so I can tie them in my hair to hunt from the karigi." She took the head up to the karigi and put him on the floor. When everybody was gathered in the karigi he said to his wife, "Throw me the way you used to when I was after you."

She went to him, grabbed his hair, whirled him around, and threw him through the door. He didn't make any noise. Before he went he told his wife, "When you hear me you can come out of the karigi." After awhile the head landed on top of the karigi. His wife came out and he said, "Let all the people go up and get caribou. I put them where nobody steps." They went up and saw a lot of caribou. Only a head had gotten them. That's how that head hunted. THE END.

I have forgotten who told me this.

F501 Person consisting only of head; T311 Woman averse to marriage. Similar to Keithahn 1958:368 (Seward Peninsula).

PM173. AKVAYYUK AND HIS WIVES

A man from Point Hope was coming towards Kotzebue. When he got as far as Ikpigaaruk (close to Sheshalik) he reached the camp of a man and his wife and their son and his wife. The son was out hunting. The Point Hope man took his wife away. The Point Hope man's name was Akvayyuk. Akvayyuk started back to Point Hope with the girl. He had one wife, but he wanted another. When they got to Point Hope the girl escaped and started walking back home. Akvayyuk used his aŋatquq and pulled her back with a string. She left another time taking one of Akvayyuk's mittens with her. Akvayyuk's first wife's name was Siiluyyuk. Akvayyuk asked Siiluyyuk, "Where's Ahliguk?" Siiluyyuk said, "She's in the bag." Ahliguk walked until she reached home. She gave the mitten to her father-in-law. THE END.

(Maybe something happened about that mitten.) Jack Henry told this.

D1711 Magician; T145.0.1 Polygyny.

PM174. SIISIIGUKRUK

Some Noatagmiut lived in Siisiigukruk (way up Noatak). One time they invited the Kobuk people to visit because one of the Noatagmiut had a wife from the Kobuk. The Kobuk people came, stayed for the night, and were leaving the next day. The Noatagmiut planned to kill them. The Kobuk girl married to a Noatagmiut told the Kobuk people what the Noatagmiut planned to do. While the Noatagmiut were helping the Kobuk people tie up their sleds they put the Kobuk people's bows and arrows under the ties so that they couldn't get them right away. Then the Noatagmiut started shooting them.

Those who were warned managed to get their bows and arrows out and killed some of the Noatagmiut. All of the Kobuk people were killed. Then the Noatagmiut grabbed ahold of the Kobuk woman and put her on top of a high cliff. It was winter and cold. They took all of her clothes off and hung her over the cliff. They said, "Why did you tell the Kobuk people?" When she got to the bottom they pulled her up and then let her slide down again. Her husband was around, but he couldn't help her. Her breasts were frozen and all cut up. They kept doing that until she died. They call that place Siisiigukruk. When it gets real cold there in the wintertime the willow bark always comes off. THE END.

I heard this story from Jennie Mitchell.

K929.9 Murder by pushing off cliff; K950 Treacherous murder; Q261 Treachery punished (MacKenzie River—Jenness 1924:87; West Hudson Bay—Boas 1907:551f.).

PM175. AHVLIIGAH

A grandmother and grandson lived in Sukmalairluk. In the wintertime they always got tomcod and smelt with a fish spear. The grandson learned how to make a spear and started fishing. One time when he went to the holes there was nobody else around. He started trying to get fish. A seal came up to the hole and he speared it. The seal was going from hole to hole. Luckily there was nobody else around, so the boy got it. He started dragging the seal home. Some women were sitting on top of the grandmother's house. She heard them say, "Ahvliigah is bringing home a seal that he speared." The old woman heard Ahvliigah, her grandson's name. She kept hearing the women say that, so she went out and saw her grandson with a seal. Those women were proud of him. THE END.

Wanda Stalker told this.

L111.4.1 Orphan hero lives with grandmother.

The first animal of a particular species taken by a young Eskimo boy was considered very important as being indicative of coming manhood and he was praised for his success.

PM176. The Indian Boy

An Indian boy lived in a village on a river. He had a bow and arrow and always shot with it. One time he went with his bow and arrow farther away from the village. He saw an eagle sitting on the ground and got close. The eagle wasn't scared of him. It didn't fly. When the boy got real close he saw that its wing was broken. He took the eagle home and tied its wing up. He had it for a pet.

The eagle got better and started moving its wings. Then it started flying around. Sometimes he would fly and not come back for a few days. Then it would come back. Finally one time it never came home. One day the boy was paddling downstream in a little boat. He had only one paddle. He noticed a waterfall a little way ahead. He tried to turn back, but the paddle broke. He started going towards the waterfall.

When he got real close he looked around and saw the eagle coming towards him. The boy got up in the boat and waited. The eagle got close and stretched its legs out. The boy grabbed them. The eagle flew with him and put him down on the riverbank. That eagle knew his master. That's why he came to save that boy's life after the boy had saved his life. The boy had a dog and when he came home the dog was glad to see him. The End.

This is a white man's story that I read in a little storybook. This is as far as I read it when my eyes were good.

I have not analyzed this tale because it is not Eskimo in origin. Had Paul not told me the source, I would not have thought the story out of place in this collection.

V. Analysis

Presently available records indicate that the Eskimos were the first of the New World peoples to be contacted by Western Europeans. According to the saga of Erik the Red, Norsemen under the leadership of Thorfinn Karlsefni met "Skraelings," now believed to be Eskimos, during the course of a voyage to Vinland in A.D. 1003–6 (Birket-Smith 1959:13). Frequent intercourse between Eskimos and Norsemen reputedly occurred in Greenland after that date, though the Icelandic sagas contain relatively few direct references to Skraelings. Hence, not until after the demise of the Norse Greenland colonies and the arrival in Greenland and the eastern arctic of British and Danish explorers and missionaries were reasonable descriptions of the resident peoples published (Cranz 1770 and Egede 1741). Interest in Eskimos has continued at a high level ever since, with the result that they are among the best known of the world's primitive peoples. Murdock's extensive *Ethnographic Bibliography of North America* (1961) lists approximately three times as many references for Eskimos as for the Navaho, the next best represented group.

Eskimo folklore, as a specialized study, also received early attention, in the form of both collections (Rink 1866–71, 1875) and treatises on geographical distribution (Boas 1904). More recent studies have dealt with personality as reflected in Eskimo mythology (Lantis 1953) and the underlying psychological motives embedded in the myths (Parker 1962). Additionally, Eskimo folktales have attracted popular attention through the works of writers such as Rasmussen (1932), Gillham (1955), and Keithahn (1958). In a 1951 bibliography of American folklore Haywood included twenty-nine pages of general and specialized publications on Eskimo folklore; numerous studies have been published since.

Even in the relatively small area of Northwest Alaska a great number of folktales have been collected and published (see the limited references in Chapter II, p. 44). Thus there is available a considerable body of comparative data and a variety of approaches to that data from which to forge a framework within which to view the Noatak folktales as well as to offer a means of discovering possible functions and meanings of the folktales to both the tellers and listeners. On the other hand, the sheer amount of comparative material and the bewildering variety of analytical approaches taken by previous researchers increase the difficulty of any comprehensive study. I do not pretend that the comments which follow encompass in any way the available avenues to understanding the distribution or meaning of the Noatak folktales.

A further difficulty in dealing with the Noatak folktales involves the size of the sample itself. Not only do the 190 tales represent one of the largest single collections from a restricted area in the arctic, but Paul Monroe's 176 stories are, as far as I know, the largest number of tales recovered from a single informant. A comprehensive analysis of all 190 folktales would be a considerable task! Of course, much of the value of the Noatak collection derives from the number of tales represented, which allows study of the range and extent of two individuals' folklore knowledge.

In the following pages I intend only to sample this folklore smorgasbord. One reason for presenting the cultural background of the informants in the form of an ethnographic sketch and autobiographies is to allow interested researchers to apply their own particular analytical approach to the tales. The stories have been published in the order and exactly as recorded—also toward this end. I do have some advantages, of course, in terms of understanding the folktales. I did record them and was able to observe facial expressions, vocal mannerisms, and other nuances that added meaning to the words being spoken. Also, living a year or more among the Noatak Eskimos has given me a feeling for the physical and human setting of the folktales. Perhaps my growing, but yet very imperfect, knowledge of what being Eskimo is, of how an Eskimo perceives the reality of his environment, and of the social and physical parameters of that environment allows some insight that others might not have.

The topics to be covered include discussions of the method of collection which may have affected the sample, the manner of storytelling among the Noatak Eskimos and elsewhere in Northwest Alaska, the range of folktale types and motifs represented in the collection, the literary conventions evident in the folktales, the folktale content and, finally, some of the possible meanings the stories may have to the Eskimos who still tell them.

COLLECTION OF FOLKTALES

In Chapter II, I briefly discussed the procedures utilized in collecting the folktales, so the reader is already aware of some of the problems which arose. Here I would like to discuss in more detail the difficulty of collecting folktales under circumstances similar to those that prevailed in Noatak Village. Researchers wishing to work with the Noatak sample should be cognizant of the methods of collection I did not employ, as well as of those I did.

Some of the problems involved in collecting folktales are discussed by Thompson (1946:406–12) and Garfield (1953:25–36). As Garfield notes, many of the available collections of folktales are adequate for the purposes of studying the basic psychological situations involved in all myth creation and, also, for making comparative and distributional surveys. These collections usually do not include descriptions of the cultural setting or considerations of the integration of mythology with the culture as a whole. Such data are necessary for folklorists who are interested in the dynamics of how myths are formulated and the function of mythology in specific cultures.

Ideally, then, folklore collectors should include sufficient information for scholars to apply both major analytical approaches. Minimal requirements include the following: (1) an adequate ethnographic description of the culture involved; (2) a range of folktales and variants of the same folktale from a number of raconteurs in the society to allow study of the personality factor in mythmaking; (3) descriptions of informants, including autobiographies if possible; (4) knowledge of the cultural context within which folktales are told, including who tells the myths, when they are told, the audience to whom they are told, if some folktales are the property of certain individuals, and so forth; (5) data on the relationship between mythology and other aspects of the culture (for example, does myth act as a charter for certain social institutions?); (6) a discussion of how folktales are passed from individual to individual within the culture; (7) description of the circumstances under which the folktales were collected, which are often quite different from those in the native setting; (8) indication of nonverbal communications that form part of the storytelling; (9) the use of a tape recorder to preserve all folktales in the native language for future study; and (10) accurate interpreters if the collector does not speak the local language (autobiographies of the interpreters and knowledge of how their personalities might affect the recitation of the folktales would be helpful).

No collection of folktales from Northwest Alaska meets all these criteria; indeed, many collections from the area are barely adequate for the first type of analysis mentioned above. The Noatak collection is no exception, though a number of the requirements were fulfilled during the process of collection.

Unfortunately, no really good, complete ethnographic description exists for any of the Northwest Alaskan Eskimo groups. The ethnographic present in Northwest Alaska, the date by which Eskimo culture had begun to change substantially in response to white influence, was approximately A.D. 1850, long before anthropologists and others deeply interested in the aboriginal way of life reached there. The available reconstructive ethnographies are sufficiently detailed to allow a general understanding of precontact Eskimo culture across Northwest Alaska. However, as indicated in Chapter I, the Eskimo population consisted of a number of localized groups and there was some, albeit minor, cultural variation among these various groups. Quite probably such differences did not affect mythology, beyond the recasting of tales in local settings, but it should be kept in mind that the Naupaktomiut and Noatagmiut are two of the least well-described Eskimo groups.

My original intention in collecting the Noatak folktales was to interview as many informants as possible so as to secure a wide range of tales. Time, the number of tales Paul Monroe knew, and the discovery that Paul and Edna were the only two individuals in Noatak who consistently told folktales curtailed this effort. Additionally, my real interest was not in compiling the total collection of folktales current in Noatak Village, but rather in the extent of individual repertories. Several variants of particular folktales are found in the present collection, and comparisons are possible with two earlier collections from the same village—Curtis (1930) and Ostermann (1952). Unfortunately, the earlier collections do not include data on the storytellers.

I have attempted to acquaint the reader with the two informants through a brief description and the presentation of autobiographies. Perhaps this information should have been supplemented with psychological tests, discussions with other villagers concerning Paul and Edna, and further autobiographical data gleaned by direct questioning of the informants. None of these approaches appealed to me and I feel the personal data available are adequate for most purposes.

The quality of the interpreters was discussed in Chapter II; I feel that Martha Burns and Herbert Onalik were the best available in Noatak for my purposes. Herbert translated PM59–69, 74–81, and 94–101, while Martha did the rest. Only minor differences are evident in their renditions of the folktales. For example, Herbert frequently used the phrase "young lady," while Martha spoke of "the girl." Beyond this their translations probably can be considered equivalent. However, I did note some hesitancy when Martha translated stories that included sexual references. I do not think that ambivalence, on Paul's part, in telling such stories was involved, but rather that Martha was slightly shy about repeating sexual material. We soon settled on several harmless euphemisms ("doing bad things"), and translating continued smoothly. Lacking texts, I have no way of checking the accuracy of either Martha's or Herbert's translations, but often adult Eskimos who spoke English listened during recording sessions and seemed satisfied with the English renditions.

In conclusion, the Noatak folktales were collected under reasonably controlled conditions, though a number of procedures were not utilized that would have increased the value of the sample. Researchers interested in distributive or comparative studies, in the meaning of the mythology of particular cultures, or in the psychological situations underlying mythology in general should be able to use this material.

If they do so, however, another issue concerning the collecting process must be considered. How did Paul and Edna collect their store of folktales? Obviously they must have heard many stories beyond those added to their repertoire by memorization. What conscious or unconscious factors controlled the choices they made? If we knew the entire range of folktales represented in Northwest Alaska over the past eighty years, and also knew to what part of that folklore Paul and Edna had been exposed, then perhaps by analyzing the stories they chose to learn and repeat, and those they did not, we might understand the motives for their choices. For obvious reasons, such research is impossible.

In an attempt to understand the sources of Paul's and Edna's stories, I asked them from whom they heard each tale. This information is summarized in Table 2. If I had had the time to contact those storytellers on the list who are still living and collect their stories and autobiographies, then some progress could be made toward a study of individual repertoire formulation.

A further problem lies in the possibility that the total folklore store of Northwest Alaska has changed drastically in the past 120 years. Preston (1964:376, 397), in a psychological study of Alaskan Eskimos, suggests on the basis of Rorschach and t.a.t. records that the Eskimos are going through a period of mass melancholy in response to acculturation, and that this psychological condition affects their responses to the outside world. If this is true, then perhaps the folktales current in a given area at a given time may reflect the psychological outlook of the people telling and listening to the stories. If the telling of myths satisfies some psychological need or expresses a particular psychological motive, changes in group needs or motives may result in the discarding of certain tales and the increased popularity of others. The total store of folktales now found in Northwest Alaska may be quite different from that of 120 years ago.

TELLING OF STORIES

I have already discussed in Chapter II the scanty information Paul and Edna possessed on the telling of folktales among the Noatak Eskimos in aboriginal and early historic times. Further knowledge of the art and practice of storytelling can be derived from the scattered comments appended to other collections of folktales from Northwest Alaska.

Where and When

Apparently nowhere in Northwest Alaska were strictures placed on when and where stories could be recounted. Spencer (1959:383) comments that winter was the primary time for telling folktales, not because the culture disapproved of storytelling in the summer but because people were scattered in small groups then and leisure time was scarce. Certainly folktales are told in the summer now in Noatak Village, though perhaps not as frequently as in the winter.

Spencer also suggests that certain storytelling sessions took on the rather formal atmosphere of a contest between two or more raconteurs. A sense of rivalry may have motivated some storytelling, but I doubt that competition was an important factor. Ingstad (1954:178) notes that the Anaktuvuk Pass Nunamiut tell stories when hunting, after a successful hunt, when everything goes wrong—or, in other words, almost any time. The same is true, today at least, in Noatak. Once I waited in a goose blind with two Eskimos and listened as they took turns telling stories to while away the time between flights.

In the past most stories were told in the *karigi*, as this was where people congregated to socialize during the winter months. However, settings as diverse as a winter house or summer tent, a boat anchored in Kotzebue Sound waiting for the beluga to arrive, or a goose blind also served as scenes for storytelling in the past as they do today.

Sequence

Paul expressed the notion that more than one story must be told at a single sitting because "one story is simply hanging and needs a stick to hold it up." Paul qualified his statement by saying that if only one man was telling stories he had to tell two or more, implying that if several storytellers were present they took turns, and each told only one story. According to Spencer (1959:384), the idea prevailing at Point Barrow was that each storyteller had to tell more than one tale because, "You can't leave it standing on one leg." Ingstad (1954:178) presents a slightly different observation on the Anaktuvuk Pass Nunamiut: "But the number of stories told in the course of one evening must not be uneven. There must always be 'two legs to stand on';

otherwise they would be forgotten later." Whatever the case, the Northwest Alaska Eskimos feel the necessity to relate more than one folktale at a single time, and, indeed, Paul always did so during our recording sessions.

On what basis did the storyteller choose the stories he wished to present on a particular occasion? Obviously Paul could not tell all 176 stories in one evening! When asked why he told a specific story Paul answered, "Because I remember this one." Only twice was the relating of a particular story possibly keyed to an outside occurrence. Once I had returned to the village from a boat trip to Kotzebue and when I met Paul he asked if I had seen the "giant Mickey Mouse" in the Little Canyons above the Noatak mouth. I answered no, and he proceeded to tell a short tale about a mythical beast that inhabited the cliffs above the river and overturned boats (see Ostermann 1952:154–57). Interestingly enough, when I began to collect his folktales Paul would not repeat this particular story, saying that he had forgotten it. I am not sure why. On the other occasion, on the day when Paul told PM104 about a piece of wood floating down the river, breakup was taking place and a considerable amount of driftwood was floating down the river past the village.

Probably the choice of stories told had to do with the raconteur's mood, or external stimuli that triggered the memory of a tale, or, perhaps, requests from the audience. Undoubtedly each storyteller had a few favorite tales that he repeated more often than others. The late Don Charles Foote collected two folktales from Paul Monroe and two from Edna Hunnicutt during the course of fieldwork for Project Chariot in 1960. In Edna's case these are EH13 and EH14, told to Foote (n.d.:188–92, 193–200) in that order. The stories recovered from Paul (Foote n.d.:209–14, 215–27) are PM144 and PM2 respectively. PM2 may have been one of Paul's favorite stories, but the position of the other three in my collection indicates no favoritism on their behalf.

The sequence in which Edna and Paul told their stories to me was controlled partially by memory factors. For example, PM27 and PM28 both involve the identification of a person by name, PM48 and PM49 both deal with plants, and the raven played a part in both PM59 and PM60. In Paul's case story order also was directed partially by his desire (discussed below) to repeat only complete stories. He claimed not to know the beginning or end of PM4, but most obvious story fragments are found toward the end of the collection. Other factors involved in choice of story order are not readily apparent to me.

Vocal and Visual Mannerisms

Eskimo folklore depends heavily on vocal and visual mannerisms to characterize the actors taking part in the story and to increase the audience's appreciation of the action. Giddings (1961:158), in describing storytelling among the Kobuk Eskimos, remarks: "Gestures, pauses, and voice modulation are used continuously for emphasis and dramatic effect. A very long pause accompanied by an almost imperceptible change of facial expression may turn the audience to bursts of laughter or expressions of pity, as the case may be. An animal or person may sometimes be identified by some imitative gesture that brings that character again onto the scene." Spencer (1959:383) notes that Point Barrow Eskimo storytellers acted out the parts of the characters and that good mimicry was as much applauded as the tale itself.

Both Paul and Edna utilized the technique of speaking in the local dialect of the people involved in the story (see Chapter II). Thus the setting of each story was immediately apparent to the interpreter and, presumably, the other Eskimo members of the audience. Acting out of the plot was difficult under the conditions prevailing when I recorded the stories, but occasionally both Paul and Edna pretended to spear a seal or flapped their arms like an eagle's wings. If the audience had been largely Eskimo and line by line translation were not involved, considerably more acting would have occurred. However, in light of Giddings' assertion concerning the subtlety of facial expressions, much of this nonverbal communication would be lost completely to a non-Eskimo-speaking recorder.

Exact and Complete Recitation

Everywhere in northern Alaska, storytellers place strong emphasis on repeating only complete stories exactly as learned. Both Spencer (1959:383) and Giddings (1961:157–58) speak of informants who refused to tell a particular story because they knew only part or were unsure of the proper wording or appropriate accompanying gestures.

The same was true in Noatak and often I was told to "ask so-and-so; he knows the whole story." Usually "so-and-so" was Paul Monroe.

Paul did repeat story fragments and episodes for me only because he knew I was interested in his total store of folklore knowledge and because I said I would clearly indicate, as he did, when a story was not complete. Sometimes I thought a particular story was complete—PM4 for one—but Paul assured me that in this and similar cases he knew part of the story was missing. Possibly these story fragments are episodes in longer tales of the PM102 type. Other stories identified as fragments by Paul (PM113 and PM157, for example) are obviously just that.

I wonder now about the genesis of the story fragments. Did Paul hear a complete story and retain only a part? If so, why that particular episode? Unfortunately I neglected to ask. One way story variants can arise is through recombination of fragments from two different folktales.

Stories were supposed to be repeated exactly as learned. Among the Kobuk Eskimos, for example, "Stories should be told in exactly the same words, and with the same father archaic wording and accompanying gestures, time after time. The stories were memorized word for word, and were passed along from one generation to another in a stereotyped form" (Giddings 1961:157). Similar strictures prevailed elsewhere in Northwest Alaska (see Spencer 1959:383) and, though not specifically noted by Paul or Edna, the Noatak storytellers presumably operated under the same rules. In the case of EH3, Paul, who was present when Edna told the story and from whom she had heard it, remarked that she had told the story exactly right, even though she had heard it only once.

One way to investigate the fidelity of folktale transmission from one individual and one generation to the next is to compare versions of the same folktale told by different individuals or by the same individual at different times. Four separate collections of folktales are available from Noatak: Curtis (1930), Lucier (1958), Foote (n.d.), and the present study. Some of the story correspondences in these collections are found in Table 3.

Two levels of comparison are possible. A tale told in 1927 or 1952 can be set against the same story as told in 1965, or a story told by Paul or Edna in 1960 can be compared with the same tale repeated in 1965. It must be remembered, of course, that any comparison is between English translations made by various interpreters and not, as would be ideal, between Eskimo texts or recorded stories.

The story called "The Serpent Killer," collected in 1927 (Curtis 1930:201–3), is virtually the same as PM4 with the following similarities and differences:

TABLE 1. Comparison of "The Serpent Killer" and PM4

PM4	The Serpent Killer
Man named Kupkuk	Young man
Brown bears as dogs	
Comes to village and marries	Comes to village and marries
	Men hunting with father-in-law disappear
Leaves	Leaves
Reaches house	Reaches house
Meat rack with human bodies	Meat rack with human bodies
K. goes in stormshed	Goes into stormshed
Living human head with labrets on; rock above door warns him not to go in	Sees living human head with labrets, flees outside
Man comes using polar bear dogs	Man comes with dogs
K. calms bears with song and kills them	Calms dogs by humming
K. pretends to go in house and rock falls	Goes to house roof
Man inside almost gets him	Man inside almost gets him
K. tries to shoot man through window; arrows break	Young man shoots through window
Finally man dies	Finally man dies
Little old man appears in house; K. kills him	
Washes in urine	Washes in urine
Goes to village, marries girl with three brothers	Goes to village, marries girl with four brothers
Bear/dog eats villager	Warns dogs not to bite villagers
K. goes to *karigi*, meets father of head with labrets	Goes to head man's house, meets father of head with labrets
Learns about man he killed	Learns about man he killed
Stays winter and asks wife about people near by	Stays awhile and asks wife about people near by
Wife tells about village with *tirichik*	Wife tells about village with serpent guarded by four youths
K. goes after telling wife he may return as fox	Goes after telling wife he may return as white fox
Reaches village, sees *tirichik* in house	Reaches village, sees serpent in house

414

Calms it with song; kills it	Calms by humming; kills it
Goes to *karigi* to sleep	Goes to playground to sleep
People miss *tirichik*; get its mother	People miss serpent; its mother comes
K. throws men into *tirichik*'s mouth	Throws men into serpent's mouth
Finally jumps in himself	Finally jumps in himself
Kills *tirichik* from inside	Kills serpent from inside
Changes into bug and gets out	Changes into bug and gets out
Changes to wolverine; goes home; almost caught by wife's brothers	Changes into human form; rubs self with snow; changes to white fox; almost caught by wife's brothers
Changes to bug; stays in mittens watched over by wife until man again	Changes to bug; stays in glove watched over by wife until man again

Some of the differences attributable to translation can be explained. Humming and singing may be the same thing. The playground mentioned in "The Serpent Killer" was probably a *karigi*, especially as the use of oil lamps for light there is mentioned. Gloves and mittens are equivalents, as are a *tirichik* and a serpent (the description of the serpent in "The Serpent Killer" is like that of a *tirichik*).

Of the other stories PM15 is almost word for word the same as "The Fisherman" in Curtis (1930:200–1). The other stories collected by Curtis vary considerably from the modern forms. Lucier's (1958:92) version of the bringing of light by Raven is considerably shorter than EH6; most of the stories in the Lucier collection seem attenuated in comparison to those in the present sample. "The Blind Boy and the Loon" (Lucier 1958:96–98), as told by Jennie Mitchell, differs from PM56 in that in the former the boy has a sister who helps him and, in the end, the cruel mother is set adrift in a boat. In Lucier's (1958:98–99) version of Ululiinah (PM100) the boy has a sister; otherwise the two are similar. Lucier's (1958:96–98) tale "Feigned Death" is represented in Paul's stories by two separate episodes (PM85 and PM122). Thus at least two of the stories collected by Curtis in 1927 are almost duplicated by their modern counterparts, baring translation variance, suggesting that sanctions for exact word-for-word transmission were strong.

This impression is reinforced by comparing the stories told by Edna and Paul in 1960 and again in 1965. EH13 and the version in Foote (n.d.: 188–92) differ in terms of the definition of the kinship term *katunun* and the placement of one episode. EH14 and its equivalent in Foote (n.d.:193–200) are virtually identical, as are PM2 and the synonymous tale in Foote (n.d.:215–17). The trap mentioned in PM144 is described in great detail in Foote (n.d.:209–14); Foote was interested in material culture and may have questioned Paul on this point. Several other minor differences between the two versions make this the most divergent of the tale pairings.

Much more impressive than the few differences, however, are the overwhelming similarities. Placed side by side, each two renditions read almost exactly the same. Five years did not dim Edna's or Paul's memory of these particular four tales. But significant variants of many folktales do occur in Northwest Alaska. For example, one might compare EH3, EH7, and PM53 and attempt to explain the differences. Some variants undoubtedly arose in the fashion described by Paul in Chapter II. Beyond this we must remember that exact recitation was / is a culture ideal, but not always a reality. Many factors, including incomplete or incorrect renderings and combination of episodes from several stories, undoubtedly were responsible for the totality of Eskimo folklore known from Northwest Alaska today.

DISTRIBUTION OF THE NOATAK TALES

The folktales of Noatak or of Northwest Alaska do not stand in isolation from other similar bodies of folklore. The tale types and motifs represented in the Noatak folktales are found in stories from elsewhere in the Arctic and beyond, and in stories of Indian as well as Eskimo origin.

Distribution Within Northern Alaska

In the paragraph following each tale I have indicated the locations in Northwest Alaska where similar stories or variants have been collected. Another way to determine distribution is to note the local setting of each tale. Of course tales frequently were recast in local settings, with the provision that a tale about whale hunting could not take place in an inland location, but a tale about an incident at Point Hope probably would not have been recast in another setting by Noatak storytellers, as Point Hope and other locations in Northwest

Alaska were within the geographical sphere of knowledge of the Noatak people. The stated locations of the folktales are found in Table 4. The total number of locations is more than 190 because I have included all locations where action took place in each tale.

The cosmopolitan nature of the Noatak sample is readily apparent from the table. Almost every center of aboriginal human habitation in northern Alaska is represented. Point Hope is by far the best represented location. This coastal village was a mecca for Northwest Alaska Eskimos in the late nineteenth century as a whaling and trading center, and many Noatak Eskimos visited there. Stories set on the coast are considerably more numerous than inland stories, and only one-sixth of the total sample deals with locations within the territory traditionally utilized by the Naupaktomiut and Noatagmiut during their yearly cycle.

The explanation lies in how the Noatak folktales were collected by Edna and Paul. The Noatak sample is not a collection of Noatak (Naupakotomiut and Noatagmiut) folktales, but tales taken from two individuals now living in Noatak. After the arrival of whites and the subsequent disorganization of aboriginal Eskimo society, Eskimos from many locations in Northwest Alaska gathered together in modern population centers, such as Kotzebue, Noatak, and Point Barrow. They brought with them and exchanged many folktales that had local ties and local meanings. Paul, in particular, drew his store of folklore knowledge from individuals who came from many disparate locales in Northwest Alaska. Undoubtedly, in the precontact period, tales were exchanged at the great trading centers like Sheshalik, but not to the extent possible in recent times.

In characterizing his collection of folktales from the Kobuk River, Giddings (1961:157) speaks of "the inland-slanted mythology of the region as distinct from that of the sea coasts." The Naupaktomiut and Noatagmiut were also inland groups, but, as just noted, the Noatak folklore was drawn from the coast as well. Giddings (1961:11) collected the Kobuk sample in 1940, long after cultural change began in response to white contact, and he did not collect entire repertoires. Admittedly, the folktales Giddings offers have an inland cast, but factors other than simple location may be responsible. At this point in time, unraveling the origin of specific folktales within Northwest Alaska appears impossible.

Types and Motifs

According to Thompson (1946:415–16), a *type* is a traditional tale that has an independent existence and does not depend for its meaning on any other tale, while a *motif* is the smallest element in a tale having the power to persist in tradition. An index by types implies that all versions of a specific type have a generic relationship; a motif-index does not make this assumption, though generic relationships may exist between tales with the same motif.

The Noatak collection has not been classified according to type. The motifs present in each tale have been recognized and ordered according to Thompson's (1955–58) *Motif-Index of Folk-Literature*. I should state that my unfamiliarity with the utilization of the *Motif-Index* may have led me to miss specific motifs present in the tales or to give a general rather than a specific motif. Additionally, I have tended to err on the side of superfluity in terms of the motifs found in each tale. If a rich man was mentioned but did not play a role in a particular story, then I did not include the motif P150 (Rich man). If the rich man was involved in the action, then the motif was appended for that tale. The motifs listed following each tale and in the List of Motifs (Appendix A) allow the folklorist to see if particular motifs occur in the Noatak collection. The lay reader can ascertain the distribution, in the arctic, of each motif by checking the reference. The reader interested in the range of certain motifs beyond the arctic can refer to the additional references listed for each motif in Thompson.

Distribution through Time

Another study of some import would be a consideration of the persistence of specific folktales through time, the modifications that have taken place over time, and the changes in the totality of folklore from the Noatak region or Northwest Alaska. As mentioned earlier, the total store of folktales in Northwest Alaska may have altered significantly in the past 120 years under the influence of acculturation. The available collections of folktales unfortunately are not really suitable for extensive studies of distribution through time, but interested researchers could make a start.

LITERARY CONVENTIONS

The analysis by Jacobs (1959) of Clackamas Chinook myths and tales includes an extended discussion of the kinds of literary conventions and devices found in an oral literature. I want to designate briefly here some of the literary conventions present in the Noatak folktales.

The setting of most stories in the collection is fixed in the first sentence or two. The location is specified. Virtually all the characters who are to play a major role in the drama are introduced and relationships between them delineated. Most characters are not named, identification of the protagonist and other actors often being in the form of an unusual physical trait. When names are given it usually is at the end of the story (see Giddings 1961:158 for a description of a similar practice in Kobuk River folktales). One of the mistakes I made in recording the Noatak tales was to ask Paul to name characters early in the story, to avoid what seemed at the time to be a circumlocution in the identifying of characters. Thus I cannot be sure now at what point the names were traditionally given in stories following PM8.

Most stories then proceed to a situation or problem which requires action by the protagonist. The denouement usually occurs very close to the story end, followed by a brief comment which stands as an equivalent to "and then they lived happily ever after." Often this consists of the hero and his wife visiting back and forth with their respective parents. Edna and Paul did not habitually say "The End," but simply fell silent at the story's close. Additional facts to substantiate the story were appended in the form of afterthoughts.

Giddings (1961:159) notes that in the Kobuk tales repetition serves to emphasize events to come or to denote time lapse, and that often such repetitions are in terms of four. A few examples of this device are present in the Noatak folklore: in EH3 the man-who-always-kills-people tries to throw the grandson three times and is thrown himself the fourth; in EH9 the villain throws three wives in the lake of worms and attempts to do the same with his fourth; in PM53 the grandson fights four men-who-always-kill-people and plays with four brown bears; in PM56 the *mulgi* carries the boy under the water four times to restore his sight; in PM78 the woman fleeing the black people goes to four different houses. As Giddings (1961:159; see also Weyer

1962:318–19) notes, four is a magic number among some Alaskan Eskimo groups. Many rules and taboos involve doing something four times or four days. Edna (Chapter III) asserts that a husband could not see his wife for four days after the birth of a male child. Unfortunately I did not ask Edna or Paul specifically about the significance of the number four in Noatak Eskimo culture.

A number of other stylistic devices are employed in the Noatak stories to further the action, to indicate that something has or is about to happen, or to clue the listener that all is not as it appears on the surface. The only such device recognized by the Eskimos was in EH8, when the translator said that by using the word "beautifully" in the phrase "the lake . . . started freezing up just beautifully," Edna was indicating that something must disturb this beauty. I could not ask for confirmation of this analysis without seeming to doubt the translator's word, so I must assume that an Eskimo audience would realize the significance of the word "beautifully."

Additional stylistic devices include: beings who appear to be, but are not, human are said to smell funny (EH5); the equation of death with being frozen and revival with thawing (PM20 and PM23); extreme emotion, particularly sadness, resulting in a feeling of weakness (PM6); the cry "Ahohohoho" to indicate the speakers are Indian (PM12); caribou being depicted by one who has never seen them as "things in the willows that have horns like trees" (EH7, PM6, PM13, and PM53, among others); people who are different physically (having big mouths, for example) or socially (a grandmother and grandson without other kin) living apart, often across the river, from the main body of the village, thus denoting by geographical separation that some other kind of separation exists (PM22, PM28, PM55, and PM114).

Close analysis of the Noatak collection would disclose further elements of literary convention, but many subtle stylistic devices are lost through translation by forcing an Eskimo narrative into the English language structure.

STORY CONTENT

Several approaches to the analysis of story content are possible: Jacobs (1946) demonstrates a general content analysis of eight Chinook myths; Lantis (1953) analyzes sixty Nunivak Eskimo stories to abstract information on personality; and Parker (1962) includes twenty-nine Alaskan Eskimo myths in a study of psychological motives. In the paragraph after each folktale I have appended a few remarks on content. The following sections are an undirected attempt to discover, by looking at story contents, indications of the character of the relationships between man and the natural/supernatural world, the essence of human relationships, and the motives underlying them and the nature of crime and punishment—all as reflected in the Noatak folktales. I hold no particular brief for the organization of the sections; the categories, material, and analyses flow as imperceptibly one into another as did the constituents of the Noatak Eskimo external and internal world.[1]

Individual, Family, and Society

Culturally idealized personality traits. Few of the Noatak folktales directly express culturally idealized personality traits. In EH2, the primary exception, the qualities of a good hunter are enumerated, including taking care to cut the throat of a dead animal to release the soul, going out to hunt or work early in the morning rather than feeding from his mother's breast when young or lying abed with his wife when married, and helping old people in various ways. Just as in Lantis' (1953:123) Nunivak myths, other culturally approved personality traits are incidently woven into the story lines. A man should be observant, brave, and aware, strive to be a good hunter, be generous to others, protect and revenge his kin, and be kind and faithful to his wife. Although not as obvious from the stories, a woman's primary role is in terms of home and family; she ought to

---

[1] Alan Dundes, who kindly read the original manuscript of this study, has pointed out that I take a literal, historical view of the folktales and deny, by omission, the inherent psychological implications. For example, in PM7 the main character enters his wife's womb and is reborn, thus equating wife with mother. In a folklore laden with the killing of fathers and father figures, such an Oedipal solution eliminates the biological necessity of a father. PM56 may also contain Oedipal elements, and EH5 suggests the Electra complex. Dundes' point is well taken. By both training and inclination, however, I feel loath to attempt an in-depth psychological analysis of the Noatak folklore. For those scholars who wish to pursue this further, I wish now that I had recovered more psychological data on the storytellers.

love and protect her children and often, later in life, protect and educate grandchildren, carry out the daily chores efficiently and cheerfully, obey her parents or elders, and accede to the wishes of her husband. As might be expected, in terms of culturally idealized personality traits, the folktales reflect the modern and, presumably, aboriginal society, except in the supernatural realm. The desire to become an *aŋatquq*, expressed or idealized in a few of the Noatak folktales, is not consciously—or at least verbally—revealed in Noatak today. Christianity and the traditional ambivalence Noatak Eskimos had toward shamans and shamanism have led the Noatak individuals who might have sought shamanistic powers in aboriginal times to find other outlets for their aspirations and psychological needs.

Interpersonal relations. The quality of the relationships between various human characters (and animals in human form who enter into relationships with humans before their true identity is known) is summarized in Table 5. I have not included PM117, PM120, PM168, and PM170 because no humans are directly involved (or PM176, which is not an Eskimo story) in this or other tables in this chapter. Table 5 is arranged in the same order as Table 2 in Lantis (1953:115) for easy comparison with her analysis of Nunivak stories.

Before proceeding with a discussion of Table 5, I should reemphasize the importance of kinship in Northwest Alaska Eskimo society. Both the coastal and inland peoples established relationships involving mutual aid and cooperation on the level of the nuclear family, the household, extensions of the household within the community, and over a wide area with those kindred who represented the extended family on both the paternal and maternal sides (Spencer and Jennings 1965:143–44; see also Spencer 1959:62–96). These were the primary bonds of interaction and cooperation. However, additional interpersonal relationships were necessary for various economic activities. A primary goal of marriage was to extend as far as possible the bonds of mutual aid and cooperation (Spencer 1959:75). Beyond marriage, formalized ways existed to extend the rights and responsibilities of kinship to those not related by blood or marriage, including the partner relationship mentioned in at least two Noatak stories (see Burch 1970 for an extended discussion of trading partnerships). The reader should remember that the great majority of the folktales came from a male informant, a fact which may skew data on interpersonal relationships and other parts of story content.

The kindred had importance beyond mutual economic aid. The primary mechanism of social control lay in the extended family (see Spencer 1959:97). By the law of collective responsibility an injury to an individual also was an injury to those in his kindred. Whenever thrust into a strange social setting an individual sought to establish that a kinship relationship, no matter how distant, existed between him/herself and someone in the local setting. A claim of kinship was a request for protection. It is no accident that in many of the Noatak folktales a traveling individual goes first to the house of a kinsman when entering an unfamiliar village. Also, if marriage was a means of extending kinship bonds, the seeds of antagonism were present, for disagreements between husband and wife could enlarge to conflict between the two separate kindreds represented.

Turning to the interpersonal relations summarized in Table 5, we find that relations between unrelated males were slightly more apt to be bad than good. Many subsistence activities required that unrelated males work together in a spirit of cooperation, but the potential for conflict with a male not in one's kin group is emphasized by the number of negative relationships in the Noatak folktales. Unrelated women were not as likely to come into contact because most of the women's economic activities did not necessitate cooperation beyond the household. Also, women traveled less and thus had fewer extra-village contacts. As with the men, relations between unrelated women were negative more often than positive.

Male-female relations, both between unmarried men and women and married couples, were more often good than bad. For the Nunivak folktales Lantis (1953:115) notes that the highest incident of conflict is associated with females, particularly in the unmarried male-female, husband and wife, father and daughter, unrelated females, a woman and her in-laws, and sisters categories. Lantis (1953:115–17) attributes this conflict at least partially to the cultural background of the Nunivak Islanders. Here, as elsewhere among the Yupik-speaking Eskimos dwelling south of the Seward Peninsula, men and boys lived the majority of their lives apart from women. All boys went to stay in the men's ceremonial house (the equivalent of the Northwest Alaska *karigi*) and spent the rest of their lives eating, sleeping, and engaged in other activities there. Their education and life as hunters, coupled with a lack of consistent contact with females and accentuated by conduct taboos between brother and sister, left men with little preparation for establishing positive relations with members of the opposite sex. The same was true for the women, who spent their younger years within the intimate circle of mother and sisters, not even having the benefit of often meeting unrelated females. A female remained in her natal household after marriage. Consequently, a woman was unprepared emotionally for marriage or for continuing contact with those other than her mother and female siblings.

In Northwest Alaska the situation was entirely different. The *karigi* served more the function of a club, where men came each day to talk, make or repair hunting equipment, engage in certain ceremonies, and prepare for the spring whale or caribou hunt. But women were not excluded from the *karigi* and men spent their nights at home, making the household, consisting of both males and females, the most important unit of social interaction. Both males and females grew up in close contact with the opposite sex. Patrilocal residence was preferred after marriage, though there was no definite residence rule. Thus a woman often was placed in a new social setting at marriage, but one for which she was somewhat prepared and, because most marriages were within a village, in close proximity to members of her own kindred.

The cultural contrasts offer one explanation for the differing quality of interpersonal relations found in folktales collected in the two regions. Generally, relationships involving females are more positive in the Noatak sample than in that from Nunivak Island. Not that conflict does not appear in the Noatak folktales, for it certainly does. The web of kinship bonds which protected the Northwest Alaska Eskimos did not preclude male-female or any other type of conflict.

The grandmother who raises her orphaned grandson (or occasionally granddaughter) figures largely in the Noatak sample. Lantis (1953:114) agrees with Himmelheber's (1951:10) comment that the grandmother figure mirrors real life in her role of companion and home provider for the orphaned. While this may be true on Nunivak Island, I am not sure about the situation in Northwest Alaska. The available evidence does not suggest that the grandmother-grandson combination living alone was very common in aboriginal times; certainly none existed in Noatak while we were there. Lantis (1953:114) adds that the grandmother probably represents a wished-for mother, as few Nunivakers reached adulthood as part of a normal family of mother, father, and siblings. For reasons discussed above I do not believe this analysis applies to the Noatak stories. The explanation for the predominance of grandmother stories must be sought for elsewhere. The Northwest Alaska orphans were more interested in revenge and the killing of deadly monsters than the Nunivak orphans, who concentrated on the attainment of wealth and status. Perhaps the theme of revenge for the death of a kinsman—an almost sacred social trust for a northern Eskimo—was best expressed through the medium of the grandmother-grandson tale.

On Nunivak Island, where wealth was consciously sought and poverty the norm, relations between the rich and poor tended to be bad. In Northwest Alaska, wealth was desired, but was not an overwhelming goal; hence rich-poor relationships were generally good. Being kind and generous to those less fortunate was also a cultural ideal.

Rich man/poor man. Rich men appear forty-one times in the Noatak folktales. Being rich, of course, means not only having possession of capital goods, such as a skin boat, but also being acknowledged as leader by others in the local group (see Spencer 1959:147ff. for a discussion of wealth among the northern Alaska Eskimos). Fifteen cases of poverty are mentioned. Actually, many more cases of poverty are implied because orphans are mentioned seventy-one times in the stories. When I began collecting the Noatak folktales the character "Ilaypuruk," translated as "poor boy," appeared frequently. Later it became apparent that Ilaypuruk really meant orphan. One who is without kin is really poor, far beyond his probable lack of material goods.

Haughty girl/boy. In eight Noatak stories a young girl refuses to marry; in four stories a young boy does the same. In all cases, by one means or another, they are brought to marriage, but not to a normal spouse. Two girls ended up marrying ravens in human form, one girl is treated meanly, one married her own grandfather, one married a wolf, one is abandoned and changes into a wolf, one marries an owl, and one a human head; one boy changed into a bird, one married an *ugruk*, one married an old woman, and the last fell sick. A number of haughty girls appear in the Nunivak stories, but haughty boys are rare (Lantis 1953:116–17). This supports Lantis' thesis that females had a difficult time with social relationships. In Northwest Alaska, where the haughty boy occurs more frequently in the mythology, the scorn Eskimo society had for those who would not marry lies in the importance marriage had to the kin group. Marriage extended the kinship network of all the individuals involved. If a child refused to marry he or she remained an economic burden on the kin group without the recompense of a wider circle of people to call upon in time of need. Lantis' (1953:119) suggestion that the haughty girl may imply a homosexual woman seems doubtful in view of the general absence of homosexuality among Eskimos (see Spencer 1959:246). Given Eskimo attitudes toward sexual matters I do not believe the idea of homosexuality would be repressed in their folklore. Three instances of identification with the opposite sex do appear in the Noatak folktales. In PM89 a woman who feigns death returns to her husband dressed as a man, in PM94 a woman hunts, and in PM66 a woman who turns out to be a polar bear also hunts.

Death or loss of loved one; remarriage when spouse dead. The extraordinary emotional closeness of the Northwest Alaska Eskimo family is emphasized in sixteen stories which deal with the reaction of characters to death or loss of a loved one. Responses include sadness, sadness leading to self-starvation, sadness to the point of death, long searches for the lost one, revenge against the killers, becoming exceedingly aggressive, and becoming a man-who-always-kills-people. Strong and lasting emotional responses to tragedy are also true in real life—at least in Noatak.

The tendency in the stories toward rapid remarriage balances the emotional outpouring at the loss of a husband or wife. In twenty such cases eighteen remarriages are mentioned. Remarriage, of course, reestablished the kinship network beyond ego's kindred, but this observation does not deny the reality of emotional feeling.

The man-who-always-kills-people. A central character in twelve stories (EH3, EH7, PM2, PM4 [implied], PM5, PM6, PM21, PM27, PM42, PM53 [four], PM102, PM113) is the man-who-always-kills-people, portrayed either as a strong, cruel man who kills strangers, presumably with pleasure, or as a man who has lost his son and takes revenge on the world by killing. In more than half the stories his activities are curtailed by the grandson character.

The function and meaning of the man-who-always-kills-people in Noatak Eskimo folktales has been analyzed by Gordon Halliday, a student who worked with the Noatak sample briefly. In summary, his analyses of EH3 and PM27 are as follows:

EH3: Starts with "There were people in Point Hope" not only to give location of story, but to remind listener that protagonist is member of specific group. Members of the group are going hunting and not returning, including the rich man's son. A grandmother and grandson also live in the community.

The rich boy and the grandson represent two different levels of communal integration. The rich man could provide his son with food and gear and give surplus to the community; the grandmother and grandson would be dependent on charity for food. The rich man was an asset to the community while the grandson was a burden. As group support is survival-oriented, the grandson runs the risk of being the first to starve if famine should occur.

Although the grandson is a member of a group, his loyalty is not to a particular group as much as it is to the concept of community. The stress involved in shifting to a new group would be more related to rational than emotional anxiety; the grandson could rationally expect to have a group reject him if he were strange to it because he could be perceived as a drain on the group's food supply. This is in opposition to the community ethic, but derives from it. The ideal is for the individual to help others, rather than for members of a community helping each other, and all strangers have a legitimate claim to assistance. To give aid to all, however, is contra-survival in times of food stress. What members of a community want is an investment, a hedge against the time that they themselves are hungry, not simply the opportunity to gain prestige. Children have to learn the lesson of sharing if group support is to be made workable. Reinforcement of the principle of sharing is part of Eskimo daily life.

The significance of the rich man's son being lost while hunting now becomes apparent. A food crisis has arisen and the rich man makes use of his implicit investment by going to the grandson for aid. The grandson is given hunting gear and told where to find caribou. Instead of locating caribou, he finds a man-who-always-kills-people. The grandson must overcome this opposition in order to eat.

That the man-who-always-kills-people represents social opposition rather than that of nature is shown by the use of sports contests in the story. As the grandson approaches the village, he watches people playing football. Upon entering the village, ego starts the deadly struggle—he must run a footrace with the man-who-always-kills-people to the flat where earlier he had been told to look for caribou. The man-who-always-kills-people tries to stab him there, implying that killing a hungry stranger helps the food supply as much as killing a caribou.

After the footrace, the grandson is joined by three boys who had been playing football, showing that his integration into and acceptance by the group has started. All four now go to meet the man-who-always-kills people, but the battle is still the grandson's. Only he can integrate himself into the group. The killer has two of the boys with the grandson bring in the sharp rock on which he throws people to kill them. The contest, as it is a social one, is again given in the image of sport, for the killer wrestles the grandson. The grandson is thrown three times, making the killer look supreme. The grandson then turns the situation about by twirling the man-who-always-kills-people and throwing him onto the rock, permanently ending the opposition. Reassurance is thus given that although the opposition may be supreme, the supremacy is temporary; the grandson triumphs. Having beaten back the opposition to his integration into the group, the grandson stays at the village for a year. When he returns to Point Hope, he is praised as the lifesaver, thus reaffirming the wisdom of the ethic-derived food sharing in opposition to the attitude that generates the man-who-always-kills-people.

PM27: Also found in Spencer 1959:347–401. Paul begins by marking off the protagonists' starting group. The man's wife disappears while out getting water. His mother packs his things and he goes to search for his wife. As he approaches a village, he becomes circumspect; this is the scene of the conflict. While spying on the village, he watches the men play football. This incident does not advance the plot, but does serve to remind the listener that ego is excluded from the social group and implies that he will contest this exclusion.

The game ends toward dark and the hero makes his approach. He goes to a house that is a little apart from the others, emphasizing that he is approaching the group but is not yet a member of it. As soon as he enters the house, he is told, "I am sorry to see you come because there is a man-who-always-kills-people here. . . ." The initial resentment for ego is clearly stated as soon as he enters the village, even though his wife's presence there gives him some claim for integration. [The taking of a second wife at this point furthers the process of integration.]

The ease with which the hero enters the village indicates that more than a simple fear of strangers is being symbolized. If the hero's struggle were with fear (of strangers who might wish to kill him because of a feud) or with ignorance (of kin relationships by which an initial claim to enter a group might be established) it should follow the quickly resolved form that the second conflict in the tale does. In that part of the tale, all that is required is an on/off decision. The hero's son approaches him with a bow and arrow at the ready, but drops them when his father proves that they are related by saying his son's name.

Instead, the first struggle with the man-who-always-kills-people is more protracted. After hearing about the killer, the hero goes the next morning to the *karigi*, the center of social activity. This detail, along with the earlier football game, emphasizes that the hero's struggle is a social one. As with EH3, although others wish to help (and do, by tying on the knife), the fight itself is strictly ego's. The hero has to fight a monster and assume the form of a polar bear to do so. Reassurance is thus given that ego will win against even supposedly overwhelming forces. With his polar bear's strength, the hero is able to kill the monster. By doing so he eliminates all opposition in his integration. Finding his wife, he happily stays in the village for several years before returning to find his son.

I have summarized at length from Halliday because I think he makes several valid points concerning the nature of the man-who-always-kills-people in Eskimo folktales, but at the same time he places too much emphasis on the social and psychological force of the food quest. Halliday's (1969:6) primary hypothesis is that the man-who-always-kills-people symbolizes the tension that ego feels when trying to integrate into a group. Strangers who wish to become part of a group can do so, but first they have to overcome the resentment of the members of the community over the depletion of their food resources.

Before accepting Halliday's analysis we must ask, as he does, if the man-who-always-kills-people does not symbolize tension, but rather appears regularly in real life and for this reason was incorporated into folklore. Halliday found no historical equivalent for the man-who-always-kills-people in the sources he consulted, but exceedingly powerful men, in both physical and social terms, were found in some coastal villages. Brower (1942:34–37, 43–68, 112–15, 149–50) details the fear and awe with which both local villagers and strangers viewed a strong man living at Point Hope in the late 1800s who killed numerous men. Thus the man-who-always-kills-people does have historical reality.

Even so, I do agree that the conflict between a stranger and a man-who-always-kills-people does represent a confrontation between an individual and a group. In PM27 the stranger attempted to enter into the group by marrying a girl from the village and thereby enlisted the aid of her kin. But, as noted earlier, kinship ties established by marriage are not as strong as consanguineal ones, and the stranger is not thus fully integrated into the village. The man-who-always-kills-people still represents the fear that ego has of an unknown group of people; to be in a position beyond the help of one's kin is to court death. Only when that death is overcome does the stranger become a friend. From the point of view of the villagers, the man-who-always-kills-people is that antagonism within all men against disruption from without. The village becomes willing to accept the stranger eventually because acceptance, sharing, and mutual cooperation beyond kin bonds is necessary for many economic and social activities.

Does group antagonism toward outsiders stem from worries over food resources? Food shortages and starvation could occur in Northwest Alaska, but according to Spencer (1959:140) starvation apparently was not an omnipresent threat. Edna, in her autobiography, does mention a period of starvation along the Noatak River, but in historic times, after the decline of the caribou. Additionally, rather than promoting stinginess, the cultural code included a sense of generosity so strong that a successful hunter and his family would feel hunger first because whatever food was at hand was given away (Spencer 1959:164).

Even if starvation was not often a real threat in the aboriginal period, the fear of food shortage might have served to solidify a group against the demands (in terms of sociocultural obligations) of outsiders who wished to become part of that group. However, if this fear is indeed the message of the man-who-always-killed-people, I would expect to find apprehension concerning food lack to be more explicit in the Noatak stories. Certainly other anxieties of the Noatak Eskimos involved in the formulation and continued recitation of the Noatak folktales are made plain in the story content.

Life in physical isolation. The strong in-group feeling of Eskimos precluded an individual living in physical (or social) isolation except under extremely unusual circumstances. In PM15, Paul comments that he does not know how the protagonist grew up alone. Fifteen of the Noatak stories depict characters spending a period of time away from society, most often as the result of an accident. While alone these individuals display remarkable resourcefulness. For example, in PM154 a young boy who lived almost a year apart from his family survived by eating roots and caribou feces. In almost all of the cases where an individual was forced into physical isolation, he or she eventually achieved a return to a satisfying social relationship.

Human physical aberrations. Unusual human physical character-
istics are listed in Table 6. Persons with such aberrations usually are
animals in human form or have some magical power that further sets
them apart from ordinary human beings. The physical aberrations
serve as indicators to the listeners that the characters will play a
special role in the story. Often these characters live in houses somewhat apart from the village proper, further exemplifying their
distinctiveness.

The characters with mouths stretching from ear to ear and the story
about the baby who ate his parents (PM79) suggest oral aggression.
Lantis (1953:136), in an elegant analysis of the element of oral aggression in the Nunivak tales, argues that the anxiety regarding oral
aggression " . . . is not a simple fear of aggression from independent
outside agents but a projection of the individual's guilt and conflict
regarding his own behavior." The Eskimo hunter is consistently forced
to be aggressive toward the animal world, to *kill* and *eat* animals that
possess souls. His very aggression may cause animals to withhold
themselves in revenge and cause starvation. For this reason hunting
and killing animals was a supernaturally and psychologically dangerous occupation involving religious supplication and many taboos. The
Noatak stories do not prove Lantis' analysis, nor do they offer a
reasonable alternative explanation.

Marriage to animal or object. Lantis (1953:119) briefly comments
that marriage to an animal may suggest emotional aberration. Sixteen
such marriages occur in the Noatak stories: four to a polar bear, three
to a raven, two to a wolf, one to a bumblebee, one to an ugruk, one
to a beetle, one to a dog, one to an owl, one to a gastropod, and one to
a piece of wood. In eleven of the sixteen cases the persons marrying
the animal was unaware of its identity, so I doubt emotional aberration is implied. Often marriage to an animal represents supernatural
punishment for refusal to marry; in these instances the original refusal may be an aberration in Eskimo cultural terms.

Warfare. In fourteen of the Noatak stories the Eskimo equivalent
of war takes place. Occasionally conflict between various groups was
part of the social scene in prehistoric times in northern Alaska (Giddings 1952:90), but references to warfare in the historic period are
scarce. Some of the Noatak stories deal with incidents that put an

end to long-standing conflict between two villages or groups. Only two tales mention Eskimo-Indian warfare, despite the possibility that the Eskimos of the upper Noatak River, as well as the Kobuk River Eskimos, lived alongside Athapaskan Indian groups during the historic period (Hall 1969).

Crime and Punishment

The presence or absence of law and legal mechanisms among Eskimos has occasioned considerable debate, much of it revolving around definitions. I have no desire to enter the lists, but will define crime as actions that deviate from the social norm and law as customary sanctions that result in patterned ways of dealing with the deviant (see Spencer 1959:97). As Spencer notes, "It is clear that the primary mechanism of social control lay in the family, the solidarity of the family being defined and enhanced by the strong sense of collective responsibility. Properly speaking, no crimes could be said to exist; offenses of any kind related to interfamily disputes. These relate almost exclusively to murder." Punishment was leveled by the wronged individual's kin. Not all the sections dealt with below fit Spencer's definition of crime, but are discussed here as representing deviations from the social norm.

Crime in social terms. Table 7 summarizes the instances of crime, as defined above, found in the present collection. As might be expected, murder predominates, along with attempted and threatened murder.

Punishment. The types of punishment described in the folktales are listed in Table 8. Some punishments are supernatural, but most emanate from the society. The usual punishment for murder is death at the hands of the dead individual's kin. In fewer than five cases does the killer escape penalty, and only once does murder go completely unpunished. Most punishments remove the deviant from a functioning role in his group, thus punishing him for not exercising the appropriate control over his actions.

Revenge. Revenge as a special agency for providing punishment occurs forty-three times in the stories. Most cases of revenge are against those who killed relatives or friends. Often revenge seems necessary as a provision of reentry into the society for a grandson whose father has been murdered (see Nelson 1899:292–93 for a discussion of the preparation of a male child to avenge his father). Other instances of revenge are against rapists, those who annoy, against a treacherous bird, and against those who do not share. Lantis (1953: 154) remarks that the theme of revenge is much stronger in Northwest Alaska folktales than in those from Nunivak, perhaps because of the strong kinship bonds in the former area.

Flight to escape aggression. Often the Eskimo solution to possible or real conflict was flight, particularly when one lacked the backing of a strong kindred. The reasons for flight are noted in Table 9. Closely allied to the theme of flight from aggression is a lack of tolerance for certain situations. The fourteen examples noted include lack of tolerance of: a man for his mother-in-law, a father for his wife's and son's sexual activities, a wife for her husband's adultery, an uncle for his nephew, an *aŋatquq* for one who annoyed, a wife for her sick husband, and an *aŋatquq* for one who borrowed an adze and did not return it.

The Natural and Supernatural World

I do not believe that the Noatak Eskimos distinguished sharply between the natural and supernatural world in aboriginal times; therefore I have not done so in this section.

Physical dangers. Most of the physical dangers faced by the folktale characters (Table 10) were real and apparent to the Northwest Alaska Eskimos and require little comment. The prospect of drifting out to sea when ice floes broke away from shore was a constant threat to coastal hunters. The Noatak Eskimos, who rarely hunt on the sea ice these days, are extremely circumspect, almost to the point of nervousness, while offshore. According to Lantis (1953:133), the image of human-consuming worms in a lake suggests food anxiety because blowfly maggots ("worms") ate a considerable amount of meat in aboriginal times. The possibility that human biting or eating reflects the dilemma Eskimos face because they are forced to eat animals that have souls has been discussed above.

Animals encountered. The list of animals encountered by characters in the folktales is a compendium of the species with which the Northwest Alaska Eskimos came into frequent contact (Table 11). The frequency of occurrence more or less corresponds to the importance of the species in terms of subsistence, though bears (as well as *tirichiks* and other "mythical" beasts) are overrepresented. Interestingly enough, a comparison of the occurrence frequencies with the diets of the Naupaktomiut, Noatagmiut, and Point Hope people best fits with the aboriginal Noatagmiut diet as reconstructed by Foote (1965). The totals of land animals vs. sea animals vs. fish support this comparison. The only major species known from northern Alaska not represented is the musk ox (*Ovibos moschatus moschatus*), which became extinct about A.D. 1858 (see Bee and Hall 1956) but was relatively common in prehistoric times. The relatively frequent occurrence of the eagle is somewhat surprising as the modern Noatak Eskimos pay little attention to this species, not even commenting specifically on the few occasions we saw one while together. Foote (n.d.:193–200) in his version of EH14 referred to a "big bird" rather than an eagle, but the Eskimo term he provides approximates the Nunamiut Eskimo term for eagle (see L. Irving 1960). The powerful eagle in the Noatak stories may be a pale reflection of the more familiar Northwest Coast thunderbird.

Man/Animal relationships. Table 12 summarizes the instances of animals helping men, animals killing men, and animals talking to men. As Lantis (1953:146) notes, bears and wolves are symbols of ferocity. Animals that kill people are often under the magic control of human villains. Animals speak by sweeping back their headskin to reveal (presumably) a human face. Often a modern Noatak Eskimo will pull back his parka hood slightly when talking, not to speak but to hear.

Man/Animal interchange. The Noatak stories contain seventy-eight instances of human/animal interchange and five cases of man/plant or man/object interchange (Table 13). Some of these transformations are explicitly the result of using magic powers, but some apparently are not. Here particularly we see the lack of a sharp dividing line between the real and unreal, animal and man, or natural and supernatural in the Eskimo conceptualization of the external world. A good part of the concept of interchangeability may derive from the nature of that external world. In a land where summer fogs blur the distinction between land and sea, where winter wind and snow can produce the condition known as "white-out"—when the land and sky cannot be separated and where the morning mist can cause a hunter to stalk a ground squirrel with the conviction he will sup on grizzly bear—the concept of an ever-changing, amorphous world is not surprising. The Eskimo world was essentially smooth, without projections or sharp corners. True, men made tools with sharp points, black mountains thrust into the clear sky in some areas, and the cold gray ocean water lapped in leads split through the winter ice. But a man clothed in a bulky caribou parka blended into the landscape, dressed in the skin of an animal and not looking like a man. The sharp dividing line between rock and sky is blotted out by the rising wind and snow. The ice lead freezes overnight and the ocean cover is again unbroken. Thus I would argue that the Northwest Alaska Eskimos' conceptualization of the natural world was preconditioned by the real external world, that apparent transformations of various kinds were always occurring, so the change of a man to a wolf was no more unbelievable or inexplicable than the merging of land and sea. If an Eskimo were tricked by lighting conditions into thinking a ground squirrel was a grizzly bear and suddenly discovered he was looking at the smaller animal, the most obvious explanation was that a bear transformed itself, probably through magic, into a ground squirrel.

Humans treated like animals. As further proof of the interchangeability between man and animal, in twenty-one of the stories (Table 14) men are treated like animals. Lantis (1953:133–34) includes incidents of this kind as evidence of her hypothesis that the human and animal world was so interwined as to cause guilt about the necessity to kill animals to survive.

Animal stories. Though animals are encountered everywhere in the collection, few of the stories feature animals as the sole or main characters. Himmelheber (1951:26) remarks that the Nunivak Island Eskimos also told few animal stories. In terms of responses to Rorschach cards, Preston (1964:365) found the proportion of animal responses to be 45 percent, close to the animal-content responses to be expected in our culture. Of course we have no idea what the expected proportion should be in Eskimo culture. Lantis (1953:134) probably best explains the scarcity of animal stories by noting that animals, in one form or another, appear in almost all of the Nunivak (and Noatak) folktales.

Shamanism and the use of magic powers. The shaman, or *aŋatquq*, was a link between the natural and the supernatural world. Shamans are explicitly identified in twenty-two stories, but examples of the use of magic powers by individuals not specifically called *aŋatquqs* are found throughout the collection. The various uses to which magic powers were put are listed in Table 15. Lantis (1953:125–27) discusses at length the Nunivak concept of magic, as expressed in folktales, and concludes that magic provides the individual with a means to escape from difficulty, in other words a way to reduce the anxiety resulting from a feeling of inadequacy in a given situation. The use of magic seems much more casual in the Noatak stories, but may have a similar psychological explanation.

Story Endings

Lantis (1953:155) has characterized the mythology collected by Nelson (1899) from the Bering Strait region as having a tragic tone, the stories recorded by Garber (1940) at Cape Prince of Wales as ending cheerfully, and, presumably, feels her Nunivak stories and Rasmussen's (Ostermann 1952) from Northwest Alaska fall somewhere between. In many cases the decision as to whether a myth is tragic or cheerful or neither is strictly a value judgment on the part of the reader (unless the storyteller ventures an opinion). I have considered stories wherein the difficulties faced by the protagonist are resolved to have a happy ending and stories wherein the protagonist dies or is unsuccessful as sad. On this basis, 117 of the Noatak stories can be classed as having happy endings and thirty-three as having unhappy endings, while the rest are neutral in tone. In general, I would submit that the mythology indicates a relatively cheerful view of the world, despite its inherent violence.

436

FOLKTALES AND NOATAK ESKIMO CULTURE

A primary and obvious function of the telling of tales among the Noatak Eskimos was for recreation, to while away idle hours. In a society where the other arts are poorly developed, oral literature has great value for self-expression and entertainment. Today, as in the past, storytellers in Noatak are rewarded for their efforts by group approbation and, often, by gifts of food or other small items.

Another obvious purpose of the folktales was to present and constantly reinforce moral precepts of the society. Listeners to EH2 were told that a man would not be a successful hunter if he lay abed in the morning or didn't cut the throat of dead animals to release the soul. At the end of the story the protagonist specifically tells the young boys and girls of his group about his adventures and cautions them not to behave as he did. Other stories warn against certain kinds of behavior. We learn that a person who is lazy may change into a porcupine, that annoying others too much may have serious repercussions, and that refusal to marry may result in an unpleasant situation for the haughty boy or girl. Some morals are less obvious. For example, the unstated force of many grandmother-grandson stories is that one who grows strong and hunts for his elders will be able to avenge his parents (be a culturally approved agent of social control) and, perhaps, become a rich man. Thus a code of proper behavior passed from generation to generation as part of the folklore.

A further function of folktales was as a medium for expressing group psychological needs. This function almost seems to be recognized consciously in the story about the *kikvik* (PM62). In this story a grandson is repeatedly kicked out of the *karigi* by the rich man because he is unable to join in storytelling. He asks his grandmother for stories, but she has none. She sends him to his uncle who gives him a magic *kikvik* (cutting board) instead of stories. When the grandson looks into the *kikvik* a scene appears showing a man tossing meat into a house; magically the meat falls beside the watcher. He takes the *kikvik* to the *karigi* and shows the rich man how it works, saying after the meat drops by them, "That's all my stories." Actually the grandson tells no story; rather, he provides the community with meat. Storytelling is thus equated with food sharing, an institution which helps the members of the community to survive. (Halliday [1969] also makes this point.)

In discussing how stories were told I mentioned that two tales must be told at a single sitting because "There must always be two legs to stand on." As man is the only animal in the arctic to consistently stand on two legs, this statement equates folktales and men. Perhaps one social and cultural measure of a man was his ability to memorize and repeat more than one folktale, as in "The Kikvik" a knowledge of folktales being necessary to maintain social ties.

The suggestion here is that Eskimo folktales in general are an institution with survival value, food for a hunger beyond that of the body. Eskimos have evolved an ingenious technology to cope with a relatively intractable environment, but sometimes that technology is not sufficient. No matter how good the whaling equipment, if one year the whales fail to come hunger must follow. Survival crises arose in the folktales too, but there the hero usually resolves the difficulties by using his strength and magic powers. The folktale hero commands greater resources than individuals do in reality, but those who tell and listen to the stories aspire to control similar resources in the same way. Thus folktales epitomize the desires of the Eskimos; if they could dominate the external world as completely as the folktale characters do, then life would be secure. If folktales are believed to be real stories about real people in real situations—and this belief persists even today—then there is hope for any individual or group in distress. The Sears, Roebuck catalogue is sometimes called the "wish book" by the Noatak Eskimos; perhaps folktales are a "wish world." The folktale world differs little from the real world, but the difference lies in the element of control, of mastery over the known and unknown fates that determine the lives of all men.

CONCLUSIONS

The present collection of Eskimo folktales, recorded in Noatak, Alaska, during the spring of 1965, consists of 190 stories, 14 recounted by Edna Hunnicutt and 176 by Paul Monroe. Brief autobiographies accompany the stories, which have been published in the order and exactly as told to me. The folktales and their content can be placed in cultural context by referring to the ethnographic sketch of the primary Eskimo groups involved. This analytical chapter is not intended to be complete, and it is not offered as a model of folklore analysis. Rather, I have commented on a few aspects of the folk-tales that interested me.

The Noatak folktales have meaning to the Eskimos who told them, to those who heard them, to me, and, I hope, to the reader. Part of the value of this or any folktale collection is that those meanings do not necessarily coincide. Folktales are important as indicators of the cultural reality, cultural values, and cultural aspirations of their originators, but the greatest value is the light such stories may cast on the human condition, the responses evoked in the reader. Some-one with little or no knowledge of the Eskimo world may draw mean-ing, based on his own world, from the Noatak folktales. At least I hope so. If the conditions of collection are accepted, the professional folklorist can utilize the Noatak folktales in his own research. Paul and Edna would have been pleased with this possibility, but for them, as for me, storytelling is part of being Eskimo, to be savored and enjoyed, not to be questioned.

TABLE 2. Sources of Folktales Told by Paul Monroe
and Edna Hunnicutt

Source	Paul Monroe	Edna Hunnicutt
Frank Burns	24½	
Carl Stalker	24	
Forgotten	17	7
Ralph Gallahorn	15	5
Daniel Walton	13½	
Wanda Stalker	10	
Jack Henry	6	
Makan	6	
Frieda Goodwin	5	
Frank Glover	4	
Charles Stalker	4	
Kenneth Flood	3	
John Adams	3	
Edna Hunnicutt	3	
Paul Monroe's mother	2	
Calvin Barger	2	
Jimmy Hawley	2	
Putumie Norton	2	
Old Man Driggs	2	
Jennie Mitchell	2	
Agnes Towkajhea's Brother	2	
Austin Thomas	2	
Charlie Goodwin's Wife	1	
Charlie Allen	1	
Jack Porter	1	
Kusick Hunnicutt	1	
Nellie Wood's half-sister's husband	1	
John Barger's uncle	1	
Ahsetjuk Kilyikvuk	1	
Marie Stalker	1	
Jack Walton	1	
Peter Carfield	1	
Abraham Lincoln	1	
William Trueblood	1	
Paul Green	1	
Edward Occut	1	
Benjamin Arnold	1	
Leonard Brown	1	
Chester Downey	1	
Edger Foster	1	
Nellie Woods	1	
Pukik	1	
From a book	1	
Paul Monroe		1
Clarence Allen's brother		1

TABLE 3. Story Correspondences in Noatak Folktale Collections

Collector:	Curtis (1930)	Lucier (1958)		Foote (n.d.)		Hall (1974)	
Year collected:	1927	1952		1960		1965	
Storyteller:	Unknown	Jennie Mitchell	Mark Mitchell	Edna Hunnicutt	Paul Monroe	Edna Hunnicutt	Paul Monroe
Story page or number:	199–200					5	34
						6	69
						9	
					215–17	13	
						14	
		92					
		101					
	201–3			188–92			2
	200–1			193–200			4
	197–98	96–98					15
		94–96					30
							56
							85,122
			98–99		209–14		100
	203–4	108					144

441

TABLE 4. Settings of Noatak Folktales

Setting	Number of occurrences
Point Hope	29
Noatak	13
Point Barrow	11
Cape Prince of Wales	10
Shismaref	10
Sealing Point (Cape Krusenstern)	6
King Island	6
Selawik	5
Kukpuk River	5
Little Diomede Island	5
Kobuk River	5
Sheshalik	4
Uḵaliḵsuk	3
Buckland	3
Kotzebue	3
Siberia	3
Sukmalarluk	2
Unalakleet	2
Point Lay	2
Utukok River	2
Noorvik	2
Oksuruk	2
Uŋgaluḵlik	1
Suttulik	1
Coast	135
Inland	56
Territory occupied by Naupaktomiut or Noatagmiut during yearly cycle	33
File Creek	1
Cape Blossom	1
Colville River	1
Ḵiḷḷikmaḵ	1
Beechy Point	1
Inland (unspecified)	20
Coast (unspecified)	32
Unknown	29

TABLE 5. Interpersonal Relations Expressed or Implied in Noatak Folktales

Relationship	Good	Bad	Unclear or neutral
Unrelated males	70[1]	87[2]	10
Unrelated females	12	14[3]	1
Unmarried man/woman	44[4]	34[5]	2
Husband/wife	44[6]	30[7]	54[8]
Father/son	11[9]	9[10]	14
Father/daughter	3	4[11]	1
Mother/son	7	2	2
Mother/daughter	3	1	2
Grandfather/grandchild	2[12]	1[13]	1[14]
Grandmother/grandchild	24[15]	2[16]	15[17]
Man/in-laws	12[18]	11[19]	4[20]
Woman/in-laws	3[21]	5[22]	—
Uncle/nephew	7[23]	4	1
Uncle/niece	3[24]	1	—
Aunt/nephew	1	—	1
Brothers	7[25]	1	5
Sisters	—	—	—
Brother/sister	9[26]	1	—
Wealthy/poor	15	3	1

[1] Turned out to be cousin in one case, polar bear in another, several men in some cases; includes one trading partnership.

[2] Turned out to be raven or wolf in some cases.

[3] Polar bear in two cases, brown bear in one, wolf in one.

[4] Cousin in one case, eagles in another.

[5] Cousin in one case, polar bear in one, dog in one, wolf in two.

[6] In six cases marriage is implied; in one the husband turns out to be a raven.

[7] Two marriages implied, one case with several marriages, one with wolf, and one with owl.

[8] One marriage implied, one case with several marriages, one with raven.

[9] In one case initial conflict was followed by good relations.

[10] One case resolved to good relations.

[11] One case implied.

[12] Grandsons.

[13] Granddaughter, probable conflict.

[14] Grandson.

[15] Twenty grandsons, four granddaughters.

[16] One grandson, one granddaughter.

[17] Twelve grandsons, three granddaughters.

[18] Seven fathers-in-law, five brothers-in-law; one father-in-law is a polar bear.

[19] One mother-in-law, eight brothers-in-law, one father-in-law, one stepfather in-law.

[20] Two fathers-in-law, one mother-in-law, one brother-in-law.

[21] Two mothers-in-law, one former mother-in-law, one sister-in-law.

[22] One mother-in-law, four brothers-in-law.

[23] One case includes three uncles and two nephews who are polar bears.

[24] All in one story.

[25] One case of conflict first.

[26] Two cases of three brothers and one sister.

TABLE 6. Human Physical Aberrations

Aberration	Number of occurrences	Aberration	Number of occurrences
Dwarf	5	Hole in hand	1
No head	3	Very long ears	1
Big mouth stretching as far as ears	3	Ghost or zombie	1
		Short penis	1
Head alone	2	Neck stretching straight from hood to shoulders	1
Heart in toe	2		
Invisible	2	Very long breasts	1
One eye	2	Funny fingernails	1
Flint penis	2	Boy with no arm	1
Head sideways on neck	1	Hole in belly	1
Shiny woman	1	Black people[1]	1

[1] An aberration in aboriginal Eskimo terms.

TABLE 7. Crime in Social Terms

Crime	Number of occurrences	Crime	Number of occurrences
Murder	27	Threatened murder	1
Disobeying orders	16[1]	Stealing boy	1
Refusing to marry	12[2]	Borrowing without return	1
Adultery	6	Treating wife badly	1
Annoying others	6	Warning blood kin against kin by marriage	1
Abandonment	6[3]		
Theft	5	Arranging for person to get lost	1
Breaking taboo	5	Scolding children	1
Attempted murder	4	Wanting woman too much	1
Stealing women	4	Being lazy	1
Utilizing supernatural powers	4	Desire for property of others	1
Making fun of others	3	Hoarding	1
Causing injury	3	Lying	1
Meanness	3	Carrying aggression too far	1
Jealousy	3	Refusing request	1
Incest	2	Not taking what is offered	1
Fighting	2	Rape	1
Refusing to share	2	Vanity	1
Making love too much	2	Not helping kin	1

[1] Seven of elders, five of spouse.
[2] Eight female, four male.
[3] Two female, one male, three family.

444

TABLE 8. Types of Punishment

Punishment	Number of occurrences	Punishment	Number of occurrences
Killed	39	Marrying own grandfather	1
Died	8	Forced to eat human head	1
Abandoned	5	Forced to spill slops	1
Almost killed	4	Loss of possession	1
Chastised	3	Tortured	1
Getting in trouble	3	Marrying owl	1
Son killed	3	Marrying wolf	1
Failure to get food	2	Children leave	1
Loss of power	2	Daughter-in-law leaves	1
Getting sick	2	Son leaves	1
Life threatened	1	Wife leaves husband	1
Wife commits suicide	1	Tricked	1
Disappears	1	Frightened	1
Thrown out of *karigi*	1	Husband gets sick	1
Treated roughly	1	Loss of woman	1
Chased	1	Killed self accidentally	1
Loss of sister	1	Marrying head	1
Loss of brother-in-law	1	Marrying raven	1
Loss of wife	1	Changed to bird	1
Loss of daughter	1	Changed to caribou	1
Getting old fast	1	Changed to porcupine	1
Getting lost	1	Changed to weasel	1
Marrying old man	1	Daughter changed to wolf	1
Marrying old woman	1		

TABLE 9. Source of Aggression Causing Flight

Source	Number of occurrences	Source	Number of occurrences
Killers or would-be killers	6	Villagers' revenge	1
Mother-in-law	2	Brown-bear people	1
Man-who-always-killed-people	2	Friend	1
Wife	2	Fire	1
Husband	2	Indians	1
Man with flint penis	2	Rich man's son	1
Black family	1	War	1
Baby	1	Man	1
Sexual advances of son's father	1		

TABLE 10. Physical Dangers

Danger	Number of occurrences	Danger	Number of occurrences
Cutting or stabbing	34[1]	Set adrift	2
Other physical combat	22[2]	Caught on fishhook	1
Eaten by animals	11[3]	Killed by top	1
Falling	10[4]	Caught in net	1
Drifting out to sea	9	To be eaten by skin	1
Blow	8[5]	Bellyache	1
Burning	8[6]	Sickness	1
Consumed by worms	7[7]	Caught in trap	1
Human biting or eating	6[8]	Threatened by whale	1
Starvation	6	Storm	1
Drowning	6	Freezing in water	1
Caught in snare	4[9]	Killed by walrus	1
Lost in fog	4	Killed by walrus' dog	1
Killed or threatened by bird	4	Crushed by ice	1
Bear hug	2[10]	Freezing	1
Pushed in boiling oil	2	Taken by beluga on line	1
Offered poison food	2		

[1] Eleven knives, nine spears, two flint penises, two ulus, two sharp rocks, two broken caribou bones, one walrus tusk, one ice chisel, one harpoon, one dagger, one human nails, one hair scraper.

[2] All cases involve bow and arrow.

[3] Three polar bears, two brown bears, two wolves, one threatened by wolf, one threatened by brown bear, one dog, one eagle.

[4] Five down cliff, two in holes, one dropped by eagle, one from sky, one through ice into ditch.

[5] Four with stick, one against rock, one against log, one with whale rib, one with fist.

[6] In one case person was insect.

[7] All in two stories.

[8] One threatened, one implied, one by men, one by baby, one actually polar bear, one actually brown bear.

[9] In one case as a caribou.

[10] One case questionable.

TABLE 11. Animals Encountered (not including insects)

Species	Number of occurrences	Species	Number of occurrences
Caribou	17	Killer whale	2
Brown bear	16	Marmot	1
Polar bear	11	Sea worm	1
Ptarmigan	10	Canadian jay	1
Wolf	9	Shiny duck	1
Dog	9	Hare	1
Small seal	8	Unusual fox	1
Bowhead whale	8	Tern	1
Ugruk	7	Rabbit	1
Tirichik	7	Woodpecker	1
Small bird	6	Gastropod	1
Walrus	5	Sheefish	1
Fish	4	Mammoth	1
Raven	4	Mountain sheep	1
Eagle	4	Muskrat	1
White fox	3	Beaver	1
Wolverine	3	Pintail duck	1
Reindeer	3	Snowy owl	1
Ground squirrel	3	Owl	1
Polar-bear head	2	Tomcod	1
Brown-bear head	2	Smelt	1
Geese	2	"Mythical" worm	1
Beluga	2	Huge seagull	1
Worm	2	Beast with teeth like shark	1
Red fox	2	Big ptarmigan	1
Spotted seal	2	Walrus dog	1
Loon	2	Dog with mouth	1
Flounder	2	Six-legged polar bear	1
Duck	2	Big fish	1

General

Land animals	69
Sea animals	49
Birds	37
Fish	9
"Mythical" beasts	22

TABLE 12. Man/Animal Relationships

Number of occurrences

Species	Animals helping man	Animals killing man	Animals talking
Raven	4	1	2
Caribou	3	—	3
Dog	2	1	—
Bird	2	2	3
Brown bear	2	1	—
Eagle	2	—	1
Wolf	1	1	2
Ground squirrel	1	—	—
White fox	1	—	1
Fly	1	—	—
Pintail duck	1	—	1
Loon	1	—	2
Beaver	1	—	1
Polar bear	—	3	1
Walrus	—	2	—
Walrus' dog	—	1	—
Fish	—	1	—
Mouse	—	—	1
Ptarmigan	—	—	1
Geese	—	—	1
Seal	—	—	1
Muskrat	—	—	1

TABLE 13. Man/Animal Interchange

Transformation[1]	Number of occurrences	Transformation	Number of occurrences
Man/eagle	6	Man/tern	1
Woman/eagle	1	Man/owl	1
People/eagle	1	Man/snowy owl	1
Man/wolf	5	Man/mouse	1
Woman/wolf	3	Man/wolverine	1
People/wolves	2	Man/dog	1
Man/brown Bear	4	Woman/dead dog	1
Woman/brown Bear	4	Woman/ugruk	1
People/brown bear	2	Woman/black whale	1
Man/polar Bear	4	Man/walrus	1
Woman/polar Bear	2	Woman/porcupine	1
Man/squirrel	4	Man/weasel	1
Man/bird	3	Woman/beetle	1
Woman/bird	3	Woman/bumble bee	1
Man/caribou	3	Woman/spider	1
Man/raven	2	People/bugs that swarm	1
Man/spotted Seal	2	Woman/caterpillar	1
Woman/seashell	2	People/fish	1
Man/gastropod	1	People/animals	1
Man/bug	1		
Woman/fly	2	Man/plant	1
Man/loon	1	Man/wood	1
Man/goshawk	1	Man/feather	1
Man/dirt	1		
Woman/cotton grass	1	Mice/caribou	1

[1] Direction unspecified.

TABLE 14. Humans Treated Like Animals

Treatment	Number of occurrences	Treatment	Number of occurrences
Snared	4	Dragged like seal	1
Trapped	4	Hung up like meat	1
Hooked or gaffed	3	Tied like dog	1
Grabbed by eagle	2	Scratched like skin	1
Bodies piled like salmon	1	Twirled on spear like salmon	1
Netted	1	Fed mice	1

TABLE 15. Use of Magic Powers

Magic power	Number of occurrences	Magic power	Number of occurrences
To kill man or beast	7	To become walrus tusk	1
Magic or jaw sled	5	To fish through floor	1
To make boat go	5	To tilt house	1
Amulet to protect from harm	3	To regenerate woman	1
To make men young	2	To go to moon	1
To become bird	2	To get rock from water	1
To make woman sleepy	2	To kill whale in stormshed	1
To kill or blind with urine	2	Magic shavings	1
Throwing back things to stop danger	2	Magic snowshoes to catch game	1
Renewable meat	2	To kill killer whale with stick	1
To change to squirrel	2	Magic like wet spring fog	1
To become dirt	1	To tip boat	1
To stop animals from coming to those who don't share	1	To paint sleds so they won't go	1
To make play whale real	1	To make house bigger	1
To call east wind	1	To get rich	1
To lift boat	1	To get young men to follow	1
To change to bug	1	To bring fire	1
Song to calm polar bear	1	Song to make weak	1
To kill with *mittikluk*	1	Magic gaff	1
To travel	1	To fly	1
To hunt	1	To make men stiff	1
To make play doll real	1	To change to weasel	1
To travel with seal skin	1	To make ill	1
To make boy big	1	To make well	1
To change leaves to clothes	1	To run on water	1
Medicine to kill bird	1	Magic snowshoes	1
To get food from *kikvik*	1	To make spear point come off	1
To split ice with wave of hand	1	Magic stick	1
To become rock	1	To bring back woman	1

VI. Epilogue

During the summer of 1968, Leona and I returned to northern Alaska. We spent the last part of June at Sheshalik, camping among the tents of the families from Noatak Village.

Late June is not yet summer along the coast. The constant wind, chill from the scattered sea ice lying just offshore, ruffles the brown grasses covering the crests of the gently rolling beach ridges. The boats of the villagers are anchored out from the beach, bows parting the incoming waves. A series of drying racks, fashioned from driftwood or from spruce logs brought by boat from the lower Noatak, run along the first beach ridge above sprayline. The tents of the Noatak villagers are pitched in traditional family locations on the second and third beaches inland from the sea. More beach ridges rise behind the tents, extending like ancient frozen waves to the lagoon which separates Sheshalik spit from the mainland.

Fewer Noatak families come to Sheshalik each year. The possibilities of wage work draw the Noatak men to Kotzebue and Fairbanks and to the fish canneries in southern Alaska. They spend only a week or two at Sheshalik hunting ugruk and beluga before leaving. Some of the families then move to Kotzebue to spend the summer in town. Others stay at Sheshalik, netting fish and picking berries. Summer is a lazy time, sitting on the warm sand looking out on the windswept sound, gossiping and telling stories, wondering how the men are doing, dreaming of other days. Children never seem to sleep, as they play away the twenty-four-hour day. Often their voices rival the wind and the waves.

We stayed with Chester and Martha Burns and their children. The high winds, fog, and rain discouraged outdoor activities during many of the days we were there, though occasionally the wind would die down and the sun come out. The silence and warmth would bring us from the tent to draw in the net and pick out the flapping trout and whitefish, feed the dogs, and walk along the beach looking for driftwood to feed the stove.

We spent the time inside reading, playing cards, or talking with Martha and Chester and visitors from other tents. The battered wood stove, handmade from a fifty-four gallon oil drum, kept us warm and dry. Every now and then Martha would roast some trout or ugruk meat, which we would eat with seal oil, pilot bread, and jam. Coffee was always heating on top of the stove. It was a happy time, happy and content, spent with people we both admire and love.

Especially the children. Martha and Chester have seven ranging in age from four to sixteen, and they were constantly in and out of the tent, accompanied by youngsters from other families. We joined in their games, wiped their tears, and loved them as if they were our own.

One afternoon as I was reading, Ethel, the youngest, flung the tent door open and stepped inside. She stood by the stove in her tattered yellow calico wind parka, staring intently at me until I looked up at her. Then she ran to me and sat in my lap, looking up into my eyes. "Are these them?" I looked down and saw some seashells in her hand. "Are these the ones you wanted?" "Yes," I answered, "do you know what they are?" "No, tell me." "They are *nahkunuks*. Do you know the story about them?" "No, tell me." "Well, a man, his wife, and their daughter lived behind Kassiituk, here at Sheshalik. . . ."

During the fall of 1968, I taught an undergraduate course dealing with the prehistory of North America. I chose to illustrate the methodological procedures a prehistorian uses in reconstructing ancient lifeways by describing in depth a prehistoric site I had excavated in the Noatak River valley. To flesh out the archaeological description I told them about the historic way of life as related by Paul Monroe and Edna Hunnicutt.

One day I picked up my mail on the way to class. To fill the few minutes before the bell rang I began to read a letter from Martha Burns. The students must have noticed my face as I scanned the lines.

Ethel just say hi to pop Ed and mom Leona. She sure talk. She's talking about three bears. She's telling stories about three bears. Now she says there are three moose. They live in a house. She sure makes the kids laugh. Now three little pigs. She tells stories about all these. I don't know where she gets the stories. She talks too much.

Oh, yes, I hate to tell you about Paul Monroe. He died this fall at Kotzebue. He was coming home with a plane. He died at the airport. Heart attack. He died the last part of September. It was so sad for us at Noatak. No more stories for us. Except for grandmother Edna. She sure cry too. We stay with her all day, when we hear about Paul. So sad, but can't help it, it's God's will.

For a moment, in my grief, I thought of canceling the class. But I felt that my students, too, knew Paul, though not by name and only through my imperfect rendering of the way of life he lived. So I told them about Paul and his stories and, in an inarticulate way, what knowing Paul had meant to me. And about a way of life now gone and remembered only in my notes and in the hearts of those who knew him. It was only when death came that I realized, both as an anthropologist and as a person, how much Paul taught me, and yet how little of the man and his life I could ever re-create for those who had not known him.

Now, as I write in February 1971, Sheshalik is deserted. The low, snow-covered beach ridges merge almost imperceptibly into the still sea, locked fast with ice. The returning summer will bring the people once more, though in fewer numbers, and the waves of summer storms will wash *nahkunuks* onto the sand.

But change is continuing in northern Alaska. During the five years since we lived in Noatak a major technological change has occurred. The snowmobile is rapidly replacing the dog team as a means of winter transportation. The acquisition of the snowmobile by the Noatak people will have wide-ranging repercussions. It will no longer be necessary to seine many salmon in the fall for winter dog food. The relatively great speed of snowmobiles will result in hunting trips of one or two days rather than a week or more. There will be more social interaction between Noatak and other northern Alaskan villages. Wage labor will become an even more permanent feature of the peoples' lives, to provide cash for purchasing the machines and for gas and maintenance.

Other changes will come. The younger Eskimos are looking only forward. Their ties to the land and to the ancient way of life become more and more tenuous with each passing year. Ethel Burns may continue to come to Sheshalik each year, but I doubt that her children will. And her children's children may well not speak Eskimo, or see the land with the eyes of a hunter, or remember the old stories. The past has value, though we often do not realize it before the ties are broken too completely to understand what came before. Thus I offer Ethel the stories of Paul and Edna, lest she forget and so she may remind her children's children of a people, a land, and a way of life that might otherwise be forgotten.

Glossary

aaluyuk	wooden tray
aanuktuk	games
agluchurak	killer whale
aġruks	two beams of light cast by the sun when it first appears above the horizon in late December
ahalik	old squaw duck
ahġun	fish gaff
ahnuk	feces
ahtalik	zombie or ghost
ahtaŋnuk	ugruk-skin mukluk bottoms
ahvariki	whale flipper; also the celebration when they eat whale flippers
aiyupak	counting stick
akham	"Wait for me"
akpahluruk	species of bird
akpatuks	guests at Messenger Feast
akutuk	Eskimo "ice cream," a dish made with seal or caribou fat and berries
alapah	cold
aŋatquq	shaman, also shaman's familiar and shamanistic power
anna	grandmother
aññuluk	shaman's tools
añyuk	magic charm
apuk	what two men with one wife call each other
atuk	namesake
auḳsauk	football
aulanguluk	seal-oil lamp

dtalik	burbot or ling
ebrulik	Naupaktomiut winter house
iilyaaruq	joking partner
iilyuk	special friends
iiŋaagiiruk	species of duck
ikaklik	seal-skin boots
iḳigut	meat rack or cache
iklukḳinik	small fish that can survive freezing
iknikḳutiilik	fire
ikusik	species of plant
ilaypuruk	orphan; poor boy; basically one without kin
illiktiuruk	species of duck
iŋagiruk	small species of sea bird
iŋaluk	gut, intestine
iñgaluk	gut cover
iññukaknaaluk	man-who-always-kills-people
innukon	stranger
inugaakaliḳurit	dwarf
inuksuk	soul
inusuk	meat rack or cache
ipnuk	pile of rocks
itnaŋniksuit	stories that happened not long ago
iuktun	boat pole
ivalu	sinew
kaichik	caribou-skin mattress
kaivtuk	wooden spoon
kalovik	Naupaktomiut summer skin tent or Noatagmiut winter house
kanichuk	stormshed
kaniuk	bullhead
karigi (pl. kariyit)	recreation and ceremonial structure
katak	waterbucket; entrance passage
katunun	two men who had shared the same wife
kavhwuk	circular throwing board for hunting rabbits
kavisik	fish scales
kavsuk	toy top
kayaḳtuking	paddling along in a kayak
kayuluich	ocean-living species of fish
keralaluk	Canadian jay
kiiligvuk	mammoth
kikvik	cutting board
kilyumlu	sky
kirgavik	goshawk

kivauk   Messenger Feast; also the runners who invite villagers to such a feast
ķuk   frozen meat or fish
ķuksik   tool box
ķumarak   bugs in salt water that eat seals
kumiġun   hide scraper
ķupuluk   sea worm
ķutliruk   a small plant species with cotton inside the stem and flowers

masu   edible root
mauraa   see: *tirichik*
miññuk   small black bug
mitik   species of duck
mitķutaylyuk   arctic tern
mittikluk   stone flipper
mukluk   foot gear
muktuk   whale skin
mulgi   loon

naakun   bead
naatigluk   dirt from ocean bottom
naguyuk   tall section of iceberg
nahkunuk   marine gastropod; also, being cross-eyed
nahviivuk   house fly
nakasuķtuķ   big bladder
naķuktukruk   small bird with black feathers on top of head
nalak   white seal skin
napaarak   sled stanchion
napuhuutlik   dark fox with white lines down back
naulaukmie   white man
naulayuk   least weasel
nauyaķ   seagull
niauk   lasso
nigrarruk   spider
niivakruuķ   bugs that swarm together
niksiiktuk   becoming unconscious through shamanistic power
niŋyuk   cottonwood
nipaluktuk   owl
nunukruķ   small bug that swims rapidly on surface of water

pamrauk   small seal
panuktuk   dried meat of any kind
patupuk   brass
pitmik   type of trap
puaak   trap for ptarmigan made from willow

pukruk	mukluks made from an old seal poke
puuyuuak	crab
saavitluk	short knife
shishauk̲	beluga or white whale
siikluk	pick
siisak	trap for foxes made from hollow tree
siksikpuk	marmot
suppuktukvik	whale's spout
tak̲u	"Thank you"
taupuk	large rocks in area with no sand
tiġgak	weasel
tiŋmak	duck
tirichik	a mythical dragonlike animal that eats people
tuakikpak	tobacco
t̲uk	ice chisel
tukpuk	killing spear
tulugak	raven
tuluvak	big upper teeth
tutuk	labret or lip plug
tutulik	footgear worn in extremely cold weather
tuutlik̲	loon
tuwak	(walrus) tusk
tuyuk	woodpecker
uk̲alik̲sugruk	arctic hare
ukpik	snowy owl
uksruk	species of duck
ulichulyak	footgear worn during wet snow conditions
ulimun	adze
ulipk̲uk̲	old true stories
ulu	semilunar woman's knife
umaylik	rich man
umaypak	large skin boat
umuk	a kinship term referring to two boys, one of whom is named after his paternal grandfather, the other after the first's paternal grandmother.
unaypak	sled
uŋnuk	seal spear
uuglugruk	ball
uuyaksak	missionary

Bibliography

Bee, James W., and E. R. Hall
 1956. "Mammals of Northern Alaska on the Arctic Slope." *University of Kansas Museum of Natural History, Miscellaneous Publication No. 8*. Lawrence, Kans.
Birket-Smith, Kaj.
 1959. *The Eskimos*. London.
Boas, Franz
 1888. "The Central Eskimo." *Sixth Annual Report of the Bureau of American Ethnology*. Washington, D.C.
 1904. "The Folk-Lore of the Eskimo." *Journal of American Folk-Lore 17*. Boston.
 1907. "The Eskimo of Baffin Land and Hudson Bay." *Bulletin of the American Museum of Natural History 15*. New York.
Brower, Charles D.
 1942. *Fifty Years Below Zero*. New York.
Burch, Ernest S., Jr.
 1966. "Authority, Aid and Affection: The Structure of Eskimo Kin Relationships." Diss. Univ. of Chicago.
 1970. "The Eskimo Trading Partnership in North Alaska." *Anthropological Papers of the University of Alaska 15*, No. 1. College, Alaska.
Chance, Norman A.
 1966. *The Eskimo of North Alaska*. New York.

Cranz, D.
1770. *Historie von Grönland,* 4 vols. Barby, Germany.
Curtis, E. S.
1930. *The North American Indian.* XX. Norwood, Mass.
Egede, Hans
1741. *Relationer fra Grønland 1721–36 og Det gamle Grønlands nye Perlustration 1741.* Copenhagen.
Foote, Don Charles
1961. *A Human Geographical Study in Northwest Alaska.* Cambridge, Mass.
1965. "Exploration and Resource Utilization in Northwestern Arctic Alaska Before 1855." Diss. McGill Univ.
n.d. Field notes.
Foote, Don Charles, and Alan Cooke
1960. *The Eskimo Hunter at Noatak, Alaska: Winter 1960—Summer 1960.* Cambridge, Mass.
Foote, Don Charles, and H. A. Williamson
1966. "A Human Geographical Study." *Environment of the Cape Thompson Region, Alaska.* Norman J. Wilimovsky and John N. Wolfe, eds. Oak Ridge.
Garber, Clark M.
1940. *Stories and Legends of the Bering Strait Eskimos.* Boston.
Garfield, Viola E.
1953. "Contemporary Problems of Folklore Collecting and Study." *Anthropological Papers of the University of Alaska* 1, No. 2. College.
Giddings, J. L., Jr.
1952. *The Arctic Woodland Culture of the Kobuk River.* Philadelphia.
1961. *Kobuk River People.* College.
Gillham, Charles E.
1955. *Medicine Men of Hooper Bay.* New York.
Golder, F. A.
1903. "Tales from Kodiak Island." *Journal of American Folklore* 20. Boston.
1907. "A Kodiak Island Story." *Journal of American Folklore* 20. Boston.
1909. "Eskimo and Aleut Stories from Alaska." *Journal of American Folklore* 22. Boston.

Gubser, Nicholas J.
  1965. *The Nunamiut Eskimos: Hunters of Caribou.* New Haven, Conn.

Hadley, Martha E.
  1969. *The Alaskan Diary of a Pioneer Quaker Missionary.* Mt. Dora, Fla.

Hall, Edwin S., Jr.
  1966. "Kangiguksuk: A Cultural Reconstruction of a 16th Century Eskimo Site in Northern Alaska." Diss. Yale Univ.
  1969. "Speculations on the Late Prehistory of the Kutchin Athapaskans." *Ethnohistory* 16, No. 4. Tucson.

Halliday, Gordon
  1969. "The-Man-Who-Always-Kills-People." Unpublished MS.

Hawkes, Ernest W.
  1916. "The Labrador Eskimo." *Geological Survey of Canada, Memoir 91, Anthropological Series, No. 14.* Ottawa.

Haywood, Charles
  1961. *A Bibliography of North American Folklore and Folksong,* 2 vols. New York.

Himmelheber, Hans
  1951. *Der gefrorene Pfad.* Eisenach, Germany.

Holm, Gustav
  1912. "Legends and Tales from Angmagsalik." *Meddelelser om Grønland* 39. Copenhagen.

Ingstad, Helge
  1954. *Nunamiut.* New York.

Irving, Laurence
  1960. "Birds of Anaktuvuk Pass, Kobuk, and Old Crow." *Bulletin 217, United States National Museum.* Washington, D.C.

Jacobs, Melville
  1959. *The Content and Style of an Oral Literature.* Chicago.

Jenness, Diamond
  1924. "Myths and Traditions from Northern Alaska." *Report of the Canadian Arctic Expedition* 13A. Ottawa.
  1952. "Stray Notes on the Eskimo of Arctic Alaska." *Anthropological Papers of the University of Alaska* 1. College.

Keithahn, Edward L.
  1968. *Alaskan Igloo Tales.* Seattle.

Kleivan, Inge
   1962. "The Swan Maiden Myth Among the Eskimo." *Acta Arctica,*
      Fasc. XIII. Copenhagen.

Kroeber, A. L.
   1899. "The Eskimo of Smith Sound." *Bulletin of the American
      Museum of Natural History* 12. New York.

Lantis, Margaret
   1946. "The Social Culture of the Nunivak Eskimo." *Transactions
      of the American Philosophical Society,* n.s., 35, Pt. 3. Phila-
      delphia.
   1953. "Nunivak Eskimo Personality as Revealed in the Mythology."
      Anthropological Papers of the University of Alaska 2, No. 1.
      College.

Larsen, Helge, and Froelich Rainey
   1948. "Ipiutak and the Arctic Whale Hunting Culture." *Anthropo-
      logical Papers of the American Museum of Natural History*
      42. New York.

Lucier, Charles
   1953. "Buckland Eskimo Myths." *Anthropological Papers of the
      University of Alaska* 2, No. 2. College.
   1958. "Noatagmiut Eskimo Myths." *Anthropological Papers of the
      University of Alaska* 6, No. 2. College.

Murdoch, John
   1892. "Ethnological Results of the Point Barrow Expedition." *Ninth
      Annual Report of the Bureau of American Ethnology.* Wash-
      ington, D.C.

Murdoch, George P.
   1961. *Ethnographic Bibliography of North America,* 3rd ed. New
      Haven, Conn.

Nelson, Edward W.
   1899. "The Eskimo about Bering Strait." *18th Annual Report of
      the Bureau of American Ethnology.* Washington, D.C.

Ostermann, H.
   1942. "The MacKenzie Eskimos, after K. Rasmussen's Posthumous
      Notes." *Report of the Fifth Thule Expedition* 10, No. 2. Cop-
      enhagen.
   1952. "The Alaskan Eskimos." *Report of the Fifth Thule Expedi-
      tion* 10, No. 3. Copenhagen.

Parker, Seymour
   1962. "Motives in the Eskimo and Ojibwa Mythology." *Ethnology* 1. Pittsburgh.
Preston, Caroline E.
   1964. "Psychological Testing with Northwest Coast Alaskan Eskimos." *Genetic Psychology Monographs* 69. Provincetown, Mass.
Rainey, Froelich
   1947. "The Whale Hunters of Tigara." *Anthropological Papers of the American Museum of Natural History* 41, Pt. 2. New York.
Rasmussen, Knud J.
   1921. *Myter og sagn fra Grønland*, 3 vols. Copenhagen.
   1932. *The Eagle's Gift*. Garden City, N. Y.
Ray, Dorothy Jean
   1968. "St. Michael Eskimo Myths and Tales." *Anthropological Papers of the University of Alaska* 14, No. 1. College.
Rink, Henry
   1866–1871. *Eskimoiske eventyr og sagn*, 2 vols. Copenhagen.
   1875. *Tales and Traditions of the Eskimo*. Edinburgh.
Saario, Doris J., and Brina Kessel
   1966. "Human Ecological Investigations at Kivalina." *Environment of the Cape Thompson Region, Alaska*. Norman J. Wilimovsky and John N. Wolfe, eds. Washington, D.C.
Solecki, Ralph S.
   1951. "Archaeology and Ecology of the Arctic Slope of Alaska." *Annual Report of the Smithsonian Institution for 1950*. Washington, D.C.
Spencer, Robert F.
   1959. "The North Alaskan Eskimo: A Study in Ecology and Society." *Bureau of American Ethnology, Bulletin 171*. Washington, D.C.
Spencer, Robert F., and W. K. Carter
   1954. "The Blind Man and the Loon." *Journal of American Folklore* 67. Boston.
Spencer, Robert F., and Jesse D. Jennings
   1965. *The Native Americans*. New York.
Stefansson, Vilhjalmur
   1951. *My Life with the Eskimos*. New York.

463

Thalbitzer, William

1904. "A Phonetical Study of the Eskimo Language." *Meddelelser om Grønland* 31. Copenhagen.

Thompson, Stith

1946. *Tales of the North American Indians.* Cambridge, Mass.

1955–1958. *Motif-Index of Folk Literature*, 6 vols. Bloomington, Ind.

Turner, Lucien M.

1894. "Ethnology of the Ungava District." *11th Annual Report of the Bureau of American Ethnology.* Washington, D.C.

VanStone, James W.

1962. "Point Hope: An Eskimo Village in Transition." *Monographs of the American Ethnological Society* 35. Seattle.

Weyer, Edward M.

1962. *The Eskimos.* Hamden, Conn.

Zibell, Wilfred

1968. *Iñupian Ukathi.* Summer Institute of Linguistics. Fairbanks, Alaska.

Index of Motifs

B210	Speaking animals—EH4, 11, PM134
B211.11	Speaking fish—PM170
B211.2.2	Speaking caribou—EH2, PM109, 112
B211.2.3	Speaking bear—PM31, 137, 139
B211.2.4	Speaking wolf—EH2, PM112
B211.3	Speaking bird—EH1, PM10, 17, 30, 50, 81, 85, 156
B211.3.6	Speaking raven—EH11, PM60, 117, 162
B282.16	Marriage of raven with another bird—PM117
B300	Helpful animals—PM13
B341	Helpful animals' injunctions disobeyed—PM112
B350	Grateful animals—PM36
B360	Animals grateful for rescue from peril of death—PM112
B390	Animal grateful for other kind acts—EH4, PM10, 156
B430	Helpful wild beasts—EH11, PM134
B435.3	Helpful wolf—EH2
B435.4	Helpful bear—PM24, 29, 33, 66, 137, 139
B443	Helpful wild beasts: ungulate (caribou)—EH2, PM109
B450	Helpful birds—EH1, PM156, 162
B451	Helpful birds: passeriformes—PM50
B451.5	Helpful raven—PM60
B455.3	Helpful eagle—PM30, 42, 73
B483.1	Helpful fly—PM150
B521.1	Animal warns against poison—EH1
B541.4.1	Boat towed by dog—PM13
B552	Man carried by bird—PM27, 73
B575.1	Wild animals kept as dogs—PM4, 24, 32, 42, 65
B600	Marriage of man to animal—PM25, 29
B600.2	Animal husband provides characteristic animal food—PM169
B601.18	Marriage to seal—PM32
B602	Marriage to bird—EH11
B615.7	Marriage to bear in human form—PM66, 92
B631	Human offspring from marriage to animal—EH6, 11, PM36
B632	Animal offspring from marriage to animal—PM36
B651	Marriage to beast in human form—PM60
B651.4	Marriage to dog in human form—PM36
B651.6	Marriage to wolf in human form—PM96
B651.7	Marriage to bear in human form—PM29, 71

D124.3	Transformation: man to wolverine—PM4
D127.1	Transformation: man to seal—PM32, 155
D127.4	Transformation: man to walrus—PM119
D150	Transformation: man to bird—EH1, PM11, 17, 26, 44, 54
D152.1	Transformation: man to hawk—PM26
D152.2	Transformation: man to eagle—EH14, PM5, 10, 22, 73, 77
D152.3	Transformation: man to owl—PM76
D180	Transformation: man to insect—PM53
D181	Transformation: man to spider—PM78
D184.1	Transformation: man to beetle—PM4, 34
D192.1	Transformation: man to caterpillar—EH5
D200	Transformation: man to object—PM47, 70
D231	Transformation: man to stone—PM70
D233	Transformation: man to shell—PM107
D275	Transformation: man to feather—PM47
D283.6	Transformation: man to whirlpool—PM28
D293	Transformation: man to star—PM45
D300	Transformation: animal to person—PM36, 140, 146
D310	Transformation: animal (fox) to person—EH1
D313.2	Transformation: wolf to man—PM21, 55, 82, 146
D313.3	Transformation: bear to man—PM29, 33, 80, 137, 140
D315	Transformation: rodent to man—PM166
D315.2	Transformation: mouse to man—EH1
D327.2	Transformation: seal to man—PM32, 44
D341	Transformation: dog to person—PM93, 159
D350	Transformation: bird to man—PM2, 44, 59, 118, 169
D352.2	Transformation: eagle to man—EH1, PM30, 72
D361.1	The Swan Maidens—PM35
D370	Transformation: fish to person—PM78, 111
D380	Transformation: insect to man—EH5, PM16
D382	Transformation: hymenoptera to person—PM16, 34, 66, 150
D382.1	Transformation: bee to man—PM16
D398.1	Transformation: marine gastropod to person—PM74
D410	Transformation: one animal to another—PM71
D430	Transformation: object to person—PM151
D437.4	Transformation: feces to man—EH6
D440	Transformation: object to animal—PM125

H911	Tasks assigned at suggestion of jealous rival—PM71
H920	Assigners of tasks—PM64
H931	Tasks assigned in order to get rid of hero—PM87
H934	Relative assigns tasks—PM35
H960	Tasks performed through cleverness or intelligence—PM47, 79
H1150	Tasks: stealing, capturing, or slaying—PM35, 47, 87
H154.0.1	Task: bringing head of animal—PM41
H1161.1	Task: killing murderous bird—PM61
H1210	Quest assigned—PM27
H1220	Quest voluntarily undertaken—PM4, 6, 12, 16, 19, 20, 28, 47, 62, 80
H1331.1	Quest for marvelous bird—PM35
H1381.3	Quest for unknown woman—PM35
H1385	Quest for lost persons—PM2, 16, 21, 25, 28, 30, 42, 71, 72, 80, 85, 100, 113, 136, 148
H1385.3	Quest for vanished wife—PM27
H1543	Contest in remaining underwater—PM71
H1562	Test of strength—EH3, 7, PM53
H1563	Test of skill—PM71
J50	Wisdom (knowledge) acquired from observation—PM84, 122, 145, 161
J130	Wisdom (knowledge) acquired from animals—EH2, PM30, 50, 60, 73, 85, 109, 137, 162
J151	Wisdom from old person—PM22, 35, 39, 43, 47, 58, 65, 71, 95
J200	Choices—PM112
J514	One should not be too greedy—PM92, 130
J552	Intemperate pugnacity—PM61
J585	Caution in eating—EH1, PM12, 81
J624.5	Warnings against certain peoples—PM95
J652.4	Warnings against certain people—PM22, 53, 66, 67
J1050	Attention to warnings—EH1, 13, PM35, 50, 51, 60, 103, 106, 131, 153
J1072	Man to be judged by his own qualities, not his clothes—PM13
J1100	Cleverness—PM87
J1110	Clever persons—PM102

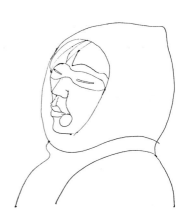

General Index

Bear
  grizzly, 3, 17, 32, 46, 117–18, 120, 132, 141–42, 178, 199–200, 204, 210, 212, 219, 242, 259–60, 262–64, 293, 295, 323, 352, 365, 367–71, 414, 419, 435, 443, 445–49
  polar, 25, 119, 122, 173, 175, 178–79, 184–87, 190–93, 195, 197, 199–200, 210, 214–16, 245–46, 262–64, 271, 273–74, 308–9, 325, 386, 414, 426, 429, 431, 443, 446–50
Beaver, 8, 301, 363–65, 394, 447–48
Bee, James W., 434
Beechy Point, 384, 442
Beluga, 13, 21, 24, 26, 32, 47, 64, 91–93, 101, 106, 134, 300, 326, 368–69, 398, 410, 446–47, 451
Bering Strait, 10, 78, 85, 102, 114, 117, 130, 137, 151, 161, 165, 175, 183, 187, 204, 232, 248, 263, 270, 274, 276, 278, 288, 309, 311, 336, 348, 352, 355, 391, 436
Berries, 21–22, 24, 32, 53, 62, 167, 199, 200, 203, 288, 328–29, 371, 393, 451
Bird, 117, 145–46, 162, 168, 176, 183, 187, 194, 210, 227, 235, 246, 251, 253–54, 274–76, 278, 295–96, 299–300, 303, 332, 348, 356, 369, 389, 395, 399, 425, 433, 445–50
Birket-Smith, Kaj, 404
Boas, Franz, 73, 78, 88–89, 91, 95, 100, 102, 114, 117, 125, 130, 134, 137, 140, 149, 152, 160–61, 163, 165–66, 175, 178, 180, 187, 190, 192–94, 200–1, 206, 211, 217, 221, 224, 228, 243, 246, 248, 262–63, 266, 269–70, 274, 276, 278, 288, 291, 293, 295, 298, 300, 304–5, 308–9, 311, 313, 315, 327, 329, 335, 349, 352, 365, 367–68, 370, 380–81, 383, 388, 391, 398, 402, 404
Bow and Arrow, ix, 17, 22, 24, 26, 77–78, 96, 98–99, 108–9, 119–20, 131–32, 137–39, 144, 149, 168, 173, 187, 193, 200, 208, 231, 238, 240, 245, 253, 264–65, 298–99, 302, 306, 312, 321, 327–28, 334–35, 351, 366, 375, 377, 385–86, 396, 402–3, 414, 428, 446

Breakup, 3, 21, 24, 32, 46, 51, 104, 116, 179–80, 196, 212, 235, 266, 305, 349, 361, 411
Brooks Range, 3, 6, 9, 28
Brower, Charles D., 429
Brown, Leonard, 372, 440
Buckland, 44, 204, 221, 224, 300, 303–4, 352, 388, 442
Burch, Ernest S., Jr., 9, 422
Bureau of Indian Affairs, 29–31, 33
Burial, 48, 60–61, 153, 175, 191, 202, 214, 222–24, 242, 247–48, 265, 285, 305, 340, 342, 345, 385, 396
Burns, Bertha, 64
Burns, Chester, 452
Burns, Ethel, xi, 453
Burns, Frank, 109, 183, 190, 194, 206, 209, 224, 228, 233, 243–44, 251, 270, 319, 323, 339, 345, 351, 357–58, 362, 396–98, 440
Burns, Frank (Aku), 64
Burns, Martha, xi, 37, 42, 66–67, 69, 81, 408, 452–53

California Yearly Meeting Friends Church, 27, 30, 63
Campbell, John M., xi
Cape Blossom, 301, 442
Cape Krusenstern (Sealing Point), 20, 51, 97–98, 104, 245, 296, 340, 353, 355, 422
Cape Lisburne, 6, 26
Cape Prince of Wales (Wales, Sagmaluruk), 21, 24, 40, 44, 52–55, 73, 92, 151, 165, 212, 249, 288, 297, 305, 346–47, 349–50, 352, 362–63, 366, 436, 442
Cape Thompson, 8, 300
Cape York, 95, 175, 187, 201, 263, 274, 309, 352, 388, 391
Carfield, Peter, 291, 440
Caribou, ix, 3, 11, 13, 17, 20, 22–28, 31–32, 34, 41, 43, 46–47, 55, 61, 65, 74–79, 81–82, 85–86, 90, 103, 106, 118, 121, 127–28, 131–33, 139–40, 143–44, 146, 148–49, 156–58, 164–65, 168, 174, 184, 196, 200, 205, 211, 225, 235, 239–41, 250, 255, 268, 285, 298, 301, 303, 306, 312–14, 317, 328, 332, 336–39, 341–42, 345, 349, 351, 353, 360–61, 370, 374, 376, 378,

The Eskimo Storyteller was manually composed on the Linotype in ten-point Caledonia with two-point spacing between the lines. L&C Hairline, a photo type face, was selected for display.

The book was designed by Jim Billingsley, typeset and printed letterpress by Heritage Printers, Charlotte, North Carolina, and bound by the Carolina Ruling and Binding Company, also of Charlotte. The paper on which the book is printed bears the watermark of the S. D. Warren Company and is designed for an effective life of at least three hundred years.

THE UNIVERSITY OF TENNESSEE PRESS
KNOXVILLE